Warrior Ascetics and Indian Empires

Many people assume, largely because of Gandhi's legacy, that Hinduism is a religion of non-violence. William R. Pinch shows just how wrong this assumption is. Using the life of Anupgiri Gosain, a Hindu ascetic who lived at the end of the eighteenth century, to explore the subject, he demonstrates that Hindu warrior ascetics were not only pervasive in the medieval and early modern Indian past, but were also an important component of the South Asian military labor market and crucial to the rise of British imperialism. Today, these warriors occupy a prominent place in modern Indian imaginations, ironically as romantic defenders of a Hindu India against foreign invasion, even though they are almost totally absent from the pages of Indian history. William Pinch's innovative and gloriously composed book sets out to correct this historiographical deficiency and to piece together the story of the rise and demise of warrior asceticism in India from the 1500s to the present. Implicit in his approach is the need to measure modern mythologies of Hindu warrior asceticism against the real-life experiences of powerful, violence-prone ascetics. This is a book which has as much to say to students of religion as to historians of empire, and will no doubt be taken up by both.

WILLIAM R. PINCH is Professor of History at Wesleyan University in Middletown, Connecticut. He is the author of *Peasants and Monks in British India* (1996).

Cambridge Studies in Indian History and Society 12

Cambridge Studies in Indian History and Society will publish monographs on the history and anthropology of modern India. In addition to its primary scholarly focus, the series will also include work of an interdisciplinary nature which will contribute to contemporary social and cultural debates about Indian history and society. In this way, the series will further the general development of historical and anthropological knowledge and attract a wider readership than that concerned with India alone.

A list of titles which have been published in the series can be found at the end of the book.

Warrior Ascetics and Indian Empires

William R. Pinch
Wesleyan University

CAMBRIDGE
UNIVERSITY PRESS

CAMBRIDGE UNIVERSITY PRESS
Cambridge, New York, Melbourne, Madrid, Cape Town, Singapore, São Paulo

Cambridge University Press
The Edinburgh Building, Cambridge CB2 2RU, UK

Published in the United States of America by Cambridge University Press, New York

www.cambridge.org
Information on this title: www.cambridge.org/9780521851688

© William R. Pinch 2006

First published 2006

Printed in the United Kingdom at the University Press, Cambridge

A catalogue record for this publication is available from the British Library

ISBN-13 978-0-521-85168-8 hardback
ISBN-10 0-521-85168-8 hardback

Contents

Illustrations

Acknowledgments

I have been on Anupgiri's trail since 1994. If these pages are set between two hard covers, it means I am no longer chasing after the Great Warlord. I have let his trail go cold and have turned to other things. But Anupgiri and I have had happy times together and I would be remiss not to acknowledge the many fine memories I owe him. Not least of all, I have flown on his back to Britain and India repeatedly these last ten years. So first of all, he has my heartfelt gratitude. I hope I have done him and his men (and women) justice in the pages that follow. God knows he did not make it easy; and God knows there is much more to be said about him. One question that I was never able to resolve, and therefore (as is the historian's wont) completely elided in the pages that follow, is the manner of his death. In a way, this is fitting given that he was, theoretically, immortal. All we "know" is that his decline was sudden and unexpected. Was he poisoned by the British, as some of his descendants today quietly claim? Or by a woman close to him, as others allege? Certainly everybody had a motive. Like the uncertainty that surrounds the location of his final resting place, his *samadhi*, the cause of Anupgiri's death is a nagging question. Perhaps someone else will have the energy to take it up.

There are many others to thank. First among the living is Kailash Jha, who puts in an occasional appearance in the pages that follow. My adventures with Anupgiri, particularly in Bundelkhand, would have been much less enjoyable – and much less fruitful – but for Kailash's companionship, friendship, and wisdom. Indeed, he became so closely associated in my mind with this work, and with Anupgiri, that in the end I could not conceive of writing the book without putting him in it. If Anupgiri still inhabits this world – and to my way of thinking this is not entirely out of the question – then a good measure of him surely resides in Kailash. He will not be the first great man said to have been "metempsychosically kidnapped" by a death-defying *yogi*.

Abha, Kailash's wife, also deserves praise and thanks. She did not complain (too much) when I stole Kailash from her, and (in any case) she did not burn our clothes, flea-ridden and stinking though they may have been, when we came back to Delhi from our jaunts in the north Indian countryside. For this, and for the constant hospitality she extended to me and my family, I bow in gratitude.

I would be remiss were I not to acknowledge the kind assistance of Dr. G. K. Rai and Dr. Ram Naresh Tripathi of Allahabad. Likewise, for research affiliation on repeated visits to London, I wish to record my thanks to Professor Peter Robb and the Department of History at the School of Oriental and African Studies.

Portions of this work have been presented in a variety of venues, including Wesleyan University, the Colegio de México, Columbia University, Dartmouth College, University of Oslo – Göteborg University consortium School of Asian and African Studies, Yale University, Goodenough College, the University of Virginia, Middlebury College, the University of California (Berkeley), Edinburgh University, the University of Pennsylvania, the School of Oriental and African Studies, and at annual gatherings of the Association for Asian Studies (San Francisco) and the American Academy of Religion (Toronto). I thank the organizers of those talks and those who offered responses and raised questions. I am especially grateful to my colleagues at Wesleyan – in particular those in the Christian Studies Cluster, the Religion and History Concentration in the History Department, the Southern Asia and Indian Ocean Cluster, the Jewish and Israel Studies Cluster, and the editorial staff at *History and Theory* – with whom I have spent many happy hours probing the problem of religion within and without the academy.

Several colleagues at Wesleyan and beyond have read portions or all of this work, sometimes more than once, in various stages over the last ten years. For their comments and suggestions, and encouragement, I take the liberty of singling out a few: Seema Alavi, G. ("Anu") Arunima, Chris Bayly, Aditya Behl, Indrani Chatterjee, Rick Elphick, Stewart Gordon, Peter Gottschalk, Sumit Guha, Walter Hauser, Jack Hawley, Monika Horstmann, Bill Johnston, David Lorenzen, Philip Lutgendorf, Bruce Masters, Dilip Menon, Phil Pomper, Peter Robb, Vera Schwarcz, Gary Shaw, Phil Wagoner, and Ann Wightman. Marigold Acland of Cambridge University Press has been a patient and congenial editor. I am grateful as well for the editorial labors of Isabelle Dambricourt, Mary Leighton, and Elizabeth Davey of Cambridge University Press, the enormously helpful suggestions of two anonymous readers, and the perspicacious copy-editing eye – and gentle copy-editing hand – of Sara Adhikari. And I thank John Hammond for creating the map.

I have been fortunate to receive funding for the research and writing that went into this book. This includes a grant from the Joint Committee on South Asia of the American Council of Learned Societies and the

Social Science Research Council with funds provided by the National Endowment for the Humanities and the Ford Foundation (1995); a US Department of Education Fulbright-Hays Faculty Research Abroad grant (1994–95); a senior research fellowship from the National Endowment for the Humanities (2001); a Wesleyan University Center for the Humanities fellowship (spring 1999); and three project grants from the Office of Academic Affairs at Wesleyan University. This generous support, in addition to Wesleyan's fine sabbatical policy, made this book possible. I am grateful for all of it.

History is, as I never tire of telling anyone who will listen, a conversation with the past. That conversation could not take place if we could not hear voices of those who have gone before us. Here again I have much to be thankful for, in India as well as Britain. When I was not wandering the byways of Bundelkhand, my most interesting conversations with the past occurred in the reading room of what used to be called, in a simpler age, the India Office Library. My children laugh when I tell them how I like to spend my vacations. If they knew the caretakers of the past at what is now known as the Oriental and India Office Collection of the British Library, they would understand my idea of a good time.

All that remains is to apologize to my wife, Jennifer, and my children, Pearse and Helen. Anupgiri has taken me from them. Maybe now he will give me back.

Vijay Pinch
Middletown, CT
26 February 2005

Glossary

[For more detailed discussion of these terms, see the relevant index entries]

akhara	lit., "exercise arena" or "wrestling pit"; refers in ascetic content to armed regiment or branch of order
atith	lit., "guest", mendicant ascetic
bairagi	lit., "bereft of emotion"; generic term for ascetic; often used for armed Vaishnava ascetic
Bhairava	a horrific form of Siva, "haunt of the cremation ground"
bhakta	devotee
bhakti	devotion, love of God
chakra	sharp-edged metal disc used as a projectile weapon by medieval and early modern *yogi*s; also yogic term for each of the seven centers of energy in the human body; from Sanskrit *chakram* (wheel)
chela	student, disciple; can also mean slave or adopted son
Dasnami	lit., "ten-named"; Saiva ascetic order said to have been founded by the ninth-century Shankaracharya
fakir	ascetic, often applied to Sufis
gosain	lit., "in control of emotions"; generic term for ascetic; often used for armed Saiva ascetic
jagir	revenue estate
jaidad	revenue assignment specifically earmarked for the maintenance of troops
kaula	of or relating to clan, *kula*; in tantric context, refers to "hardcore" of religio-sexual practices that predated philosophical, or "high-caste," tantra
kumbha mela	pilgrimage festival that alternates every three years between Allahabad, Ujjain, Hardwar, and Nasik, the centerpiece of which is the procession of armed ascetics known as the "*Shahi Snan*" (imperial swim)
mahant	abbot, chief, commander

mandir	temple
masjid	mosque
math	monastery, structure that houses ascetics
mazar	grave
naga	warrior ascetic; thought to connote nakedness, from Sanskrit *nagna* (naked)
nath	lit., Lord; often used to signify a *yogi* who follows in the tradition of the eleventh-century Gorakhnath
pindari	marauder, usually associated with Maratha wars
Rajput	lit., progeny of kings; extended clans of warrior-rulers (Kshatriya) with many branches throughout northern India
Ramanandi	follower of Ramanand (*c.* 1400?)
Ramcharitmanas	lit., "Tale of the Sacred Pool of Rama"; the story of Rama as told by Tulsidas, *c.* 1600
randi	prostitute
sadhu	monk, anchorite; from Hindi *sadhana* (discipline, concentration)
samadhi	deathless meditative state achieved by the most adept *yogi*s; also a stone marker to signify the location at which such a state was achieved
sangam	confluence
sanyasi	lit., "renouncer"; generic term for ascetic; often used for Saiva ascetic
tapas	austerities that generate supernormal power
tawaif	courtesan
vajroli	urethral suction, an ascetic sexual practice thought to generate supernormal power, particularly when employed during intercourse with a *yogini*
yogini	a ravenous, bloodthirsty female consort of Bhairava, able to confer supernormal powers to those human sexual partners skilled enough to couple with her

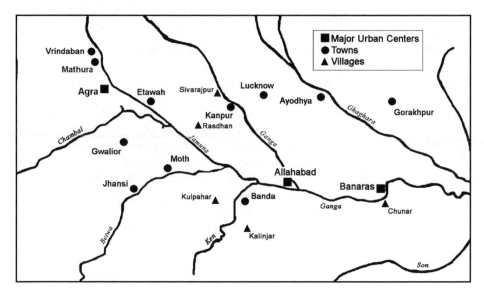

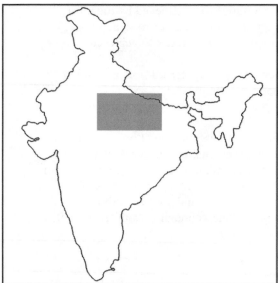

Map 1. Anupgiri's India.

Introduction

Delhi, 1788

The Mughal throne was a shadow of its former glory in 1788. Shah Alam, the emperor, was important only for the mantle of authority he represented. His predecessors, men like Akbar and Aurangzeb, the "great Moguls," had been rightly regarded as the most powerful men on earth in their time. By the 1750s their power had migrated to regional principalities, or "successor states," as they have come to be known. To make matters worse, the devolution of Mughal power meant that progressively less of the fabled wealth of India, which began in the rich soil of the countryside, made its way back to the center by way of taxation and annual tribute. The new men of consequence ruled from capitals like Hyderabad, Kabul, Jaipur, Mysore, Lucknow, Poona, and Calcutta. Some came from families that had served the Mughal throne for generations. Others were the heirs of rebel chieftains who had long chafed at Mughal dominance. Some, indeed, were a little of both: imperial politics, in India and in Europe, depended on the military subordination – and incorporation – of difference. And some were relative newcomers, men of trade from Europe who had brought not only an endless supply of New World silver but also new kinds of military organization and, eventually (but not just yet), new ways of understanding governance and the state.

Shah Alam possessed little power but he retained considerable authority. Over the course of the sixteenth and early seventeenth centuries, the Mughal emperor and his Indo-Persianate nobility had crafted a culture of imperial politics that enabled an expanding circle of political-military elites from diverse ethno-racial, religious, and linguistic backgrounds to work together in the interests of the empire. By the eighteenth century, and particularly during its latter half when India was the most diverse place on earth, the Mughal throne symbolized the distant potential of that subcontinental empire, that language of power which is authority. In 1788 Shah Alam was still the sun around which competing interests orbited, maneuvering for advantage, each against the others.

1

His decisions still conferred an air of legality, the impress of legitimacy, if little else.

Nevertheless, Shah Alam was approaching a crisis. Delhi's Shahjahan-abad, the grand imperial city within a city that the Mughal emperor had built in the middle of the seventeenth century, was a viper's nest of warlords and intrigue. Circling above were vultures, the major pow-ers, the English and the Marathas prominent among them, waiting for the emperor – the system – to falter and collapse so that they might feed on his carcass. They had plenty of cause to expect a ready feast. The weaker Shah Alam had become, the more he strove to retain his independence: and the more he attracted to his side men without clear allegiances, dangerous men, men with nothing to lose. Of particular concern to Shah Alam, and to all interested observers, in late July of 1788 was Ghulam Qadir Khan, an Afghan warlord who held the emperor prisoner in his own palace. Ghulam Qadir was unpredictable: his hatred for the emperor, fueled by the humiliation his family had suffered years earlier, was matched only by his thirst for treasure. But the emperor was not forthcoming on the location of the secret storerooms in the palace. Infuriated, the Afghan ordered Shah Alam's eyes pierced with needles. The next day, he person-ally carved one eyeball out of its socket and ordered a fellow Afghan to extract the other.

Not far from Delhi was another unpredictable warlord, the Maratha Mahadji Shinde. Shinde had remained aloof in the summer of 1788 while Ghulam Qadir had his way with the emperor and his family. Finally, late in the day, he decided to act. He soon took Delhi and captured Ghulam Qadir in the process. In 1789, at the repeated demands of Shah Alam, Shinde ordered the Afghan's eyes removed and sent in a casket to the restored imperial court in Delhi. But the damage had been done. The Afghan's atrocities, as Jadunath Sarkar justly remarked, "ruined the prestige of the empire beyond recovery."[1] They also cleared the way for open competition between the two major powers with subcontinental designs, the English and the Marathas.

If Delhi was the decaying inner city, the urban jungle of late eighteenth-century India, many of the "Vice Lords"[2] who prowled – or policed – its dark, narrow lanes in 1788 were *gosain* warriors commanded by the

---

[1] Jadunath Sarkar, *Fall of the Mughal Empire*, 4th edn (New Delhi 1991), vol. III, p. 263. Sarkar's narrative of Ghulam Qadir's rise and fall is on pp. 257–280. For an account of the atrocities committed by Ghulam Qadir, see Fakir Khairu-d Din Muhammad, '*Ibrat-Nama*, trans. H. M. Elliot and J. Dowson in *The History of India as Told by its Own Historians*, vol. VIII (London 1873), pp. 249–254.

[2] R. Lincoln Keiser, *The Vice Lords: Warriors of the Streets* (New York 1969). The Vice Lords are a powerful North American gang founded in the 1950s in the Lawndale section of Chicago.

shadowy figure of one "Himmat Bahadur." Indeed, Himmat Bahadur was as responsible as anyone (although Shinde comes a close second) for the depths to which Delhi had sunk in 1788. He had been secretly colluding with Ghulam Qadir since early August of 1787.[3] When the emperor's palace guard had withdrawn later in that year, Himmat Bahadur was left with the responsibility of patrolling the walls of the city. He withdrew his forces in mid-July, just as Ghulam Qadir was entering Delhi, thereby abandoning the Mughal emperor to his fate. It turns out that he was motivated not by hatred for the emperor, but by a desire for revenge – against Mahadji Shinde. Four years earlier Himmat Bahadur had engineered every aspect of Shinde's foray into and ascendancy over Delhi,[4] but he was rewarded with treachery. Shinde had brushed him and his men aside and had tried to take away their massive revenue estates near Delhi and pension them off to a paltry assignment in rugged Bundelkhand.[5] Himmat Bahadur would have none of it: Ghulam Qadir, it would appear, was his way of trying to lure Shinde into a close-quarter battle the Maratha could not win. It almost worked, but in the end Shinde would not take the bait. So Himmat Bahadur withdrew his forces so as to avoid blame for the ugly consequences that were sure to follow.

Shinde sought to imprison Himmat Bahadur in the summer of 1789, ostensibly for his role in the degradation of the emperor but mostly because the Maratha despised the *gosain*. Among other allegations, Shinde blamed him for his own failure to gain a permanent ascendancy over the Mughal throne in 1785 – even though the real cause of Shinde's frustrations was Shinde himself, particularly his rash decision to engage in a military contest with the kingdom of Jaipur to the west soon after gaining Delhi. But there was another fuel that stoked Shinde's wrath that summer: He suffered from a painful case of the boils which, he claimed, was caused by Himmat Bahadur's "magical arts."[6] Shinde's

---

[3] Kirkpatrick to Governor General Cornwallis, letter received 17 Sept. 1787 (dated 5 Aug.), Bengal Secret and Political Consultation (BSPC), Oriental and India Office Collection (OIOC), British Library, London.

[4] See Major James Browne, "Memorandum for Mr. Hastings, respecting the State of Affairs in Hindostan, January 1, 1785" (Add. MS 29,209, Hastings Papers, Manuscripts Reading Room [henceforward MRR], British Library, London), esp. fols. 161b–177a.

[5] See, for example, letters from Anderson, the Resident with Shinde at Dig, to Cornwallis, letter received 8 February 1786 (dated 18? Jan. and 9 Mar.), BSPC; and "Copy of an arzie from Rajah Omrou Gir Behadre, written to the Nawaub Vizier," enclosed in a letter from Harper, the Resident at Lucknow, to Governor General Cornwallis, letter received 17 Sept. 1787 (dated 14 Aug.), BSPC. Omrou Gir Behadre was Himmat Bahadur's brother, better known to us as Umraogiri.

[6] Ives to Cornwallis, letter received 12 Aug. 1789 (dated 30 Jul.), BSPC. The full episode is narrated in Jadunath Sarkar, *Fall of the Mughal Empire*, 4th edn (New Delhi 1991), vol. IV, pp. 6–10.

men even produced a woman who gave evidence to this effect, and who appeared able to ease his symptoms. Himmat Bahadur escaped from Shinde's guard, however, and took refuge with another Maratha warlord, Ali Bahadur, the "illegitimate" grandson of the *peshwa* who had recently arrived in the neighborhood seeking to make his fortune out of the chaos of Delhi politics. Eventually, through the intercession of Ali Bahadur – who stood to gain much from the armed men and political information that Himmat Bahadur could provide – Shinde was forced by the *peshwa* to make peace with the *gosain*. An unusual scene followed, in which Shinde presented himself at Ali Bahadur's camp and invested Himmat Bahadur with a *khilat*, a robe of honor. Normally, the Mughal ritual of *khilat* signified the subordination of the recipient, in this case Himmat Bahadur. But normally such gifting takes place in the *darbar* of the person giving the robes. However, Himmat Bahadur had refused to go to Shinde's *darbar* as a suppliant, begging for pardon. So, instead, Shinde was forced to go to him – in effect, to do the begging himself. This constituted a public humiliation of massive proportions for the Maratha warlord. But he had no choice: the only other option was a robe of honor for Himmat Bahadur from the *peshwa* himself. It was a blow from which Mahadji Shinde would not recover.

The remarkable sequence of events in 1788–1789 was a typical turning of the tables orchestrated by Himmat Bahadur. Indeed, the more one examines the succession of events that marked Mughal (and Maratha) decline in the late eighteenth century, and the concomitant rise of British power, the more one sees the outline of Himmat Bahadur in the background. On several occasions he emerges into the light. He fought on the side of the Mughal emperor and the Afghans against the Marathas at Panipat in 1761; he was present with the Awadhi and Mughal forces against British forces at Buxar in 1764, and helped Shuja ud-Daula escape after his defeat; he was instrumental in the downfall of Bharatpur and the rise of Najaf Khan, the Persian adventurer, at Delhi in the 1770s; he engineered Mahadji Shinde's foray into Delhi politics in the 1780s; he was the force behind Ali Bahadur's conquest of Bundelkhand in the name of the *peshwa* in the 1790s. His last act, at the end of his life in 1803, was to enable the Maratha defeat at the hands of the British in Bundelkhand and the Doab and, thereby, the British capture of Delhi, an event that catapulted the Hon'ble Company into the role of paramount power in southern Asia – and ultimately the world.

Himmat Bahadur was ubiquitous because he was the kind of person that everyone needed. He was reviled because he was the kind of person that everyone hated needing. He was the inside operator people turned to when they wanted troops, an ear to the ground, a deft negotiator, or a dirty job done quietly. His genius lay in his ability to parlay his indispensability into power. He was aided in his work by the fact that he was not high-born, and he did not suffer the illusions of the high-born: he knew how and when to fight – and when to run. He knew how to convince his opponents and allies alike that he had nothing to lose. And though he commanded thousands of men, he never suffered from the Achilles' heel that plagued warlords like Shinde: the constant clamor of troops demanding their arrears in pay. Himmat Bahadur was, arguably, the most successful military entrepreneur of the late eighteenth century. He certainly had better staying power than any other late eighteenth-century actor, save the corporate body of John Company. And, perhaps, that is why he joined it in the end.

This book was written, in part, out of a desire to understand Himmat Bahadur. But in order to understand him we must peel away a succession of veils. The first veil to be removed is the name "Himmat Bahadur." This was a "Persianate" nickname of sorts meaning "great courage," awarded to him for an act of bravery in the service of the Nawab of Awadh in the 1750s.[7] It is the name that tends to show up in Company and Persian correspondence from the eighteenth century. The name he went by both before and after his *nom de guerre* gained currency in official correspondence, and the name I tend to use in this book, is Anupgiri Gosain – or simply Anupgiri. This earlier name brings us closer to who he was: like the men he commanded, Anupgiri was a *gosain*. This fact means that in addition to being India's most successful military entrepreneur in the eighteenth century, Anupgiri was also a "Saiva ascetic" – or, for those who find these two words obscure, a Hindu renouncer who worshipped Siva. As I make clear in the chapters that follow, the words Hindu, renouncer, worship – even Siva – are not as straightforward or simple as they appear.

But the name Anupgiri Gosain, too, is a kind of veil. It conceals the fact that we do not – and cannot – know his first name, the name his mother and father gave him at birth. This is because his father's death left his mother destitute: she sold her two children in their infancy to the man who became, in Saiva sectarian memory and in fact, their guru and commander.

If these sentences convey an impression of Indian religion and asceticism that is at odds with the model the reader was raised with, it is because that model was based on wishful thinking. One object of

---

[7] This according to Bhagvandin, the editor of Padmakar's *Himmatbahadur Virdavali* (Banaras n.d.), xxi. Bhagvandin gives no source, but it is likely that his account of Himmat Bahadur's life was based largely on legend and the stories told by the warlord's descendants. He adds that Himmat Bahadur was wounded in the thigh while protecting Shuja during the Battle of Buxar in 1764.

this book, and this introduction, is to reflect on the possibility of a better model.

Killing ascetics

Anupgiri Gosain, alias Himmat Bahadur, was a Saiva ascetic warrior and warlord. The chapters that follow are also an attempt to understand, often through him, what it meant to be a Saiva ascetic warrior and warlord in a late medieval world that was being catapulted by global transformations into the modern. More generally, this book is a history of Hindu ascetics who kill – and of the slow rise and demise of those killing ascetics between 1500 and the present. Armed Hindu ascetics have been known across the centuries by various names. I first came across them as *naga*s, a term that is said to refer to their nakedness in battle, from the Sanskrit *"nagna."* However, the first use of the term *naga* for such men that I am aware of is from the eighteenth century. Sixteenth and seventeenth-century authors tended to speak of *yogi*s (or *jogi, ioghee*) when describing these kinds of men, sometimes in a disparaging manner. The eighteenth century saw the increased use of the terms *sanyasi* (*sannyasi, sunnasee*) and *fakir* (*faquir, fukeer*), particularly by British officials in Bengal. To the west, toward Allahabad, Lucknow, and Delhi, the term *gosain* (*gossye, gusain, gusaiyan*) prevailed. Further west still, toward Jaipur in particular, the term *bairagi* (*byragee, vairagi*) gained prominence. This terminological variety is due partly to sectarian distinctions: *bairagi*, for example, tends to refer to ascetics oriented toward Vishnu or one of his avatars, Rama or Krishna. But much of it reflects the fact that observers did not, and still do not, know what to make of these armed men on the margins of religion and society.

This is not the first time warrior ascetics in India – or Anupgiri and his men, for that matter – have appeared on the radar screens of modern historians. The first scholarly attempt to explain warrior ascetics in Indian history was the work of the Scottish missionary–scholar, J. N. Farquhar, in particular in an article he authored in 1925 entitled "The Fighting Ascetics of India."[8] The timing of this article (and Farquhar's interest in warrior ascetics generally) is significant, coming as it did in the wake of Mohandas Gandhi's revolutionary rise to power in Indian nationalist politics after 1919. The rising profile of Gandhi's own ascetic repudiation of violence, particularly in the West, meant that warrior ascetics were

---

[8] J. N. Farquhar, "The Fighting Ascetics of India," *Bulletin of the John Rylands Library* 9 (1925): 431–452. See also his "The Organization of the Sannyasis of the Vedanta," *Journal of the Royal Asiatic Society* (July 1925): 479–486.

increasingly seen as a "problem" that Western scholars needed to resolve – particularly if they were to be able to properly understand the social and religious depth of Gandhi's civilizational claims. For Farquhar the particular challenge was explaining how the peaceful ascetic order created by the ninth-century sage Shankaracharya evolved a numerically dominant military wing, a wing that would have been on prominent display during his visit to the Allahabad *kumbha mela* in 1918.[9] His explanation pointed to the rise of Islam in South Asia – and more particularly to the persecution (according to sectarian legend) of non-violent Hindu *sanyasi*s by fanatical Sufi warriors, *ghazi*s intent on stamping out pagan religious practices. The historiographical significance of Farquhar's assertions is that it inaugurated in the Western academy a communalist explanation of Hindu warrior asceticism that has not, to date, received a serious challenge. It is not difficult to see why: officials and historians, Indian as well as British, had long cited Hindu–Muslim difference – and its corollary, violence – as a defining feature of Indian history and society; the explosion of Hindu-versus-Muslim antagonism and communal violence after 1920, and the institutionalization of that antagonism and violence in Partition and the divided nation-states of India and Pakistan after 1947, only served to further embed the communalist understanding of the Indian past.[10] Even David Lorenzen, whose important 1978 essay did much to dispel the simplistic notion that the initial arming of Hindu ascetics was a response to Muslim atrocities, himself suggested that the coming of Muslim rule in India – and with it broad legal, political, and cultural sanctions in Islam for the persecution of non-Muslims – probably acted as the catalyst that resulted in the formal militarization of Hindu ascetic orders.[11]

For my part, it is not my intention to argue against Farquhar (or Lorenzen for that matter), that Muslim persecution, legal or otherwise,

---

[9] In his essay, "The Historical Position of Ramananda (part 1)," *Journal of the Royal Asiatic Society* (April 1920): 185, Farquhar reports that he attended the 1918 Allahabad festival. The *kumbha mela* is a massive pilgrimage festival that alternates every three years between Allahabad, Ujjain, Hardwar, and Nasik. It attracts millions of lay pilgrims and tens of thousands of ascetics from throughout India and is the occasion for the initiation of thousands of young men into the major armed orders. The central spectacle of the *kumbha* is the procession of the *naga akhara*s to sacred water (at Allahabad, the *sangam*) during astrologically pre-ordained moments; these processions are known as "*shahi snan*", or "the imperial immersion" – a term that reflects, as I argue in chapter 1, the involvement of the Mughal imperial court in the affairs of the armed ascetic orders.

[10] See Gyanendra Pandey, *The Construction of Communalism in Colonial North India* (Delhi 1990); Peter Gottschalk, *Beyond Hindu and Muslim: Multiple Identity in Narratives from Rural India* (New York 2000); and Peter van der Veer, *Religious Nationalism: Hindus and Muslims in India* (Berkeley 1994).

[11] David Lorenzen, "Warrior Ascetics in Indian History," *Journal of the American Oriental Society* 98 (1978): 68.

had nothing to do with the original arming of non-Muslim Indian ascetics. This is because we do not, I believe, possess sufficient evidence to argue the case one way or the other. What we do possess is evidence that calls into question the hard boundaries posited between Hindu and Muslim in the late medieval, early modern period – particularly in reference to armed ascetics. To some degree, this renders the original, communal question moot. Nevertheless, I feel the communalist oral tradition upon which Farquhar relied does transmit an important kernel of meaning, and I draw upon it in chapter 1 to argue that what we later come to know as Hindu warrior asceticism *was* in some – perhaps unexpected – ways a product (though not an anachronistic or antagonistic one) of Mughal rule. Hence the title of the chapter, "Mughal *yogis*." Similarly, I argue in chapter 2 that Saiva ascetic guru-commanders were well placed tactically, socially, and culturally – and even religiously – to respond to the need for increasingly well-trained, mobile, and inexpensive bodies of men in the changing military economy of the eighteenth century. Moreover, some of these Saiva commanders were particularly well positioned to respond to and take advantage of Company expansion out of Bengal and up the Gangetic Plain toward Delhi. Hence the title of chapter 3, "Company *gosains*." Similarly the title of chapter 6, "Indian *sadhus*," is intended to characterize the ways in which armed ascetics refashioned themselves in (and were refashioned by) the nineteenth and twentieth centuries in response to the religious forces of imperialism and nationalism, particularly devotionalism.

The goal in all of this is not to suggest that armed ascetics were simply a product of their times – indeed, far from it. Such an impulse is an unfortunate by-product of the reasonable desire of scholars in the academy to combat "primordialism" and "essentialism" in the wider world. Rather, the goal is to counter the pervasive popular and occasionally scholarly tendency to accept uncritically a distinctly modern oral narrative of armed asceticism that begins with the organizational genius of Shankaracharya in the ninth century, and begins again with the violent arrival of Muslims in the eleventh century.[12] While I agree – indeed, I argue – that we cannot understand what we now know as Hindu warrior asceticism without recourse to religion, that religion may not be recognizable as distinctly or exclusively Hindu, or even necessarily anti-Muslim, especially given the complex history that swirls around it between 1500 and 2000. There is something else, beneath and beyond Hindu and Muslim, that we need to

---

[12] See, e.g., Jadunath Sarkar (and Nirod Bhusan Roy) *History of the Dasnami Naga Sanyasis* (Allahabad n.d. but probably mid 1950s); G. S. Ghurye, *Indian Sadhus* (2nd edn, Bombay 1964); and Sadananda Giri, *Society and Sannyasin (A History of the Dasnami Sannyasins)* (Rishikesh 1976). I will have more to say about Jadunath Sarkar's work in chapter 3.

put our finger on – to take the pulse of, as it were. I return to this point momentarily, and to religion more generally.

Though the scope for the application of their craft is today much constrained, warrior ascetics continue to exercise considerable influence in modern India, particularly in the nationalist imagination. This stems in large part from the literary genius of the Bengali nationalist writer, Bankim Chandra Chatterji. Beginning in the 1870s, Bankim depicted armed Hindu ascetics as proto-modern Indian patriots, sprung from the soil to defend Hinduism against Muslim and British invasions.[13] For the *naga sadhu*s of the present, and those middle-class nationalists who idealize them in their imaginations, the emotional appeal of this chivalric role as defenders of a beleaguered religion (and religious nation) is that it papers over their (the *akhara*s' [confraternities][14]) much more complicated investment in the Mughal and Company past. More pragmatically, by accommodating themselves to the image of the patriotic Hindu ascetic, opportunistic *naga* chiefs (or *mahant*s) have gained access to a newly emergent north Indian power base, namely, urban middle-class Hindu nationalism and the political plums that have recently accrued to it. This was a two-way street: if *naga mahant*s eyed middle-class Hindu nationalism with a desire to expand their influence among Vaishnavas, Hindu nationalists also eyed the *naga mahant*s with their own, wider political agendas. The recruitment of the *akhara*s by Hindu nationalists began in the early twentieth century, but the real political payoff only came in the late 1980s when several *naga mahant*s allowed themselves and their organizations to be swept up in the movement to reclaim the remembered birthplace of Rama at Ayodhya. Untangling the knotted threads of the "*Ramajanambhumi*" movement is not a goal of this work – indeed, the more I examined that knot, the more it metamorphosed into a red, or rather saffron, herring, not really that revealing in the longer history of warrior asceticism.[15] And in any case, it seems clear that despite the continued persistence of "godmen" in Indian politics, the Hindu right

---

[13] *Anandamatha* (Calcutta 1882), trans. as *The Abbey of Bliss* by Nares Chandra Sen (Calcutta 1906). For a more detailed discussion of this and the other issues raised in this paragraph, see William Pinch, "Soldier Monks and Militant Sadhus," in David Ludden (ed.), *Contesting the Nation: Religion, Community, and the Politics of Democracy in India* (Philadelphia 1996), pp. 140–162; and chapter 6, in this volume.

[14] See chapter 1, fn. 15.

[15] Save to note that beneath the remembered Hindu–Muslim fractures in Ayodhya today lies a deep, and oblique, Saiva–Vaishnava fault line. This is certainly a question worth more research, and any inquiry should begin with three facts: first, the presence of numerous *gosain* followers of Anupgiri and Umraogiri in Awadh in the eighteenth century; second, the increasing involvement of Jaisingh II of Jaipur and his successors (and of ascetics headquartered in Galta) in the religious affairs in the Vaishnava pilgrimage centers of north India, including most notably, Ayodhya, also in the eighteenth century; and third, the gradual accommodation of Saiva ascetics to Vaishnava institutionalization through the course of the nineteenth century.

no longer possesses, in the twenty-first century, the monopoly on Indian *sadhu*s that it did in the twentieth. Many *akhara*s, and many *mahant*s, have learned that political success means not putting all your eggs in one basket – and that the religious understandings of middle-class Hindu nationalism do not necessarily accord with their own.

The contentious politics that swirled around armed ascetics in the nineteenth and twentieth centuries were what first attracted me to them as a subject for study. Despite the popular assumptions concerning the organic patriotism of armed Hindu ascetics,[16] the details of their past, as I show in the first three chapters, are much more complicated and contradictory. Far from thinking of themselves as the last line of defense against foreign invaders, armed ascetics in the seventeenth, eighteenth, and early nineteenth centuries served any and all paymasters, including the Mughals and the British. Nor did they understand themselves as fundamentally or exclusively Hindu in the modern sense of the term, but rather drew on multiple martial and political idioms, including idioms we normally associate with the British and the Mughals. Despite the claims of twentieth-century oral tradition (the examination of which forms the introduction to chapter 1), the origins of the *naga akhara*s are not to be found in the imputed civilizational conflict between Muslim and Hindu. It seems much more likely, as I suggest in chapters 2 and 5, that weapons (and the art of violence) were part of a *shaktiyoga* repertoire that centered on harnessing supernormal forces both within and beyond the human body. This might be read as an overly idealist account, given Lorenzen's emphasis on material factors – especially the need to protect religious endowments from treasure-hungry monarchs – in the early manifestations of warrior asceticism in the latter part of the first millennium CE.[17] As I see it, Lorenzen's quite convincing materialist account nevertheless begs the question of where the wealth came from in the first place, especially if we acknowledge that the dominant religious culture was not necessarily a devotionalist, dualist one. In any case, the distinction between idealist and materialist causality tends to dissolve in the face of monistic sensibilities.

---

[16] And in case there are any doubts about the persistence of those assumptions, one need only tour the new Museum of Indian Independence in Delhi's Red Fort. A caption describing early resistance to English East India Company rule reads as follows: "In eastern India, displaced peasants and Bengal soldiers joined hands with religious monks and uprooted zamindars rose up [sic] in the Sanyasi revolution (1763–1800). 'Bande Mataram' the patriotic song composed by Bankim Chandra Chatterjee in his novel Anand Math, inspired greatly the Sanyasi Movement." I am grateful to Peter Gottschalk for this information.

[17] Lorenzen, "Warrior Ascetics in Indian History," 64–65.

As should be evident from the foregoing paragraph, any history of armed ascetics in India is also, at some level, a history of Indian religion. But as also should be evident from the preceding paragraph, there was no monolithic "Hinduism" in the period under review. Historians of religion in India have been arguing for some time now that the presumed holistic systematicity of modern Hinduism conceals (and is a product of) social and political shifts, especially over the last two centuries. The varied strands that are thought to operate as complementary (if occasionally controversial) sources of Hindu belief and practice today were often, even as late as the nineteenth century, ranged in fierce opposition to one another – or, at best, were so mutually unpalatable as to require careful distancing and concealment in the lives of practitioners. Likewise with Indian Islam. Armed ascetics were, I argue, in the thick of these controversies, and in some ways were the products of them.

Looking to pre-modern religion for answers to political and military questions in India is a risky analytical venture for another reason. Scholars working on religion in recent years, and particularly historically minded cultural anthropologists, have begun to take note of the fact that the Western understanding of religion reflects the Enlightenment's proximity to Christianity, or more precisely, to private belief in a distant, inscrutable, loving God. As historian John Bossy put it, religion had become by 1700 "a worshipful attitude to God or a respect for holy things."[18] One possible response to this insight, particularly in light of recent postmodernist trends in South Asian historiography, would be to conclude that armed *gosain*s, *sanyasi*s, and the like were not "religious" at all but were constituted as such by the British as part of a process of discursive disarmament. And indeed, there is a certain amount of truth to this line of reasoning: the British did bring a certain Christian, Enlightenment disposition to their understanding of religion – with belief in and distance from an inscrutable, loving God at its ontological core – to the epistemological challenges that India posed for them (and they contributed thereby to the intellectual evolution of what came to be described as "Hinduism"). The assumptions about religion that British officials brought to their work, grounded in a dualist understanding of God as A Thing Apart, could not begin to encompass men

---

[18] John Bossy, *Christianity in the West, 1400–1700* (Oxford 1985), p. 171; for the argument that the hermeneutic dilemma, especially as it prevails in anthropology, renders the term "religion" contingent and invalid, see Talal Asad, "Anthropological Conceptions of Religion: Reflections on Geertz," *Man* n.s. 18, 2 (June 1983): 237–259; later published, with modifications, as "The Construction of Religion as an Anthropological Category," in his, *Genealogies of Religion: Discipline and Reasons of Power in Christianity and Islam* (Baltimore 1993), pp. 27–54.

bent on the bodily cultivation of supernormal power – in other words, men who would be gods. Certainly the heirs of Anupgiri Gosain did not measure up to the British application of an Enlightenment yardstick of religion during the course of the early nineteenth century – and the British used this fact against them in the 1840s, as I show in chapter 4.

This does not mean, however, that armed ascetics had nothing to do with religion – and that therefore an analytic category of religion should not be used to understand them. The British application, unconscious or otherwise, of a normative conception of religion served to structure their own actions and decisions with respect to armed ascetics. The British were not, in the main, overly concerned with the task of convincing them of the correctness of their Enlightenment conception of religion. They did not have to be: a major strand of Indian religious reform was tending in the same general direction as late medieval, early modern Christianity, and had been for some time. And the purveyors of that Indian religious reform also took a dim view of men who encroached upon the terrain of God. I will return to this point in the following section, and it is the subject of part of chapter 5. For the present, however, it is important to distinguish between understanding how the British (and how Indian religious reformers) understood armed ascetics, and how armed ascetics understood themselves.

In order for the armed ascetic to make sense, in order for the "ascetic archer" (to use a pejorative label that was launched at him by some of his Indian critics [see chapter 5]) to be more than a contradiction in terms, we need an understanding of religion that takes us beyond the pious Enlightenment posture of "a worshipful attitude to God or a respect for holy things." But we must again proceed with caution: "religion" should not be understood to be so inclusive as to make room for every potent symbol-system that makes sense of the world, confers meaning, and enables group activity. At best, understanding religion as simply a system of symbols has the effect of reducing core tenets and practices to an ontological level of unreality, to mere representation – which most of their adherents-*cum*-practitioners would do well to dispute.[19] At worst, it has the potential to elevate that which is trivial yet pervasive in culture (e.g., American football) on to a par with that which billions of people regard as central to their very existence – to their life

---

[19] Brad Gregory, "The Other Confessional History," Wesleyan University Snowdon Lecture on the Study and Teaching of Religion, 1 May 2002, pp. 7–9; I am grateful to the author for allowing me to cite this unpublished essay. See also Brad Gregory, *Salvation at Stake: Christian Martyrdom in Early Modern Europe* (Cambridge, MA 1999), introduction.

and their death. Even if religion has become a "second-order generic concept"[20] to be brought to bear in investigation and analysis as scholars see fit, it still possesses roots in the European and Christian past.[21] Cutting those roots may not trouble some social scientists (again, historically minded cultural anthropologists come to mind), particularly those whose primary concern is with the politics of the now, for whom the past is a land inhabited by distant adversaries who must be remade to suit the needs of the present. But for those who understand history to be, at least in part, a conversation with the past – for those who are taught to temper their own theoretical and methodological dispositions with the thoughts and actions of the people in the past so as to arrive at an understanding across time – it is a fatal choice. It deprives the past of language, and renders the conversation wholly one-sided.

The issue, then, is which past we should look to for our reformulation of religion as a "second-order generic concept" – and whether it must be simply European and Christian. Clearly it should not be the remarkable post-Reformation Christian moment that produced the Enlightenment – that annoying wellspring of all our hermeneutic dilemmas, including postmodernism itself. As appealing as Enlightenment Christianity is to our modernist sensibilities, our devotion to Reason, and our desire for religious tolerance, this would only return us to "a worshipful attitude toward God and a respect for holy things" – neither of which soldiering *gosain*s seemed to possess to any significant degree. But neither should it be so remote from that Enlightenment Christianity as to be unrecognizable to it. We need to look to older, less compartmentalized understandings – both within the Christian tradition and within traditions against which Christianity defined itself. Here it is appropriate to let the objects of study take a hand in our understanding of religion – to become, for a time, subjects in their own representation.[22] Late eighteenth-century *gosain*s – moments away from being subsumed in the expanding Enlightenment (and thus becoming, as "other", part of the European, Christian past) – explained the decision to take up arms in the following way: a young ascetic was guarding a cave, inside which was his guru who had entered

---

[20] Jonathan Z. Smith, "Religion, Religions, Religious," in Mark Taylor (ed.), *Critical Terms for Religious Studies* (Chicago 1998), p. 281.

[21] I am concerned not with the etymological puzzle represented by the term religion, which is properly elaborated as a "cautionary parable" in Benson Saler, "*Religio* and the Definition of Religion," *Cultural Anthropology* 2, 3 (Aug 1987): 395–399 (396 for the quote), but with the Christian experience that shaped understandings of it.

[22] In other words, my preference is to tinker with the language of analysis, not the object of study. I am aware that the very act of examining something causes it to change, but it is better to burden the reader with only one layer of hermeneutic complexity rather than two.

the deathless state of *samadhi*. A stranger approached and tried to enter the cave but the young boy blocked the entrance. The visitor, it turned out, was no ordinary mortal: he was the undead guru of the boy's guru's guru. Impressed by the devotion of the child to his master, the undead visitor granted a boon. The boy replied that he wished to be a great king. The visitor pronounced that the boy and his *chelas* (disciples) would one day rule. The boy's name was Rajendragiri. He would grow up to be a warlord in Bundelkhand: and while on the march one day he would come upon a destitute widow who would sell to him her two infant children. One of those children would grow up to become Anupgiri Gosain, alias Himmat Bahadur.[23]

The significance, for us, of this foundational episode is not the prophecy about power but the detail about immortality. Today "*samadhi*" is understood to refer to the deep meditation that is required in order to achieve union of the self, *atma*, with ultimate being, or *adhyatma*. In the premodern context in which it is intended here, however, *samadhi* refers to the *yogi*'s achievement of immortality through discipline – his (and sometimes her) conquest of death. The guru of Rajendragiri's guru's guru had long since entered this undead state; his arrival at the entrance to the cave indicated that Rajendragiri's guru, too, had just achieved immortality. Conquering death, as becomes clear in chapters 1 and 2, is what medieval *yogis* do. As the great sage and *yogi*-master Svatmarama put it in the penultimate verses of the fifteenth-century *Hathayogapradipika*,

107. The yogi who has passed beyond all the states and is freed from all thoughts and who appears as if dead is liberated without doubt.
108. A yogi in samadhi is not swallowed up by death [*kal*]; he is not affected by action [*karman*]; he cannot fall under the influence of others.
109. A yogi in samadhi apprehends neither smell, taste, form or colour, touch, or sound; he does not cognize himself or others.
110. One in whom the mind is neither asleep nor awake, whose mind is free of memories and of forgetfulness, which neither goes into oblivion nor into activity – such a one is indeed liberated.
111. A yogi in samadhi is not affected by heat or cold, pain or pleasure, honour or dishonour.
112. Verily, he is a liberated one, who is clear-minded, who is in the waking state, yet appears to be in sleep, devoid of inhalation and exhalation.
113. A yogi in samadhi is not vulnerable to any weapons, not assailable by any persons, not subject to control by the use of magical incantations.[24]

[23] Man Kavi, "Anupa Prakasa," Mss.Hin.D.9(a), OIOC, 1a; see also the more accessible Hindi translation by Lala Bahadur Bhatt (1894), Mss.Hin.D.9(b), 1a. I am grateful to Kailash Jha for ensuring the accuracy of this translation.

[24] *The Hathayogapradipika of Svatmarama*, with the commentary *Jyotsna-* of Brahmananda and English translation (Madras 1972), pp. 82–83. I have improved the translation slightly.

From the perspective of the *yogi*, the key objective was victory over death. With a little work, this objective can be massaged into a serviceable, and – dare I say it – even universal, definition of religion. All living creatures face the problem of death; all sentient creatures reflect, at some point, on the approach of death. Religion is to find a way through death, to cheat its temporal finality and to thereby conquer it. It is necessarily subjunctive, infinitive. In retrospect it is easy to see that the problem of death and the desire to conquer it has given rise to practices, disciplines, ideas, and institutions that the globalized European Enlightenment chose to describe, and circumscribe, with the inherited term "religion." To the surprise of many of the heirs of the Enlightenment, religion has a nasty way of bursting the seams that modernity seeks to sew around it. Death is why. More on that in a moment. For the *yogi*, the conquest of death (and, by extension, the limitations of time and space) is an end in itself; it is the product of esoteric knowledge and practices, available to the select few. It is a way of self-transformation, elevation, of becoming a god. For the Christian the conquest of death is thrown open to all by Christ incarnate on the cross; that conquest is structured not as an end in itself but a doorway, a way-station en route to a timeless, blissful existence in the presence of a loving God. This is not at all unlike the dualist devotional religious vision of the *bhakta* or Hindu "devotee," for whom love of Sita–Ram or Radha–Krishna is the vehicle that transports him across "the ocean of existence" so that he may sit "in the lap of the Lord."

What, then, of the postmodernist claim, by now a commonplace, that "there cannot be a universal definition of religion, not only because its constituent elements and relationships are historically specific, but because that definition is itself the historical product of discursive processes."[25] Upon close examination, the objection is not tenable. This is because it can refer properly only to definitions of religion that descend, whether consciously or unconsciously, from the privatized, belief-centered understanding produced by post-Reformation Enlightenment Christianity. As noted, there is much to recommend this specific critique. But it simply does not follow that there cannot be a trans-historical

---

[25] Asad, *Genealogies of Religion*, p. 29. It is instructive to compare Asad of 1993 with his far more equivocal position of 1983 ("Anthropological Conceptions of Religion," 238): "there cannot be a definition of religion which is universally viable because and to the extent that the effects of these processes are historically produced, reproduced and transformed." Enlightenment discourse – or, rather, a particular reading of Enlightenment discourse – has emerged as so central as to render the very possibility of a universal definition moot. In any case, Asad's more recent statement has become the gold standard for the postmodernist critique of Enlightenment "religion" and its corollary, the impossibility of a universal definition. See, e.g., Richard King, *Orientalism and Religion: Postcolonial Theory, India and "the Mystic East"* (London 1999), pp. 10–12.

and trans-cultural phenomenon that includes Christianity and is denoted by the term "religion." There is no better evidence for this than the fact that the authors and adherents of the postmodernist critique themselves maintain the objection because the abstraction "religion" produced by the Enlightenment cannot, in their view, help but fail to properly apprehend non-Western and pre-Enlightenment Western "religious phenomena."[26] Much as they seek to avoid essentialist nominalism, they themselves admit by implication the existence of a common denominator. "Religion" has been used in many different ways over many centuries. One might even argue that it has been functioning as a "second-order generic concept" practically from the time Greek meanings began to suffuse the Latin term.[27] The casual Enlightenment usage of the term "religion" to denote – even if we long have not realized it – the varied technologies of immortality across cultures and time may have produced semantic confusion. But we should not allow that semantic confusion to empower those who would sow epistemological chaos. Let us speak truth to power. There are certain universals that bind us. Death is one of them. We are not bound by how we choose to confront it. But confront it we must. And when we confront it and conquer it, we enter the province of religion.

The denial of the possibility of a universal definition of religion has been articulated in terms of the historical contingency of Enlightenment Christianity, but it is grounded in the conviction that a universal definition is a mask for asserting an "essence" to religion – and that somehow that "essentialising" move "invites us to separate [religion] from the domain of power."[28] But is this a valid presumption? What if the definition we settle upon allows wide latitude for the conjunction of religion and power? Surely such a definition answers the original, justifiable complaint. As the "essence" of religion, victory over death is precisely such a definition – because not only does it allow for power, it is rife with it. With death as the common denominator, the armed *yogi* is not a contradiction in terms: his conquest of death requires that we see him as religious, and his conquest of death guarantees worldly power. As a soldier he is simply someone who may possess, or may be feared to possess, the tactical advantage of being invulnerable. At the very least, his skeptical opponent would nonetheless be concerned that the armed *yogi* possesses the battlefield confidence that such corporeal invulnerability would confer. Likewise the crusader monk in Europe, who is akin to an armed *sadhu*, may possess, or may be feared to possess – or be feared to possess a belief in – a different kind of

---

[26] King, *Orientalism and Religion*, p. 10.

[27] Hans Dieter Betz, "Christianity as Religion: Paul's Attempt at Definition in Romans," *The Journal of Religion* 71, 3 (July 1991): 315–344.

[28] Asad, *Genealogies of Religion*, p. 29.

tactical advantage, the favor of the Lord. It is only natural that, prior to the emergence of the modern state, such men might parlay that tactical advantage into institutionalized forms of power. But whereas the worldly trappings of that power would pose a problem for the dualist, devotionalist Christian monk, for whom all glory must go to God, it would pose no problem for the monist, yoga-tantric Saiva ascetic, precisely because all glory must go to gods.

Mughal, British, and Vaishnava

The reader may notice that in the pages that follow I avoid use of the term "colonial" to describe British India. This is primarily because India was not a British colony in the strict sense of the term. Despite this indisputable historical fact, the term "colonial" (and derivatives of it) has become a commonplace in the historical study of British India. This stems – or at the very least takes sustenance – from what may be called a historiographical "bifocalism," namely, the tendency to project the political ruptures over racial and national identity of the late twentieth century on to earlier periods, particularly in the form of historical discontinuity and essential cognitive difference between Indian and European.[29] I am by no means the first to raise this point.[30] What matters is "that a careful reading of pre-British historical data can turn up historical continuities where postmodernist and postcolonial scholarship, inclined as it is to privilege European discursive traditions and the epistemological

:s only discontinuities."[31] One of the
itish are thought to have occasioned is
nassaging Indian religion into a shape
ment dispositions.

rtant for precisely this reason: he both
, tectonic shifts in the religious and

n India and Europe," *History and Theory* 38, 3

. A. Bayly, particularly *Empire and Information:*
iication in India, 1780–1870 (Cambridge 1996),
's: North Indian Society in the Age of British Expan-
well. Sumit Sarkar, dismayed by the increasing
nd discourses to the neglect of the "subaltern,"
ned to have brought about an absolute rupture:
een literally constituted by colonialism alone."
n Subaltern Studies," in his *Writing Social His-*
>wever, that the ubiquity of the term "colonial"
l Bayly's.
:rness: A Postmortem for the Postmodern in
(2000): 74. Eaton raises the issue of termino-
"colonial" on 70, n. 44.

military landscape of southern Asia. A glimmer of the epistemology that confronted him in the British-Indian nineteenth century could be seen as early as 1773 in Warren Hastings' proclamation banning all "Biraugies and Sunnasses" from Company Bengal, save for those "fixed inhabitants" who "quietly employ themselves in their religious function."[32] Central to Hastings' ban, as has been noted, was an Enlightenment conception of religion that allowed no maneuvering room for the freewheeling, death-defying, transgressor ascetic. But such a religion already existed in India well before Robert Clive's coup at Plassey and the Company acquisition of Bengal. Hastings, in delivering his proclamation, was adding fuel to an engine of religious reform that had been gathering steam in seventeenth and eighteenth-century northern India, where *gosain*s were, paradoxically, becoming strongest. The increasing military strength and political influence of armed ascetics was paralleled by an increasing desire on the part of these Indian religious reformers, especially those promoting a loving relationship with the divine and all that that implied, socially as well as politically, to rein them in. Hastings was aware of this, since he himself invoked sedentary Ramanandis – the primary authors of that reformist sentiment – as emblematic of the kind of monastic-priestly ideal he had in mind.

By the late eighteenth century, in other words, Company agents were arriving at policies that major *bhakti* reformers found entirely appropriate. From their perspective, the British had joined an ongoing Indian project of religion.[33] Many examples can be adduced to describe this Indian project of religion (see chapter 5), but one particularly significant episode involved the battle for control over Galta, a shrine connected to a natural spring near present-day Jaipur. The struggle for Galta is remembered in Vaishnava legend as a confrontation between two early sixteenth-century men – one a shape-shifting *yogi* named Taranath who, along with his unruly followers, enjoyed the patronage of the local raja; the other a wandering Krishna devotee named Paihari Krishandas.[34] The climax

---

[32] Foreign Department, Secret Proceedings (FDSP), National Archives of India, New Delhi (NAI), nos. 5 and 6 of 21 January 1773.

[33] The degree to which this religion of love, *bhakti*, was able to speak to an analogous sentiment in Christianity, and in the process clear a base from which to mount an internal critique of Empire in the early twentieth century is the subject of a separate essay. See Pinch, "*Bhakti* and the British Empire," *Past & Present* 179, 1 (May 2003): 159–196.

[34] Sitaramsharan Bhagvan Prasad, *Goswami SriNabhaji krita SriBhaktamala Sri Priyadasji pranit Tika-Kavitta*, 7th edn (Lucknow 1993), p. 305. This work, upon which the crystallization of Vaishnava religion can be mapped, consists of three interwoven texts: Nabhadas' *Bhaktamala* (c. 1600), Priyadas' expansion and gloss (c. 1712), and Bhagvan Prasad's commentary (c. 1903–1909). For discussion of this textual corpus, see William R. Pinch, "History, Devotion, and The Search for Nabhadas of Galta," in Daud Ali (ed.), *Invoking the Past: The Uses of History in South Asia* (Delhi, 1999), pp. 367–399.

of their confrontation occurred when Taranath magically transformed himself into a tiger and lunged to attack Paihari Krishandas. The latter's response was to simply remark, "what a jackass," upon which Taranath was miraculously transformed into a donkey. Then, just as suddenly, the distinctive ivory earrings worn by Taranath's followers – from which they took their appellation, *kanphat* (ear-pierced) *yogi*s – clattered to the ground; their owners, terrified by this more powerful magic, fled to the surrounding hills. The local ruler, Prithviraj (King of the World), then shifted his loyalty to the pious Paihari Krishandas, who established a monastic lineage of Ramanandis from Galta.

Something new was taking shape when Paihari Krishandas defeated Taranath at Galta. Love of God (*bhakti*) itself was not new. But the harnessing of *bhakti* to Mughal imperial expansion, or more precisely, to the widely dispersed Rajput clans (prominent among which was that of Prithviraj's descendants, beginning with Mansingh), who provided the lion's share of the military manpower of the Mughal state, was. The evolution of this new religious-political formation defies easy observation, not least because the religious combatants – ascetics and devotees – resembled each other in many ways despite their mutual enmity. (Paihari Krishandas came to the attention of Taranath because he was a wandering ascetic who, while visiting Galta, wanted to warm himself by a fire surrounded by Taranath's *yogi*s. Both relied on their ability to effect supernormal transformations during their combat.) The key difference that separated them was the manner in which they conceived of and related to God. Taranath affected a yoga-tantric asceticism, the sole purpose of which was to cultivate supernormal power within – in effect, to turn himself into a god. Paihari Krishandas, by contrast, only appeared to conjure Taranath's transformation into a jackass. In fact, this was the work of a distant yet ever-present Lord, his God as a thing apart, God with an upper-case 'G' – a being who inspired total self-abandonment, and offered a sheltering refuge of love in return.

To Taranath's followers, Paihari Krishandas' magic was more powerful than their master's, and this perception assisted in their marginalization and gradual incorporation into the new Vaishnava cult at Galta (they would be reduced to the menial role of providing firewood for the new guru and his expanding community of followers). A similar pattern has been noted in the interpenetration of religion and magic in early modern England. "Conversions to the new religion, whether in the time of the primitive Church or under the auspices of the missionaries of more recent times, have frequently been assisted by the belief of converts that they are acquiring not just a means of other-worldly salvation, but a new and more powerful magic." This appropriation of magic in the service of religion does not in any way weaken the larger point that by the end of his period "one could draw a distinction between magic and religion which would not have been possible at the beginning" – and that the former was being socially and politically marginalized by the latter.[35] A word of caution is called for, since it is not clear that yoga-tantric ascetics such as Taranath lacked the "comprehensive view of the world" that distinguishes, for many sociologically minded historians, religion from magic. Nevertheless, it is possible to discern the socio-political advantages that Paihari Krishandas offered, from the instrumentalist perspective of the state, advantages that depend on the positioning of God in the religious imagination. Taranath's reputation was based on his ability to generate supernormal power within himself: not only did this render him an unpredictable and unruly ally, it meant that his power (and popular appeal) could always be challenged by other *yogi*s. Paihari Krishandas, by contrast, disclaimed any hint of ascetic wizardry. His great act of asceticism, we are told, was to subsist only on milk. His reputation was based on his love for Krishna, pure and simple. This not only made him a predictable ally, it offered a conception of a loving God who was ready and willing to tend to the needs of even the most destitute supplicant. All things being equal, Paihari Krishandas' religion – a religion of temples, monasteries, and physical symbols – promised significant political dividends.

The claims of Vaishnava hagiography would bear this out: By 1600, Prithviraj would be remembered as having "plant[ed] the standard of religion among the people of the world," his body miraculously emblazoned with an image of the conch shell, the symbol of Krishna, through the agency of his new guru. By the early 1700s, the retelling of the hagiography had evolved further: when the maharaja emerged on his balcony at dawn, after a miraculous nightlong encounter with Krishna, "there was a great uproar among the people at his great devotion, crowds collected, monks and abbots from the area all came to pay homage and were greatly pleased at seeing the conch symbol on his body. Gifts were brought, a flattering song was sung, all of which embarrassed Prithviraj greatly. He had a temple built, installed an image of the Lord, and the entire world sang his glory." According to another verse, describing advice given by Siva to a blind and destitute Brahman, even the sweat from Prithviraj's body had curative powers.[36] During the same period that saw the evolution of this hagiography, namely the seventeenth and eighteenth centuries, the

---

[35] Keith Thomas, *Religion and the Decline of Magic: Studies in Popular Beliefs in Sixteenth and Seventeenth Century England* (New York, 1971), pp. 25, 640. Thomas adopts a "Malinowskian" position, though not without reservations; see esp. pp. 636–637, 656.

[36] *Bhaktamala*, pp. 302 (on Paihari Krishandas), pp. 427–428 (on Prithviraj), pp. 724–727 (on Prithviraj and Paihari Krishandas); for Paihari Krishandas' monastic heirs during the reign of Mansingh, see esp. pp. 309–311 (Kilhdev) and pp. 312–315 (Agradas).

devotionalist sentiment nurtured at Galta (and at nearby religious centers like Mathura–Vrindaban) expanded east and north into the agriculturally rich swathe of territory that runs from the Punjab and Bundelkhand to Bihar and Bengal. By the end of the eighteenth century, Ayodhya (north of Banaras) and Mathura–Vrindaban were displacing Galta as the centers of Vaishnava *bhakti* catholicity. Banaras itself, long regarded as Siva's city, was well on its way toward becoming a major center of Vaishnava *bhakti* as well.

This was the lay of the land when the Maratha Mahadji Shinde was trying his hand at Mughal politics, when Anupgiri Gosain was headquartered in Vrindaban, the playing fields of Krishna, and when the Mughal emperor's eyes were being removed by the Rohilla Afghan, Ghulam Qadir Khan. This was what north Indian religion looked like when the English East India Company was on the verge of capturing an empire in southern Asia.

Vrindaban, 1999

Vrindaban is a small pilgrimage town that abuts the Jamuna, about two hours' drive south from Delhi. It has long been regarded as the place where Krishna spent his childhood and youth and, as such, its sacred landscape is packed with temples and shrines dedicated to the mischievous, flute-playing, amorous, cowherd God. According to F. S. Growse, a District Magistrate in the late nineteenth century who was fascinated by Krishna *bhakti* in the Mathura–Vrindaban region, Himmat Bahadur built a *ghat* on the banks of the Jamuna in Vrindaban.[37] (The term *ghat* refers to the point where the water meets the shore; when someone builds a *ghat*, it means that they have sheathed that embankment in stone or concrete, either as a ramp or as steps – or a combination of both.) In early November of 1999, I decided to set off in search of that *ghat*. If I could find a structure that bore the imprint of the man, I reasoned to myself, it might help me better understand his world, perhaps even who he thought he was. In any case, I was intrigued: the idea that a Saiva warlord would build a *ghat* in a Vaishnava pilgrimage center struck me as odd. And there was no better person to help me find this place than Kailash Jha.

We decided to make a family pilgrimage out of the adventure. Kailash's wife, Abha, and their daughter, Archita, would come along to see the land of Krishna. Upon arrival in Vrindaban, we separated: Archita and Abha went off in search of interesting temples, while Kailash and I went off

[37] F. S. Growse, *Mathura: A District Memoir* (1882; reprint New Delhi, 1993), 307–308.

in search of Anupgiri's *ghat*. On the waterfront, as Kailash and I soon discovered at some cost to our raiment, was an array of exquisite late Mughal architecture sorely in need of historic preservation. Nevertheless, after much searching up and down the mile or two of embankment, we had little to show for our labors on the Anupgiri front. No one had heard of the *gosain*, let alone a *ghat* built by him. Dejected, we decided to try the Vrindaban Research Institute on the main road into town. There we met Dr. Gopal Chandra Ghosh, who immediately lifted our spirits by recognizing the name of Anupgiri – but he added that this name is not spoken of in Vrindaban because he was the enemy of Vaishnavas. Ghosh regaled us with legends concerning the enmity between Saiva *gosain*s and Vaishnava *bairagi*s, and added that the Mughal emperor Jahangir (r. 1605–1627) had been a devotee of one Jadrup Gosain who came to live in Mathura–Vrindaban and who was himself an inveterate opponent of the *bairagi*s.[38] He added that "Gosain Ghat" was located directly behind the well-known Shah-ji *mandir* (temple) and right beside Chir Ghat, where Krishna is said to have stolen the saris of the bathing cowherdesses and hidden them in the large tree that still adorns the embankment. Nearby, Ghosh added, is the Chaitanya Prem Sansthan (Chaitanya Love Institute): surely Srivats Goswami, its director, would be of assistance given his well-known interest in the history of the *ghat*s and his desire to see them preserved.

Armed with this information, we headed back to the river. We quickly found the Chaitanya Prem Sansthan; happily, Srivats Goswami was willing to meet with us. After we explained ourselves, he confirmed that the *ghat* was in fact nearby, and added that the Shah-ji *mandir* contained portions of the structure that was built by Anupgiri. Srivats Goswami then phoned the owner of the Shah-ji *mandir*, Shah K. S. Gupta, and asked him if he would be willing to show us the sections behind the temple that dated to Anupgiri's time. Gupta, as it turned out, had long been curious about the history of Himmat Bahadur. His family had owned the temple since the mid-nineteenth century, and he had been reared on tales of the *gosain*'s nefarious deeds. We arranged to meet him at the temple at 10 a.m. the following morning. After taking our leave of Srivats-ji, and with our heads swimming in disbelief at the sudden reversal in our fortunes,

---

[38] The *Jahangirnama* as well as two separate Mughal paintings document the visits of Jahangir and even Akbar to Jadrup Gosain. "Jahangir visiting Jadrup Gosain," att. to Govardhan, *c.* 1616–20, from a *Jahangir-nama ms.*, at the Musee Guimet in Paris. The image may be viewed in Amina Okada, *Indian Miniatures of the Mughal Court*, trans. Deke Dusinberre (New York, 1992), p. 40. A similar painting, dating to 1625–1630, depicting a visit of Akbar to the *gosain* is held in Harvard's Sackler Museum. See also Walter Smith, "Hindu Ascetics in Mughal Painting under Akbar," *Oriental Art* n.s. 27, 1 (1981): 67–68.

we decided to have a look at Gosain Ghat. We immediately found Chir Ghat, with its tell-tale tree. (As we walked under the tree, some monkeys tried to steal my glasses – confirming in my mind that this was, in fact, the place where Krishna played his tricks on the naked, cavorting *gopis*.) Next to Chir Ghat was the back of Shah-ji *mandir*, facing the water. By now it was approaching evening and the light was starting to fade. We recognized the rear of the temple as one of the distinctive – and one of the few well-maintained – late Mughal buildings we had encountered earlier in the day. After poking around a bit, we discovered a small shrine in the bottom corner of the structure. To our surprise, the Hindi sign above the entrance read: "Himmatgir Bahadur Mandir." Below, also in Hindi, was written, "Ghat, Mandir, and Nand Kila [Nand Fort, presumably a reference to the imposing structure of the Shah-ji *mandir*] established in Samvat 1430." A passerby explained the local formula for converting the date to the Christian calendar, which placed the alleged construction date in 1686 – fully ninety years before Anupgiri shifted his base of operations to Vrindaban. Puzzled, we resolved to come back early in the morning, before our ten o'clock meeting with Gupta.

The next morning, half an hour before our meeting, we ventured into the Himmatgir Bahadur Mandir. No one was about, so we hazarded a glance at the shrine itself, which featured a black marble statue of Krishna playing the flute. Next to Krishna stood a portrait of a man, showing his head and torso. In his hands was a musket (see figure 1). This, I felt sure, was a portrait of Anupgiri Gosain. Unfortunately, however, the shrine was locked behind a retractable metal gate, so all we could do was peer through from a distance. Aside from us, the grounds were empty. Again we resolved to return, after our tour of the larger temple above. A few minutes later, we were upstairs, in the office of the Shah-ji *mandir*, meeting its proprietor, Shah K. S. Gupta. The Shah-ji *mandir*, he explained, occupied the western two-thirds of the entire structure; Anupgiri's palace-fort occupied the remaining third on the eastern side, facing the river. His ancestors had acquired the property, including the palace-fort, in the 1850s; they laid the cornerstone to their temple in 1860. Gupta then showed us around the luxurious gardens, terraced rooms, and balconies in which Anupgiri spent his days and nights in the 1770s and 1780s. Whatever may be said about the *gosain*, there is no question that he lived well. The grounds were comprised of a long courtyard surrounded by buildings – long, narrow, one-storey structures to the north and south, and a large two-storey structure on the eastern edge, by the river. Anupgiri would have occupied the two-storey portion, facing the waterfront. Upstairs was a large, airy room with ornate marble lacework screens, flanked by two smaller rooms to the north

Figure 1. Himmat Bahadur Anupgiri Gosain, Himmatgir Mandir, behind Shah-ji Mandir, Vrindaban. Photographed by the author.

and south, a balcony overlooking the courtyard to the west, and an expansive terrace to the east overlooking the Jamuna. Also of note were the waterworks: two shallow channels intersected to form a cross in the middle of the courtyard; water was fed into the channels from the eastern end via an ornate marble waterfall that spilled over a series of small recessed compartments designed to hold candles. The effect at night would have been exquisite, with the sound of the water gurgling over the stonework combined with the candlelight streaming through the pane of falling water and dancing off the surrounding walls. According to Gupta, Anupgiri enjoyed resting on the balcony above, watching the light reflect off the water. It was easy to see why: the place was a late Mughal idyll. I had to keep reminding myself that the point of Saiva asceticism was not world denial.[39]

After wandering about some more, and visiting the main Radharaman (Radha and Krishna) image in the Shah-ji *mandir*, about which I will have more to say in chapter 5, we took our leave. While on Anupgiri's terrace we had been able to look down at the small patio beside the shrine in the Himmatgir Bahadur *mandir*. Pilgrims had gathered on the patio and a *purohit* (priest) was holding forth. We proceeded down to the entrance by the north side of the exterior of the fort. As we entered, the *purohit* was concluding his discourse about the importance of the shrine. We asked him who was pictured next to Krishna. He replied that it was a great maharaja from Rajasthan who came to this place 700 years ago, had a dream, decided to give up everything, and became a great mahatma. After the crowd dispersed, we introduced ourselves and explained what we knew about Anupgiri Gosain. The *purohit*, Syam Babu, explained that his is the oldest temple in Vrindaban, and that the image of Krishna belonged to the maharaja. The temple used to be much bigger, he said, gesturing toward the palace-fort of Anupgiri above, but it is no longer in the possession of "his side." There used to be a passageway that connected to the rest of the "temple," but this has been walled up. He told us other things as well: one Rani Man Kunwar from Kanpur, the wife of Himmatgir's grandson, used to write letters here, expressing concern about the upkeep of the shrine. She paid a surprise visit in the 1930s (by this time, we had all dispensed with the 700-year story), and was dismayed by the situation – namely, the fact that the Shah-ji people were in possession. A court case ensued, and Syam Babu's ancestors managed to become the priests in this small temple. The acrimony of those days had

---

[39] Indeed, the closer I looked (see chapter 5), the more I realized that, as with late medieval Europe, "asceticism was an effort to plumb and to realize all the possibilities of the flesh." See Caroline Walker Bynum, *Holy Feast and Holy Fast: The Religious Significance of Food to Medieval Women* (Berkeley 1987), pp. 189–276 and 294 (for the quote) – 296.

gradually passed. Syam Babu made it clear that he thought very highly of Gupta-ji. Evidently the two sides had come to an easy co-existence.

Syam Babu showed us Himmatgir's *samadhi* marker on the edge of the patio, an octagonal stone-marble plaque embedded in the floor and embossed with iconic symbols. Here, then, Himmatgir lives on. Strange things have happened according to Syam Babu, things that he himself has witnessed. Many years earlier he had constructed a makeshift room for himself above the *samadhi*, in which he lived for seven years. Gradually he fell ill, half his body became paralyzed. Despite visits to many doctors, no one could cure him. One night Himmatgir visited him in a dream and asked: "Why have you built this structure? I enjoy living out in the open. Tear it down and throw it in the Jamuna." Syam Babu did as he was told, and was immediately cured. Another story concerned a visitor who decided to sleep in front of the image of Krishna inside the shrine itself. In the middle of the night, this person was lifted bodily by an unseen force and heaved out of the sanctum sanctorum. A third encounter involved some steps that led down to the river from the patio. Worried that these afforded access to thieves, Syam Babu decided to fill the aperture with stone. No sooner had he done this than Himmatgir visited his dreams and ordered him to remove the stone so that he (Himmatgir) could continue to use the passage for bathing in the river early in the morning. Needless to say, Syam Babu complied.

We left Vrindaban later that afternoon and headed for Sadabad, a small town to the east where Anupgiri was said, according to a later gazetteer, to have built a small fort.[40] We eventually found it, but it is unremarkable – mostly it is a utilitarian structure geared toward supervising the collection of revenue and billeting armed men. It has long since been taken over by the local administration and used for a police headquarters. The local officials showed us a Hindi document dating from 1978 claiming that the fort was built by "Sindhiya Himmat Rao Bahadur." Clearly a late Mughal past that pitted Hindu against Hindu is not what people have wanted in recent years. Mahadji Shinde and Anupgiri Gosain, who had suffered a bitter falling out in the 1780s, had been reunited into one personality in the 1970s.

A host of questions raced through my mind as we made our way through the fog-shrouded darkness into Delhi that night. Had I gotten any closer to Anupgiri as a result of the previous two days' encounters? Certainly there was some value to touching the bricks and mortar that this remarkable man had conspired to erect around himself in a troubled time. And

---

[40] *Uttar Pradesh District Gazetteers: Mathura*, comp. and ed. Esha Basanti Joshi (Lucknow 1968), p. 344.

I did now know, more or less, what he looked like. Indeed, if Syam Babu was telling the truth – and there seemed no reason to doubt him – I had spoken to a man who is occasionally visited in the night by the great war-lord himself. This was about as close as one could get to one's subject without actually encountering him in person. Indeed, if I worked at it, perhaps I too could be visited by Anupgiri in the night. It was also reassuring to know that some vestige of the *gosain*'s late Mughal, Saiva moorings had survived the smothering embrace of Vrindaban's Krishna-*bhakti*. His house may have become a Vaishnava temple within a Vaishnava temple, but at least one late Mughal image of Siva remained – the image of Anupgiri himself.

1   Mughal *yogi*s

The asceticism of most of these men arises from the world's having turned its back on them, and not from their having become cold-hearted to the world.

– Abu'l Fazl, c. 1595 (re Thaneswar, 1567)[1]

A strange thing happened to Akbar in 1567. The young Mughal sovereign was returning to Agra from a wide-ranging hunting expedition in the Punjab, which (as was the Mughal wont) he had combined with a punishing raid into a recalcitrant prince's territory. He ordered camp to be set at Ambala, near the shrine of Thaneswar, a popular watering hole long favored by Sufi and Saiva ascetics. The timing was auspicious: an eclipse was occurring, and many wealthy pilgrims had gathered to immerse themselves in one of the sacred tanks at the site. But trouble was brewing. Two bands of Saiva ascetics had squared off and were ready to come to blows, each convinced that the other had usurped the choice location for collecting the silver and gold coins being distributed. The groups were not evenly matched – a large band of *yogi*s, numbering 500, faced a smaller group of *sanyasi*s less than half its size. A slaughter appeared imminent. The leader of the *sanyasi*s, one Kisu Puri, decided to appeal to the emperor for justice on behalf of his weaker party. He insisted that the *yogi*s had come belatedly and ejected his band from the spot – and though they "had not the strength to encounter them, yet they would, trusting in God, engage in fight with them, and would either shed their own blood or take the place from them." The *yogi*s for their part insisted that "the place belonged to them by inheritance, though the Puris [the *sanyasi*s] had settled there for some time. Now they would sit there, and the site would remain theirs as long as there was life in their bodies."

Akbar sought in vain to reason with the disputants. As his friend and adviser Abu'l Fazl would later put it, "he flung out the jewels of advice and counsel to those vain spirits, [but] it was like casting pearls on the ground,

---

[1] Abu'l Fazl, *Akbar Nama*, trans. H. Beveridge (Calcutta 1902–1939), vol. II, pp. 423–424.

and their absurdity and error only increased." Finally, Akbar granted them permission to settle the dispute through combat and ordered the two sides to opposite ends of a field. The battle commenced in a kind of ritualized fashion. To quote Abu'l Fazl again, "The two sides drew up in line, and first one man on each side advanced in a braggart fashion, and engaged with swords. Afterwards, bows and arrows were used. After that . . . stones." It was clear that the outnumbered *sanyasi*s would be defeated. Suddenly, Akbar intervened, ordering some of his footsoldiers to assist the weaker party. As a result the *yogi*s were quickly routed and their leader, Anand Kur, beheaded. According to Nizamuddin Ahmad, who was probably present, "The Emperor greatly enjoyed the sight."[2]

Ripples from Thaneswar

The unusual events at Thaneswar were recorded by four separate court historians: Nizamuddin Ahmad, Badauni, Abu'l Fazl, and an anonymous writer. The accounts by the latter two included lavish illustrations of variously attired ascetics engaged in combat, with Mughal soldiers intervening and much spilling of blood (see figures 2 and 4). Though there are slight discrepancies between the accounts, the four authors agreed that: (1) Akbar's entourage encountered at Thaneswar two bands of "Hindu"[3] ascetics, each of which was armed and claiming the right to occupy the most auspicious location at the shrine. (2) The shrine in question was a

---

[2] This episode is recorded in four Persian accounts. The most detailed is Abu'l Fazl, *Akbar Nama*, vol. II, pp. 423–424, written some two or three decades after the event from eyewitness accounts. Nizamuddin Ahmad, *Tabakat-i Akbari*, trans. Elliot and Dowson, *The History of India*, vol. v, p. 318, and the anonymous "Tarikh-i-Khandan-i-Timuriya" (Khuda Baksh Oriental Public Library, Patna), fols. 322a–322b, are the two earliest versions; the former may have been present and was probably one of the sources for Abu'l Fazl's history. I am grateful to Dr. Behrooz Ghamani for help with the translation of the anonymous account. The event is also noted in Abdul-Qadir ibn-i-Muluk Shah, known as al-Badauni, *Muntakhabu't Tawarikh*, trans. by George S. A. Ranking (Calcutta 1898; reprint New Delhi 1990), vol. II, p. 94. The last quote is from Nizamuddin Ahmad; the preceding quotes are Abu'l Fazl.

[3] From the Mughal perspective, the term "Hindu" referred to the religious practices and beliefs of the people of *al-Hind* who were not Muslim, nor Christian, Jewish, Zoroastrian, Buddhist, or Jain. It could also be used to simply refer to the people of *al-Hind*, irrespective of religion. This blanket grouping tended, of necessity, to mask the considerable divisions, religious and otherwise, among Hindus – of which observers, Muslim or non-Muslim, were generally aware. Useful reflections on the problem include Y. Friedmann, "Medieval Muslim Views of Indian Religions," *Journal of the American Oriental Society* 95, 2 (1975): 214–221; H. von Stietencron, "Hinduism: On the Proper Use of a Deceptive Term," in G. D. Sontheimer and H. Kulke (eds.), *Hinduism Reconsidered* (New Delhi 1989), pp. 11–27; Cynthia Talbot, "Inscribing the Other, Inscribing the Self: Hindu-Muslim Identities in Pre-Colonial India," *Comparative Studies in Society and History* 37, 4 (October 1995): 692–722; and David Lorenzen, "Who Invented Hinduism?" *Comparative Studies in Society and History* 41, 4 (October 1999): 630–659.

large body or "tank" of water, to which people from throughout north India flocked to ritually immerse themselves and to make valuable offerings. (3) After some discussion, Akbar granted permission for an armed contest between the ascetics to decide the issue. (4) As the contest escalated, the emperor ordered some of his footsoldiers to assist the smaller group. (5) The smaller group prevailed after considerable violence.[4]

A very different picture of a meeting between Hindu ascetics and the Mughal emperor is recorded in *sanyasi* oral tradition. Though the details differ markedly from the Mughal accounts, I would argue that it derives from the same 1567 episode. The earliest recorded version of the oral tradition, as retold by the missionary–scholar J. N. Farquhar in 1925, runs as follows:

In the sixteenth century there were in North India thousands of Muslim *faqirs* who went about armed, took part in the wars of the time, and, when there was no regular war, fought for their own hand. One of their practices, as good Muslims, was to attack and kill sannyasis as representatives of Hinduism. As ascetics, these faqirs held a privileged position, and were thus protected from mob violence and also from interference on the part of the government, which was then Muhammadan. Thus, when sannyasis were killed, no one was punished, while sannyasis themselves were prevented from taking violent measures against their enemies by their vow of *ahimsa*.

Madhusudana Sarasvati, a well-known sannyasi scholar of the Sarasvati sub-order [of Dasnamis], who lived in Benares in the middle of the century, at last went to Akbar to see whether anything could be done for the protection of the ancient order to which he belonged. Raja Birbal was present at the interview and suggested the way out of the difficulty. He advised Madhusudana to initiate large numbers of non-Brahmans into the sannyasi order and arm them for the protection of Brahman sannyasis. The Emperor agreed that armed sannyasis should be protected by their sacred character from government interference. Madhusudana, therefore, went and initiated large numbers of Ksatriyas and Vaisyas into seven of the sub-orders [of the Dasnamis], Bharati, Vana, Aranya, Parvata, Sagara, Giri and Puri.

Farquhar recounted this tradition in an article published in the *Journal of the Royal Asiatic Society* in 1925; he gave a similar version in a

---

[4] The remarkable level of agreement between the four authors may be due – at least in part – to the fact that they relied on a relatively small circle of informants. Abu'l Fazl himself did not join the emperor's entourage until after 1570, so he was not present at Thaneswar and consequently relied on the reminiscences of the emperor as well as other eyewitnesses, prominent among whom was (probably) Nizamuddin Ahmad and (possibly) the anonymous author. That Badauni depended heavily on Nizamuddin Ahmad is well known. See H. Elliot's introduction to the *Tabakat-i Akbari*, in Elliot and Dowson, *The History of India as Told by its Own Historians*, vol. v, p. 177. "Badauni . . . professes his work to be simply an abridgement of this [Nizamuddin Ahmad's work], and acknowledges himself to be chiefly indebted to it for the relation of all events down to A.H. 1002 (1593 AD)." On the high quality of Nizamuddin Ahmad's history, see pp. 177–178.

Figure 2. Thaneswar, 1567, detail. *Tarikh-i-khandan-i Timuriyya*, Khuda Baksh Oriental Public Library, Patna. Reproduced with permission.

separate piece published in the same year in the *Bulletin of the John Rylands Library*.[5] It was reported to him by members of the Chausastha monastery

---

[5] Farquhar, "The Organization of the Sannyasis of the Vedanta," 482–483 (for the quote); "The Fighting Ascetics of India," 442. As noted in the introduction, Farquhar's work established a pattern of understanding that would stand unbroken for many decades. See Pinch, "Soldier Monks," esp. 148–152. Farquhar's questions were directed mainly to

in Banaras and by members of "a Giri monastery near Allahabad."[6] In addition, he attended the Allahabad *kumbha mela* in 1918 and had numerous discussions concerning the historical origins of the various ascetic orders there.[7] Farquhar did not treat the story as fanciful legend but as "a piece of history which has been faithfully preserved by tradition."[8]

Readers will not find this agreement between Akbar and Madhusudana Sarasvati mentioned in any historical work. So far as I know, it has not been recorded anywhere. I picked up the information from the lips of sannyasis, who told it me to explain how large numbers of their order came to be fighting men. But though it has come down to us by tradition, there can be no doubt about its truth. All sannyasis in North India hold the tradition; and we may also be certain that the Emperor who had given the Hindu an equal place with the Muslim in his empire would at once recognise the justice of Madhusudana's appeal and would respond to it.[9]

In one respect, Farquhar was correct: there is no mention of a meeting between Madhusudana Saraswati and the emperor in any written record of Akbar's reign. In seeking to make historical sense of the oral tradition, Farquhar concluded that the Madhusudana interview with Akbar and his courtiers took place well prior to the emperor's visit to Thaneswar. He settled, rather arbitrarily, on 1565, two years earlier. The ascetic battle at Thaneswar, he argued, "fits so well into the tradition that I am sure every historical mind will at once acknowledge that it ought to be accepted as full corroboration of the story." According to Farquhar, Akbar "must have chuckled inwardly to see [Hindu ascetics] turn their swords against each other," having just recently "agreed to their organization, in order that they might fight Muslim foes."

Farquhar's treatment of the *sanyasi* oral tradition and the Mughal history as descriptive of two distinct and separate events is due, in large part, to the fact that the central leitmotif of the oral tradition was Hindu–Muslim antagonism. For most British and many Indian observers in the

---

issues of chronology and how the arming of *sanyasis* corresponded to a reading of Hindu monastic history "proper" in India. His general understanding of Hinduism relied in large part on the oral traditions of ascetics, monks, and religious reformers, with whom he had extensive and prolonged contact between 1890 and 1920. See his *Modern Religious Movements in India* (reprint New Delhi 1977 [based on a series of lectures given in 1913 at the Hartford Seminary in Connecticut]), pp. viii–ix.

[6] Farquhar, "The Organization of the Sannyasis of the Vedanta," 483. Baidyanath Sarasvati and Surajit Sinha, *Ascetics of Kashi: An Anthropological Exploration* (Varanasi 1978), p. 247 (Appendix 2), identify "Chausastha monastery" as "Chausatthi *Matha*," a "*Dandi*" or orthodox (non-*naga*) Dasnami monastery.

[7] Farquhar, "The Historical Position of Ramananda (part 1)," 185.

[8] "The Organization of the Sannyasis of the Vedanta," 483.

[9] "The Fighting Ascetics of India," 443 (also for the following quote).

twentieth century, Hindu–Muslim antagonism – known by the shorthand "communalism" – was a timeless certainty of the South Asian past since the arrival of Islam in the eighth century. We now know, by contrast, that this was a flawed premise. Religious antagonism and assertions of difference between Hindus and Muslims were not the norm; more often the practices and beliefs that we today associate with "Hindu" or "Muslim" were, in fact, seen to be complementary – particularly when it came to asceticism. An excellent example of this complementarity may be found in the "Rishi movement" in medieval Kashmir, a home-grown Sufism grounded in the region's Saiva mysticism.[10] Richard Eaton has documented similar kinds of complementarities in medieval Bengal and the Punjab, and has argued moreover that they were crucial for the gradual process of religious accretion and transformation that later historians came to perceive, in retrospect, as a sudden moment of "conversion."[11] That Hindu and Muslim asceticism shared common ground was a commonplace for contemporaries. Jahangir enjoyed visiting a *gosain* of Ujjain (later Mathura) named Jadrup, of whom he remarked offhandedly, "He is not devoid of learning and has studied well the science of the Vedanta, which is the science of Sufism."[12] Such examples can be found in abundance. Thus it is as well to hold in abeyance allegations of difference grounded in Hindu-ness and Muslim-ness, particularly when speaking of the early modern period. Claims of one or the other usually reveal more about the solidification of a conscious religious identity in the mind of the claimant (or the group to which the claimant belongs) in the present than about the nature of the religious beliefs or practices of the person (or group) being described in the past.

If we strip away the communalist presumptions, it is not only possible but advisable to treat the two historical narratives – the *sanyasi* oral tradition and the Mughal written record – as ripples in a pond emanating from the same central event, the 1567 meeting and skirmish at Thaneswar. At the same time, my reconciliation of the Mughal and *sanyasi* accounts grants primacy to the written record over the oral tradition. I locate the original event at Thaneswar and in 1567. In doing so I am recognizing that the oral transmission of history allows (indeed, requires) the details to change in a way that the written transmission is able (indeed, mandated) to resist. This poses problems for the historian who wishes to mine

[10] Mohammad Ishaaq Khan, *Kashmir's Transition to Islam: the Role of the Muslim Rishis* (New Delhi 1994).

[11] Richard Eaton, *The Rise of Islam and the Bengal Frontier, 1204–1760* (Berkeley, 1993).

[12] *The Jahangirnama: Memoirs of Jahangir, Emperor of India*, translated, edited, and annotated by Wheeler M. Thackston (Washington DC, New York, 1999), p. 209. According to Jahangir, many years earlier Akbar "also paid him a visit in this very place [Ujjain] and often mentioned it with fondness."

the oral tradition for historical insights, but it also offers opportunities for those who take the proper precautions.[13] What is noteworthy is that the late sixteenth-century Mughal account and the early twentieth-century oral tradition agree on three basic points: (1) the overarching context is one of persistent violence between two categories of ascetics, (2) an interview takes place between the emperor and a representative of one group of ascetics who seeks the emperor's intervention by way of a solution to this persistent violence, and (3) the emperor grants permission to use force to arrive at a concrete solution. What remains unsupported by the Mughal account is the assertion in the oral tradition that previously unarmed Hindu ascetics took up arms, with the permission of Akbar, to defend against attacks by Muslim ascetics. The ethical claim of the oral tradition is that the turn to violence by Hindu ascetics was a departure from previous non-violent behavior, and that this departure was in response to Muslim aggression. (This also served to explain, for early twentieth-century *sanyasi*s and Farquhar as well, the all-too-apparent fact of the recruitment of non-elites – or *sudra*s – among the Dasnami order. Both the communal and social dimensions of the tradition found a receptive audience in northern India in the twentieth century.) Two components of this main assertion of the oral tradition are clearly contradicted by the Mughal accounts. First, *sanyasi*s were armed well before Akbar came on to the scene.[14] All the Mughal accounts observe that the two parties were itching for a fight, and both the narrative accounts as well as the paintings make clear that they possessed a variety of weapons. Indeed, the author of the "Tarikh-i-Khandan-i-Timuriya" asserted that "squabbles often broke out on the edge of the tank between the *jogi*s and the *sanyasi*s. In recent years these had even become battles [*jang*] and a few were killed. This now appeared to be occurring again. A sizable group had gathered and was preparing to wage war." Second, in contrast to the assertion of communal causation in the oral tradition, it was not Muslim attacks on Hindus that was at issue, but an attack by one group of Hindu ascetics against another.

[13] On the appropriate use of oral tradition by historians, see Jan Vansina, "Recording the Oral History of the Bakuba," *Journal of African History 1, 1* (1960): 43–51, and 1, 2: 257–270; and his "Once upon a Time: Oral Traditions as History in Africa," *Daedalus* 100, 2 (1971): 442–468.

[14] This observation is made as well by Lorenzen, "Warrior Ascetics," 69, and G. S. Ghurye, *Indian Sadhus*, 2nd edn (Bombay 1964), p. 103. Though both express doubts about the oral tradition, neither probes the broader historiographical and historical questions raised by the contrast with the written record. Lorenzen concludes that "it is best to suspend judgment about the whole question," presumably referring to the veracity of the oral tradition. In any case, the testimony of Ludovico de Varthema, cited in the next chapter, would serve to confirm that armed *yogi*s preceded the arrival of Mughals in northern India.

The contrasting images of the paradigmatically non-violent Hindu and the pathologically hyper-violent Muslim were standard tropes of twentieth-century historiography, so we need not look far to find the source of the communal content in the oral tradition. Such assertions were in the air and their inclusion in the narration would have endowed the story with an undeniable political currency and cultural authenticity. Nevertheless, despite this deficiency, we should not discount the oral tradition altogether: after all, it did manage to record a glimmer of a meeting between Hindu ascetics and the Mughal emperor over the question of violence. What else might it tell us? If we continue to remove the communalist gloss, we are also left with the perception – indeed, the assertion – that the meeting with Akbar had a decisively transformative effect on the organizational dynamics of *sanyasi*s. This point is confirmed by two later recordings of the oral tradition, one in 1954 by a government official conducting an inquiry into a disaster that occurred earlier that year at the Allahabad *kumbha mela* (see chapter 6), the other reported by two anthropologists collecting ethnographic data on the ascetic institutions of Banaras in the 1970s. The head of the 1954 government inquiry reported that "Madhusudan Saraswati Ji of Banaras, possibly with the assistance of Birbal and Abdul Rahim Khankhana, the well-known Ministers of Emperor Akbar, and with the approval of the Emperor, had put the organisation of these Akharas on a proper footing."[15] This information was based on interviews with the head of the Mahanirvani Panchayati *akhara*, an ascetic order in Daraganj (adjacent to the festival ground in Allahabad). Two decades later, a slightly different version was collected from ascetics of the Juna *akhara*, a related ascetic institution in Banaras.[16] According to this version:

From ancient times the Naga ascetics were peregrinating in the country in groups, called *Jhundi*. During the reign of Akbar, the Moslem Malanga *faquirs* were troubling the Hindu villagers, because the Hindus used to receive the Naga sannyasis respectfully while the Malanga *faquirs* were more feared than respected. This eventually exploded into an open clash between the Nagas and the Malangas.

[15] *Report of the Committee appointed by the Uttar Pradesh Government to enquire into the mishap which occurred in the Kumbha Mela at Prayaga on the 3rd February 1954* (Allahabad 1955), p. 105. The author of the report was the renowned judge and legal scholar, Kamalakant Verma. *Akhara* is a particularly fertile term. Usually translated as wrestling pit or arena, it has become a metonymy for the wrestling club or team that uses a particular pit. See Joseph Alter, *The Wrestler's Body: Identity and Ideology in North India* (Berkeley 1992). Similarly, *akhara* was the training ground for armed ascetics, and came to signify the armies or subordinate organizational units of those armies. Today, in the post-military Dasnami context, the term *akhara* refers to a particular sub-order or lineage.

[16] Saraswati and Sinha, *Ascetics of Kashi*, pp. 94–95. Both the Mahanirvani Panchayati and the Juna *akhara*s are armed lineages within the overarching Dasnami order, about which I will have more to say below.

The Malangas were already equipped with swords, they killed the Naga ascetics mercilessly. When the Hindus approached Akbar for justice, the latter said: two cows are fighting, which indicated his helplessness or non-interference in this religious matter. On this the princes of Rajputana *sent some soldiers in the guise of ascetics* to defend the Hindu *sannyasis* and villagers from the ravages of the Malanga *faquirs*.[17] It was on this occasion that for the first time the Naga ascetics were supplied with arms by Hindu kings. These ascetics gradually trained themselves in fighting, and subsequently fought many battles and took part in many a skirmish.

Taken together with Farquhar's 1925 account, all three oral traditions make the assertion that the imperial intervention was in some way instrumental in ascetic military organization and institutionalization. This is probably the most important historical assertion that can be made about the interaction between Akbar and Hindu ascetics. It speaks not simply of a sequence of events, but of long-term change – the meat and potatoes of the historical profession. The fact that it is not transmitted in the Mughal record is not surprising: the broader implications of Akbar's decision to intervene in the affairs of Hindu ascetics would probably not be felt for some time, if they were felt at all, and certainly would not be the concern of Mughal chroniclers intent to record for posterity the emperor's doings.

Of course, the oral tradition may have been asserting rather than recording a link between institutional transformation and the agency of Akbar. Nevertheless, there are several possibilities as to the nature of the transformation, whether or not Akbar was the cause of it. The 1925, 1954, and 1978 versions of the oral tradition were told from, as Farquhar put it, "the lips of sannyasis," and were given as an explanation for how it was that large numbers of armed men populated the lower ranks of India's largest ascetic order, the Dasnami, who claim descent from the ninth-century sage, Shankaracharya. We may conclude then, that the various Dasnami *sanyasis* interviewed in the twentieth century were (or at least saw themselves as) the institutional descendants of the *sanyasi* victors at Thaneswar in 1567. Pinning a firm institutional identity to their *yogi* adversaries is, by contrast, more difficult. The term *yogi* today usually refers to ascetics who claim descent from the ninth-century master, Gorakhnath. But as applied in the medieval and early modern periods, the term signified a loose band of ascetics connected with the emulation and worship of Bhairava, a form of Siva that haunts the cremation ground. As David White has noted in his study of the "*nath siddha*" tradition:

---

[17] This detail is particularly reminiscent of the Mughal accounts, which held that the emperor ordered some of his footsoldiers to smear themselves with ash and enter the fray on the side of the *sanyasi* party.

'Yogi' or 'jogi' has, for at least eight hundred years, been an all-purpose term employed to designate those Saiva religious specialists whom orthodox Hindus have considered suspect, heterodox, and even heretical in their doctrine and practice. On the one hand, the Yogis are defined (like the tantrikas of an earlier time) by their nonconformity to and exclusion from orthodox categories: they are that troubling aggregate of sectarian groups and individuals whose language and behavior subvert the canons of Vedic, devotional, and 'high' tantric religion. On the other hand, they are defined by certain features of their sectarian affiliations and practices: heirs to the heterodox Pasupatas and Kapalikas of an earlier age, they are devotees of terrible forms of Siva (usually Bhairava) who besmear themselves with ashes, leave their hair uncut, and continue to adhere to the practices of 'primitive' tantrism. As such, their 'yoga' is more closely identified, in the jaundiced eyes of their critics, with black magic, sorcery, sexual perversion, and the subversion of alimentary prohibitions than with the practice of yoga in the conventional sense of the term.[18]

A closer examination of Dasnami tradition suggests how the conflict at Thaneswar may have been a chapter in a long process of institutional evolution that involved both *sanyasi*s and *yogi*s. Dasnamis today claim descent from Shankara, the great ninth-century sage of south India, and adhere generally to the *advaita* (non-dualist) Vedanta that he espoused. *Advaita* Vedanta gained institutional strength, political respectability, and theological direction in Vijayanagar in the fourteenth century, when the well-connected theologian Vidyaranya began asserting genealogical *parampara* (traditional guru–disciple descent) links to Shankara and linking him as well to the temple complex at Sringeri.[19] As *sanyasi*s gained influence in northern India after the fourteenth century, their followers eventually came to be known by one or another of the titles that today make up the "*das-nami*" (ten-named) enumeration. Not surprisingly, twentieth-century Dasnamis insist that the term "Dasnami" dates from the time and intention of Shankara. However I have yet to discover a specific reference to the term that is earlier than the nineteenth century. Indeed the earliest mention of any permutation of the tenfold enumeration (that I am aware of) is around 1600 in Sanskrit texts that describe the proper ritual investiture of a *sanyasi*. The relevant excerpt is as follows: "tirthasrama-vanaranyagiriparvatasagarah sarasvati bharati ca puri nama yaterdasa," which may be translated as "Tirtha, Asrama, Vana Aranya, Giri, Parvata, Sagara, Sarasvati, Bharati, and Puri are verily the ten names one can give

---

[18] David G. White, *The Alchemical Body: Siddha Traditions in Medieval India* (Chicago 1996), pp. 8–9.

[19] See Hermann Kulke, "Maharajas, Mahants and Historians: Reflections on the Early Historiography of Early Vijayanagara and Sringeri," in his *Kings and Cults: State Formation and Legitimation in India and Southeast Asia* (New Delhi 1993), esp. pp. 226–239.

to the ascetic."[20] The phrase *"nama yaterdasa"* (literally, "names ascetic ten") is the closest the authors come to the term "Dasnami." Nor is the term specifically invoked in the tenfold enumeration that is noted in the mid-seventeenth-century Persian text *Dabistan-i-Mazahib*.[21]

The generic quality of the tenfold enumeration and its relatively late arrival in descriptive accounts suggest that it was connected to a process of incorporation and institutionalization that was underway in northern India, namely, of regional varieties of ascetic practices and styles into a more cohesive, institutionally self-conscious monasticism. The bands of *yogi*s who wandered the countryside – unruly, ash-besmeared, naked, armed and dangerous – would have posed an obstacle to this process of monastic institutionalization. The main hagiography of Shankara, the *Shankaradigvijaya* (the world-conquest of Shankara), confirms this apprehension. Authored by Vidyaranya in the mid-fourteenth century, the text describes in a major concluding episode the strong (though fruitless) opposition offered to Shankara by one "Krakacha" and his followers, armed *kapalika yogi*s, in what is now Karnataka. This contest of power is worth recounting in some detail, since it affords a picture of an armed ascetic band in the centuries just prior to Thaneswar:

Thereupon the acharya [Shankara], along with his disciples, entered into the heart of this region of Kapalikas with a view to controvert their vicious doctrines. He was soon opposed by Krakacha, the leader of the Kapalika cult. Krakacha's body was smeared all over with the ashes from the cremation ground, and in his hands were a skull and a trident, the emblems of his cult.

After being verbally repulsed by Shankara's royal patron, "Krakacha declared, flourishing his battle axe, 'I am not the famous Krakacha unless I reap a harvest of the heads of you fellows!' He then dispatched a large band of well-equipped Kapalikas, who approached the party with fierce

---

[20] The Sanskrit texts are Visvesvara Saraswati, *Yatidharmasamgraha*, p. 103, and Vaidyanath Dikshita, *Smrtimuktaphala*, p. 182, discussed in P. V. Kane, *History of Dharmasastra: Ancient and Mediaeval Religious and Civil Law* (Poona 1974), vol. II, part 2, p. 948 n.2172, in the context of Shankara and the Dasnamis. Kane dates the *Smrtimuktaphala* to 1700 in *History of Dharmasastra*, vol. I, part 2, p. 815, but David Pingree, *Census of the Exact Sciences in Sanskrit*, vol. v, (Philadelphia 1970), p. 743, has Vaidyanatha Dikshita flourishing in 1600. Kane does not date the *Yatidharmasamgraha*, but Karl Potter, *Encyclopedia of Indian Philosophies*, vol. I, bibliography, 2nd revised edn (Delhi 1983), p. 382, dates Visvesvara Sarasvati (through a separate text) to 1600. Significantly, Abu'l Fazl does not use the term Dasnami, nor does he mention a ten-fold nomenclature for *sanyasi*s, suggesting that it (the nomenclature) only came into vogue around 1600. I am grateful to Professor Christopher Minkowski of Cornell University for his crucial bibliographic assistance on these Sanskrit references, and for translating the relevant Sanskrit passages.

[21] *Dabistan-i-Mazahib*, trans. David Shea and Anthony Troyer (Paris and London 1843), p. 244.

and angry roars like a turbulent sea. The king put on his mail, and seated in his chariot resisted the approaching Kapalika horde with his bow and arrows." Meanwhile "Krakacha sent another batch of his followers to attack the party of Shankara's disciples and the entourage of devotees from the rear." However, "with the utterance of the mystical syllable '*hung*,' the Acharya [Shankara] reduced to ashes" the enemy. Krakacha, undeterred,

stood still with eyes closed, and a skull in his hand. As he continued to meditate, the skull became full of liquor. He then drank half of it, and again continued to meditate on the Bhairava. Then there appeared before him the great Kapali (Bhairava) [the fierce Siva] with a garland of skulls, long matted locks, and a trident in hand, bellowing out wild laughter and fierce roars. Addressing this deity, the Kapalika said, 'O Lord! Destroy this persecutor of Thy devotees!' Then the great Kapali said: 'Am I to destroy myself?' and with that he cut off Krakacha's head. Then the Acharya sang a hymn in praise of the great Kapali, who forthwith disappeared from the sight of men. On the discomfiture of these sordid types of men, good folk everywhere praised the Acharya in great joy.[22]

The image of Krakacha's defeat by Shankara, and more generally the incorporation and ordering of unruly *yogi*s, is the context in which we should understand the tenfold enumeration that came to constitute Dasnami classification – and, by extension, is the context in which we should examine the 1567 skirmish at Thaneswar. Two of the names are terms for forest (*aranya* and *van*), two are terms for mountain (*giri* and *parvat*), three refer to or derive from generic ascetic places (*puri*/settler, *asrama*/hermitage, and *tirtha*/shrine), and one means ocean (*sagar*). The remainder, *bharati* and *sarasvati*, possess a variety of religious and geographic connotations. Sarasvati is both the goddess of learning as well as the subterranean river that is said to run beneath much of northern India and feed its sacred waters and springs, including Thaneswar and the Prayag *sangam* at Allahabad. (For this reason the *sangam* is often referred to as *triveni*, or the "triple-braid" of the Ganga, Jamuna, and the Sarasvati.) Bharati is another name for the goddess Sarasvati; as Dasnami names, both Bharati and Sarasvati connote great learning. Taken together, the terms suggest a naturalization of not simply a compelling if treacherous frontier, but the wild frontier men who inhabited it. The Krakacha episode makes clear that followers of Shankara perceived *yogi*s as wild men in tune with the elements; the emergence of a Dasnami enumeration is suggestive of how they were managed, sedentarized, and

---

[22] Madhava-Vidyaranya, *Sankaradigvijaya, The Traditional Life of Sri Sankaracharya*, trans. Swami Tapasyananda (Madras 1978), pp. 177–179. See also Ghurye, *Indian Sadhus*, p. 100.

tamed over time through proper world renunciation (*sanyas*). As perhaps a reflection of the demographic importance of *yogi*s to *sanyasi* institutionalization, the author of the *Dabistan-i-Mazahib*, Mubad Shah, appends his seventeenth-century discussion of the latter to his treatment of the ascetic practices of the former. But he does so in a way that suggests there was no necessary theoretical divorce of asceticism and worldly power. "As the Sanyasis are also pious men, I will join an account of them to that of the Yogis. The Sanyasis make a choice of abnegation and solitude; they renounce all bodily enjoyments; some, in order that they may not be invested with another body, and migrate from body to body; a great number, in order to go to heaven; and a multitude, in order to acquire dominion, that is, to become kings, or very rich men."[23]

There is more conventional evidence of the absorption and incorporation of *yogi*s into a Dasnami monastic framework throughout northern India, particularly in the context of the *naga akhara*s. This evidence refers not to *kapalika*s as such, but to ascetics generally understood as their close evolutionary heirs, the *nath* or *Gorakhnathi yogi*s. A Dasnami lineage chain discovered in the early 1980s in an Ayodhya monastery showed a shift in about 1300 from preceptors whose names ended in *nath* to preceptors whose names ended in *giri*.[24] Terminologically, *nath* connotes "lord," "protector," or "master," and refers typologically to the internal Siva that each *yogi* cultivates within. Hence these *yogi*s are often referred to as *nath yogi*s. *Giri*, by contrast, is one of the ten suffixes that Dasnami *sanyasi*s append to their names and, along with *Puri*, it is the term most commonly adopted by *naga*s. According to anthropologists Baidyanath Saraswati and Surajit Sinha, a similar if more recent shift in nomenclature from *nath* to *giri* occurred in the lineage of *mahant*s at a prominent *samadhi* (internment) shrine at Chunar fort, on the south bank of the Ganga about thirty miles southwest of Banaras.[25] In both cases, significantly, the institutions in question are not only under the control of Dasnami *sanyasi*s but belong to the Juna *akhara* – generally regarded as the oldest of the Dasnami military lineages. Saraswati and Sinha cite

---

[23] *Dabistan*, 244. On the question of this text's authorship, see S. H. Askari, "Dabistan-i-Mazahib and Diwan-i-Mubad," in Fathullah Mujtabai (ed.), *Indo-Iranian Studies Presented for the Golden Jubilee of the Pahlavi Dynasty of Iran* (New Delhi 1977); and Nabi Hadi, *Dictionary of Indo-Persian Literature* (New Delhi 1995), pp. 360–361; both cited in Aditya Behl, "An Ethnographer in Disguise: Comparing Self and Other in Mughal India," in Laurie Patton and David Haberman (eds.), *Notes from a Mandala: Essays in Honor of Wendy Doniger* (New York, 2003).

[24] Peter van der Veer, *Gods on Earth: The Management of Religious Experience and Identity in a North Indian Pilgrimage Center* (London 1988), pp. 146–147.

[25] Saraswati and Sinha, *Ascetics of Kashi*, pp. 93–94. *Samadhi* shrines mark the internment spot of *yogi*s and *sanyasi*s.

numerous other shared features of *nath yogi* and Dasnami *sanyasi* religious culture, as manifest in the Juna *akhara*. These include the continued use of the suffix *nath* for monastic officials, worship of both Bhairava and the ancient *yogi* Dattatreya (depicted as bearing a conch, discus, and club), an emphasis on the maintenance of a continuous fire (*dhuni*), and aspects of outward appearance such as common earrings, ochre-robes, ash-besmeared bodies, and use of the human skull as a ritual drinking vessel.[26]

A similar shift from *nath yogi* to Dasnami *sanyasi* seems to have occurred at Thaneswar itself. There is no question that Dasnamis are the dominant sectarian force at Thaneswar today.[27] The Dasnami institution that exercises the greatest amount of influence is the Mahanirvani Panchayati *akhara*, the subcontinental headquarters of which lie adjacent to the *kumbha mela* grounds in Allahabad. The Thaneswar branch of the Mahanirvani Panchayati *akhara* is a large, fortress-like structure that is known as the Dera Baba Sravan-nath-ji Sthan, or the place of Baba Sravan-nath-ji. Sravan-nath, a prominent *baba* or charismatic mystic, is said to have built the structure in the seventeenth century. As with the shrines in Ayodhya and Chunar, described above, the *mahant*s today go by the name of "*giri*." A legend related by a local historian hints at the reason for the shift.

The story goes that once Baba Lachchman Giri visited this place and asked for milk. The pupils of Baba Shravannath poured *maund*s [gallons upon gallons] of milk in the alms pot but could not fill it. Then Baba Shravannath himself came out and started pouring milk from his *kamandal* [water jug]. The milk came out in an endless stream but neither the kamandal nor the alms pot was filled. Both the Babas recognised each other as having been possessed of supernatural powers and embraced each other.[28]

Though the legend glosses over what must have been a considerably more complex sectarian transition, we may presume that following the embrace of the two great personalities, control of the shrine shifted to Dasnamis connected to the Mahanirvani Panchayati *akhara*. There is

---

[26] Ghurye makes a similar argument about the yogic antiquity of the *Juna akhara*, based in particular on the shared worship of Bhairava and Dattatreya; see *Indian Sadhus*, pp. 103–104.

[27] I visited the several shrines and tanks of Thaneswar on 19 March 1995, and gathered the information related in this paragraph. Among those I met were the newly installed *mahant* of Dera Baba Sravan-nath-ji Sthan, Syam Narayangiri, and Kesavgiri of Sannehit Sarovar. The latter regaled me with stories of warrior *naga*s in the employ of the Rajput kings in centuries past, including Jaipur, Udaipur, Gwalior, and Jodhpur.

[28] Bal Krishna Muztar, *History of Kurukshetra* (Kurukshetra, Haryana, nd.), p. 23. This text is an abridged version of *Kurukshetra: Political and Cultural History* (Delhi 1978), by the same author, and is intended for pilgrims and tourists.

also, it should be noted, a Gorakhnathi *mandir* and *math* (temple and monastery) nearby, but it is a much less imposing structure and the occupants are extremely wary of their Dasnami neighbors.

That *yogis* of various stripes were including Shankara in their *parampara* genealogies (and thereby being absorbed into the Dasnami order) is, in fact, widely accepted.[29] But what was the process whereby such absorption and ordering occurred? The Mughal account of Akbar's intervention at Thaneswar in 1567, I argue, represents a glimpse of one possible mechanism at work at one point in time. The standard translation of Abu'l Fazl's account appears to confuse the picture, however, but in a way that may well reflect and shed light on this process of absorption and ordering. In this account the combatants are described as "two parties among the Sanyasi: one is called Kur, and the other Puri" – the latter receiving the decisive imperial assistance of Akbar. "Puri" is easily explained, since it is one of the ten names that Dasnamis append to their own and is particularly favored (along with *giri*) by members of the *naga akharas*. Explaining "*kur*" is more difficult. Clearly the term is meant to indicate the group identified as *yogis* in the other Mughal accounts; on this point there is no ambiguity, since the "*kur*" group is the one that suffers defeat in Abul Fazl's narrative. The theory that has been favored by most modern authors is that the term "*kur*" is synonymous with "*gir*" (or, more formally, "*giri*"), the other main Dasnami *naga* marker.[30] In support of this interpretation, it is noted that in addition to sounding more or less alike, the terms "*gir*" and "*kur*" appear almost identical in the Perso-Arabic script. It is entirely possible that later transcribers and translators misread the term, not being sufficiently familiar with Dasnami nomenclature and the ascetic context. A similar misreading certainly occurred with the transcription and translation of Mubad Shah's mid-seventeenth-century *Dabistan-i-Mazahib*, wherein the tenfold Dasnami list includes "*kar*" in the place of "*giri*."[31] Mubad Shah writes, "They [*sanyasis*] are distinguished by names, and divided into ten classes, namely: *Ban, Áran, Tírthah, Áshram, Kar, Parbatah, Sákar, Bhárthy, Perí*, and *Sarsatí*." Since it is obvious that "*sákar*" should be "*ságar*," the Sanskrit–Hindi term for ocean, we may conclude that at some point in the process of transcription or translation the Perso-Arabic *gaf* or "g" was misread as *kaf* or "k" – and

---

[29] At the same time, there is no standard historical treatment of the process. See e.g. Ghurye, *Indian Sadhus*, p. 108; and George Grierson, "Rukhada," in James Hastings (ed.), *Encyclopædia of Religion and Ethics* (New York and Edinburgh 1908–1926), vol. x, pp. 866–867.

[30] See Ghurye, *Indian Sadhus*, p. 102; Lorenzen, "Warrior Ascetics," p. 69, and Farquhar, "Fighting Ascetics," p. 443.

[31] *Dabistan*, p. 244.

the same error would have been made with respect to *kar*. If the *kaf* of *kar* was, in fact, a *gaf*, then the term may be read as *gar*, *gir*, *giri*, *gor*, *gur*, and even *guru*, depending on the context.

A *giri–puri* reading of Abu'l Fazl's narrative would suggest that the 1567 conflict was a Dasnami affair on both sides.[32] This would be squarely at odds with the Dasnami *sanyasi* versus *nath yogi* interpretation argued by me and suggested by the remaining Mughal accounts. Another possible reading, however, is that Abu'l Fazl meant *kur* to be *gor*, as shorthand for "Gorakh" (or "Gorakhnath"), the *yogi* master who was, in competition with Shankara, being included in an increasing number of *yogi* guru genealogies after the twelfth century. Another possibility that does not preclude an affinity for Gorakhnath, is that the term *kur* was employed to link *yogi*s to the broader geo-cultural associations of the Thaneswar setting. Introducing the event, Abu'l Fazl noted that "Formerly there was a wide plain there known as *Kurkhet* [from the Sanskrit *Kurukshetra*, the field of the *Kurus*] which the ascetics of India have reverenced from ancient times." This is, of course, a reference to the epic conflict known as the *Mahabharata*. Abu'l Fazl later noted that the "*kurs*" made an ancestral claim to the spot: "The Kurs represented [to Akbar] that the place belonged to them by inheritance, though the Puris had settled there for some time." (Likewise, one could speculate about the orthographic similarity between Kurkhet/Kurukshetra and Gorakh-khet/Gorakh-kshetra.) Badauni was more explicit about the *Mahabharata* connections of Thaneswar, possibly because he was more familiar with the epic, having been ordered by the emperor to translate it into Persian. Acerbic juices in full flow, he observed that near Thaneswar, "at the lake [called] *Kurk'het*, a host of Kurus and Pandus, (curse on them!) more than 4,000 years ago, according to the opinion of the Hindus, to the number of seven or eight hundred millions of persons[,] were killed in a tumult (and they went by way of water to hell-fire)."[33] Badauni, however,

---

[32] Thus Pramod Chandra argued, on the basis of Abu'l Fazl's identification of the leader as Anand Kur, that the scene depicts the "Death of Anandagiri". Pramod Chandra, "Hindu Ascetics in Mughal Painting," in Michael Meister (ed.), *Discourses on Siva: Proceedings of a Symposium on the Nature of Religious Imagery* (Philadelphia 1984), pp. 312–316.

[33] These observations led Beveridge to equate the 1567 combatants with the feuding family branches from the *Mahabharata*, despite the fact that neither Badauni nor Abu'l Fazl made such a direct assertion. See *Akbar Nama*, vol. II, 422, n.1. In any case, there existed in the late sixteenth century an awareness of the *Mahabharata* past, and it served as a frame for Muslims seeking to understand internecine "Hindu" combat in the present. This is one important reason there was an increased desire to translate such texts as the *Mahabharata* and *Ramayana* into Persian during and after the reign of Akbar, since these texts would be thought to provide some clues to the nature of the people the Mughals had come to rule. This implies that there was more to Mughal interest in "Hinduism" than simply benign curiosity. In fact, Mughal imperial inquiry into the culture of the

did not equate either combatant party with the ancient antagonists of the *Mahabharata*.

One final point from Abu'l Fazl's narrative supports the identification of *kur*s as *yogi*s. Abu'l Fazl describes the leader of the *kur*s using the Sufi designation, "*pir*" : "They [the *puri*s] came up with their [the *kur*s'] *Pir* and head, who was called Anand Kur, and slew the miserable creature." It is possible that Abu'l Fazl was simply employing a Sufi lexicon that would aid a Muslim reader in making sense of the scene. But it is worth noting that the term *pir* was (and still is) used by *nath yogi*s to indicate the head of an ascetic band.[34] Moreover, nineteenth-century observers reported that *nath yogi*s had formerly recruited novitiates without regard to caste or religion and consequently attracted many Muslims, but that this practice was, by the late 1800s, falling out of favor.[35] Such Hindu–Muslim interpenetration among *yogi*s (both in terms of language and recruits) may have, over time, led Dasnami *sanyasi*s to think of them as Muslims. This in turn may help to explain the twentieth-century oral tradition that Akbar intervened to assist Hindu *sanyasi*s against attacks by Muslim *fakir*s.

Yogi Akbar

The episode at Thaneswar raises several important questions, not least among them being why Akbar, well on his way to becoming the architect of the most powerful imperial state southern Asia had witnessed in many a generation, would choose to involve himself in the tawdry affairs of a handful of Hindu ascetics – men who, judging from Nizamuddin Ahmad's observations, smeared their bodies with ashes and wore rags. Was it simply out of his love for blood sport and his desire to see an evenly matched contest, as one early twentieth-century biographer contended?[36] Nizamuddin Ahmad tells us that the emperor greatly enjoyed the spectacle; Abu'l Fazl likewise reports that Akbar "was highly delighted with this sport." Perhaps. But what, then, do we make of the detailed assertion, also by Abu'l Fazl, that the emperor tried to reason with the disputants? Indeed, the manner in which the scene unfolds suggests a subtle intentionality on the part of the emperor, that there is more to his intervention than the leveling of a playing field. Akbar waits until the

people of Hindustan is remarkably similar to later British "Orientalist" investigations, both in tone and scope, a point made in Bayly, *Empire and Information*.
34 See Ghurye, *Indian Sadhus*, pp. 138–139; G. W. Briggs, *Gorakhnath and the Kanphata Yogis* (Calcutta 1938, reprint Delhi 1989), e.g. pp. 8, 20, 26, 35, 37–38, 42.
35 Briggs, *Gorakhnath*, pp. 26–27.
36 Vincent Smith, *Akbar the Great Mogul*, 2nd edn (Oxford 1919), pp. 78–79.

skirmish is underway before making a choice between the two parties. By intervening on the side of the *sanyasi*s, Akbar is letting it be known that the *sanyasi* victory is really *his* victory. By waiting, he puts the *sanyasi*s in his debt in a way that is far more dramatic than had he simply favored the *sanyasi*s at the outset and thereby prevented bloodshed. Furthermore, had he decided against the *yogi*s at the outset and thereby forestalled the skirmish, the *yogi*s would have harbored resentment – possibly an organized resentment. His intervention during the fight itself, the killing of Anand Kur and the decimation of the *yogi* band, lent his victory a punctuated finality that any pre-conflict adjudication surely would have lacked. The vanquished are not simply defeated, they are eradicated. There was, it would appear, a calculus at work in the mind of the emperor.

There is another other odd feature to the unfolding of the scene. According to Abu'l Fazl, only one of the two leaders, the *sanyasi* Kisu Puri, appealed to Akbar prior to the battle. By contrast, we only learn of the identity of the *yogi* leader, Anand Kur, when that "miserable creature" is suffering decapitation at the hands of his adversaries. The wording of the competing claims of the two parties prior to the battle is also worthy of note: one party makes an appeal to God, the other does not. Kisu Puri and his *sanyasi*s, "trusting in God," would stand up for their rights and be killed if necessary. The *yogi*s would hold their ground as long as there was "life left in their bodies." Is this just a casual distinction on the part of Abu'l Fazl? Unlikely, since he introduces the scene with the observation that "The asceticism of most of these men arises from the world's having turned its back on them, and not from their having become cold-hearted to the world." This would appear to be a barb aimed in particular at the *yogi*s. In Abu'l Fazl's estimation, the *sanyasi*s may have presented a more appealing religious prospect.[37]

Bedraggled though they were, the ascetics at Thaneswar may have intrigued Akbar for reasons other than the question of their piety. For one thing, they were ubiquitous. His grandfather Babur had heard tell of *yogi*s who frequented a dangerous cave near Peshawar, and he finally managed to visit the site in 1519.[38] Moreover Akbar was not blind to the

[37] A complicating factor in all this is that Abu'l Fazl, alone among the authors, does not identify the combatant factions as *yogi* and *sanyasi*, but rather "*kur*" (or possibly "*gur*," depending on one's reading of the Perso-Arabic characters for *kaf* and *gaf*) and "*puri*" – which he understood to be "two parties among the Sanyasis." See the preceding section for discussion.

[38] *The Baburnama: Memoirs of Babur, Prince and Emperor*, trans., ed., and annot. Wheeler M. Thackston (New York and Washington, DC, 1996), pp. 186–187, 285. This is the cave of Gurh Kattri, near Jam and Bigram in the vicinity of Peshawar. Babur was ultimately disappointed with the place, and did not mention having seen any *yogi*s there. However, the two paintings that illustrate this event in a British Library Baburnama MS (1580)

fact that these men were greatly esteemed by the people of India – the Hindus – and that they seemed to possess privileged access to important pilgrimage sites. One of those sites, the *sangam* at Prayag, was particularly important; indeed, it may rightly be regarded as the geo-strategic center of northern India. As Abu'l Fazl would later report, "For a long time [Akbar's] desire was to found a great city in the town of Piyag [Prayag], where the rivers Ganges and Jamna join, and which is regarded by the people of India with much reverence, and which is a place of pilgrimage for the ascetics of that country, and to build a choice fort there."[39] Akbar would build this fort in the early 1580s and name it Illahabas, or "blessed by God," which over time evolved to Allahabad, "abode of God." The distinction is not, as I will suggest later, an idle one.

The subcontinental ubiquity of Hindu ascetics also meant that they might be usefully employed as spies. In India ascetics had long been used as agents of espionage and spies had long adopted ascetic disguises. The *Arthasastra* of Kautilya, an ancient Indian manual of statecraft, makes frequent reference to the political utility of ascetics, as well as men and women disguised as ascetics: they should be used to foment dissension among the ranks of the enemy; to lure rival kings into ambush; to ascertain the honesty or dishonesty of cultivators, merchants, clerks, revenue collectors, and high officials; to report on strangers on the roads and at roadside inns; to gather bazaar rumors; to administer poison; and to carry out countless other nefarious deeds. "Merchant spies inside forts; saints and ascetics in the suburbs of forts; the cultivator and recluse in country parts; herdsmen in the boundaries of the country; in forests, forest-dwellers, *sramanas* [Buddhist ascetics], and chiefs of wild tribes, shall be stationed to ascertain the movements of enemies."[40] Kautilya's text was widely translated over the centuries and was well known to the Mughals. Abu'l Fazl mentions it as one of "the eighteen sciences of the Hindus" in his own treatise on Mughal statecraft, the *Ain-i-Akbari*. Indeed, he seems to have acknowledged the early modern utility of Kautilya's ancient advice. He urged the "Provincial Viceroy" or "Commander of the Forces" (*sipah salar*) to "hold in honour the chosen servants of God, and entreat the assistance of spiritually-minded anchorites and of mendicants of tangled hair and naked of foot." Of a similar tenor was his advice for the *kotwal*, or prefect of police: "Religious enthusiasts, calendars

---

show many more, and many more different kinds of, ascetics than Babur encountered. As Walter Smith notes ("Hindu Ascetics in Mughal Painting," 70), this reflects Akbar's growing fascination with Hindu asceticism.

[39] *Akbar Nama*, vol. II, p. 616.

[40] Kautilya, *Arthasastra* (Mysore 1929), p. 22 (for the quote).

[i.e., *qalandars*, wandering and dissolute Sufi mendicants], and dishonest tradesmen he should expel or deter from their course of conduct, but he should be careful in this matter not to molest a God-fearing recluse, or persecute barefooted wandering anchorites."[41]

Evidence of an entirely different sort suggests that soon after Thaneswar the image of the barely clad Hindu ascetic and subcontinental spy were fused in the Mughal imagination. Among the earliest paintings commissioned by Akbar were illustrations of the *Hamzanama*, the fantastical and immensely popular Persian romance of the globe-trotting Hamza, the legendary uncle of the Prophet Muhammad. One such painting, entitled "Songhur Balkhi and Lulu the Spy are received by Baba Baksha, a Former Spy Living in Aqiqinagar", attributed by John Seyller to Dasavanta and Mukhlis and dated to *circa* 1570, features a host of male figures resting in a kind of open pavilion in the forest (see figure 3).[42] These men are armed and have weapons hanging in the background; they sport bare torsos and legs, and some wear distinctive round earrings. A tiger skin – a key marker of Saiva asceticism – is prominently displayed in the background, and the leader is seated on another such skin. In short, these men, hosts to the spies at Aqiqinagar, are similar in many ways to the battling ascetics pictured at Thaneswar (compare with figure 4, a detail from the Victoria and Albert *Akbarnama* manuscript, as well as figure 2, the Khuda Baksh image). This association is more deeply evident in a second *Hamzanama* image, entitled "Misbah the Grocer brings the Spy Parran to his House," also dated to about 1570.[43] In this painting (figure 5) the spy himself is draped in a tiger skin, wearing an earring, and displaying a nearly bare torso and legs. An additional detail, not included in the previous image, is the matted hair wrapped like a helmet around the head.[44]

---

[41] *A'in-i-Akbari*, trans. H. Blochmann, H. S. Jarrett, with corrections by Jadunath Sarkar (Calcutta 1927–1949, reprint Delhi 1989) vol. II, pp. 40, 45 (vol. III, p. 235 for the reference to the eighteen sciences).

[42] For recent color reproductions, see S. C. Welch, *Imperial Mughal Painting* (New York 1978), p. 45; and John Seyller, *The Adventures of Hamza: Painting and Storytelling in India* (London and Washington, DC, 2002), p. 199. Seyller's summary translation (p. 198) is additionally illuminating: Baba Baksha, known also as "World Traverser," is "a veteran spy" – "a grizzled but still vital man." His establishment is "a spy's paradise, stockpiled with weapons of all sorts and staffed by youths honing their skills in guerrilla warfare."

[43] For recent color reproductions, see S. Kossak, *Indian Court Painting: 16th–19th Century* (New York 1997), p. 33; Seyller, *The Adventures of Hamza*, p. 169.

[44] Seyller, *The Adventures of Hamza*, p. 168, describes Parran's head covering as "a rakish fur cap," but when compared to the headgear of other warrior ascetics (e.g., figures 6 and 9, below) it is clear that this is simply Parran's way of arranging his *jata*, matted hair, on his head.

Figure 3. Songhur Balkhi and Lulu the spy are received by Baba Baksha, a former spy living in Aqiqinagar. *Hamzanama*. B.1 8770/59, MAK – Austrian Vienna Museum of Applied Arts/Contemporary Art. Reproduced with permission.

Figure 4. Akbar and the battle of Sanyasis. *Akbarnama*. Detail from right folio. CT8104, Victoria & Albert Museum, London. Reproduced with permission.

Whatever may have been Akbar's intentions at Thaneswar in 1567, by the 1570s he (or, rather, the artists in his atelier) saw more in them than a ragged, ash-besmeared rabble. The utility of ascetics as spies was not simply the empty rhetorical advice of a political theorist, whether Kautilya or Abu'l Fazl. The seventeenth-century Venetian physician and soldier of fortune, Niccolao Manucci, related the tale of a *yogi*-spy told to him by a condemned man on whom Manucci had operated, a rebel chieftain near Lahore. The chieftain had been asked by a friend and neighboring "rajah *faujdar*" (a local notable who held a Mughal military assignment) to demonstrate the cleverness of his spies. "After the lapse of some days, there appeared at daybreak in front of the rajah's tent a *Jogi* penitent seated

Figure 5. Misbah the grocer brings the spy Parran to his house, detail. *Hamzanama*. Rogers Fund, 1924 (24.48.1), Metropolitan Museum of Art, New York. Reproduced with permission.

on a tiger-skin, with flowing hair, a huge beard, his arms raised on high, having long twisted nails, his body smeared over with ashes." The rajah's army "thronged to see him" and offered him food and drink (which he refused). Finally, the rajah himself approached the *yogi*, "prayed him to have compassion on him and his army," and offered to have him fed from the hand of one of his own wives. The *yogi* consented. "At once the rajah sent for a tent, and caused all his women to appear. These did the *faqir* great reverence, and in his presence prepared the food. The principal wife of the rajah as a sign of worship placed a morsel in his mouth, and he refused to eat more. Thus all were satisfied, and when night descended the *Jogi* disappeared." When the rebel chieftain and the "rajah-*faujdar*" met some months later, the latter complained that his friend's spies had yet to demonstrate their ability. The spy, "standing by clad as a soldier," stepped forward and announced, "'I am the man to whom your wife gave [food] to eat,' and told the whole of what had passed. The rajah was in astonishment, praying them another time not to play him such tricks."[45]

A third factor prompting the imperial intervention at Thaneswar may have been Akbar's own evolving sense of self, what his critic Badauni secretly perceived as the emperor's straying from the straight and narrow of Islam. Akbar's increasing "apostasy" – and Abu'l Fazl's fanning of the heretical flames in the service of expanding imperial power – became particularly evident to Badauni in the mid-1570s.[46] Events reached crisis proportions in 1584 when, according to Badauni, Akbar instituted some of his "new-fangled decrees . . . to please the Hindus" – such as periodic prohibitions on the killing of animals, daily sun worship, fasting, and vegetarianism. The slide into apostasy was complete when the emperor began visiting the haunts of lowly ascetics and dabbling in their practices.

His Majesty [had] built outside the town [of Agra] two places for feeding poor Hindus and Musalmans, one of them being called *Khairpura*, and the other *Dharmpurah*. . . . As an immense number of *Jogis* also flocked to this establishment, a third place was built, which got the name of *Jogipurah*.

His Majesty also called on some of the Jogis, and gave them at night private interviews, enquiring into abstract truths; their articles of faith; their occupation; the influence of pensiveness; their several practices and usages; the power of

---

[45] Niccolao Manucci, *Storia do Mogor, or Mogul India, 1653–1708*, trans. W. Irvine (London 1907–1908, reprint Delhi 1990), vol. II, pp. 428–429. Manucci's tale leaves open the question of actual identity: we are not told (and presumably Manucci was not told either) whether the spy was a soldier pretending to be a *yogi*, or a *yogi* pretending to be a soldier. This need not be read as an omission, unless we subscribe to the notion that ascetic archer is a contradiction in terms (see the opening paragraphs of chapter 5, below).

[46] The religious experiments on the part of the emperor and those around him have been understood in modern historical writing either in terms of political status – the political status of non-Muslims (primarily Hindus) in an empire led by Muslims, or the political status of individuals gathered around the emperor's person – or in order to ascertain their philosophical and religious origins. The literature is too voluminous to detail, but see Sri Ram Sharma, *The Religious Policy of the Mughal Emperors* (London 1940); S. A. A. Rizvi, *The Religious and Intellectual History of Muslims in Akbar's Reign* (New Delhi 1975); M. Athar Ali, "Suhl-i Kul and the Religious Ideas of Akbar," *Studies in History* 4, 1 (1982): 27–39; Douglas Streusand, *The Formation of the Mughal Empire* (Delhi 1989), esp. pp. 130–138, 148–153. This modern scholarship is structured in large part by the importance of religion as a basis for political belonging in the twentieth century. Scholars have either looked to Akbar as an exemplar of Indian secularism, or they have sought to show the ways in which he used a cult of personality as an instrument to forge new loyalties across the boundaries of religion and ethnicity. However, there has been little attempt to understand the *yogi*s themselves and why the Mughal emperor may have been interested in them.

being absent from the body; or into alchemy, physiognomy, and the power of omnipresence of the soul. His Majesty even learned alchemy, and showed in public some of the gold made by him. On a fixed night, which came once a year, a great meeting was held of Jogis from all parts. This night they called *Sivrat*. The Emperor ate and drank with the principal Jogis, who promised him that he should live three or four times as long as ordinary men. His Majesty fully believed it, and connecting their promises with other inferences he had drawn, it became impressed on his mind as indelibly as though it were engraved on a rock.[47]

The exact date of these meetings is difficult to discern. Since they are not mentioned in Nizamuddin Ahmad's account, it would appear likely that they occurred after 1593, toward the end of Akbar's life. Finally, as noted earlier, by the late 1590s both Akbar and his eldest son Salim (later known as the emperor Jahangir) were visiting a *sanyasi* recluse named Jadrup Gosain, who lived in a cave near Ujjain and, later, Mathura. In any case, by the 1590s the emperor was confronting his own mortality. The advice of *yogis* could be useful – as was confirmed by Badauni, much to his dismay. Apparently they convinced Akbar to adopt many of their bodily practices.

[The emperor] limited the time he spent in the Harem, curtailed his food and drink, but especially abstained from meat. He also shaved the hair of the crown of his head, and let the hair at the sides grow, because he believed that the soul of perfect beings, at the time of death, passes out by the crown (which is the tenth opening of the human body) with a noise resembling thunder, which the dying man may look upon as a proof of his happiness and salvation from sin, and as a sign that his soul by metempsychosis will pass into the body of some grand and mighty king.

It is difficult to know what to make of Badauni's claims, especially given Akbar's hand in the defeat of the Thaneswar *yogis* in 1567. It is clear, nonetheless, that the emperor was adopting new behaviors toward the end of his life, and that those behaviors were influenced by his association with *yogis* as well as other ascetics. Abu'l Fazl celebrated the personal and public religious innovations of the emperor, such as sun and fire-worship, vegetarianism, sexual abstinence, and the giving of *darsan* (or public appearance). But he cast Akbar's association with ascetics not in terms of the benefits that accrued from them to the emperor, but in terms of the emperor's own advanced spiritual state and the benefits that accrued to those who came within range of his glow: "Many sincere inquirers, from the mere light of his wisdom, or his holy breath, obtain a degree of awakening which other spiritual doctors could not produce by repeated

---

[47] Badauni, *Muntakhabu 't Tawarikh*, vol. II, pp. 334–336. The passage is partially translated in Elliot and Dowson, *The History of India*, vol. V, p. 538.

fasting and prayers for forty days. Numbers of those who have renounced the world, as *Sannasis, Jogis, Sevras, Qalandars, Hakims,* and *Sufis,* and thousands of such as follow worldly pursuits as soldiers, tradespeople, mechanics, and husbandmen, have daily their eyes opened to insight [by the emperor], or have the light of their knowledge increased."[48]

Most scholars agree that Abu'l Fazl, as Douglas Streusand puts it (paraphrasing S. A. A. Rizvi), "combines the Timurid model of kingship and the Sufi doctrine of illuminationism" in his conceptualization of Akbar's religious eclecticism, and that an important political result of that conceptualization was a "new sovereign cult" understood as "*sulh-i kull* (general peace), the principle of universal toleration."[49] But Abu'l Fazl's imperial propaganda should not be confused with what Akbar was actually up to – what his motives were in his religious and political experimentation – nor with how people responded. It is difficult if not impossible to arrive at any certainty with respect to the former: no matter how close we get, we always run up against the fact that Akbar did not write his memoirs. How people responded to Akbar's eclecticism, however, can be discerned. Badauni's response was unambiguous: Akbar's eclecticism was dangerous and boded ill for Muslims. The best way to condemn that eclecticism, in the eyes of an orthodox Muslim, was to elevate the paradigmatic unbeliever, the heterodox *yogi,* as the main source of Akbar's decline into apostasy. And to condemn the emperor as a perverse Mughal *yogi.*

Later stories about Akbar indicate that the emperor's reputation as a Mughal *yogi* extended beyond the level of the court. An example is the fabulous tale told to John Marshall, an East India Company trader living in Patna in 1670, who recorded it in his notebook as "*Jougee-Eckbar*" (or *Yogi*-Akbar).[50] According to "the Moores" who recounted it for him, during Akbar's reign there was said to have lived a *yogi* who could fly through the air with the aid of a pellet of quicksilver that he held in his mouth.[51] One day, en route to the shrine of Jagannath in Orissa, this *yogi* chanced to alight on the terrace of the emperor's harem for a nap. While the *yogi* slept the pellet of quicksilver slipped from his mouth.

[48] Abu'l Fazl, *Ain-i-Akbari,* pp. 172–173. As Streusand argues, *Formation of the Mughal Empire,* pp. 123–153, esp. pp. 130–132, Abu'l Fazl was careful to represent the emperor's bodily constitution as the vehicle of a penetrating light descended to him through his ancestors from God.

[49] Streusand, *Formation of the Mughal Empire,* pp. 130, 137.

[50] *John Marshall in India: Notes and Observations in Bengal 1668–1672,* ed. Shafaat Ahmad Khan (London: Oxford University Press, 1927), p. 371; see "Marshall MSS," Harl. MS 4254, fols. 31b–32a, British Library, London, for the original text.

[51] For more on the alchemical, physiological, and psychosexual efficacy of mercurial pellets, or *gutika*s, see White, *Alchemical Body,* esp. pp. 315, 336–337, 349–352.

Akbar chanced by, sized up the situation, and seized the pellet. When the *yogi* awoke, he assured the emperor that he had not meddled with his women and begged him to return the quicksilver, without which he could not fly. The emperor demurred, demanding instead that the *yogi* teach him a few tricks. The *yogi* agreed and offered to put his soul into any living creature. Akbar had a deer brought forth, upon which the *yogi* demonstrated. Apparently unconvinced, the emperor requested that his own soul be put into the deer. The *yogi* complied with the request and then brought the emperor back into his own body. Akbar was so frightened by the power of this *yogi* that he quietly ordered his guards to kill him. This order was duly carried out but afterwards people began noticing a change in the emperor's demeanor. To quote Marshall:

Immediately after [the execution of the *yogi*] the King was extremely altered, and all his life long after lived a retired life, which was for about 10 or 11 yeares, and as to all his disposition hee was perfectly altered, and any that went to him would not have knowne by his discourse or actings that hee was the same man as before. So that the Moores say That when hee ordered the Jougee to be killed, that the Jougee changed soules with the King, so that it was the Kings soule that was gone, and the Jougees soule remained in the King.

At one level, we may read the "Moores'" tale as a late seventeenth-century updating of Badauni, right down to the emphasis on metempsychosis. And the end result was the same: "the King was extremely altered."[52] Marshall's tale makes clear that not only did Muslim anxiety over Akbar's eclecticism persist well after the emperor's death – and not surprisingly, since that eclecticism marked the multi-ethnic and multi-religious character of Mughal imperial state well into the seventeenth century – but *yogis* also remained central to the expression of that anxiety. There are some important twists, however. Instead of the emperor becoming a *yogi*, a *yogi* becomes the emperor. And he does this, the "Moores" tell Marshall, by trading souls with him. Whereas Badauni scoffed at the claims of the *yogis* – even though "His Majesty fully believed it" – Marshall's "Moores" were willing to grant, at least for the purposes of a good story, the possibility that *yogis* could practice not only metempsychosic kidnapping but even quicksilver-aided flight. That ordinary Muslims in Aurangzeb's north India could imagine such things possible is

[52] Marshall also reported a discussion with "a Sober, Serious Fuckeer, a Hindoo," who claimed that "Some [*fakir*s, by which he meant *yogi*s] live 2 or 300 years of age, and when their bodies are therewith decayed, they acquaint their friends that they desire to leave that body and assume another. So without any violence offered to their body, after their prayers said, they sit downe and die voluntarily and at what time they please, but before do acquaint their relations at what place they desire to assume a Body, at Agra or Dilly, or the like. And then they leave their old body and go into the belly of a woman, and so it is borne againe." See "Marshall MSS," fol. 18b.

not nearly as outlandish as it may seem: Mughal documents from a *nath yogi* institution north of Delhi indicate that Aurangzeb himself was given, in the 1660s, to purchasing quicksilver from *yogi*s.[53] In one letter, Aurangzeb complained that the quicksilver sent to him "is not so good as Your Reverence [Anand Nath] had given us to understand," and he graciously requested that some better quicksilver be sent "without unnecessary delay." We do not know what use Aurangzeb had for the substance, but the very fact that he was corresponding solicitously with north Indian *yogi*s – and during a period in his reign that is normally associated with intense persecution of Hindus – raises questions about the precise meanings of Aurangzeb's religio-political policies. At the very least it suggests the possibility that *yogi*s were not, in the eyes of some late seventeenth-century Muslims, purveyors of a competing religion, but of magical esoterica that transcended (or sublimated) religion. Such a reading is consistent with the details of Marshall's story, which make no reference to the changes in religious policy enacted by Akbar, or his own personal religious eclecticism. All the "Moores" tell Marshall is that "the King was extreamely altered."

Then there is the legend of Mukund Brahmachari, a very different kind of ascetic from Marshall's flying *yogi*. Mukund lived on the south bank of the Yamuna, directly across from the *sangam* where Akbar was to build the Allahabad fort. Mukund was well known for his rigid diet, which consisted of nothing but milk. One day, however, he forgot to strain his drink and accidentally swallowed a single hair of a cow. Immediately realizing his error, he decided to commit suicide – a ritual practice permitted at Prayag in those days. Since he had defiled himself (or become a *mlechha*) by eating beef, he decided that in his next life he would be a Muslim. But not just any Muslim: he chose to be born as Akbar. Mukund-Akbar eventually would return to the *sangam* where he had immolated himself, and would order the construction of the fort over the site, "to prevent others reaping similar fruit by their self-sacrifice."[54] As with Marshall's metempsychosic *yogi*, there is a hint of Badauni here. The Mughal chronicler would have

---

[53] See B. N. Goswamy and J. S. Grewal, *The Mughals and the Jogis of Jakhbar: Some Madad-i-Ma'ash and Other Documents* (Simla 1967), pp. 120–124.

[54] Related in R. Chatterjee, *Prayag or Allahabad, A Handbook* (Calcutta 1910), pp. 57–62, who introduced the tale with the observation that "the Hindus have a curious legend in connection with the building of the Allahabad Fort by Akbar." Chatterjee reported that versions of the story had been told for generations. According to Lucinda Dhavan, a former resident of Allahabad and expert on local legend, B. N. Pande read a version of this story in a December 1910 issue of the *Modern Review*. The story was earlier reported in 1882 in the *Pioneer* newspaper as part of a series entitled "Kumbh Mela Notes," penned by a "Native Correspondent." Kama MacLean, personal communication, 15 March 2001.

been pleased by this last sentiment, if not the transmigratory manner in which he was said to have carried it out. He wrote that "The infidels consider this [the *sangam*] a holy place, and with a desire to obtain the rewards which are promised in their creed, of which transmigration is one of the most prominent features, they submit themselves to all kinds of tortures. Some place their brainless heads under saws, others split their deceitful tongues in two, others enter Hell by casting themselves down into the deep river from the top of a high tree . . ."[55]

Afterword

Akbar's interactions with *yogi*s and *sanyasi*s, and the stories that emanate from them, are significant not simply because they reflect the emperor's open-mindedness when it came to matters of religion (as contrasted to the bigoted Badauni, quoted above). Rather, they matter because they show the degree to which the world of early modern India cannot be reduced to Hindu versus Muslim. This is not to say that the categories "Hindu" and "Muslim" lacked meaning and relevance in the early modern period – only that they do not exhaust the range of possibilities for what constituted the religious or the political. Cutting across the political, civilizational meanings that adhered to the categories Hindu and Muslim were the practices and attitudes associated with ascetics, particularly *yogi*s. *Yogi*s were concerned not with the niceties of group identity in relation to an external God, but with how to cultivate supernormal powers within and thereby attain immortality. Whatever we may make of their claims, it is clear that many (and, as we shall see to an even greater extent in the following chapter, many besides the Mughal emperor) regarded *yogi*s as both dangerous and compelling.

Understanding *yogi*s as "Mughal" should not be seen as an attempt to claim that they were somehow not religious. *Yogi*s were, by my definition, deeply religious precisely because they were concerned with and consumed by the question of how to cheat death. Indeed, I would even go so far as to suggest that they stood at the center of religion – and it was precisely that posture that attracted the Mughal emperor to them. By calling *yogi*s "Mughal" I wish to emphasize the degree to which their history, and the history of the warrior ascetics who are tied to them, was shaped by Mughal imperial politics and culture. This does not mean they were born of the Mughal experience; it does mean that they cannot be understood independently of it. Even the Dasnami order, which links itself back to the agency of the great south Indian *Vedantin* Shankara (beyond whom

[55] Badauni, *Muntakhabu-t-Tawarikh*, p. 179.

it is difficult to imagine anyone being regarded as more central to Hindu self-understanding), seems to bear the imprint of the Mughal experience. There is, of course, much that we cannot know about the intricacies of *yogi* involvement in Mughal affairs, or Mughal involvement in *yogi* affairs for that matter. But it is clear that the Mughals, and not simply Akbar and Jahangir, but certainly Aurangzeb and probably Shah Jahan as well, were interested in *yogi*s, and *yogi*s were interested in them. Secondarily I hope to jolt us out of the notion that *yogi*s were fundamentally Hindu or Muslim, and to prompt, besides, a reflection on the question of what precisely constitutes being Hindu or Muslim. As I suggest in the chapters that follow, the devotional meanings and styles that we today associate with being Hindu were coming into shape in the Mughal and late Mughal period.

One final point bears mentioning, in part because it also foreshadows images and themes that emerge more fully in chapters 4 and 5. If we look closely at the detail of the Victoria and Albert image of the Thaneswar skirmish between *yogi*s and *sanyasi*s (described by Abu'l Fazl as a battle among *sanyasi*s only), we notice a turbaned figure running toward Anand Kur (or Anandagiri) from the right, as Anand Kur's right shoulder is being cleaved open from behind (on the left) by a determined-looking Mughal swordsman. The face of the figure rushing toward Anand Kur is a mask of horror. Upon close inspection, it becomes evident that the figure is different than the other combatants: the figure is that of a woman, and though she carries a sword, it is sheathed. As we shall see in the following chapter, women were part of *yogi* establishments. Ludovico di Varthema, the Bolognese traveler of the early sixteenth century, for example, mentioned a wandering "Gioghi king" of Gujarat whose large entourage included "a wife and children." Not surprisingly, the presence of women among *yogi*s occasioned critical commentary by some later observers. The traveler Pietro Della Valle, who encountered ash-besmeared *yogi*s near Ahmedabad in the early 1620s, reported that though "they do not marry, and they profess strict chastity," it was an open secret that "many of them behave basely when given the chance."[56] It did not help matters that their "spiritual exercises" included a kind of "carnal intercourse" with supernatural women who, in recompense, could afford the *yogi*s "marvelous" powers. Indeed, even *yogi*s who avoided women attracted them: John Marshall, the East India Company merchant who recorded the tale of "*Jougee-Eckbar*" in 1670, heard reports that women afforded great respect and veneration to naked *yogi*s: "the Hindoo women will go

[56] *The Pilgrim: The Travels of Pietro Della Valle*, abridged edn, trans. G. Bull (London 1989), p. 238.

to them and kiss the Jougees yard. Others ly [sic: lay] somthing upon it when it stands, which the Jougees take to buy victualls with; and severall come to stroke it, thinking that there is a good deale of vertue in it, noe [nothing] having gone out of it as they say, for they ly [sic: lay] not with women nor use any other way to vent their seed."[57] But whether *yogis* were "behaving basely" with loose women, engaging in ritual copulation with bloodthirsty goddesses, or attracting the attention of female devotees with their virtuous bodies, what is clear is that sexual discipline was central to the cultivation of their ascetic power. The question to which we will return in chapters 4 and 5 is how sexuality and women figured in the constellation of warrior ascetic religious and military culture in the centuries after the skirmish at Thaneswar.

---

[57] "Marshall MSS," Harl MS 4255, fol. 16b; Khan, *John Marshall in India*, pp. 196–197, gives the incorrect folio.

2 Warlords

These yogis are not such by descent, but by choice, just as with our religious ministers.

– Pietro Della Valle, *c.* 1624 (near Ahmedabad)[1]

The written and oral accounts of Akbar's encounter with *yogi*s and *sanyasi*s at Thaneswar in 1567 represent the earliest record of a distinct group of armed ascetics told from multiple perspectives. They are not, however, the earliest historical evidence of *yogi*s carrying weapons. Probably the oldest reference to armed *yogi*s occurs in the seventh-century *Harsacharita* authored by Banabhatta.[2] Bana described here the enlistment of two *yogi*s, adherents of one Bhairavacharya, who join the personal guard of King Pushpabhuti of "Sthanisvara" (or Thaneswar), the founder of a royal lineage that would eventually produce the great seventh-century monarch, Harshavardhana. Thaneswar, it would seem, was a breeding ground for armed *yogi*s in search of young nobility on the make.

Bhairavacharya is celebrated in Bana's text as a great Saiva ascetic of the Deccan, "whose powers, made famous by his excellence in multifarious sciences, were, like his many thousands of disciples, spread all over the sphere of humanity."[3] According to Bana, Pushpabhuti was himself a fervent devotee of Siva and, "immediately on hearing of this saint Bhairavacarya . . . conceived towards him, though far away, a deep

---

[1] Della Valle, *The Pilgrim*, p. 238.

[2] Banabhatta, *Harsa-carita*, trans. E. B. Cowell and F. W. Thomas (London 1897), pp. 83–99. Older still are the references to ancient sages such as Visvamitra and Vasistha in the *Ramayana* and Dronacharya in the *Mahabharata*. See chapter 5 for discussion of these sages.

[3] *Harsa-carita*, p. 85. The name Bhairavacharya indicates a sectarian affiliation with Bhairava – or malevolent Siva, depicted as naked, intoxicated, and bearing arms, with a garland of skulls draped around his neck. Given the association with Bhairava, it is likely these were *kapalika yogi*s (the term '*kapalika*' is derived from *kapali*, a representation of Siva holding a skull), whose loose sectarian identity would be associated with and overtaken by the followers of the sage Gorakhnath in the twelfth century (see the previous chapter). The followers of Gorakhnath would come to be known generically as *kanphat* (or split-eared) *yogi*s, denoting the initiatory practice of piercing the earlobe and inserting a large circular disc. On *kapalika*s and Gorakhnathis, see Ghurye, *Indian Sadhus*, ch. 7.

affection as towards a second Civa, and desired even with longing by all means to see his face." One day Bhairavacharya camped at Sthanisvara and dispatched a "recluse" to present Pushpabhuti with gifts (five silver lotuses) and to request a meeting. On the following day Pushpabhuti met Bhairavacharya and declared himself the great *yogi*'s disciple. Bhairavacharya in turn presented the monarch with an additional collection of silver lotuses and, most importantly, a magical sword. Some days later Bhairavacharya asked the monarch to accompany three of his armed disciples to a funeral ground where he had made ready the performance of a dark ritual involving the lighting of a ceremonial fire in the mouth of a corpse. The successful completion of the ritual required "victory over a goblin" by a Kshatriya (a warrior of royal blood). The goblin emerged from the burning mouth of the corpse; Pushpabhuti stepped forward and destroyed the beast with his new sword. At this a goddess appeared and foretold the future glory of the prince's descendants. Meanwhile, by successfully completing the ritual destruction of the demon, Bhairavacharya was elevated to a new level of accomplishment as a *yogi*-wizard. The tale concludes with Bhairavacharya ordering two of his disciples to join Pushpabhuti's personal guard. These two, one Patalaswamin and a "Dravidian" named Karnatala, would be "elevated to a fortune beyond their wildest dreams, drawing their swords in the midst of the royal guard, [and] occupying the front rank in the battle," eventually to "[arrive] at old age by the king's side."

More frequent – and more mundane – descriptions of armed *yogis* occur after 1500, occasioned by the arrival of European travelers in (and travel literature describing) the Indian subcontinent. I begin this chapter by mining these accounts for a picture of armed ascetics in the sixteenth and seventeenth centuries. These accounts, when set alongside the Mughal record and oral traditions reviewed in the previous chapter, not only make clear that armed *yogis* were a regular feature of the early modern Indian landscape, but also suggest that the seventeenth century was a time of ascetic military expansion, both in terms of tactics and in number – that armed *yogis* were finding service in the Mughal system. It is also during this period that the terminology describing armed ascetics begins to multiply, suggesting both a sectarian branching out process as well as tactical specialization. The eighteenth century, the period that saw the dramatic weakening of the Mughal throne if not the Mughal system, was an extremely lucrative time for all kinds of military entrepreneurs, and armed ascetics were no exception. In fact, the rising cost of technology and the expanding military labor market created an increased demand for an inexpensive but disciplined soldiery. Judging by the variety of references to them in eighteenth-century literature, armed *yogis* seemed to step into this niche with abandon. The best example of armed ascetic military entrepreneurship is the army of Rajendragiri Gosain and his *chela*s (disciples), Anupgiri and Umraogiri. The military career of this army, which climaxes with a crucial alliance with the Company in 1803, occupies center stage in the following chapter. I conclude this chapter, by contrast, with what I regard as the last gasp of the Mughal *yogi* phenomenon: the "*Sanyasi* and *Fakir* Rebellion" in Bengal.

Old world encounters

Though it lacks the occult quality of Bana's account, the first European depiction of armed *yogi*s is nonetheless vivid. Ludovico di Varthema of Bologna, who traveled in India and the Moluccas between 1503 and 1508, encountered near the coastal town of Surat a "Ioghe" (he later renders the term "Gioghi") who was said to be in a prolonged state of war with Sultan Mahmud of Gujarat. According to Varthema, this "Ioghi king" would set off every few years on a tour "through the whole of India," accompanied by "three or four thousand of his people," his "wife and children," and "four or five coursers [chargers], and civet cats, apes, parrots, leopards, and falcons."[4] He would travel "like a pilgrim, that is, at the expense of others." Though their dress was "*à là apostolica*," the higher ranking among them wore many jewels and scented themselves with sandalwood powder. The *yogi* king himself wore only a goatskin in front and back, with the hair turned outwards. His followers wore a horn around their necks (see, for example, the *Hamzanama* image of the spy Parran in the previous chapter, figure 5) with which they announced their arrival in, and readiness to receive alms from, the leading persons of a town or village. And many of these men were armed.

Some of them carry a stick with a ring of iron at the base. Others carry certain iron diskes which cut all round like razors, and they throw these with a sling when they wish to injure any person; and, therefore, when these people arrive at any city in India, every one tries to please them; for should they even kill the first nobleman of the land, they would not suffer any punishment because they say that they are saints.

Varthema also noted that "the liberty they enjoy, and their sanctity," enabled them to "go where jewels are produced, and carry them into other countries without any expense."[5]

---

[4] *The Travels of Ludovico di Varthema (1503–1508)*, trans. and ed. John Winter Jones, notes and introduction by George Perry Badger (London 1863), pp. 111–112. Varthema claimed that the *yogi* lord had approximately 30,000 "subjects," but these should not be taken to be armed followers.

[5] Varthema, *Travels*, p. 113.

Varthema encountered the *yogi* king and his armed men again on the Malabar Coast in southwest India, while the Bolognese was trying to aid in the defection of two wealthy Portuguese artillery makers from Calicut to Cochin (the ruler of which had allied himself to the Portuguese). Word of their plans to escape Calicut, with all their wealth,[6] reached the ears of the "Moorish Cadi" or *qazi*, the Muslim legal authority and head of the Muslim merchants of Calicut. He convened a council of all the "Moorish merchants" of the town, collected a small sum which "they carried to the king of the Gioghi who was at that time in Calicut with three thousand Gioghi." The Muslims asserted that the Portuguese merchants were spies for the Portuguese, and asked the *yogi* to kill them. "The king of the Gioghi immediately sent two hundred men to kill the said two Christians, and when they went to their house, they began by tens to sound their horns and demand alms." The Portuguese merchants, alarmed, attacked and killed some *yogi*s, whereupon "these Gioghi cast at them certain pieces of iron which are made round like a wheel, and they threw them with a sling, and struck Ioan-Maria on the head and Pierre Antonio on the head, so that they fell to the ground; and then they ran upon them and cut open the veins of their throats, and with their hands they drank their blood."[7]

If nothing else, Varthema's account confirms that Akbar was not responsible for arming Hindu ascetics, as was alleged by *sanyasi* oral tradition in the early twentieth century (see the previous chapter). Nevertheless, not all *yogi*s went about armed. While traveling through the environs of Delhi in the early sixteenth century, the Portuguese, Duarte Barbosa, encountered large bands of "jogues" wandering about "like the gipsies," but "naked, barefooted, and bareheaded," their only covering tight brass belts and heavy chains draped about their necks and waists and legs.[8] In addition to the metal adornments,

---

[6] Among their many possessions was said to be a diamond weighing thirty-two carats, worth 35,000 ducats, a pearl weighing twenty-four carats, and 2,000 rubies weighing between a carat and a carat-and-a-half each.

[7] Varthema, *Travels*, pp. 273–274. See figure 4 for the disc weapon described here.

[8] Duarte Barbosa, *A Description of the Coasts of East Africa and Malabar in the Beginning of the Sixteenth Century*, trans., notes, and preface Henry E. J. Stanley (London 1866), pp. 99–100. According to Barbosa, "in their own speech they are called Zoame [*swami*], which means servant of God." Barbosa asked them "many times why they went in this fashion. And they answered me, that they wore those chains upon their bodies as penance for the sin which they committed for allowing themselves to be captured by such bad people as the Moors, and that they went naked as a sign of dishonour, because they had allowed their lands and houses to be lost, in which God brought them up; and that they did not want more property since they had lost their own, for which they ought to have died; and that they smeared themselves with ashes in order to remind themselves perpetually that they were born of earth and had to return again to earth, and that all the rest was falsehood." Francois Bernier also encountered, over a century later, ascetics laden with

they smear all their bodies and faces with ashes. And they carry a small brown horn at their necks, after the fashion of a trumpet, with which they call and beg for food at the door of any house where they arrive: chiefly at the houses of great kings and great lords and at the temples . . . They are brown, very well made and proportioned, of handsome faces; they wear their hair without ever combing it, and made into many plaits, wound round the head.

Barbosa added that "all the Gentiles of the country honour them greatly, and receive from them some of these ashes, and put it on their heads, shoulders, and breasts, making a few lines with it. And throughout all the country the Gentiles are in the habit of doing this. And so also throughout all India among the Gentiles, many of them turn jogue; but most of them are from the kingdom of Dely." [9] Similarly, in 1623–1624, the Italian traveler, Pietro Della Valle, encountered in and around Ahmedabad two large groups of *yogi*s who "go wandering about the world with no settled abode." These too were unarmed. Like Barbosa's *yogi*s, they were mostly naked and "smeared with ashes, earth and colours . . . their beards and long hair untrimmed, roughly bound up."[10]

More often than not, however, *yogi*s went about in groups that included men both armed and unarmed. A comprehensive picture is given by the English merchant, Peter Mundy, who was astonished by the variety of ascetics in Banaras, "Mussellmen or Moores and Hindooes, then Jooguees, Ashemen, etts. [and other] Hindooes." These were men "of great meanes, whoe for their devotion have renownced all, chuseinge voluntarie povertie."

They generally have noe trade, but live by what is given them, most of them travellinge from Countrie to Countrie. Others sett by the high wayes att the entrance in or goeing out of Townes or Citties and begg of passengers. Others amonge Tombes, there care beinge to looke to dicto tombes in keepeing them cleane etts., alwaies amonge greene trees, many tymes a well by them, a litle garden, a Cabban [temporary shelter] and a Chowtree [*chabutra*, or raised platform], another with a mightie Crooked Copper Instrument in forme of a horne, with which they make a strange sound blowing in it. And most comonlie they goe in Companies, without any other weapons but staves (that I could see), and for the most part every one a bunch of peacocks feathers in their hands, some with a Leopards skinne, which they sitt uppon. Ashmen are soe called by us, because they doe all their bodies over with ashes. Jooguees are another sort, comonly in Yallowish Clayish

---

chains "such as are put about the legs of elephants." Francois Bernier, *Travels in the Mogul Empire, AD 1656–1668*, trans. I. Brock and A. Constable, 2nd edn, rev. and ed. V. A. Smith (London 1934, reprint Delhi 1994), p. 317.

[9] Barbosa was employing the term "gentile" to mean "heathen" or "pagan" – in the north Indian context, non-Muslim and, hence, Hindu.

[10] Della Valle, *The Pilgrim*, p. 238. The quotes in the following paragraph are from pp. 239–240.

Coulored Clothes. Wee have mett others with greate Chaines of iron about their midle, to which is fastned a broad plate of the same, which is made fast over their privities to take from them the use and very thought of weomen. They all weare their haire longe, made upp about their heads, whereof I have seene to contain two yards in length, but it is knotted and growne together. There are not soe many several sorts as there are Customes. Some of them, when they would have any thinge, will stand right before you without speakeing untill you bidd them begone. Many of them professe secretts in Medicine, etts., and some reputed holy; many times neere great men.[11]

Likewise Francois Bernier, thirty years later, wrote of encountering in Hindustan bands of naked *"Jauguis,"* "hideous to behold." Again, some of these were armed, some were not.

Some had their arms lifted up in the manner just described [to atrophy the musculature]; the frightful hair of others either hung loosely or was tied and twisted round their heads; some carried a club like to Hercules; others had a dry and rough tiger skin thrown over their shoulders. In this trim I have seen them shamelessly walk, stark naked, through a large town, men, women, and girls look-ing at them without any more emotion than may be created when a hermit passes through our streets. Females would often bring them alms with much devotion, doubtless believing that they were holy personages, more chaste and discreet than other men.[12]

For his part, Mundy concluded that "there is so much more to be said That I knowe not when I should make an end; And this that I have said is but superficiallye." Who can blame him? Armed *yogi*s crop up with such regularity in early modern material – Indian as well as European – that they must have been a consistent feature of the early modern landscape. It might be argued that European travelers remarked with such frequency on *yogi*s (and other ascetics) simply because they were one-dimensional metonyms of civilizational difference.[13] In point of fact, however, when European observers – even occasionally hostile observers like Bernier and Della Valle – encountered *yogi*s they were reminded of both the European present and the European past. They saw not simply creatures "hideous

[11] *The Travels of Peter Mundy, in Europe and Asia, 1608–1667*, vol. II, *Travels in Asia, 1628–1634*, R. C. Temple (ed.) (London 1914), pp. 176–178.

[12] Bernier, *Travels in the Mogul Empire*, p. 317.

[13] As I argue below, this would be a superficial, modern view – a product of a particular strand of nineteenth- and twentieth-century European scholarship on Indian religion that saw, for a variety of often conflicting reasons, India and Europe as polar opposites and Indians and Europeans as inhabiting fundamentally incompatible mental worlds. Ironically it is a view that persists in postmodern guise. See Pinch, "Same Difference in India and Europe."

to behold," but a tradition and practice of asceticism that was similar in many ways to that of Europe, the Mediterranean, and the Christian lands of western Asia and northern Africa. Bernier reflected, tellingly, that "Our *Friars* and *Hermits* must not suppose that on these points [fasts and other austerities] they surpass the *Jauguis* or other Asiatic religionists. I can, for instance, appeal to the lives and fasts of the *Armenians*, *Copts*, *Greeks*, *Nestorians*, *Jacobins*, and *Maronites*; compared to these people our European devotees are mere novices . . ."[14] Della Valle evinced a subtler or, perhaps, unconscious understanding of Indian and European (or rather Hindu and Christian) religious comparability: he was given to understand that "the ashes with which they [*yogis*] sprinkle their bodies come from burnt carcasses, and that they go bedaubed like that all their lives as a constant reminder of death." The day after he encountered these *yogis*, he made a point of noting, was Ash Wednesday.[15] Was this an ironic literary device? Or was he simply being a faithful Christian and taking note of a key moment in the religious calendar? He left it to his audience to draw conclusions.

If we resist the urge to dismiss the European evidence out of hand as just another sensationalist "othering" of the Orient, it becomes difficult to avoid the conclusion that early modern *yogis* were regarded as potent, powerful beings by ordinary and not-so-ordinary people. Many European observers understood this in terms of Christian veneration of saints. Recall Barbosa's observation that "all the Gentiles of the country honour them greatly." Della Valle likewise noted that the "archimandrite" of the *yogis* near Ahmedabad "was so venerated for his reputation of saintliness, not only by the priests of their religion but also by the other secular Indians, that I saw many grave persons go to make profound reverence to him and kiss his hand, and stand humbly before him, to hear just a sentence."[16] And, as noted above, Bernier observed that women "often bring them alms with much devotion, doubtless believing that they were holy personages, more chaste and discreet than other men."[17] If we look to Bana's description of the relationship between Pushpabhuti and Bhairavacharya, however, it becomes apparent that *yogis* did not aspire to saintliness in the conventional, Christian sense: they were not remarkable for their intense love for God, and did not seek to bask in the glow of God's special love for them. Rather, they aspired to become gods on

---

[14] Bernier, *Travels in the Mogul Empire*, pp. 320–321. Similar comparisons were made by Thomas Roe's chaplain, Edward Terry, *Voyage to East India* (London, 1655, reprint London 1777), p. 264.

[15] Della Valle, *The Pilgrim*, pp. 236, 237.   [16] Della Valle, *The Pilgrim*, p. 238.

[17] Bernier, *Travels in the Mogul Empire*, p. 318.

earth – to become, as it were, "a second Civa." Bernier seemed to sense the difference: he confessed to "amazement" at the "gross superstition" that attended their performance of austerities. At first he believed *yogi*s to be akin to and even descended from "the ancient and infamous sect of *Cynics*," but found them lacking the proper mental equipment – particularly the capacity for rational thought. At other times he suspected them to be "honest though deluded enthusiasts," but discovered them to be "in the widest sense of the word, *destitute of piety*" [emphasis added]. Finally he came to accept, however incredulously, their own claim that they "exercise painful austerities in the confident hope that they will be Rajas [kings] in their renascent state."

The magical supernormality of *yogi*s – their ability to effect personal transformation, whether real or imagined – had important political implications. As Varthema put it, "should they even kill the first nobleman of the land, they would not suffer any punishment because they say that they are saints." His description of events in Calicut would seem to bear this out. The Muslim merchants who requested the assassination of the Portuguese artillerymen considered the *yogi* king an extra-legal authority – and, apparently, so did the *yogi* king himself. The *samudri* (secular ruler) of Calicut, referred to in European sources as the *Zamorin*, was conspicuous by his absence from the scene. Varthema reported that the *samudri* had, in fact, been warned of the impending defection by a slave of the Portuguese, and had taken the limited step of posting five guards to watch over them. "The slave, seeing that the king [*samudri*] would not put them [the Portuguese] to death, went to the Cadi of the faith of the Moors, and repeated to him those same words which he had said to the king, and moreover, he told him that they [the Portuguese] informed the Christians [of the *Estado da India*] of all that was done in Calicut." Whereas the *samudri* would not interfere with the European residents, the merchant-*qazi* and the *yogi* king were only too willing to act, and act with deadly force.

The *samudri*'s reluctance to interfere with what appears to our modern eyes as a merchant-*yogi* partnership in crime may have been in part due to a necessarily *laissez-faire* attitude adopted by rulers of important coastal emporia along the Indian Ocean littoral. As K. N. Chaudhuri has noted, "In any other place than a trading emporium the concourse of foreign nationals on such a scale would have presented the urban authorities with severe problems. But in the Indian Ocean, as also in the Mediterranean, there was already an ancient and honoured law of reciprocity. Rulers and princes refrained from interfering in the commercial affairs of merchants from abroad, and they in turn guaranteed good behaviour through their own law-enforcing agencies."[18] *Yogi* gangs may have represented, in this sense, a particularly effective "law-enforcing agency" in the coastal emporia not simply because of their facility with iron discs but because of the veneration-cum-fear with which *yogis*, as a generic type, were regarded. On top of this was their subcontinental mobility, which would have made them attractive agents for people of means to project force, inflict punishment, carry valuables, or transmit valuable information – all over long distances. In this context, it is worth noting that while Surat and Calicut may appear to be far removed from each other in Indian land-based geographic terms, they were close neighbors as Indian Ocean coastal emporia. The periodic movement by the *yogi* lord and his entourage overland between the two cities paralleled seasonal shipping by merchants on the water.

Varthema's early sixteenth-century *yogi*-king is usefully set alongside a mid-seventeenth-century description of armed ascetics by the French jewel merchant, Jean Baptiste Tavernier. Tavernier encountered in 1640 a party of "Fakirs, or Muhammadan *Dervishes*," while he was *en route* from Surat to Agra.[19] Possibly Tavernier assumed that the group was generically Muslim, based on the leaders' claim of having been formerly attached to Mughal imperial service: The "Chief or Superior had been master of the horse to Shah Jahangir" (Akbar's heir to the Mughal throne, r. 1605–1627), and "There were four others who, under the Superior, were Chiefs of the band, and had been the first nobles of the court of . . . Shah Jahan." Tavernier's religious categorization notwithstanding, the appearance and weapons of these men, and the baggage that they carried, suggest that they were armed *yogis* who had accommodated themselves culturally, linguistically, and militarily to Mughal service. "The only garment of these five *Dervishes* consisted of three or four ells of orange-coloured cotton cloth, of which they made waistbands, one of the ends passing between the thighs and being tucked between the top of the waistband and the body of the *Dervish*, in order to cover what modesty requires should be concealed, both in front and behind. Each of them had also a skin of a tiger upon the shoulders, which was tied under the chin." Their baggage included "four boxes full of Arabian and Persian books," and the chief used the Persian term "*Aga*" (nobleman) when referring to Tavernier. The entire party consisted of fifty-seven men, the remainder of whom

[18] K. N. Chaudhuri, *Trade and Civilisation in the Indian Ocean: An Economic History from the Rise of Islam to 1750* (Cambridge 1985), p. 112.

[19] Jean Baptiste Tavernier, *Travels in India*, trans. V. Ball (London 1889), vol. I, pp. 81–84. The encounter occurred about sixty miles north of Ahmedabad, in the town of Sidhpur.

had for their sole garment a cord, which served as a waistband, to which there was attached a small scrap of calico to cover, as in the case of the others, the parts which should be concealed. Their hair was bound in a tress about their heads, and made a kind of turban. They were all well armed, the majority with bows and arrows, some with muskets, and the remainder with short pikes, and a kind of weapon which we have not got in Europe. It is a sharp iron, made like the border of a plate which has no centre, and they pass eight or ten over the head, carrying them on the neck like a ruff. They withdraw these circles as they require to use them, and when they throw them with force at a man, as we make a plate to fly, they almost cut him in two. Each of them had also a sort of hunting horn, which he sounds, and makes a great noise with when he arrives anywhere, and also when he departs . . . There were three of these *Dervishes* armed with long rapiers, which they had received, apparently, from some Englishman or Portuguese.

The similarities between these men and the *yogi*s encountered by Varthema a century earlier are striking. Of particular note are the *chakra*s (metal disks), the "hunting horns," the relative lack of clothing, the animal skins worn by the leaders, and the long, matted hair. Moreover, Tavernier's itinerants were either feared or venerated, or both, by the people whose villages and towns they passed through. "The Governor of the town [Sidhpur] came to pay his respects to these principal *Dervishes*, and during their sojourn in the place sent them rice and other things which they were accustomed to eat. When they arrive in any place the Superior sends some of them to beg in the towns and villages, and whatever food they bring, which is given them out of charity, is immediately distributed to all in equal portions, each being particular to cook his own rice for himself. Whatever they have over is given every evening to the poor, and they reserve nothing for the following day." A small incident reveals that they were accustomed to getting their way. When they arrived at Tavernier's encampment, "the Chief or Superior of the troop, seeing me well accompanied, inquired who that *Aga* was; and asked me subsequently to give up to him the position I occupied, it being more commodious than any other about the place for camping with his *Dervishes*." Tavernier, "informed of the quality of this Chief and the four Dervishes who followed him," was "willing to do them a civility, and to yield that which they asked with a good grace."

While there are similarities to Varthema's *yogi*s, there are also differences. The main one is that the band encountered by Tavernier appeared to be better armed. In addition to the metal disks (wielded as well by Varthema's *yogi*s), Tavernier's *yogi-fakir*s carried muskets, pikes, and swords of European make. In short, they appeared to be adopting new military styles and expertise. Such diversification would continue apace. By the eighteenth century large numbers of armed ascetics, the institutional descendants of armed *yogi*s, were becoming professional soldiers in *gosain* armies whose commanders would sell their military services and military intelligence to the highest bidder. This eighteenth-century phase, embodied best by the Dasnami warlords, Anupgiri and Umraogiri Gosain, and their *naga* armies, is taken up in chapters 3 and 4. The seventeenth century may be seen as a period of transition to that full-scale, eighteenth-century military entrepreneurship on the part of strategically located lineages of armed *yogis*. In fact, the evolution from *yogi* to Dasnami seems to have provided the institutional hierarchy requisite for expansion to wider military service. Thomas Broughton, who encountered some of Anupgiri's *chelas* near Gwalior in 1809, wrote:

Having attained such [military] distinction, Gosaeens are commonly styled Gurus with their chelas, the eldest chela succeeding to the 'Guruship' on the former's death. When in military formation the leader often carries the title 'muhunt': they then retain but little of their original manner and appearance; distinguishing themselves alone by the *jutta*, or long matted hair folded like a turban on the head, and having some portion of their dress dyed of a kind of orange colour, called *Geroo*, peculiar to their sect.[20]

Encountered at random by the postmodern scholar, any of the accounts of *yogi* lords and their armed followers might be dismissed, in the long aftermath of Edward Said's *Orientalism*, as a fanciful traveler's tale – a "marvelous encounter" that tells us more about the demons that inhabited the mind of early modern Europe than the real meanings and practices that helped to shape religious and political culture in early modern India.[21] Such a reading perceives Varthema's bloodthirsty *yogis* as yet another sensationalist European "othering" of an Orient destined for colonized monstrosity. But when set alongside the preponderance of evidence culled from other sources, Indian as well as European, killer *yogis* migrate from the imaginary to the real. They may have reverberated in the European mind, but they were first and foremost Indian flesh and bone. If we dismiss them out of hand as literary devices intended to communicate European mastery we blind ourselves to the fact that the past was in one way radically different than the present – and that that difference was, in large part, a function of popular religious understanding. A world in which armed *yogis* could operate with such wide license was a world

---

[20] Thomas D. Broughton, *Letters Written in a Mahratta Camp During the Year 1809, Descriptive of the Character, Manners, Domestic Habits, and Religious Ceremonies of the Mahrattas* (London 1813), pp. 129–130.

[21] Cf. Stephen Jay Greenblatt (ed.), *New World Encounters* (Berkeley 1993); and Stephen Jay Greenblatt, *Marvelous Possessions; The Wonder of the New World* (Chicago 1991). For a more straightforward approach to Europe's pre-modern experience of "the other," see Jerry Bentley, *Old World Encounters: Cross Cultural Contacts and Exchanges in Pre-Modern Times* (Oxford 1993).

in which all *yogi*s were held (or feared) to be what they claimed to be: humans who had conquered death.

Naga foot and horse

The shift from the armed *yogi* bands of the sixteenth century to the soldiering *naga akhara*s of the eighteenth century was both demographic and tactical. By the late eighteenth century the sheer size of the *naga* armies was of an entirely different order compared to the numbers given in sixteenth-century accounts. Anupgiri and Umraogiri commanded upwards of 20,000 men in the late 1700s. At Thaneswar Akbar encountered, by comparison, small bands of between 300 and 600 men. Varthema's early sixteenth-century description of the 30,000 followers in the entourage of the *yogi* king may appear to confuse this picture until it is recalled that many of those individuals were not armed. When the *yogi* king agreed to the merchant *qazi*'s request to assassinate the Portuguese artillerymen of Calicut, he sent 200 armed *yogi*s to carry out the deed.[22]

More important, however, is the tactical shift that occurs, from small-scale guerilla action to larger-scale infantry and cavalry service. The former can be seen in Varthema's description of the *yogi* assassins armed with sharp-edged metal disks. These disks are also a prominent feature of the illustrations depicting the Thaneswar skirmish. Abu'l Fazl's account of that skirmish adds some tools to their repertoire: "first one man on each side advanced in a braggart fashion, and engaged with swords. Afterwards, bows and arrows were used. After that the Puris attacked the Kurs with stones."[23] Sword and dagger, bow and arrow, metal disks and stones – this may seem like a descent into barbarity to a modern reader steeped in John Keegan's evolutionary account of warfare.[24] In fact, these weapons were the tools of a specific trade, namely, engaging an enemy at fairly close quarter and rapidly closing in for the kill. This was not the *matériel* that made an Indian empire in the sixteenth century. For that task, cannons were required, primarily to breach the walls of forts built prior to the days of field artillery and secondarily to overawe the opponent.[25] Of equal importance, when opposing armies were amassed on the open field, was a well-trained archery – some men specializing in long-distance accuracy with massive bows, others trained in dispatching arrows in rapid succession and with an astonishingly high degree of accuracy while mounted and at full gallop. When properly deployed in

---

[22] Varthema, *Travels*, pp. 111–112, 274.   [23] Abu'l Fazl, *Akbar Nama*, p. 424.

[24] John Keegan, *A History of Warfare* (New York 1993). Keegan's narrative progresses from stone to flesh to iron to fire.

[25] See A. J. Qaisar, *The Indian Response to European Technology and Culture: (A.D. 1498–1707)* (Delhi 1998); and John Richards, *Mughal Empire* (Cambridge 1993).

tandem, such a force could quickly harass the enemy into submission. Sword, arrow, disk, and stone had utility – not for making empire, but for keeping it. Akbar recognized this and retained men expert in the art of stone combat. Again, according to Abu'l Fazl: "As the Puris were few in number, [Akbar] signified to some men who understood fighting with stones, such as the *Petamcaha*, of Turan, and the *Cirus* of India, to assist the Puris."[26]

It is a curious turn of phrase, "men who understood fighting with stones." Abu'l Fazl alludes to stones again in his description of the Mughal infantry in the *Ain-i-Akbari*. Part of that unmounted force consisted of *Pahluwans* (from Hindi *pahelwan*, or wrestler). "There are many Persian and Turani wrestlers and boxers at Court, *as also stone-throwers*, athletes of Hindustan, clever *Mals* from Gujarat, and many other kinds of fighting men."[27] They were not only well paid but also the recipients of gifts on the occasion of their daily matches. In addition to several famous combatants from central Asia, Persia, and Africa, Abu'l Fazl listed the names Sadhu Dayal, 'Ali, Sri Ram, Kanhya, Mangol, Ganesh, Anba, Nanka, Balbhadra, and Bajrnath. Unlike those from beyond Hindustan, he did not identify these men as belonging to a particular region, which suggests they hailed from northern India. The generally Hindu sounding names, with the exception of 'Ali, would seem to confirm this. Particular attention should be directed, however, to the first and last names on the list, Sadhu Dayal and Bajrnath, since each includes terms suggestive of north Indian ascetic culture. The former, *sadhu*, related to *sadhana* (discipline), is a generic term for an ascetic; *nath* means "lord" and is a suffix often used by *yogis*. This does not necessarily mean that large numbers of such ascetics populated the ranks of court wrestlers and, by extension, the irregular infantry (though neither does it preclude the possibility).[28] But it does give us an idea of the type of hand-to-hand combat skills martial ascetics could be expected to possess.

If small bands of armed *yogis* had a tactical specialty in the sixteenth century, it was close-quarter combat. The seventeenth century saw an expansion in weapons, tactical specialization, and scale of recruitment. By the 1640s, judging from Tavernier's account, the numbers were still small but there was a greater variety of weaponry. "They [Tavernier's *dervishes*] were all well armed, the majority with bows and arrows, some with muskets, and the remainder with short pikes, and a kind of weapon which we

---

[26] According to the anonymous author of the "Tarikh-i-Khandan-i-Timuriyya," "His Majesty ordered the Samarqandis who were nearby to assist the smaller group."

[27] *A'in-i-Akbari*, vol. I, p. 263.

[28] It is worth noting, however, that the Abbé Carré mentions Mughal soldiers who are "almost naked" and "a terrifying sight." Barthélemy Carré, *The Travels of the Abbé Carré in India and the Near East, 1672–1674* (London 1947–1948), p. 457. I am grateful to Casey Quinn, a former student, for bringing this reference to my attention.

have not got in Europe," namely, the ubiquitous *chakra*. Toward the end of the seventeenth century the numbers had expanded dramatically. The Mughal emperor, Aurangzeb, issued a decree in 1692–1693 authorizing five Ramanandi commanders of what is now eastern Rajasthan "to move freely about the whole Empire with standards and kettledrums, at the head of companies both of horse and foot." Local landlords and military officials were warned "that no obstacle or hindrance be put in their way, so that they may travel without molestation from one province to another."[29] The Neapolitan traveler, Gemelli Careri, who visited western India in 1695–1696, had much that was scandalous to say about "jogis," whom he also called "fakirs;" but he did confirm that "they march in companies with banners, lances and other weapons."[30] When Rajendragiri Gosain took up service under Safdar Jang of Awadh in 1751, it was on the condition that, first, he not be required to salute and, second, he be allowed to beat his kettledrums in his master's retinue.[31]

These descriptions suggest large numbers of men. This was unsettling for some since it connoted wider social access to what were normatively religious orders. When the religious order was a pillar of state legitimacy, as was the case with the Vaishnava *akhara*s in Amber-Jaipur, such uncontrolled access posed ideological problems. This was the dilemma that confronted Jaisingh II in the 1730s, who not only sought to block the entry of the low-born into the *akhara*s but to disallow arms among Vaishnava ascetics generally.[32] He solicited and received four separate bond agreements containing pledges from prominent Vaishnava *mahant*s, nine

[29] This *farman* is in the possession of the Balanand *math* and *mandir* in Jaipur and is translated in W. G. Orr, "Armed Religious Ascetics in Northern India," *The Bulletin of the John Rylands Library* 25 (1940): 87. On the previous page, Orr suggests the early sixteenth century for the arming of Ramanandis, citing the rise to dominance of Vaishnavas at Galta in the early 1500s and the decline of *nath yogi*s there. Farquhar ("Fighting Ascetics," 444–445) proposes 1600, but also offers little in the way of supporting documentation. Ghurye (*Indian Sadhus*, p. 178) was told by Ramanandis in the early 1950s that *naga* organization among them was 250–300 years old, suggesting a date between 1650 and 1700. See Pinch, *Peasants and Monks in British India*, pp. 27–30, for a discussion of the contradictory historical trajectories of the various sources.

[30] *The Indian Travels of Thevenot and Careri*, ed. Surendranath Sen (New Delhi 1949), p. 258.

[31] A. L Srivastava, *The First Two Nawabs of Oudh* (Lucknow 1933), 169n.

[32] See Monika Thiel-Horstmann, "Warrior Ascetics in 18th-Century Rajasthan and the Religious Policy of Jai Singh II" (unpublished essay, no date). I am grateful to Professor Horstmann for providing me a copy of this essay and allowing me to cite it. In addition, see Gopal Narayan Bahura and Chandramani Singh, *Catalogue of Historical Documents in the Kapad Dwara, Jaipur* (Amber-Jaipur 1988), pp. v–vii, on Jaisingh II's growing attraction to the Bengali Vaishnavism of Chaitanya and the Gauriya Vaisnava Goswamis of Vrindaban which, in part, accounts for his interest in Vaishnava affairs. The *Kapad Dwara* collection has long been under lock and key pending a legal settlement to determine ownership. Fortunately, the heroic labors of Bahura and Singh have ensured that the general contents of many of the documents therein remain available to scholars.

of whom identify themselves as "Ramanandi," to give up the practice of keeping arms and to boycott or otherwise punish those who continued to do so.[33] (The use of weapons did not conform to his notion of what a religious order should be; for more on Vaishnava *bhakti* and unruly, armed ascetics, see chapter 5.)

By the late eighteenth century, not only had the numbers of armed ascetics increased dramatically, there was much greater tactical variety. *Sanyasi*s, *gosain*s, *bairagi*s, *fakir*s, and (especially) *naga*s, as these soldiering ascetics were increasingly known, generally carried muskets and served widely in infantry as well as cavalry units. There is abundant evidence of this, not least of which are the celebrated careers of Rajendragiri, Anupgiri, and Umraogiri Gosain and their *naga* armies of Bundelkhand, Awadh, and the Delhi–Agra hinterland (see the next chapter). There is a variety of anecdotal evidence as well of the increasingly routine participation of armed ascetics in the military economy of northern India. Lieutenant-Colonel Valentine Blacker included "gossyes" (*gosain*s) in his reflection on the rise of infantry forces in India in the 1700s. He described them as "a Hindoo cast of peculiar habits, scattered over different parts of India," who "have been always considered as good troops" on a par with Rohillah Afghans, Jats, and *khalsa* (military) Sikhs.[34] Thomas Broughton remarked in 1809 that, "as soldiers, they [*gosain*s] are accounted brave and faithful."[35] The veteran Rajput-Scottish cavalry chief James Skinner noted the inclusion of *naga*s in the Maratha-led armies in which he served prior to joining forces with the Company after 1803. In preparation for a battle against the forces of Jaipur in 1798, he recalled that "Our horse amounted by the smallest calculation to 60 thousand, Infantry 40 thousand, 10 thousand Gossains called Naggas with Rockets, and about 150 pieces of cannon."[36] Skinner also included a portrait (see figure 6)

---

[33] Document Nos. 1176 (undated, from the nine Ramanandi *mahant*s), 1483 (also undated), 1277 (referring to *bairagi*s, dated 29 April 1733), and 1275 (dated 28 March 1736), listed in Bahura and Singh, *Catalogue of Historical Documents*. From separate correspondences (nos. 1506 and 1507, both undated), it is evident that the Maharaja also solicited opinions from Bengali Vaishnavas regarding the rights of *sudra*s and other low classes. He also obtained pledges (nos. 1518 and 1520, both undated) from *Ramanandi mahant*s and other Vaishnavas not only to maintain strict caste rules in commensal relations but to no longer accept *sudra* and other low-born disciples. See also A. K. Roy, *History of Jaipur City* (New Delhi 1978), p. 26, where these latter documents are reproduced.

[34] Valentine Blacker, *Memoir of the Operations of the British Army in India, During the Mahratta War of 1817, 1818, & 1819* (London 1821), p. 22.

[35] Broughton, *Letters Written in a Marhatta Camp*, p. 130.

[36] "Skinner Papers," Photo.Eur.173, Oriental and India Office Collection (hereafter OIOC), British Library, London, 46 (f. 21b). This is a photocopy of the original MS held at the National Army Museum, London. The substance of this MS is published in *Military Memoir of Lieut.- Col. James Skinner*, ed. J. B. Fraser, 2 vols. (London 1851, reprint Mussoorie 1955); see vol. I, p. 141 for the (slightly altered) quote.

Figure 6. *Naga*, "Tasrih-al-Akvam," ["Account of Peoples"] credited to James Skinner, Add. 27,255, British Library, London, fol. 386b.

Figure 7. Two *naga*s, "Silsilah-i-Jogiyan," Ethe 2974, British Library, London, ff. 9a, 22a.

of a *naga* soldier in his early nineteenth-century caste compendium. This formidable warrior wears what appears to be a leather belt from which is suspended a saber and pouches for gunpowder, ammunition, and flint. He is otherwise naked and barefoot, and his long, matted hair is wrapped around his head like a helmet; he holds a long double-ended spear or lance over his right shoulder and a long-barreled musket over his left. Similar if less sophisticated martial images accompany an anonymous early nineteenth-century Persian manuscript entitled "Silsilah-i-Jogiyan," or "The Chain of the Jogis," also held in the British Library (see figure 7). One shows a seated Vaishnava "naugah" with one leg tucked beneath him, holding over his right shoulder a sheathed saber and in his left hand a small shield. Save for a loincloth and a few necklaces of what appear to be *rudraksha* beads (*Elaeocarpus ganitrus Roxb*), he is naked. His matted hair is tied into a kind of stylish forelock-helmet. On his forehead is painted the vermillion *tilak* (or symbol) known as the *urdhvapundra*, a U or V-shaped parabola emblematic of Vishnu. The other, described as a Saiva "naugha," is shown standing with a musket in his left hand, a saber hanging by his side, and a shield on his back. He is completely naked save three necklaces of *rudraksha* beads and shoulder and belt straps with which to secure the sword and shield to his body. On his arms, neck, and forehead are painted the *tripundra*, the three horizontal stripes widely recognized as the mark of Siva.

The shift into a more conventional infantry and cavalry role does not mean that *naga*s altogether abandoned the close-quarter combat and small-scale guerilla action of their *yogi* predecessors. Quite to the contrary, *naga*s remained conspicuous for the hand-to-hand skills they could bring to bear. This is evident in the observation of Francis Buchanan, the Scottish surveyor of the early nineteenth century, that "Nagas [are] a description of rogues who from going quite naked[,] close shaved and well rubbed with oil are so slippery that no one can seize them while they force their way with a dagger pointed at both ends and held by the middle."[37] Buchanan wrote this in his account of Dinajpur District, a region that now straddles Bangladesh and West Bengal, but the observation applied equally to *naga*s in the other districts that he surveyed to the west, in western Bengal, Bihar, and beyond.[38] Likewise the Capuchin friar, Marco della Tomba, writing in about 1773 about skirmishes between the Company army and the forces of Shuja ud-Daulah in the aftermath of Buxar (1764), described the "*fakiri nudi*" (naked *fakir*s) as "skilled cut-throats on their own account" whose opposition was "the strongest that the English ever had." "These [men], not caring for the artillery, nor the English fire, advanced with sabers in their hands up to the bayonets . . ." Della Tomba argues that but for the steadfast quality of the Company forces, the English "would have been undone."[39]

Given their skills at close-quarter combat, armed ascetics excelled in surprise raids, whether on enemy encampments in the light of day or over walled fortifications under the cover of darkness. For example, according to the lengthy chronicle left by the Bengali courtier, Ghulam Husain Khan:

---

[37] Buchanan's Dinajpur Account, in R. Montgomery Martin, *The History, Antiquities, Topography, and Statistics of Eastern India* (London 1838), vol. II, p. 517.

[38] Buchanan noted in 1811 that many *naga*s of Bihar had found employment "in the armies of the Rajas beyond the Yamuna." *An Account of the Districts of Bihar and Patna in 1811–1812* (Patna 1934, reprint New Delhi 1986) vol. I, p. 375. This raises the startling possibility that *naga*s driven out of greater Bengal by Company arms by 1800, during the repression of the "*Sanyasi* and *Fakir* Rebellion," had found service with Anupgiri in Bundelkhand, and then allied to and working for the Company after 1803. I elaborate this point in the following chapter.

[39] Marco della Tomba, "Viaggio," Borg.Lat.524, Vatican Library, Rome, fol. 35. I am grateful to David Lorenzen for generously providing me with his translation of this fascinating Italian account. For more on the Capuchins in Bengal and Bihar, see Lorenzen, "Europeans in Late Mughal South Asia: The Perceptions of Italian Missionaries," *Indian Economic and Social History Review* 40, 1 (2003): 1–31.

There happened to be then [1750–1751] on the shores of the Ganga, and quite close to the castle of Ilah-abad, a certain Saniassi-fakir, very brave and well accompanied, who spent his time in his devotions to Maha-deoo [Siva]. This man shocked to see the ravages committed by the Afghans, he had, without any invitation, resolved to join his cause to that of Baca-ollah-qhan [the Awadhi defender of the Allahabad fortress], and of the others, that were shut up in the castle; but although he was requested to come within its walls, he constantly refused it, and contented himself with encamping his brave slave-boys and his people at a small distance from it. Every day he used to set out with the bravest of his people, all mounted on excellent mares, and to gallop about the Afghan camp, from whence he never returned without having killed several of the bravest of the enemy, and brought away both their arms and horses with him; so long as the siege lasted he did not miss a single day, and always did some execution.[40]

A schematic painting that depicts the siege of Bhiwai (c. 1750?), a fortress in the Shekhavati region of northern Rajasthan, provides additional evidence of *naga* versatility in eighteenth-century warfare. The painting, held in the royal archives of Jaipur, shows a variety of forces arrayed against the fort. Most of the besieging regiments are placed at a distance, behind earthworks, and many are aided by heavy artillery. The *naga*s, by contrast, are stationed near the fort, in what appear to be tunnels. They would represent the first wave of attack once the cannonade and sappers' explosives breached the walls. They are naked, save for their loincloths, and carry muskets.[41]

The key point here is that by 1800 armed ascetics were a familiar and valued component of the military economy of northern India. They fought in a variety of capacities, from small tactical units and personal guards to large, disciplined regiments of foot and horse. From the perspective of the military historian, this is not surprising. All successful Indian armies had made what is often characterized in the European context as a "revolutionary" shift to well-disciplined musket-based infantry as well as cavalry in the eighteenth century. Compare, for example, the above quote from Ghulam Husain describing the *sanyasi* attacks on Afghan encampments at Allahabad in 1751 to an account of the wheeling

---

[40] Gholam Hossein Khan, *Seir Mutaqherin, or a Review of Modern Times*, trans. Nota Manus (nom de plume of M. Raymond, also known as Hajee Mustapha) (Calcutta 1789, reprint Delhi 1990), vol. III, pp. 298–299. These particular *sanyasi* soldiers are the focus of the next chapter on Anupgiri and Umraogiri Gosain – whose guru, Rajendragiri, was the "*saniassi-fakir*" celebrated in the above quote.

[41] This map painting is reproduced in Susan Gole, *Indian Maps and Plans, From the Earliest Times to the Advent of European Surveys* (New Delhi 1989), p. 149, where it is said to be stored in the City Palace Museum, Jaipur. It is not included in G. N. Bahura and C. Singh, *Catalogue of Historical Documents in Kapad Dwara, Jaipur: Maps and Plans* (Jaipur, 1990), but a "fort of Shekhawati" (s. no. 83, o. no. 72) is included in an appendix listing the "Potikhana Collection," p. 148.

cavalry charges employed by Afghans against Marathas ten years later at Panipat:

Ahmad Shah saw that his troops were now very hard pressed; he summoned the *Bash Ghul* squadrons – which means his slaves who numbered 6000 men – and cried out: 'my boys! This is the time. Encircle these men.' The three squadrons of slaves moved from three sides and brought the vanguard of the Bhau's army under musket fire all at once, and swept away their firm stand. The Maratha vanguard retreated and mixed with the division under the Bhau himself. A great tumult arose; men turned their faces to flight. The Bhau's personal guards showed some firmness and kept standing at some places. One squadron of slaves, numbering 2000 men, came from the right and after firing off their muskets went away to the left. Another squadron which came from the left, after emptying their muskets, went away to the right. The third squadron which came from the front, discharged their muskets at the Bhau's vanguard and then turned to the rear. Before the enemy could recover, these men had loaded their muskets again and arrived, the left squadron on the right wing and the right squadron on the left wing, while the squadron that had been originally in front fell on the rear. During this circular manoeuvre, they quickly discharged their muskets from one side and went away to the other. It looked as if on all four sides troops were attacking the Marathas simultaneously.[42]

The military shift to increased group discipline made new demands on soldiers and commanders alike. The result of large groups of men armed with muskets and acting as a single, coordinated organism rendered Indian warfare a far bloodier, noisier, and more expensive business. The battlefield toll paid by late eighteenth, early nineteenth-century European infantrymen, such as the 27th or Inniskilling Regiment of Foot at Waterloo (after 1881 part of the Royal Inniskilling Fusiliers), is a good indicator of the new, more total warfare that slowly overtook older, more personalized styles of combat through the period. War was becoming a total and all-encompassing hell in the eighteenth century, in India as well as Europe.[43] Warriors had to be able to endure that hell and remain intact, mentally as well as physically. This required a new kind of bonding – almost a kind of parenting, with intimacy tempered by discipline – between field commanders and the rank and file. Surviving the drill alone,

---

[42] Nur ud-Din Husain Khan Fakhri, "An Original Account of Ahmad Shah Durrani's Campaigns in India and the Battle of Panipat" (*Tawarikh-i-Najib ud-Daulah*), trans. J. Sarkar, *Islamic Culture* 7, 3 (1993): 452–453, cited in Jos Gommans, "Indian Warfare and Afghan Innovation During the Eighteenth Century," *Studies in History* 11, 2, NS. (1995): 272.

[43] See John Keegan, *The Face of Battle* (New York 1976), ch. 3, esp. pp. 141–143; Seema Alavi, *The Sepoys and the Company: Tradition and Transition in Northern India, 1770–1830* (Delhi 1995); D. H. A. Kolff, *Naukar, Rajput, and Sepoy: The Ethnohistory of the Military Labour Market in Hindustan, 1450–1850* (Cambridge 1990); and Jos Gommans, *The Rise of the Indo-Afghan Empire, c.1710–1780* (Leiden 1995).

to say nothing of the chaos of battle, required strict self-control if not total self-abnegation – on both sides of the service line. Some scholars have understood this self-disciplining to be restricted to the new gunpowder infantry soldier. David Ralston argued, for example, that

The way an organized infantry [as opposed to cavalry] force operated presupposed a much different attitude on the part of the fighting men, one stressing a sense of abnegation and even selflessness. To be a foot soldier, an ordinary person had to be conditioned through rigorous training before he and his fellows were capable of maintaining a tight, orderly formation when they moved forward into the chaos and slaughter of battle. Overcoming, even if but momentarily, their fear of death and dismemberment, and retaining presence of mind under the most shattering circumstances, they were able to act as integral, obedient members of a single, coherent body.[44]

For Ralston, "a body of mounted men may have been able to keep a reasonably cohesive formation as they charged against the foe," but at "the moment of impact" they would "lose their unity" and "become involved in a series of man-to-man duels." While this may have conformed to patterns of warfare in medieval Europe,[45] it certainly does not capture the discipline implicit in the wheeling attack motion displayed by Ahmad Shah's mounted slave soldiers at Panipat in 1761. The point at Panipat was to avoid "the moment of impact," and, rather, to inflict devastating blows at high speed, veer off, and regroup for successive attacks. This enabled Indian cavalry (which included Afghans, Europeans, and others) "to act as integral, obedient members of a single, coherent body."

Nevertheless, Ralston's point is a good one. It only needs to be applied more widely. Also valuable is his insight about discipline, though it too needs to be generalized to include gunpowder cavalry.

Although it has been an essential element in the development of the infantry, discipline is not a force intrinsic to or originating within a military unit by virtue of the simple fact that a body of troops has been organized. Rather, discipline must be consciously inculcated in the soldiers, its ultimate source generally lying outside the armed forces in some preexisting social or political authority, one capable of imposing it through fear if the men cannot be inspired to support its demands voluntarily.

---

[44] David B. Ralston, *Importing the European Army: The Introduction of European Military Techniques and Institutions into the Extra-European World, 1600–1914* (Chicago 1990), p. 3. On gunpowder empires, see William McNeill, *The Pursuit of Power: Technology, Armed Forces, and Society since A.D. 1000* (Chicago 1982); and on the "military revolution" generally, see Geoffrey Parker, *The Military Revolution: Military Innovation and the Rise of the West* (Cambridge 1996).

[45] For a complicating view, see Keegan's description of Agincourt in *The Face of Battle*, esp. pp. 94–96.

Table 2.1 *Sixteenth and seventeenth-century famines.*

Year	Region	Source
1554–1556	**Agra/Delhi/Bayana**	**Badauni, Abu'l Fazl**
1563–1567	Gujarat	Frederick, Purchas
1572–3/74–5	Sirhind/Panjab, Gujarat	Sirhindi
1596–1597	Kashmir	Abu'l Fazl, Jarric
1613–1615	Doab/Delhi	Jahangir
1630–1632	**Gujarat**	**Mundy, Qazwini**
1636–1637	Panjab	Lahori
1641–42, 44–7	Kashmir	Lahori, Sadiq Khan
1647	Marwar	Factories
1658–1663	Agra/Delhi/Lahore/Sind	Alamgirnama
1670–1671	**Bihar [Benaras to Rajmahal]**	**Marshall, Bowrey**
1691, 1694–5	Gujarat, Orissa	Wilson
1702–1704	**Deccan, Maharashtra**	**Mannucci**

[Source: Irfan Habib, *Agrarian History of Mughal India*]

The new demands of military conflict help to explain how *yogi* bands could expand so rapidly into widespread military entrepreneurship in the eighteenth century. *Yogi*s were accustomed to physical disciplines; their bodies were hardened by ascetic austerities and itinerancy, and habitual exposure to the elements. Organizationally, the non-biological bonds of loyalty that tied *chela*s to their gurus would have enabled smaller bands of armed ascetics to expand over time into larger and more institutionally complex – Dasnami or Ramanandi – regiments and armies. Gradations of discipleship could evolve seamlessly into a military hierarchy of soldiers, subalterns, field officers, and commanders. All that was needed was a ready population of "recruitable" boys, a requirement that could not have been difficult to meet in an agrarian region dependent on uncertain rainfall and lacking any widespread social safety net in times of seasonal stress. Seventeenth and eighteenth-century north India was just such a place. The 150 years between 1554 and 1704, encompassing the reigns of Akbar, Jahangir, Shah Jahan, and Aurangzeb, saw four major famines (shown above in boldface) and numerous more localized dislocations and general food shortages.

Clearly there was no shortage of agrarian dislocation in Mughal India. A typical observation is made by the seventeenth-century Jesuit historian, Pierre du Jarric, describing the visit of the Mughal encampment to Kashmir in 1596–1597: "Whilst they were in the kingdom of Caximir there was so grievous a famine that many mothers were rendered destitute, and having no means of nourishing their children, exposed them for sale in the public places of the city."[46] These conditions persisted well into the eighteenth century, particularly during its latter half. A period of severe "weather instability" hit northern India particularly hard in the decade of the 1680s and during the two decades between 1769 and 1790 – with the years 1769–1770 (Bengal) and 1783–1784 (Awadh–Agra–Delhi) representing major regional demographic crises. Added to the climatic uncertainty in the early eighteenth century was the fact of increased warfare, unpredictable spikes in taxation (particularly during the establishment of Company rule in Bengal), and sporadic cycles of economic dislocation and relocation that occasioned the refashioning of the Mughal system.[47]

Only recently has the effect of such ecological and political shifts on South Asian families received historiographical attention, particularly the incidence of selling or abandoning children into the care of local corporate institutions or into the extended families of landed magnates.[48] One important demographic result was (and is) the production of various forms of domestic and agrestic slavery. It is telling, in this context, that Ghulam Husain Khan should have described the *sanyasi* soldiers that accompanied Rajendragiri on his daily raids of Afghan encampments near the Allahabad fort in 1751 as "slave boys." In addition to the fact that central and west Asian military slavery shared a strong family resemblance to ascetic soldiering, Anupgiri and Umraogiri, Rajendragiri's two most famous *chela*s present at Allahabad, were themselves said to have been delivered as young children into a world of ascetic soldiering by their destitute mother in the 1730s (see the following chapter). According to Abu'l Fazl, the Mughal emperor, Akbar, recognized the shared ground occupied by slavery and discipleship. Akbar, however, was uncomfortable with the coercive aspects of slavery in the face of the all-too-clear loyalties and affections that masters and slaves felt for one another. In a section entitled "The *Chelas*, or Slaves," Abu'l Fazl wrote that, "His Majesty, from religious motives, dislikes the name *banda*, or slave; for he believes that mastership belongs to no one but God. He therefore calls this class of men *Chelas*, which Hindi term signifies a *faithful disciple*."[49] Significantly, this passage occurs just after Abu'l Fazl's description of wrestlers, in a larger chapter on the infantry (ch. 6). In the following paragraph,

[46] Pierre du Jarric, *Akbar and the Jesuits: An Account of the Jesuit Missions to the Court of Akbar*, trans. C. H. Payne (New York 1926), pp. 77–78.

[47] An excellent summary narrative is Bayly, *Rulers, Townsmen and Bazaars*, esp. ch. 1; see also pp. 85–86 on seasonal calamity.

[48] See Indrani Chatterjee, *Gender, Slavery and Law in Colonial India* (Delhi 1999).

[49] *A'in-I-Akbari*, vol. I, p. 263. I am grateful to both Jos Gommans and John Richards for pressing this point with me.

Abu'l Fazl makes clear that the choice of the term *"chela"* was not simply fortuitous, but seems to suggest that some ascetics traded in human chattel.

Various meanings attach to the term *slave*. *First*, that which people in general mean by a slave. Some men obtain power over such as do not belong to their sect, and sell and buy them. The wise look upon this as abominable. *Secondly*, he is called a slave who leaves the path of selfishness and chooses the road of spiritual obedience. *Thirdly*, one's child. *Fourthly*, one who kills a man in order to inherit his property. *Fifthly*, a robber who repents and attaches himself to the man whom he had robbed. *Sixthly*, a murderer whose guilt has been atoned by payment of money, in which case the murderer becomes the slave of the man who releases him. *Seventhly*, he who cheerfully and freely prefers to live as a slave.

Abu'l Fazl does not provide any hint as to which among these classifications were employed in the Mughal infantry. He simply states that "the pay of Chelas varies from 1 R. to 1 d. *per diem*," and that "His Majesty has divided them into several sections, and has handed them over to active and experienced people who give them instruction in several things." But, at the very least, the phrasing in his first definition – "some men obtain power over such as do not belong to their sect" – seems to imply that leaders of ascetic bands were trading in human flesh. Tavernier's testimony four decades later, describing the *yogi-fakir* commander of horse and his band near Surat, suggests that some of those literal slave-*chela*s may have entered Mughal service.

*Sanyasi*s and *fakir*s in Bengal

The popular religious world that the English East India Company encountered in the seventeenth century was defined less by Hinduism and Islam than by asceticism. Ascetics would, over time, appropriate for themselves increasing degrees of Hindu and Muslim coloring; but judging by the previous chapter's comparison of the Mughal and *sanyasi* record of Akbar's involvement in the affairs of ascetics in 1567, that process of "civilizational" differentiation was only beginning in the sixteenth century. The terms "Hindu" and "Muslim" may have communicated deep meaning to Badauni in 1567; they did not appear to matter to *yogi*s and *sanyasi*s until the early 1800s. The degree to which asceticism in the eighteenth century still worked by the blurred religious definitions of the Mughal world may be seen in the regional response of armed ascetics in Bengal and Bihar to the English intrusion into Indian politics. This response is known to historians as the *"Sanyasi and Fakir* Rebellion." It would become, after the 1870s, a rallying cry of resistance for Indian nationalists – or the Bengali *bhadralok* (gentlefolk), who were in the Indian nationalist forefront – in search of a model of insurgency and seeking to resolve for themselves their forebears' myriad Empire-building collaborations with the British during the long nineteenth century.

Thanks to the literary efforts of the Bengali writer Bankimchandra Chatterji, who popularized the insurgency as a rebellion in the early nationalist novel, *Anandamath* (1882), the fact of *sanyasi* and *fakir* opposition to the onset of British rule in Bengal is well known. Bankim, who as a lower-level official (*babu*) in British imperial service was struggling with his own budding nationalist demons, may be forgiven for endowing the insurgents with a patriotic consciousness they did not possess. Likewise we may forgive Jamini Mohan Ghosh, the official government historian of the insurgency, for having portrayed the insurgents as little more than a disorganized and occasionally rapacious rabble, largely devoid of a broader subcontinental significance. What is lost in the pyrotechnics of the political representations of the insurgent *sanyasi*s and *fakir*s in Bengal is the fact that they – or important figures among them – were not necessarily opposed to Company rule. Servants of the Company were mindful of the political intelligence (not to mention military influence) possessed by armed ascetics. Well before Robert Clive made his way to Calcutta to engineer his famous coup of August 1757 at Plassey, officials at Fort St. George in Madras were busily gathering information on the political lay of the land in Bengal. Among the many pieces of intelligence they amassed was a "List of the principal officers of the Nabob, Allyverdy Cawn's [Alivardi Khan's] court at Moxudavad [Murshidabad], and of the Governors and Rajas subject to him in the Provinces of Bengal Bahar and Orissa." This remarkable list was provided by one "Nimoo Goseyng." Though he is described in the records as "Gentoo [Hindu] Priest of the first order now residing at Calcutta," he appears, in fact, to have been a leading *gosain* of Bengal. This point, and an assessment of his knowledge and influence, emerges in the following excerpt from a letter of intelligence written by Charles Frederick Noble and received by the "Select Committee" at Fort St. George in late September 1756:

There is a man nam'd Nimo Gosseyng the high priest of the Gentues, who has a great influence among the Jentue Rajahs, and with a particular cast of people go up and down the Kingdom well arm'd in great bodies, of the Facquier or religious beggar cast, who might possibly be of service to us if they could be engag'd to our interest, which by Nimoo Gooseyngs means, I have particular reason to believe might be done.

This priest gave Colonel Scott very good information and advice, relating to the affairs of that country, and told him he could bring 1000 of these men to assist the English in four days warning, when needful. The Colonel did him some service while he liv'd and I dare say he has a respect for his memory to this day.[50]

---

[50] Orme. MSS VI, OIOC, item 12 ("Nimoo Goseyng"), fols. 1500–1502. This document is described in detail in the *Catalogue of Manuscripts in European Languages Belonging to*

Company officials in Bengal chose not to avail themselves of the aid of the easily mobilized, highly mobile network of armed ascetics after the formal acquisition of the Mughal *diwani* (the right of civil and revenue administration) in 1765.[51] Quite to the contrary, they decided, particularly under the leadership of Warren Hastings (from 1772), to expend every effort in the suppression of the mobile bands of heavily armed ascetics in Bengal. On 21 January 1773 Warren Hastings would issue a proclamation banning all such men from entering and traversing the province of Bengal.[52] Hastings' proclamation came amidst a series of Company reports of skirmishes with large bands of armed *sanyasis*. The formal notice is worth quoting in full, since it brings into focus a number of the themes raised in the course of this and the previous chapter.

No. 5 of 21 January 1773, Foreign Department, Secret Proceedings
The president delivers in the following minute on the subject of the Sinasses –
The President reports that also by late advices from Rungepore and the other northward districts he is informed that the Sinasses infest the country in great numbers, different bodies of these having entered and ravaged the districts of Rungepore, Gooragaut, Silberris, and Purnea, that the Nazir Deo or minister of Coochbahar has 500 of these people in his pay and is suspected of holding an intelligence with the rest, that it is now become an object of important attention to government not only to repel the present incursions but to adopt such expedients as shall hereafter prevent them and therefore recommend that an additional force of one battalion of sepoys be ordered on this service from Dinapore cantonments [near Patna], which is the most convenient for securing the districts of Tirhoot and Butua [Batwa] from the Maradars [sic], that he cannot learn that the Sunasses have any fixed abode but that they chiefly frequent the countries lying at the foot of the chain of mountains which separate Indostan from Tibbet, wandering continually from the Gogra river in the domains of the Vizier [Awadh] to the Burrampooter [Brahmaputra River], and from this line occasionally penetrating into Gorukh [Gorakhpur], Butua, Tirhoot, Purnea, and Rungpore, that to pursue them beyond the borders of our own territories would prove of no effect, since it would be scarce practicable for infantry to overtake them as they have no fixed place of residence where we might retaliate the injuries sustained from them, that having taken some pains to inform himself of the state and institutions of

---

the Library of the India Office, vol. II, part 2: Orme Collection, by S. C. Hill (London 1916), p. 298. It is important to note in this Bengali context, however, that the armed ascetics that came to be known generically as *gosains* throughout northern India in the eighteenth century and after were not the same as the *gosains* (lit. "*goswamis*") of the *Gauriya sampraday*, the followers of the sixteenth-century Vaishnava singer-saint, Chaitanya. The two communities may well have had institutional relations, may have shared reverence for particular pilgrimage shrines, and may have shared a proclivity for trade and occasional administrative posts, but the former were and are distinctly Saiva in their outlook, the latter Vaishnava.

[51] The Mughal emperor's *farman* granting *diwani* to the Company covered the territories of present-day Bihar, West Bengal, Bangladesh, Orissa, and parts of Assam.

[52] "Minute on the Subject of the Sinasses," nos. 5 and 6 of 21 Jan. 1773, FDSP.

the different sects of these people he finds that except one sect among them called Hijoohars [?] who never mix with the herds which infect the more civilized neighbours they neither marry or have families but recruit their number by the stoutest of the children which they steal in the countries through which they pass. That some among them carry on a trade in diamonds, coral, and other articles of great price and small compass and often travel with great wealth. Some subsist by gratuitous alms and others, the far greater part, by plunder; that the various sects of them travel at fixed periods on religious pilgrimages to the Burrampooter, Byjuant [?], and Ganga Sangam [Allahabad], besides those who in all the dry months of the year pass through the provinces on to Juggernaut. That individuals of them are at all times scattered about the villages and capital towns of the province and where the bigotry of the inhabitants affords them an access to their houses and every right of hospitality which they are suspected of abusing in the most treacherous manner by reuniting their corps whenever they enter the country and giving information both of the most substantial inhabitants and of the place where the wealth is deposited, a suspicion confirmed by the success which they have met with in the late ravages and ready choice which they have been known to make of the persons who have been the objects of their rapacity. That at this time there are many hundreds of them in the town of Calcutta, the roads being thronged with them as must have been apparent to all the members of the Board, that the president has met them on the road armed, they are continually armed with swords, lances, and matchlocks and generally loaded with heavy bundles, rice, firewood and other burthens which he concludes to be the plunder of the neighbouring villages, that from all the circumstances premised, it appears that the most innocent of these people are a nuisance to the country and that in general they do the greatest injury to the population and revenue of these provinces, and therefore recommends it to the consideration of the Board whether it would not be expedient to pass a general order to banish them the country and to forbid them permission to enter into it on any pretence hereafter. That if the Board concur in this opinion he further recommends that the following advertisements translated from and drawn by the Roy royam,[53] whose religion and attachment to the duties of it induced the President to consult him on the subject, as the most likely means to secure him from proceeding to a degree of vigour which might prove offensive to the people or an oppression to individuals, be immediately published at Calcutta and in the cucherry [courthouse] of every district the casts of Rammaninder [Ramanandi] and Goorca [see following para.] are excepted as they are held in great reverence by the Gentoos and they are neither vagrants nor plunderers but fixed inhabitants and quietly employ themselves in their religious function. It will be further necessary if this regulation should be adopted that patrols be stationed in different parts of the towns to prevent any disturbances which the Sunnases may be provoked to raise in opposition to it and that their arms be taken from them.

[53] This should read "Roy Royan," which is the Persianized Bengali title, "Rai Raiyan" (but pronounced Roy Royan), meaning "King of Kings." The title refers to Maharaja Nandkumar, who was the chief deputy to Muhammad Reza Khan, the finance minister under the East India Company's administration in Bengal. I am grateful to Sumit Guha for clarifying the meaning of the title and the identity of its owner.

No. 6 of 21 January 1773, Foreign Department, Secret Proceedings
Notice is hereby given to all Biraugies and Sunnasses who are travellers strangers
and passengers in this country excepting such of the cast of Rammanundar and
Goraak [Gorakhnath] who have for a long time been settled and receive a maintenance in land money or [illeg.] from the Government or the Zemindars of the
province, likewise such Sunasses as are allowed charity ground for executing religious offices etc. to leave the town of Calcutta its precincts or any other place of
residence in it with in seven days from the publication of this advertisement and
depart from the soubahs of Bengal and Bahar in two months.
    It is further declared that if any of the above mentioned sects shall be found
in Bengal or Bahar at the expiration of two months they are to be seized and put
on the roads for life made to work at the public buildings and have their property
confiscated to the Government. If any one with a view of evading the intent of
this publication shall claim donations of land and his claim be falsified he will be
punished as above directed. Resolved that the proposals made by the President
in the above minute be carried into execution.
    [Signed] Warren Hastings, Pres.

Hastings' council minute and subsequent proclamation was an early
legislative salvo in what would become a three-decade long suppression of
armed *sanyasi*s and (increasingly) *fakir*s, in Company-controlled Bengal.
His legislative "prose of counter-insurgency"[54] may well strike the reader
as long-winded. In fact, it (and the considerable body of official correspondence that the "*Sanyasi* and *Fakir* Rebellion" generated in the
decades after 1773) represents a breath of fresh air after the asphyxiat-
ing lack of social-historical detail in earlier records. Armed *sanyasi*s and
*fakir*s were antithetical in every way to the world that Hastings and his
successors sought to create in late eighteenth-century India – namely, a
modern agrarian empire that would happily disgorge endless streams of
cash revenue to support an ever-growing military and bureaucratic organism dominated by Britons and staffed by Indians. It is not surprising that
they emerge, then, in Hastings' prose as the epitome of unruly barbarity.
The image offered up by Hastings and his subordinates has the advantage, however, of descriptive specificity. Thus he serves to confirm our
earlier patchwork of sources: *sanyasi*s and *fakir*s were creatures of hill and
jungle, and in the case of Bengal, Himalayan hill and jungle; they carried
state-of-the-art weaponry and knew how to use it; they moved about constantly in large bands with little regard for state authority, largely because
the state they were familiar with was a limited affair; they demanded payment and sustenance from the populations through which they traveled;
and they dabbled in the gem trade and in local intelligence. In addition,

---

[54] The reference is to Ranajit Guha, "The Prose of Counter-Insurgency," in Ranajit Guha
(ed.), *Subaltern Studies: Writings on South Asian History and Society*, vol. II (Delhi 1983),
pp. 1–42.

the routes they followed connected the dots of widely dispersed shrines and pilgrimage sites – often connected to bodies of water including, most importantly, the *sangam* at Allahabad. The recruits that populated their ranks were gathered up (or stolen, and probably not just in Hastings' imperial prose) as young boys from areas through which the *akhara*s marched. We get some new images from Hastings as well, including the entertaining prospect of Hastings himself and members of the executive council having to contend with armed and boisterous *sanyasi*s in the streets of their very own city, Calcutta.

These and other familiar themes run through the Bengal records of the English East India Company between 1763 and 1800. The first inkling of the threat, ideological as well as military, that armed ascetics posed to the young Company-state was noted in 1763, when Calcutta first received word from Dacca that "faquirs" had briefly taken over the city and wreaked substantial damage on the Company's factory-warehouse.[55] This "rabble of Fakirs," as Robert Clive referred to them, was quickly dealt with and the captured offenders were made to provide "Cooley" labor for the repair of the damaged buildings. Subsequent incursions would prove less easy to repel, in part due to the mobility of the ascetic bands that moved quickly out of reach and often across frontier boundaries to evade capture, in part due to their high level of military discipline. In 1767, for example, a "body of 5000 Sinnasees" entered Saran District in northwest Bihar and handily defeated two companies of sepoys sent by the local *faujdar* (commander) to meet them. "The Sinnasees stood their ground and after the sepoys had fired away part of their ammunitions, fell on them, killed and wounded near eighty and put the rest to flight."[56] This party of *sanyasi*s eventually moved on, but probably not because of the Company reinforcements sent from Patna. Periodic sightings of and encounters with varying numbers of armed *sanyasi*s and *fakir*s continued, with occasional reports of extremely large bands. In late November 1770, for example, information began circulating that a "considerable body of Senassy Fakirs (to the amount of about 10,000) have assembled at Benares and that their intentions are to pass throughout these Provinces [of Bengal]." Company officials began organizing a force to oppose them, only to see the threat evaporate in the following month.[57]

---

[55] No. 322 of 25 Jul. 1763, and nos. 355 and 454 of 5 Dec. 1763, Home Department, Public Proceedings, NAI. See also Jamini Mohan Ghosh, *Sannyasi and Fakir Raiders in Bengal* (Calcutta 1930), pp. 36–37.

[56] James Long, *Selections from Unpublished Records of Government for the Years 1748 to 1767 Inclusive* (Calcutta 1869), p. 526, cited in Ghosh, *Sannyasi and Fakir Raiders*, p. 39.

[57] Letter from General Robert Barker, Dinapur, received 29 Dec. 1770 (dated 30 Nov. 1770), Foreign Department, Select Committee Proceedings, NAI. See also Ghosh, *Sannyasi and Fakir Raiders*, 43.

In addition to the fact that Calcutta was suddenly overrun with armed *sanyasi*s in the winter months of 1772–1773, two events seem to have finally precipitated Warren Hastings' proclamation of 21 January 1773. The first was the wholesale defeat of a company of sepoys and the death of its commander, Captain Thomas, near the town of Rangpur in what is now northern Bangladesh. Thomas and his men had been dispatched to deal with a band of 1,500 *sanyasi*s who had entered the district and, "under the pretended mask of a religious pilgrimage to perform ablutions in the Berhampoota [Brahmaputra] and worship at the island of Sagur[,] make it an [sic] uniform practice to oppress and plunder the country." Thomas crept up on the *sanyasi*s in the early hours of 30 December 1772 and ordered a surprise attack under the cover of darkness. The *sanyasi*s immediately retreated from the open plain into the cover of nearby jungle, into which Thomas and his small party pursued them and "expended all their ammunitions without doing the least execution." But "When they [the *sanyasi*s] perceived the ammunition spent, the Sinassies rushed in upon them in very large bodies from every quarter and surrounded them." Facing certain defeat, the sepoys then refused their commander's desperate order to charge with bayonets mounted. Thomas then "received one wound by a ball through the head which he tied, and next he was cut down." Only twelve men from Thomas' party of about 100 eventually returned to report on the engagement. The rest were either killed or captured. An interesting feature of this encounter was the support given to the *sanyasi*s by the local population. "The ryots [peasant–cultivators] gave no assistance [to the sepoys] but joined the Sannyasis with lathies and showed the Sinassies those whom they saw had concealed themselves in long grass and jungle and if any of the sepoys attempted to go into their villages they made a noise to bring the Sinnasies and they plundered the sepoy's firelocks."[58]

The second event that gave Hastings and his Calcutta committee considerable pause involved the arrival on 8 January 1773 of a party of 2,000 *sanyasi*s at the town of Bogra, forty miles south of Rangpur in what is now north-central Bangladesh. In addition to being well armed, this force possessed "one hundred horses and eighty bullocks laden with ammunition." The *sanyasi*s had already demanded and received a sum of money from subordinate officials in a nearby village, and likewise informed J. M. Hatch of Bogra that "they must have a sum of money paid them otherwise they should remain in the Pergunnah until they had taken a sufficiency to

---

[58] Letters from P. M. Dacres, J. Lawrell, and J. Graham, no. 1 of 10 Mar. 1773, FDSP (not to be confused with Foreign Department, Select Committee Proceedings, cited above), NAI. See also "Extracts from letters from Mr. Charles Purling to the President [Warren Hastings]," dated 29 and 31 Dec. 1772, cited in Ghosh, *Sannyasi and Fakir Raiders*, pp. 50–51.

pay their charges." Since Hatch only had five sepoys in Bogra to protect the Company treasury, he and the *sanyasis* settled on 1,200 rupees – "on receipt of which they [the *sanyasis*] passed quietly through this Pergunnah to Sibgunge [Sivganj] where I hear is another party of about four thousand men."[59] This bold (and successful) threat to the treasury was apparently the last straw, since it is at this point in the official proceedings of the Foreign Department that Warren Hastings set forth his lengthy "minute on the subject of the Sinasses," quoted in full above.

Hastings' proclamation would take time to disseminate throughout the province, and would have little immediate effect in any case. Reports soon arrived from Dacca that a band of 3,500 *sanyasis* demanded and was paid 3,500 rupees from local landlords, "in order to withhold their hands from committing further outrages," and that this band was headed north toward Mymensingh. Meanwhile, another large band led by a *sanyasi* named "Jurawalghar" (Jawahargiri?) had arrived by fifteen boats at Chilmary – "through dread of whom the *zemindar* (landlord) his family, and many of the inhabitants have fled into the jungles." The collector at Dhaka observed in his letter to Hastings "that there are a great number of this vagrant race in this city who carry on some trade and it is not improbable that many of them act as spies."[60] In Mymensingh District, meanwhile, a band of 5,000 *sanyasis* led by one "Darreangheer" was reported to have already extorted 1,600 rupees from a local *zamindar*, and was looking to rendezvous with another band of 6,000 "well armed with matchlocks, spears and other instruments of war" and headed by one "Moitegeer" – reputed to be the victor over Captain Thomas a month earlier. Soon after this another large band under the command of "Omoonuntagheer," operating around Pakulla in the vicinity of Dacca, seized an agent of some European "Gentlemen" at Dinajpur and relieved him of 4,200 rupees.[61]

---

[59] Letters from Dacres and Lawell at Dinajpur to Calcutta, and letters from Hatch at Bogra to Dinajpur, nos. 1, 2, 3 (for the quotations), and 4 of 21 Jan. 1773, FDSP.

[60] Letter from N. Grueber, Collector at Dacca , no. 4 of 4 Feb. 1773 (dated 29 Jan. 1773), FDSP.

[61] Letters from Grueber, nos. 2 and 9 of 10 Mar. 1773 (dated 26 Jan. and 10 Feb. 1773), FDSP. See also Ghosh, *Sannyasi and Fakir Raiders*, pp. 55–57. Holding wealthy individuals hostage and extorting money from those close to them was standard operating procedure. See Della Tomba, "Viaggio," 25–26, when he and his brother Capuchin Michelangelo were briefly held hostage by "*fakiri nudi*" in the employ of the Raja of Bettiah in what is now Bihar. They were only released when the Raja arrived with the chief ("maestro") of the *fakirs*, who ordered his men to desist. "The *fakirs*, very respectful of their master, all departed without saying a word." Nevertheless, once their master had moved on, several *fakirs* returned later to attempt a recapture; but Michelangelo had already fled to Patna via the jungle, "having more trust in the tigers than in the fakirs," and Della Tomba hid himself so expertly that he was not discovered. Again I record my gratitude to David Lorenzen for providing me with his translation of this rare material.

Another territory that had long experience with armed *sanyasis* – and had, consequently, long been on Hastings" radar screen – was Cooch Behar, a small border principality between Company Bengal and the Himalayan foothill kingdom of Bhutan. A large band of *sanyasis* under the leadership of Ramanand Gosain had seven years earlier assassinated the infant maharaja, forced the expulsion of his guardian and commander-in-chief, the "Nazir Deo" Rudranarayan, and given their support to Darup Deo, who became the new raja. The expelled Nazir Deo, whose followers also included some armed *sanyasis*, had sought and received the support of the Company. This led to skirmishes with Company forces in mid-1766 involving, most famously, James Rennell, who would become the official cartographer for Hastings (see his description of the dust-up in the following chapter). Matters remained at a relative standstill until January 1773, when Darup Deo's *sanyasis* began receiving reinforcements from the wandering bands that suddenly had started frequenting the province. This prompted the Nazir Deo to request renewed Company support. Charles Purling, the collector at Rangpur, traveled to Cooch Behar in January 1773 and immediately insisted on the dismissal of the Nazir Deo's *sanyasis* who – Purling claimed – "were only a useless expense." This was, however, easier said than done. The Nazir Deo was willing to consider the proposal, but only if Purling's force would "come and encamp with us." Once Purling did so and informed the Nazir Deo of Hastings' determination to offer substantial armed support, the Nazir Deo "proposed of himself the dismissal of the Sunasses and his own troops excepting a few about his own person." Purling pretended not to press this point because, as he explained in his letter to Hastings, "the Sunasses have been so much alarmed since my arrival, as imagining we shall attack them that they had been three nights under arms and have themselves proposed to leave the country."[62]

Hastings then dispatched over three separate sepoy battalions, one from Rajmahal, a portion of one from Rangpur, one from Berhampur, and one from Dinapur, to act as pincer arms converging on Cooch Behar. The Rangpur force, under Captain J. Jones, was the first to encounter resistance. On 28 January Jones reported an 11 a.m. engagement with

the Sunasses with whom were joined some of Durrup Do's people. They immediately advanced and endeavored by their numbers to surround us at a distance. I detached parties on the flanks and rear which prevented them. They kept retiring as I advanced out of the reach of our firelocks and threw their rockets pretty thick amongst us by which I had one man killed and four dreadfully wounded.

---

[62] Letter from Charles Purling, no. 8 of 17 Feb. 1773 (dated 12 Jan. 1773), FDSP. See also Ghosh, *Sannyasi and Fakir Raiders*, pp. 51–52 (and pp. 37–39 for events in 1766).

The discipline of Jones' sepoys, "who shewed great steadiness and kept their ranks and advanced without firing a musket," finally caused the *sanyasi*s to take flight. Jones "thought it dangerous to attempt pursuing them."[63] The next encounter in Cooch Behar, on 2 February, was between the Rajmahal battalion under Captain Robert Stewart and a party of 4,000 *sanyasi*s at Jalpaiguri. The *sanyasi*s, who had been surprised by Stewart, tried (as against Jones) to surround the Company sepoys. Stewart countered by attacking their stronger left flank, but "their station was very secure and it was impossible to make any impression on them with my musketry till I carried the bank that covered their front." Once Stewart's men had advanced to close range and began preparing for a heavy fusillade, the *sanyasi*s "took to flight with the utmost precipitation. We pursued with the utmost briskness but they used speed in their flight much superior to our pursuit." The speed of the *sanyasi* retreat was aided by the fact that they threw away many of their heavier weapons, including "five muskets taken from Captain Thomas' detachment as likewise several cartridge pouches and bundles of English ammunition."[64] Nevertheless, the pace at which *sanyasi*s moved through the countryside, with or without weapons, was remarked upon frequently. Nicholas Grueber, Collector of Dacca, complained only a few days later of "the marches of these people being so very rapid."[65] Or as Hastings would remark a year later, "these ravagers seem to pay little regards to our sepoys, having so much the advantage in speed on which they entirely rely for their safety."[66]

Another feature of *sanyasi* mobility that frustrated Company efforts in Bengal was the practice of dividing up into small bands only to rendezvous in large congregations at prearranged points. An eloquent demonstration of this was reported in 1775 from the westernmost outpost of Company arms in Bengal, the fort at Chunar or Chunar*garh*, thirty miles downriver from Banaras on the southern bank of the Ganga (and, as noted earlier, the very site of an old *nath*-Dasnami shrine connected to the Juna *akhara*).[67] On 20 March 1775 Lieutenant-Colonel Muir, commanding

---

[63] Letter from Capt. J. Jones, no. 6 of 17 Feb. 1773 (dated 28 Jan. 1773), FDSP.

[64] Letter from Capt. R. Stewart, no. 5 of 15 Feb. 1773 (dated 2 Feb. 1773), FDSP.

[65] Letter from Grueber, no. 7 of 10 Mar. 1773 (dated 7 Feb. 1773), FDSP.

[66] *Memoirs of the Life of the Right Hon. Warren Hastings, First Governor-General of Bengal*, vol. I (London 1841), p. 395, cited in Atis K. Das Gupta, *The Fakir and Sannyasi Uprisings* (Calcutta 1992), p. 88.

[67] Letters from Lt.-Col. Muir, Chunar Gur [*Garh*, fort], nos. 4 and 5 of 30 Mar. 1775 (dated 20 Mar. 1775), and no. 2 of 20 Apr. 1775 (dated 9 Apr. 1775), FDSP. See also Das Gupta, *Fakir and Sannyasi Uprisings*, p. 88, who makes a similar point, citing a 1784 Revenue Department correspondence: "Their techniques appear to be closer to guerilla tactics, as their 'followers are taught to disperse when pursued and unite again at appointed stations so that it seldom happens that they can be apprehended.'"

the garrison at Chunar, reported "having had information of a numerous body of armed men assembling at Allahabad [about sixty miles upriver]," said to be "on a religious pilgrimage." Doubtless this was the periodic gathering of ascetics at the Prayag *sangam*, referred to today as the *kumbha mela*. From Muir's perspective, even though "their pretensions be ever so religious," he "thought it prudent to station spies to bring the most speedy advice of their departure from that city." The upshot of that advice was that

their pilgrimage portends no good; they have for some weeks past given out that their design was to bend their route directly homewards from Allahabad whereas I have this instant most positive advice of their being now in motion to the Eastward; and in order to pass this station in the most private manner, they have divided themselves into small bodys [sic] not exceeding 50 whereas report makes them out when assembled near 20,000.

Muir decided to communicate with the *sanyasi*s directly by dispatching a *harcarah*, or intelligence agent, with a message ordering the leader to "come singly with him [the agent] to wait on me at Chunar Gur," before which "the multitude must remain where it is and cannot pass this way." Muir's resolve seemed, according to a later correspondence in April, to have had some effect. His *harcarah*s "had actually stopt the first party amounting to 40 foot and 10 horse." Consequently, "the main body although they [sic] had crossed the Ganges at Allahabad and had begun their march downwards, yet they thought it most prudent, to alter their first intentions and I now have information of their having separated in small bodys [sic] and are bending their rout [sic] homewards."

In the meantime, Muir had proposed that the increasingly dependent Raja Chait Singh of Banaras be instructed to "issue his orders to all his Fhoujdars and Zemindars [along] the frontier of his country . . . to keep a vigilant watch and endeavor to transmit the earliest notice they may from time to time have of any body of armed men or Sunnassies approaching and to specifie their force and intentions." This suggestion had emerged out of Muir's belief, probably based on the advice of his *harcarah*s, that were "Rajah Cheyt Sing to oppose their passing through his country," the measure "would entirely answer this purpose without the necessity of employing troops in this garrison." Hastings and company evidently approved of this course of action, particularly insofar as it could oblige Chait Singh to rely increasingly upon Company sepoys in occasionally repulsing *sanyasi* bands. And, in fact, there may have been something to the suggestion that Chait Singh be brought to bear in the matter of *akhara* perambulation. Adjacent to Chait Singh's old residence, on the bank of the Ganga in Banaras, are the Banaras headquarters of the Mahanirvani,

Niranjani, and Juna *akhara*s. It is difficult to date these structures, which are clustered together at Sivala and Hanuman Ghats, let alone the establishment of the *akhara* organizations.[68] But it would not be unreasonable to presume that Chait Singh had had armed *sanyasi*s – or more precisely, *gosain*s – in his employ. Prior to and coincident with his status as a tributary prince to Company Bengal, Chait Singh was under the sway of the nawabs of Awadh, namely, Asaf ud-Daula, his father Shuja ud-Daula, and his father, Safdar Jang. *Gosain*s had entered the service of Awadh under Safdar Jang in 1751 and remained a major component of the armed force of the nawabs until 1775–1776 when Company policy forced them out of the Awadh service.[69]

The Company records of Bengal over the next three decades are replete with reports of sepoy skirmishes with armed *sanyasi*s as well as *fakir*s, often fighting in unison. There is occasional confusion in the records as to the particular identity of the combatants, since (as we have seen) the term *fakir* was employed as a generic descriptor for individuals who were simultaneously described as *sanyasi*.[70] Further complicating matters is the fact that *sanyasi*s and *fakir*s were occasionally belligerents, but for reasons that appear to have had less to do with macro-communal (Hindu and Muslim) identities than with locally specific disputes, some of which may have had sectarian overtones. For example, in Purnea District of northeast Bihar in October 1770 150 sepoys commanded by Lieutenant Sinclair captured a party of armed but peaceable Madari *fakir*s en route to a *dargah* or Sufi

---

[68] The embankment at Chait Singh's residence is now known as "Chait Singh Ghat." On the site is a plaque that reads "This was the residence of RAJA CHAIT SINGH where he was arrested by the order of WARREN HASTINGS on the 16ᵗʰ August 1781 and where on the same date after the massacre of two companies of native troops with their British officers he was rescued by his adherents." In Hindi on the river-facing walls of the Niranjani and Mahanirvani *akhara*s are the words "Niranjani Ghat" and "Mahanirvani Ghat," suggesting that the *akhara*s are seeking to lay claim to the embankment usually regarded as Sivala and Hanuman Ghats. The exteriors of the structures are certainly new, built or renovated within the last thirty years and painted in a garish fortress motif even more recently.

[69] See Richard Barnett, *North India Between Empires: Awadh, The Mughals, and the British, 1720–1801* (Berkeley 1987), p. 111. I review this episode in the following chapter. Further suggestive of a link between the *akhara*s and the Banaras maharajas is an oil painting that adorns a wall of the Ramnagar Palace Museum. It depicts the *akhara*s at the Prayag *sangam* festival, military banners unfurled. The painting is undated, but appears to be a work of the nineteenth century.

[70] See, for example, the letter from J. Jones, no. 7 of 17 Feb. 1773 (dated 30 Jan. 1773), FDSP: "Late last night I was informed that the *Sunasses* had all crossed the Tusta and sunk the boats they made use of, this precluded the necessity of my marching after them to Bhoothant [Bhutan] etc. I now propose taking possession of the fort of Rothimgunge, from whence if the situation of Beyhar with regard to the Boutains [Bhutanis] of which Mr. Purling will advise me, does not render it dangerous, I shall proceed to cross the river to Galpygeree a principal fort belonging to Darrup Do, where I learn he is inciting the *Facquirs* to make another stand." Italics added.

shrine near Maldah. The local people vouched for their good behavior, however, and the *fakir*s, themselves insisted that "they had come in large numbers and with arms owing to the quarrel with the Sannyasis who lately put to death a number of their people." As a result, Company officials allowed them to proceed – but only after disarming them and keeping five or six hostage for the duration of their stay in the district. There are oral traditions from Bogra District, now in Bangladesh, about an epic clash in 1777 between *fakir*s, led by the increasingly famous Majnu Shah, and *naga sanyasi*s. The *naga*s were "said to have been well mounted on large horses and to have been armed with long swords. They and the follow-ers of Majnu met in battle at daybreak and fought till noon . . . The swords of the Nagas are described as lopping off the heads of the robbers with as much ease as if they were cutting the stalks of plantain trees."[71] It is likely that the memory of this clash had gained a grandiose quality through constant retelling during the nineteenth-century, in tandem with the demonization of Majnu himself in poetic representation.[72]

A particularly revealing episode of internecine violence is the 1794 assassination of a *fakir* commander named Chiragh Ali by a rival *sanyasi* leader. The catalyst of the dispute was, apparently, an unpaid debt. Basant Lal Amin, deputed by C. A. Bruce, Judicial Officer of Cooch Behar, to gather information on local bands of *fakir*s, offered the follow-ing explanation:

---

[71] Ghosh, *Sannyasi and Fakir Raiders*, p. 42 (for the Purnea account), p. 74 (for Bogra). For the latter, Ghosh cites the *Bogra District Gazetteer*, no page number given, which itself relies on a brochure published in Bogra town in 1861, entitled *Shetihas Bagurar Brittanta*. Other prominent *fakir* commanders included Chiragh Ali, Musa Shah, Shamsher Shah, Sobhan Shah (also known as Sobhan Ali), and Parigullah Shah. See the first letter from Bussunt Lall Aumeen (at first misidentified as "Bastiram Aumeen") enclosed in C. A. Bruce, Judicial Officer, Cooch Behar, to George H. Barlow, no. 7 of 19 Sep. 1794 (dated 27 Aug. 1794), Bengal Judicial Department, Criminal Proceedings (hereafter BJDCP), OIOC.

[72] See *Majnur Kabita*, or the "Song of Majnu," reproduced in Ghosh, *Sannyasi and Fakir Raiders*, Appendix, 160–161 and translated on pp. 109–110. "Listen, all of you, to a new poem. Majnu the *Burhana* [a kind of Madari] is the ruin of Bengal. A fakir is he? The monster is as destructive as Yama, the god of death. In fear of him, the ruler trembles and the people have no peace. His march is well ordered like a king's. See how the standards and banners precede him. Behold his retinue of camels, horses and elephants with sturdy Telingas [soldiers dressed in European fashion] armed to the teeth. Majnu himself is mounted like a warrior on an Arab steed, with his escort of mounted archers . . ." See also the valuable comments in this context by Das Gupta, *Fakir and Sannyasi Uprisings*, p. 3. Whether historians may cull countervailing meanings from verse of a much later date, such as the nostalgic *Majnu Shaher Hakikat* by Jamiruddin Dafadar of Birbhum in 1873 is, however, debatable (e.g. Das Gupta, *Fakir and Sanyasi Uprisings*, pp. 5, 90). What requires emphasis here is that a popular literature was growing in the nineteenth century concerning the "*sanyasi* and *fakir* uprising," that may have taken on communal dimensions, and that that literary history needs to be taken into account when seeking to understand the writings of Bankim Chandra Chatterji.

Cheraughally . . . lived at Rungaily [and] had some transactions with Motty Sing [a.k.a. Motigir], a Sonassy who lived in Tirhote [Tirhut]. The sonassy sent people to recover the money which Cheraugally owed to him but without success, for the latter treated them rudely, and refused an answer – when they returned and complained to Mooty Sing, he was greatly enraged, and set about collecting people to take his revenge. He then marched by night, till he waylaid him, and then cut him off. His body was taken to the cutcherry [courthouse] at Mosufferpore [Muzaffarpur].[73]

The facts of the assassination and details about its perpetrator were confirmed by a later sheet of intelligence from Purnea. The main informant, identified as a "gentleman resident near Morung," noted that he had passed through the Morung border region two years earlier and had been impressed by the discipline and quality of Chiragh Ali's force. Significantly, a major portion of that force was composed of *sanyasi*s. "About two years ago [when] I was in Morung and encamped near Cheraug Allie's chownee [camp] at Quilah, he drew out his people about four hundred, half sonasses dressed in orange, and half Molungs [*malang*, or "robust" or "martial Madaris"] in blue jackets; they made a good appearance, went thro' their platoon firing better than I could have expected, and gave an excellent volley."[74]

Despite the occasional animosities that flared up into violence, wandering bands of *fakir*s and *sanyasi*s (as well as the occasional *bairagi* and even sepoy detachments formerly in the pay of *zamindars*) did manage to fight in tandem against an increasingly implacable Company army. This story has been narrated in some detail, first by Jamini Mohan Ghosh in 1930, cited above, from the official perspective, but more recently in the trenchant analytical work of Atis Das Gupta and Suranjan Chatterjee.[75] The *sanyasi* side of the insurgency was, as noted above, the basis for the major work of Bengali nationalist fiction in the early 1880s, *Anandamath* by Bankim Chandra Chatterji. Bankim cast the prolonged series of skirmishes as an organic nationalism of patriotic Hindu ascetic *santan*s ("children") – and the occasional householder temporarily become an ascetic – seeking to throw off the yoke of foreign tyranny – a foreign

[73] Bussunt Lall Aumeen's second letter enclosed in C. A. Bruce, Judicial Officer, Cooch Behar, to George H. Barlow, no. 7 of 19 Sep. 1794 (dated 27 Aug. 1794), BJDCP. For more details on the breakdown of relations between *fakir*s and *sanyasi*s, see also Das Gupta, *Fakir and Sannyasi Uprisings*, pp. 98–100.

[74] "Extract of a letter to Mr. Y. Burges," Purnea District Collector, dated 18 Jan. 1795, enclosed in Burges to Edmonstone, dated 24 Jan. 1795 (no number), BJDCP. See the discussion below for more on the term "*malang*."

[75] Suranjan Chatterjee, "New Reflections on the Sannyasi, Fakir and Peasants War," *Economic and Political Weekly* 19 (28 January 1984): PE2–PE13 (PE stands for "Review of Political Economy," a special insert); and Das Gupta, *Fakir and Sannyasi Uprisings*.

tyranny that he cast, ironically, as Muslim. Bankim's demonizing of Muslims in *Anandamath* was in part a way of avoiding official censure as a compromised subordinate official to the British, and in part a way of catering to the increasingly communal religious sensibilities of his Bengali *bhadralok* audience. It is possible, furthermore, that Bankim was responding to a burgeoning popular literature in Bengali that celebrated various protagonists in terms of macro-religious identities.[76] Bankim's was a work of fiction, however, even if it did become the ideological template for the early nationalist movement in Bengal and has remained influential in Indian (and Hindu) nationalism generally. The Hindu and nationalist stridency of his prose should be examined for the literary liberties that it took. It should not, however, cause us to err too far on the side of caution – particularly insofar as nationalism is concerned. Though armed *sanyasi*s and *fakir*s were not Indian nationalists, they did possess a consciously articulated tie to the land and country through which they traveled and, more importantly, to sacred geographic points on their routes. The homage that some people paid them suggests, moreover, that they themselves were regarded as an integral part of a sacred landscape – rendering them less proto-nationalists perhaps than a physical feature of the proto-nation (and, hence, the object of proto-nationalist "territorial" devotion).[77] In any case, *sanyasi* and *fakir* clashes with Company arms were, at least in part, predicated on the desire to retain periodic access to that sacred landscape and to the moneyed people in it.

The fact of joint *sanyasi* and *fakir* operations may strike some readers as exceptional given the legacy of communal violence between Hindus and Muslims in modern South Asia. As I have argued throughout this and the previous chapter, Hindu–Muslim communalism is not a useful framework in which to understand warrior asceticism, let alone the viability of *sanyasi–fakir* alliances. If it appears as a religio-political backdrop to histories of *sanyasi–fakir* military activities in Bengal, it is because the story of those activities is invariably told as an early (and often first) act in the story of Indian nationalism – a narrative topos that is, in large

---

[76] See Tapan Raychaudhuri, *Europe Reconsidered: Perceptions of the West in Nineteenth-Century Bengal* (Delhi 1988), p. 117. Bankim was careful to depict the British as benevolent (if occasionally reckless) caretakers of ancient Indian glory, who must be allowed to nurture Aryan India back to greatness. This dissimulation did not suffice, and his career still suffered from official censure. He was passed over for promotion and remained a deputy magistrate until his retirement. A. N. Chandra, *The Sannyasi Rebellion* (Calcutta 1977), attempts to render Bankim's argument in a traditional historical narrative framework. For a succinct if overly materialist refutation of these communalist interpretations, see Chatterjee, "New Reflections," PE2.

[77] On "territoriality" see C. A. Bayly, *Origins of Nationality in South Asia: Patriotism and Ethical Government in the Making of Modern India* (Delhi 1998), as well as the review of this volume by Sumit Guha, *Journal of Asian Studies* 60, 1 (February 2001): 256–258.

part, the historiographical legacy of Bankim.[78] This is, in part, why I have chosen to describe late eighteenth-century Bengal as the closing act of the story of "Mughal *yogis*". *Sanyasi–fakir* agency-cum-insurgency in Bengal is as much (if not more) a product of older understandings of asceticism and its connections to landscape as it is a portent of the subaltern insurgencies that were yet to come. Communal difference was not so sharp in the middle and late eighteenth century, despite the rise in Bengal and elsewhere of Vaishnava *bhakti* devotionalism, as to render concerted interaction between people we may later describe as Hindus and Muslims a matter of historical note. Non-Muslim military service under Muslim commanders and vice versa was the rule rather than the exception in Mughal and late-Mughal India (and has, in fact, remained so in India to the present, despite all the communal water that has flowed under the bridge). The occasional success of joint *sanyasi–fakir* military action reflects, in my understanding at least, the location of historical armed asceticism beyond the boundaries of fixed, modern religious identities (though this too would change).

Macro-religious classification as Hindu or Muslim was, in the main, irrelevant to the world of Mughal ascetics, armed or otherwise. Sufis and *yogis* interacted constantly on an individual basis – and interpenetrated on a communal basis – in the centuries preceding the upsurge of violence between Company arms and joint *sanyasi–fakir* bands.[79] Of greater importance than macro-religious categories of Hindu and Muslim were specific techniques for inculcating individual access to supernormal experience – whether understood as a pathway to realizing God with a capital "G" or the cultivation of an inner wellspring of energy. As has been noted by many observers of medieval yoga and Sufism, the differences in form were outweighed by the similarities in substance. The pragmatics of gaining access to the supernormal gave rise to many shared social and cultural forms, including sectarian allegiances (especially those embodied and embedded in guru–*chela* lineages), sacred places, and the presumed right to collect donations from ordinary people, whether at those sacred places or en route to them. The Madari *malang* of Bengal were, in fact, especially emblematic of this generic sharing. An early nineteenth-century account described a *malang* as "any unattached religious beggar who drinks and smokes hemp to excess, wears nothing save a loin-cloth, and keeps fire always near him. They are said to wear their hair long and tied into a knot behind . . . They resemble in many ways the Hindu Gosain ascetics, wander through deserts and mountains, visit shrines of Saints, and wherever

---

[78] See, e.g., Das Gupta, *Fakir and Sannyasi Uprisings*, pp. 114–115, where the intercommunal cooperation message intersects with subaltern romanticism.

[79] This interpenetration is described at length in Eaton, *Rise of Islam and the Bengal Frontier*.

they sit down they light a fire (*dhuni*) and sometimes rub ashes on their bodies."[80] Mubad Shah, author of the seventeenth-century *Dabistan-i-Mazahib*, held that the particular sectarian features of Madaris were, in fact, a result of the fact that Sufis had

> heard that there are ten classes of Sannyasis and twelve of yogis, [so] they also pretend to be divided into fourteen classes . . . [Among these,] the *Madarians*, like the Sannyasi *Avadhuts* [hermits], wear the hair entangled; and the ashes which they and the Sannyasis rub upon their bodies are called 'bhasma'; besides, they carry iron chains on their heads and neck, and have black flags and black turbans; they know neither prayers nor fasts; they are always sitting at a fire; they drink a great deal of *bhang* and the most perfect among them go about without any dress in severe cold in Kabul and Kashmir and such places. They say when Badiu-d-Din Madar came to Hindostan, he became a Yogi, whom the Hindus held in great esteem and who had a large number of followers. Madar settled in Makhanpur in Cawnpore district. The Madaris come there as many as possible from all parts of the world once a year.[81]

Mubad Shah's account is no doubt apocryphal in seeking to explain the complementarities as the conscious invention of one or more visionaries. More likely those complementarities were the product of a gradual, almost imperceptible transformative process, namely, the accommodation of pre-Muslim ascetic techniques and practices to the increasingly cosmopolitan Islam that was overtaking the Bengal countryside, beginning about 1200 but especially after 1600.[82]

The historical fact of joint *sanyasi–fakir* military operation in Bengal between 1770 and 1800 is revealing for other, more mundane reasons: it brings us face to face with the mechanics of mobilization, recruitment, and soldiering that informed ascetic military action in this period. This emerges with particular clarity in a deposition of a *sanyasi* captured in Cooch Behar in 1794, enclosed in a letter of intelligence.

Deposition of one of the Fakeers

My name is Govindgeer, I come from Surat and attended Shumshur Saw and Jory Saw who live at Rungaily and Rwaliah in Napaul. These people are now

---

[80] Ja'far Sharif, *Islam in India, or, the Qanun-i-Islam*, trans. G. A. Herklots, rev. edn (London and New York 1921; reprint Delhi 1997), p. 290. This account was written in 1832.

[81] *Dabistan-i-Mazahib*, vol. II, pp. 223–224; this passage is quoted in Ghosh, *Sannyasi and Fakir Raiders*, pp. 20–21, and Das Gupta, *Fakir and Sannyasi Uprisings*, p. 15. Makhanpur or Makanpur is, incidentally, quite close to Rasdhan and Sivarajpur, where the descendants and commander-*chelas* of Anupgiri and Umraogiri would settle (see chapter 4). In addition, a village named Madaripur is just south of Rasdhan, across the Jamuna River, in Jalaun District. This raises the intriguing possibility that the connection of the *gosains* to the place was based on the nearby presence of the Madari shrine. I am grateful to Aditya Behl for drawing my attention to this point.

[82] The best work here is, of course, Eaton, *Rise of Islam and the Bengal Frontier*.

at Nidantarrah where they come on business, and will soon return back to their dwellings. They have between them above one thousand people, of which number there are four hundred Mussulmaun Fakeers, one hundred Hindoo Sonassies, four hundred Seapoys, twenty Byragies and the rest are people of different descriptions. They lead these people into Bengal to plunder the country, and they live upon the Booty which they can take there, for they have no landed property at their residencies. There is a Soubah [subadar] on the part of the Napaul Rajah at Gurnidantarrah [or at the *garh* (fort) of Nidantarrah], and when the Fakeers brought home any plunder they presented him with the warlike implements they had taken, and also with money, they generally went there and staid some time, the last place pillage in Bodah [sic]. I cannot tell the name of it, it is about two days journey from Gurnidantara. Shumshur Saw and Jory Saw generally take all the booty to themselves, and pay to their adherents wages[.] The party I was enrolled with, consisted of 100 Sonassies and they paid us 1500 Rupees per mensem, they paid us when we took property and they then divided the spoils equally between them. Sonassygottah in Bykunthpore, is one coss [approx. two miles] distant from Gur Nidantarrah, the Soubah will not allow this place to be touched. The Napaul Rajah's residence is a month's journey distant from Nidantara. There are thirty Napaul seapoys at Nidantara and twenty at Hurchundergurry. We took five people away from one place we attacked in Bodah and conducted them to Nidantarrah, on purpose that by flogging them we might make them deliver as much money as they could give to us. Rungaily is four or five coss distant from Kwalliah and is distant three munsils from Nidantarah. Kwalliah is about the same distance from Nidantarrah. When Jory Saw and Shumshur Saw after a plundering excursion return home, they dismiss the most of the Fakeers and Sonassies, they retain however about 100 or 150 always in their employ – and those who are discharged have no habitations at Rungaily, or at Kwaliah, but live elsewhere. Jory Saw and Cheraugally are cousins (it has in another place been said they were uncle and nephew) and live at Rungaily they are both chelahs of Mudjons Saw [Majnu Shah] – Shumsheer Saw and Sobanny Saw are brothers, and live at Kwaliah, they were slaves of Modjno Saw but now have set up for themselves, and pillage Bengal. These proceedings are not known to the Napaul Rajah, but the Soubah of Gurchundgurry knows them and receives a present of Horses, or camels, or money from the spoils of the Fakeers.[83]

As with Hastings' minute and proclamation of 1773, with which this discussion began, Govindgeer's deposition of 1794 confirms and, in some cases, elaborates themes we have already touched upon in this and the previous chapter. The first is the assertion that Govindgeer hailed from Surat, on the western coast north of Bombay, confirming the subcontinental scope of armed ascetic networks. This may occasion surprise, but it should not. The entourage of Varthema's sixteenth-century *yogi* king, who was based in Gujarat, traveled as far as Calicut to the south, a

---

[83] "Deposition of one of the Fakeers," enclosed in C. A. Bruce, Judicial Officer, Cooch Behar, to George H. Barlow, no. 7 of 19 Sep. 1794 (dated 27 Aug. 1794), BJDCP. This document is also reproduced in Ghosh, *Sannyasi and Fakir Raiders*, pp. 111–112.

distance of some 800 miles. This is the same distance from Surat eastward to Banaras, which is just west of Bihar (which constituted the western tract of the Company province of Bengal). Clearly these men were not put off by long distances. Also noteworthy is the apparent interchangeability of the terms *chela* and slave for Govindgeer, in describing the relationship of Jori Shah, Chiragh Ali, Sobhani Shah, and Shamsher Shah to their late guru/*pir*, Majnu Shah. Other interesting features of the deposition are the regular pay the men received and the periodic nature of their employment, suggesting again that ascetics were not only a standard feature of the military economy but were easily alerted to plans for upcoming forays. Nidantarra was clearly a center of activity, partly accounted for by the complicity of the local *subadar* who received gifts from the *fakir* leaders. This is confirmed in a later deposition, recorded in 1798, which also depicts Nidantarra/Nezamtarrah in Nepal as the site for assembling prior to raiding into Bengal.[84] It was also where Govindgeer and his companions took their more wealthy captives, to torture (or "flog") them and "make them deliver as much money as they could give to us." A later intelligence report, provided by "a gentleman resident near Morung" who passed through the region some months later and spoke with some of the mounted followers of the *fakir* commanders, gives a slightly different spin on this kind of extortion. According to this report, the men "thought it strange we [the English] should object to their easing the richer few of the ryots of money they had not the heart to spend, and seemed to make a merit in not molesting those who had little or nothing to lose."[85] We may conclude from this that *fakir–sanyasi* crime had an in-built class dimension, though it would be difficult to parlay such remarks, even with the occasional report of assistance rendered by peasants, into an argument for subaltern insurgency or all out peasant war.[86]

According to a related paper of intelligence, Nidantarra was adjacent to jungle lands "full of elephants, rhinocerosses, tigers and other wild beasts."[87] The *sanyasi*s and *fakir*s inhabited these and similar "jungles hard of access," in "encampments in the woods." A feel for that jungle

---

[84] "Extract from the examination of Teerut Gir, taken 5th April 1798," no. 4 of 4 May 1798, BJDCP.

[85] "Extract of a letter to Mr. Y. Burges," dated 18 Jan. 1795, enclosed in a letter from Burges to Edmonstone (no number), dated 24 Jan. 1795, BJDCP.

[86] This is not to say that attempts to do so have not been made. See Chatterjee, "New Reflections"; cf. Das Gupta, *Fakir and Sannyasi Uprisings*, p. 2, who notes that Chatterjee's essay is "too didactic in approach and incomplete in essential details on insurgency."

[87] "Letter from Bastiram Aumeen, 18th Afsan 1201" [later identified as Bussunt Lall Aumeen], first enclosure in C. A. Bruce, Cooch Behar, to G. Barlow, no. 7 of 19 Sep. 1794 (dated 27 Aug. 1794), BJDCP.

landscape is revealed in a harrowing report submitted by a Company messenger, one Shaik Kullum, who was dispatched with a small party to complain to the Nepal *subadar* at Nidantarra about the incursions of the *sanyasi–fakir* bands into Bengal. The *subadar* rebuffed the messenger's complaint, and replied that "there are so many Fakeers residing in the jungles, that I shall never be able to prevent them." He then provided a guide to take them to a neighboring district, but this person promptly led them down "very complicated paths and bye roads into jungles, so thick that the breath of heaven could not penetrate." After spending the night in trees to protect themselves from the wildlife, they were abandoned by their guide who claimed to have "lost the road." After waiting some time, they decided to proceed on their way. "But losing the route, we wandered about three coss [six miles] in great terror and apprehension for our safety" until they stumbled upon the outskirts of the *sanyasi–fakir* encampment of Jori Shah and Shamsher Shah. Their fear of the outlaws apparently paled in comparison to their fear of another night in the jungle, so they entered the encampment. They had the presence of mind to pretend to be in search of a lost brother who had gone this way a year before, consequently the unsuspecting jungle outlaws offered them hospitality. If nothing else, the scene is reminiscent of the late sixteenth-century *Hamzanama* portrait, "Songhur Balkhi and Lulu the Spy are received by Baba Baksha, a Former Spy Living in Aqiqinagar," discussed in the previous chapter. Still, the messenger managed to salvage some meager benefit for his Company employers: "while we stopt we obtained the following intelligence: – the Fakeers have 100 Tillungahs [*telingas*] and Sonassies, about 150 Rajpoots from Benares, they had two *Kynchies of Baun* (or forty-eight rockets) and lived in tents made of cloth plundered in Bengal."[88]

Mughal *yogi*s and Company *gosain*s

By 1800 *sanyasi–fakir* raids into northern Bengal had slowed to a trickle. The combination of a tightening Company administration beginning in 1793 under Cornwallis had pushed the arena of military operations into the northern districts of Bengal and Bihar, along the frontier with Nepal. The slowly improving trade relationship with Nepal, beginning in theory in 1792 but in effect after 1795, provided an added incentive for the Nepalese authorities to clamp down on the raids. Two points are left unanswered by the historiography: why it was that leadership in Bengal

---

[88] "Deposition of Shaik Kullum – the messenger," enclosed in "Letter from Bastiram Aumeen" (see the previous footnote).

came mostly from *fakir*s in the 1790s, and what became of armed *sanyasi*s and *fakir*s once, as Jamini Mohan Ghosh so aptly phrased it in 1930, they "ceased to be a feature of the countryside in Northern Bengal"?[89] Answering these questions requires a different vantage point than that which is usually adopted in historical considerations of the "*Sanyasi* and *Fakir* Rebellion," one that takes us to a higher altitude so as to see beyond the artificial boundaries that defined the Company Province of Bengal, into what is now Uttar Pradesh, Madhya Pradesh, Maharashtra, and Rajasthan. (A higher altitude is only appropriate given the subcontinental scope of armed ascetic networks.) This vantage point allows us to better appreciate the careers of Anupgiri and Umraogiri Gosain, two of northern India's most successful warlords of the eighteenth century, and to understand the fate of their institutional as well as biological descendants – topics which we take up in the following chapters.

Anupgiri and Umraogiri will aid us as well in answering a question that is begged by our review of the *sanyasi* and *fakir* insurgency in Bengal in the context of the "Mughal *yogi*" history that preceded it. That question is: namely, whether the process of military institutionalization over the seventeenth and eighteenth centuries eroded the ascetic self-understandings that had informed their martial existence and activities in prior centuries. Another way of stating the question is: did armed ascetics become, particularly as a byproduct of their remarkable success in the military economy of the seventeenth and eighteenth centuries, the caricatures of themselves that religious critics – both Hindu and Muslim – had long leveled at them? Some brief recapitulation is called for to bring this question into better focus. Prior to 1600 many itinerant *yogi*s carried weapons and knew how to use them. I have argued that the martial prowess of *yogi*s was enhanced by a widespread belief in their superhuman qualities – more precisely, a belief in the ability of *yogi*s to discipline their bodies in such a way as to afford them enormous transformative power. The question for us, then, as we arrive at the end of the eighteenth century, and as we close the book on Mughal *yogi*s, is whether those beliefs still mattered – to armed *yogi*s, to the chieftains, princes, and kings that employed them, and to the ordinary folk upon whom they relied for sustenance, intelligence, occasional plunder, and recruits. The Bengal experience seems to suggest that they mattered less and less to ordinary people – that ordinary folk were looking increasingly to a more predictable religious world, to Hindu and Muslim devotionalism. But this may well be a function of the volume of official noise that drowns out all other sounds. In any case, it practically

---

[89]   Ghosh, *Sannyasi and Fakir Raiders*, p. 137.

goes without saying that the new sovereigns of Bengal were not moved by yogic claims to supernormality.

Crucial to the transition to wide-scale military entrepreneurship in the eighteenth century was the ability of the *yogi* to be many things at once – to be Muslim and Hindu, emperor and mendicant, ascetic and archer, soldier and spy. If there is a central lesson in this extended reflection on the historiographical ripples that emanate outward from Thaneswar in 1567, it is that fundamental ambiguities plague any attempt to give precise religious and sectarian definition to armed ascetics in the Mughal period. Were they Hindu, or Muslim, or Hindu and Muslim, or something else altogether? Clearly they were not consumed by the question. The desire of observers to pigeonhole them runs up against their reluctance to be pigeonholed. This should be, for us, the more mundane import of the tales of metempsychosic, transmigratory *yogi*s who inhabit the previous chapter, namely, their ability to transform themselves at will – to appropriate identity and, in the process, exercise complete corporeal elasticity.

3   Company *gosain*s

> He scorches his humbled enemies in their jungle hideaways.
> He touches the poor with long-armed compassion and ritual sacrifice.
> He gives endowments to support dharma and is the clothing that covers Hindu shame.
> He is the embodiment of radiant splendor, but an insatiable demon when his anger is provoked.
>
>   – Padmakar, singing the praises of Anupgiri Gosain, *c.* 1795[1]

In 1766 James Rennell joined in the pursuit of a large band of *fakir*s, "a kind of sturdy Beggars," said to be plundering the countryside of northern Bengal. Sent to reconnoiter a nearby village, he and his small cavalry escort suddenly found themselves surrounded and badly outnumbered. He managed to escape without being touched by the constant musket fire of the enemy, and even killed one "hardy fellow" who had pursued him too doggedly. Nevertheless, when he pulled up, he found he had lost the use of both arms. A saber had slashed through his right shoulder and "laid me open for near a foot down the back cutting thro' or wounding several of the ribs." On his left arm, another stroke had taken off a large portion of muscle – about "the breadth of a hand" – near the elbow. The same arm had also received a stab wound and "a large cut on the hand which deprived me of the use of my forefinger." Rennell would later remark that "Providence surely strengthened my Arms whilst I was retreating." He would never recover the full use of his left forefinger and his right arm was permanently weakened, the severed arteries and nerves in his right shoulder having rendered a large portion of his right side numb. These were harsh wounds for the man who would become Britain's first and most celebrated imperial cartographer. But it could have been worse: Rennell's regimental broadcloth coat had saved his back "from a cut which must in all probability have finished me if

---

[1] *Himmatbahadur Virdavali*, ed. Bhagvandin, 2nd edn (Banaras n.d., but probably early 1920s), p. 2 (vv. 5–6).

I had happened to have had on the thin Cloathing which is generally worn here."[2]

The Cooch Behar encounter was an early skirmish in the long confrontation known to later historians, desirous of a sequential narrative to describe the march of British imperial power, as the "*Sanyasi* and *Fakir* Rebellion*.*" As I have argued in the previous chapter, this four-decade long series of skirmishes was less a conscious rebellion than a prolonged clash of cultures. Both groups, that is, the Company and the ascetics, perceived Bengal as a source of ready cash, whether they termed it revenue or tribute. But unlike their Mughal predecessors, whose philosophy of statecraft did not disqualify wandering ascetics from a share of wealth from the countryside, the new East India Company men perceived themselves and the landed gentry whom they recognized – the middlemen *zamindar*s – as the only legitimate claimants to the product of the land. Any skimming of the revenue by wandering armed bands, especially armed bands claiming religious sanction, was cast as an illegitimate oppression of a vulnerable, subject peasantry. It could only be met with violence.

But what may have been unsettling to Company officials in 1766 was that not all armed *sanyasi*s and *fakir*s were vagrant plunderers. Indeed, the men who surrounded and nearly killed Rennell were probably a contingent under the control of the warlord Ramanand Gosain who, in 1759, had been behind the assassination of Cooch Behar's infant maharaja and the installation of a rival, Darup Deo, on the throne. The newly emergent Company (Clive's own successful coup at Plassey having occurred only two years earlier, in 1757) had subsequently taken the side of the deposed royal guardian and commander-in-chief, Rudranarayan, the "Nazir Deo". To Company men in Calcutta, the entrepreneurial *gosain*s of Cooch Behar may have looked a little too familiar. Such apprehensions would only have been accentuated by events in the principality of Awadh to the west, where two *gosain* warlords, Anupgiri and Umraogiri, had risen to positions of military and political prominence. Awadh under the nawabs Safdar Jang and Shuja ud-Daulah had evolved into the mainstay of Mughal power in northern India during the 1750s and 1760s and, as such, represented one of the primary rivals to the Company for control over the Delhi throne. When in 1763 Shuja joined forces with

---

[2] Major James Rennell to the Reverend Gilbert Burrington, then Vicar of Chudleigh, 30 Aug. 1766, in "Typescript Copies of Personal Letters from Maj James Rennell (1742–1830), to his Guardian, Reverend Gilbert Burrington," MSS Eur.D.1073, OIOC. An abbreviated version of the passage can be found in *Hobson-Jobson: A Glossary of Colloquial Anglo-Indian Words and Phrases, and of Kindred Terms, Etymological, Historical, Geographical and Discursive*, comp. Col. Henry Yule and A. C. Burnell (London 1903), s.v. Sunyasee (p. 872).

the rebellious Mir Qasim of Bengal on behalf of the Mughal emperor and confronted the Company army on the open field at Buxar in western Bihar in the following year, the bulk of his opposition to Company forces came from Anupgiri Gosain's *naga* troops. And not simply during actual combat: just prior to the Battle of Buxar, a "*fakir*" was arrested on suspicion of having been sent among the sepoys by Shuja "to corrupt our men." This individual was "accused by a European of offering his services to the revolted party [of sepoys] . . . promising to conduct and supply them with provisions on the march up the country."[3] Though the records do not go into sufficient detail, this man was almost certainly dispatched by Anupgiri.

The Battle of Buxar did not go well for Anupgiri: the *gosain*s failed to break through the Company lines and Anupgiri himself was badly wounded in the thigh during the combat. But he once again had demonstrated *gosain* loyalty to the first family of Awadh and, by extension, to the Mughal empire: his self-sacrifice in battle earned him the sobriquet "Himmat Bahadur" from the nawab. Meanwhile, Mir Qasim was captured and executed for his notorious murder of Company men in Patna ("Qasimabad") the previous year. Shuja, with the aid of Anupgiri, fled westward – an escape that would further cement the bond between the nawab and the *gosain*. Though the terms of the subsequent "subsidiary alliance" between the Company and Awadh would force a meddlesome British "resident" on subsequent nawabs, it would take another decade of Company intrigue – and the death of Shuja – before a permanent wedge could be driven between Shuja's son, Asaf ud-Daulah, and the *gosain*s. By then, however, the *gosain*s, and particularly Anupgiri, had bigger plans: Anupgiri would embark on a career path that would take him from king-maker in and around Delhi (some of the travails of which are summarized in the introductory pages of this book) to self-made king of Bundelkhand, a rugged and strategically crucial swath of undulating upland on the southern edge of the Gangetic Plain. It was during the Bundelkhand years, in the early or mid-1790s after Anupgiri's defeat of the Rajput warlord and pride of the Bundelas, Arjun Singh, that the bard Padmakar composed the ballad from which the eulogistic epigraph for this chapter is drawn. Anupgiri's final stroke of mercurial brilliance (or treasonous stupidity, depending on one's perspective) would occur about a decade later, however, in the lead up to the Anglo-Maratha War of 1803–1805: despite the considerable Maratha connections that he had forged in the previous decades, the

---

[3] Letter from Capt. Jennings at Sasaram, received 12 Mar. 1764 (dated 20 Feb. 1764), FDSP.

gosain decided to throw his support to the Company under Richard Wellesley.

From the British perspective, the alliance with Anupgiri in 1803 was crucial: the Bengal Army under Lord Lake was making significant advances up the Gangetic Plain to Delhi, thus certifying itself as the major power in subcontinental politics and guaranteeing a supply of troops that would enable Britain to retain and extend its global influence in the early nineteenth century despite the loss of the American colonies.[4] Bundelkhand, rugged though it may have been, represented the strategically soft underbelly of the Gangetic north. By allying with Anupgiri, the British prevented the Maratha armies from using the region as a staging ground in the coming Anglo-Maratha conflict for attacks on Company supply lines passing through nearby Allahabad – particularly along the Jamuna, the northernmost extremity of the Bundelkhandi frontier. It may reasonably be argued that but for Anupgiri's complicity, the British Empire in India would have been a short-lived affair, at best constrained to Bengal. This alone would explain Wellesley's willingness to do business with a *gosain* warlord, a category of military entrepreneur so despised by his predecessors – and, as we shall see, by most of his contemporaries. Clearly Wellesley and Lake did not let questions of image concern them; what mattered was power, and Anupgiri possessed lots of it. There may have been an additional spin-off from the alliance: the "*Sanyasi* and *Fakir* Rebellion" was still under way in Bengal in the opening years of the nineteenth century; but suddenly, after the outbreak of Anglo-Maratha hostilities in 1803, we hear much less about rapacious *sanyasi*s and *fakir*s in Bengal. A clue to why this is so may be found in Francis Buchanan's cryptic observation in 1811, during his surveys of Bihar, that many *naga*s there had recently found employment "in the armies of the Rajas beyond the Yamuna."[5] It would seem that the *akhara*s in greater Bengal (which at the time included Bihar) saw the prospect of military employment in Anupgiri's pay and in the service of Company interests too lucrative to pass up. And for their part, those British officials who were put off by *gosain*s and their ilk (and as we shall see, there were still plenty of those around) were willing to swallow their distaste for the likes of Anupgiri for the services that only he and his men could provide in the rugged ravines of Bundelkhand.

In this chapter I examine the career of Anupgiri Gosain, in part to clear up the question of why he chose to turn his back on his considerable

---

[4] See C. A. Bayly, *Imperial Meridian: The British Empire and the World, 1780–1830* (London 1989) and, on military labor, Alavi, *The Sepoys and the Company.*

[5] Buchanan, *An Account of the Districts of Bihar and Patna,* vol. I, p. 375.

Maratha connections and join forces with the British, but also because a close investigation of Anupgiri and his men, particularly as they emerge in Company records, affords a level of detail on Indian warrior asceticism that has heretofore not been available. This is not, it should be noted, the first time Anupgiri has been harnessed to the task of better understanding Indian warrior asceticism. Toward the end of his life the historian, Jadunath Sarkar, was commissioned to do precisely this by the Mahanirvani Panchayati *akhara* of Allahabad – or, at the very least, to produce a book that celebrated both the *gosain* warlords and the *akhara*. The result, Sarkar's (and Nirod Bhusan Roy's) *History of the Dasnami Naga Sanyasis*,[6] may have been more than what the *akhara* bargained for. The first half (pp. 1–120), authored by Sarkar, is a description of the practices and structure of the Dasnami order, sectarian traditions regarding the remembered founder of the order, Shankaracharya, and the supposed (and in Sarkar's discerning opinion, highly suspect) origins and dates of the various military *akhara*s. The second half (pp. 121–284) was authored by Nirod Bhusan Roy of Santiniketan University, using Sarkar's notes and manuscripts and drawing extensively as well on Sarkar's earlier, if sporadic, discussion of Anupgiri (usually referred to by his *nom de guerre*, Himmat Bahadur) in his four-volume *Fall of the Mughal Empire*. While Roy's account is extremely valuable, particularly for its extensive use of Persian and Marathi manuscripts, he simply assumes the Shankaracharya-derived Hindu ascetic identity on the part of the protagonists. He does not investigate their asceticism, or seek to call into question what precisely Saiva warrior asceticism may have consisted of using Anupgiri and Umraogiri as examples if not exemplars. The result is that when Anupgiri and his associates are shown to be allying themselves with non-Hindus in the narrative, or turning against allies who were Hindu, the invariable implication is that these were yet additional instances of how these highly successful *gosain*s had let wealth and power deflect them from the straight and narrow of acceptable Hindu behavior. Anupgiri's alliance with the British at the end of his life, interestingly, is given extremely short shrift in Roy's account, perhaps because it is perceived as a betrayal of the nation as a whole. But as we shall see, Roy's is not the first nationalist reading of Anupgiri.

Another question not taken up by Roy, but central to my consideration of Anupgiri in this chapter, is why Anupgiri chose to think of himself, or at least present himself, as a maharaja in the last decade of his life, and

[6] Published by the headquarters of the Mahanirvani Panchayati *akhara*, Daraganj, Allahabad, n.d. (but probably mid-1950s). Sarkar is listed as the sole author on the title page, but it becomes evident early on that the work was a shared enterprise. This volume has been reprinted by the *akhara* on numerous occasions.

what that tells us about the ascetic institutions and ideas that ostensibly gave shape and meaning to his life in prior decades. As I will argue below, the presentation of Anupgiri as a great king, a *maharajadhiraj* – as part of a royal lineage passed down through biological, genealogical descent (which runs directly counter to the non-biological descent of ascetics) – was not simply a function of poetic license invented by the likes of the bard Padmakar. Anupgiri's pretensions to kingship should be interpreted, I argue, as a growing awareness on his part of the changes overtaking the political culture of India with the rise of the British. Despite his successes, or perhaps because of them, he seems to have sensed that the days of military entrepreneurship were numbered and positioned himself accordingly. If Anupgiri was able to read the modern handwriting on the wall, another question that emerges is whether he died before he could do much about it – whether, in fact, the crown he had fashioned for himself was meant to be hollow, and why.[7] The beginnings of an answer, I argue, are to be found by juxtaposing the voluminous Company record to sectarian tradition and bardic panegyrics dedicated to Anupgiri in the last decade of his life.

Bundelkhand, the setting for much of this chapter, has long acted as an important geo-cultural frontier between the Gangetic north and the Deccani south. This is a fact of great significance given the importance of frontiers in the germination of identity and political-military cultures.[8] Bundelkhand was well known by Anupgiri's time as the homeland of the Bundela Rajputs, a hyper-extended clan of warrior-chieftains that had established itself in the region by the sixteenth century, particularly during the reign of the Mughal emperor Akbar. Since that time, and with the assistance of the Mughal emperor, the Bundelas had claimed Kshatriya or royal status and linked themselves to the worship of Ram.[9] The Bundelas, however, were simply the most recent Rajput soldiering clan to dominate the region: earlier lineages that had settled in Bundelkhand included the Gahrwars and Pratihars (prior to the ninth century), the Chandels (by the twelfth century), and the Baghels (in the thirteenth century). Bundelkhand would gain added political notoriety in the eighteenth century as the tip of a wedge of rising Maratha influence in the north: in

---

[7] Cf. Nicholas Dirks, *The Hollow Crown: Ethnohistory of an Indian Kingdom* (Cambridge 1987), and the important argument that in the process of rendering Indian princes militarily dependent on the British and certifying their royal legitimacy so as to incorporate them symbolically into colonial rule, the British severed the multiple cultural and social interstices that linked society to the royal lineages, thus rendering Indian royalty politically impotent.

[8] For a comparative discussion of frontiers and "ethnogenesis" in India and Europe, see Talbot, "Inscribing the Other, Inscribing the Self," 700–710.

[9] Kolff, *Naukar, Rajput and Sepoy*, ch. 4, esp. pp. 120–123, 140.

the 1730s the Bundelas under Chhatrasal would ally themselves with the *peshwa*, Bajirao I, and thereby establish Bundela independence from the Mughal Empire; the price for Maratha assistance was one-third of Bundelkhandi dominions in the western portion of the province.[10] Bundela independence, and the Rajput martial pride that fueled it, would be undermined decisively by Anupgiri's own entrance into (and return to) the province in the 1790s. How that occurred, how the military asceticism in which Anupgiri thrived contrasted with the Rajput martial culture of Bundelkhand, and how Anupgiri would refashion himself as a result of his political and military ascendancy there, are themes to be explored in this chapter.

Anupgiri between empires

A native speaking of him, said he was like a man who in crossing a river kept a foot in two boats, ready to abandon the one that was sinking.

– Thomas Brooke, 4 June 1804

According to an early twentieth-century Hindi biography, Anupgiri was born in Bundelkhand around 1734 into a *Sanadhya* Brahman family from Kulapahar village.[11] Soon after his birth, his father died. His mother, left destitute, sold her two children, Anupgiri and his elder brother, who came to be known as Umraogiri, to Rajendragiri Gosain of Moth in Bundelkhand, who made them his *chela*s. We know nothing of Anupgiri's childhood and adolescence, aside from a quaint and probably apocryphal story that when not engaged in guru-*seva* (serving the guru) he spent his time playing with clay soldiers, ordering them about in mock campaigns. Consequently, it is said, Rajendragiri arranged for his martial training. Indeed, little is known of Rajendragiri himself. According to the late eighteenth-century poet Man Kavi, he was descended from a long line of Saiva gurus and rose to military and political prominence after receiving

---

[10] On the rivalries in Bundelkhand, a useful background is given in Tapti Roy, *The Politics of a Popular Uprising: Bundelkhand in 1857* (Delhi 1994), pp. 78–82. For the Maratha incursions into the north generally in the eighteenth century, see Stewart Gordon, *The Marathas, 1600–1818* (Cambridge 1994), ch. 5.

[11] The stories of Anupgiri's childhood are described by Bhagvandin in his introduction and notes to Padmakar's eulogistic ballad, *Himmatbahadur Virdavali*, esp. pp. xix–xx; see also vv. 44–45, p. 7. Bhagvandin does not indicate the sources upon which he based his treatment of Anupgiri's life. The ballad, which begins with an extensive panegyric and then describes the battle of Anupgiri and Arjun Singh in 1792, itself does not provide biographical details of this sort. Possibly Bhagvandin had gathered up legend and lore from descendants in Bundelkhand. I discuss Bhagvandin and his Hindu nationalist sensibilities later in this chapter; the religious semantics of Anupgiri's birthplace is taken up in greater detail in chapter 5.

a boon from an apparition of the guru of his guru's guru.[12] John Baillie, who figures prominently in this chapter and in the fate of Anuupgiri and his *gosains* generally, relates a different and more mundane tale. Rajendragiri had originally been a respectable banker of Jhansi but had, as a result of "some disturbances [that] arose between the people of Rajinder Geer and certain turbulent persons," abandoned his property and shifted to the village and fortress of Moth, about forty miles to the east. After rebuilding the fortifications there, Rajendragiri began committing depredations against lands held by Naru Shankar, who ruled Jhansi on behalf of the *peshwa*. Eventually Naru Shankar expelled Rajendragiri from the place, whence the *gosain* crossed the Jamuna and entered the service of the Nawab of Awadh.[13] Whatever the truth of Rajendragiri's origins, his shift north in 1751 occurred simultaneously with (and largely enabled) Safdar Jang's gradual alienation from the Mughal aristocracy and the concomitant rise of Awadhi regional autonomy.[14] For Anupgiri and Umraogiri, service with the heirs of Safdar Jang – and Shuja-ud-Daulah in particular – represented a springboard to a succession of direct and indirect alliances with virtually all the major players of north Indian politics in the latter half of the century, including the Marathas Mahadji Shinde and Ali Bahadur, the Mughal Emperor Shah Alam, the Jat prince Jawahir Singh, the Persian adventurer Najaf Khan, and, of course, the expansionist British under Governor-General Richard Wellesley.[15]

If there is a recurring theme in the *gosains*' careers up to 1790, it is that they not only outwitted but also outlived many of the princes for whom they ostensibly worked. Perhaps because of this fact, not to mention their obscure origins, they (and particularly Anupgiri) seem to have been reviled at one time or another by almost every major political figure

[12] Lala Bahadur Bhatt, "Anupa Prakash" (1894), MSS Hin. D.9(b), OIOC, London, fol. 1f (this is an 1870s' rendering of Man Kavi, "Anupa Prakasa" (1791–1792), MSS Hin. D.9[a]). See the introduction for a retelling of this episode. According to Man Kavi, Rajendragiri's guru genealogy was as follows: Sadanandgiri, Ankargiri, Narsinghgiri, Sotamgiri (of Anantpur), Bhimgiri, Santoshgiri, Sobhagiri, Narharnathgiri, Manohargiri, Chandangiri, Narayangiri, Sanathangiri, Dhyangiri, Rajendragiri.

[13] The Soobadar of Jhansee to Baillie, enclosure no. 4 in Baillie to Edmonstone, no. 1 of 26 Feb. 1807 (dated 10 Feb. 1807), Bengal Political Consultations (hereafter BPC), OIOC. The *subadar*'s narrative matches more or less (minus any details about banking) with that of William Irvine, the nineteenth-century historian and Persian linguist, who held that Rajendragiri seized by force the area around Moth (east of Jhansi) in 1745 and came into possession of 114 villages there; see W. Irvine, *A History of the Bangash Nawabs of Farrukhabad, from 1713 to 1771 A.D.* (Calcutta 1879), p. 79.

[14] See Srivastava, *The First Two Nawabs of Awadh*, pp. 214–215, 227–236.

[15] In addition to Sarkar (Roy), *History of the Dasnami Naga Sanyasis*, pp. 123–261 (based on a combination of Persian, Marathi, Hindi, and English sources), a good summary (based mostly on Company correspondences) is P. N. Bhalla, "The Gosain Brothers," *Journal of Indian History* 23, 2 (August 1944): 128–136.

with whom they came into contact. Even the unorthodox appearance of their soldiers came in for severe criticism on occasion: in the battle of Panipat (January 1761), when Shuja ud-Daulah faced the Marathas, the Afghan Ahmad Shah Abdali, Shuja's main ally, was so taken aback by the spectacle of the unclothed troopers with whom he was indirectly allied, that "He prudishly lectured Shuja on the impropriety of unrestrained kafirs, naked in front and behind . . . parading and lounging in front of Muslims, and ordered them removed to a distance from his camp."[16]

A more revealing case is that of Jawahir Singh, the Jat ruler of Bharatpur who employed Anupgiri and Umraogiri in the mid-1760s. Suspecting the gosains of intriguing with the Marathas while encamped on the banks of the Chambal in Malwa, Jawahir Singh ordered an assassination attempt on Anupgiri and Umraogiri under the cover of darkness.[17] Also in the Jat service at this time, and probably responsible for poisoning Jawahir Singh's mind against the gosains, was Ramakrishna Mahant, a powerful Vaishnava bairagi[18] commander of Jaipur and chela of the well-known Balanand Swami. The brothers would elude the wrath of the Jat and eventually have the last laugh on both Jawahir Singh and his bairagi commander: Anupgiri would dismantle part of a pavilion honoring the Jat king on the outskirts of the Vaishnava pilgrimage center of Mathura and use the materials for the construction of a ghat at Vrindaban to commemorate his own name.[19] (The insult here to Jawahir Singh requires no elaboration. The affront to Ramakrishna Mahant and his bairagis is only discernible in the context of the acrimonious rivalry between armed Saiva and Vaishnava ascetics that, from at least the seventeenth century, had erupted into violence and bloodshed – particularly at large pilgrimage festivals held periodically at alternating locations in the north and west.[20] Indeed, according to sectarian traditions connected to both Vrindaban and Galta, near Jaipur, Vaishnava ascetics are said to have armed themselves in the first place in order to respond to attacks by Saiva ascetics

---

[16] Ghulam Ali Khan Naqawi, 'Imad us-Sa'adat (Lucknow 1864), p. 84, translated in Barnett, North India between Empires, pp. 56–57. Barnett notes that the directness of the original Persian does not allow a printable translation; Roy's rendering in Sarkar, History of the Dasnami Naga Sanyasis, p. 158, is a tad closer to the original: "how could the Kaffirs have so much liberty as to walk with their things and buttocks exposed (peshopas barhana Kardah) before the Moslems." In any case, the gosains did comply with Abdali's request, moved their tents to a polite distance, and, notwithstanding the Durrani affront, acquitted themselves well on the battlefield.

[17] See Roy in Sarkar, History of the Dasnami Naga Sanyasis, pp. 174–175.

[18] An ascetic term describing Vaishnavas, analogous to gosain, meaning "bereft of emotion."

[19] See F. S. Growse, Mathura: A District Memoir (Allahabad 1882; reprint New Delhi 1993), pp. 307–308.

[20] See James Lochtefeld, "The Vishva Hindu Parishad and the Roots of Hindu Militancy," Journal of the American Academy of Religion 42, 2 (Summer 1994): 593–598; and Pinch, "Soldier Monks", pp. 154–156.

in Ayodhya at the end of the seventeenth century,[21] and as I note in the introduction, the memory of Anupgiri's affronts to Vaishnava ascetics lives on. Hence the architectural contribution of the Saiva Anupgiri to the predominantly neo-Vaishnava sacred topography of the Mathura–Vrindaban region would surely have occasioned remark.) To add injury to insult, in 1776 Anupgiri would undermine a renewed Jat-Vaishnava alliance (in the form of Naval Singh and his successor Ranjit Singh – not to be confused with the Sikh Ranjit Singh of the Punjab – and their Jat troopers, on the one hand, and Balanand and his 12,000 *bairagi* soldiers, on the other) by attaching himself to the rising star of the Persian adventurer Najaf Khan in Delhi, who was gaining in influence with and control over the Mughal emperor, Shah Alam. Since 1773 Najaf had been engaged in a series of protracted engagements in and around Dig against Naval Singh and Balanand; Anupgiri's arrival in the Delhi–Dig environs with his massive force, estimated now at about 20,000 horse and foot, would tilt the scales in this war decidedly in Najaf's favor, both vis-à-vis the Jats and with respect to imperial politics. As Jadunath Sarkar and Nirod Bhusan Roy put it, "as the star of Anupgiri rose, that of Balanand set."[22]

The rise of Anupgiri's star in and around Delhi beginning in the late 1770s was countered by its declining altitude in Awadh, partly as a result of the machinations of the English residents at Lucknow. Company officials reviled the *gosains* and doggedly strove to distance them from the service of Nawab Asaf ud-Daulah. Part of their distaste was due to the ongoing skirmishes with similarly accoutered *sanyasis* and *fakirs* in Bengal during the latter part of the eighteenth century. But much of it had to do with British apprehensions about the "undue" influence (and mischievous intentions) of the *gosains* in north Indian affairs. John Bristowe, the Resident at the court of Lucknow from 1775 to 1783, lost no opportunity in turning the young Asaf against the *gosains*, despite (or, given the dynamics of the subsidiary alliance, precisely because of) the fact that they commanded a major component of the Awadhi

---

[21] See Richard Burghart, "The Founding of the Ramanandi Sect," *Ethnohistory* 25, 2 (Spring 1978): 130. But see also the detailed examination of the historical evidence regarding Vaishnavas in Galta by Monika Horstmann, "The Ramanandis of Galta (Jaipur, Rajasthan)," in Lawrence Babb, Varsha Joshi and Michael Meister (eds.), *Multiple Histories: Culture and Society in the Study of Rajasthan* (Jaipur and New Delhi 2002), pp. 141–197.

[22] On Anupgiri's alliance with Najaf Khan and its ramifications for the Jats and Balanand, see Sarkar (Roy), *A History of Dasnami Naga Sanyasis*, pp. 187–193 (the quote is from p. 193). According to Roy, Balanand "quitted the service of the Jat Rajah presumably after the fall of Dig and entered the service of the Jaipure State." The account here is confused somewhat by the tendency of the author to refer to both Anupgiri and Balanand's followers as "*gosains*."

army.[23] James Browne, Warren Hastings' envoy to the Mughal emperor, Shah Alam, in the mid-1780s, took an even stronger disliking to Anupgiri, distrusting him so completely that he deputed two spies to observe and report on the *gosain*'s every movement and conversation.[24] Similarly Anderson, the resident with Mahadji Shinde in 1784–1785, when Shinde was introducing himself into north Indian politics around Delhi, viewed any attachment on his part with Anupgiri in the most negative terms and expressed himself to Shinde accordingly.[25] In retrospect, Shinde may have wished that he had followed Anderson's advice when it came to the *gosains*, since the Maratha warlord would boil over with hate for Anupgiri in the late 1780s – as recounted in the introduction to this book.

English distrust of Anupgiri would persist right through the time of Wellesley's alliance with the warlord in 1803. This is best captured in the private letters of Thomas Brooke, second judge of the Court of Appeal in Banaras, to Major M. Shawe, secretary to Wellesley, in 1804. Brooke fancied himself an amateur spymaster and dabbled in local intelligence gathering;[26] he very much sought to ingratiate himself with the Governor General by offering up through Shawe advice on Bundelkhand affairs, emphasizing, in particular, his dim view of Anupgiri (notwithstanding the fact that the Company had already joined forces with the *gosain* in Bundelkhand in the previous year). In a letter of 4 June 1804, unaware of Anupgiri's death on the previous day, he observed:

Himmut Behadhur is not to be trusted, by the inhabitants of every class he is detested, and whilst he stays in Bundelcund we can never prosper. A native speaking of him, said he was like a man who in crossing a river kept a foot in two boats, ready to abandon the one that was sinking. I suspect him as being the cause which has given the *Kiladar* [fort commander] of Calinger dissatisfaction. He finds it I believe profitable to fish in troubled waters; were all at peace, the nature of his jagheer might be enquired into. I am misinformed if it does not exceed by the double his estimation of it.[27]

---

[23] Letters from Bristowe to Calcutta, received 24 Jul. (undated), 11 Sep. (dated 22 Aug.), 8 Nov. (dated 11 Oct.), and 20 Nov. (dated 4 Nov.) 1775, Bengal Secret and Military Consultations (hereafter BSMC), OIOC, serve as sufficient examples. On the political and military dimensions of the relationship with the British residents at this time, see Barnett, *North India between Empires*, chs. 3 and 4.

[24] Bhalla, "The Gosain Brothers," 130. Bhalla notes Hastings' own cognizance of Browne's distrust of Anupgiri, and the extent to which that distrust invariably tainted the intelligence that his envoy transmitted to Calcutta.

[25] See, in particular, Anderson to Hastings, received 19 Feb. (dated 1 Feb.) 1785, BSMC; cf. Bhalla, "The Gosain Brothers," 131.

[26] Bayly (*Empire and Information*, p. 148) remarks that Brooke "was given to superabundant conspiracy theories" and describes how on one occasion he was duped by an Indian informant seeking to garner rewards for fabricated information.

[27] "Correspondence of Thomas Brooke at Benares with Major M. Shawe, Secretary to Lord Wellesley, 1803–1805," Add.MSS 37,281 (Manuscripts Reading Room, British Library, London), fols. 228b–229f. Though he uses the term "jagheer," Brooke refers

The censorious view of Anupgiri evinced by Indian and British observers has seeped into twentieth-century writing on the *gosain*'s exploits. Jadunath Sarkar, in his *Fall of the Mughal Empire*, resorted to such terms as "faithless", "unscrupulous", and "selfish" to describe him. According to Sarkar, "Himmat Bahadur lacked personal courage and bore a low character for his faithfulness [sic] and love of secret intrigue." Remarking on Anupgiri's reaction to being brushed aside by Shinde in 1785–1786 after the *gosain*'s usefulness had run its course in inserting the Maratha into Delhi politics, Sarkar notes: "He [Anupgiri] began to spit venom in his rage and vexation and tried his sole weapon of treachery and intrigue for regaining his ascendancy in the state by spiting Sindhia."[28] Even the more sympathetic P. N. Bhalla (1944) felt compelled to apologize in his narratives for the "lack of loyalty or fidelity" for which the *gosain*s were allegedly "notorious."[29] In their defense, however, the moments when the *gosain*s seemed to succumb to treacherous impulses can easily be interpreted in their favor as responses in kind to acts of bad faith on the part of their patrons and allies. Their disaffection from Awadh in 1775–1776 should be understood in large part as the result of Bristowe's influence over the new and inexperienced nawab, Asaf ud-Daulah; the "venom" which Anupgiri "spat" after being brushed aside by Shinde in 1785–1786 was understandable given that the Maratha's ascendancy in Delhi affairs was primarily attributable to Anupgiri's indefatigable efforts in the previous two years;[30] and, as we shall see, Anupgiri's decision to ally with the British in Bundelkhand after Ali Bahadur's death in 1802 can easily be understood as the result of his own well-founded apprehensions of Maratha intentions once the *peshwa*'s protection (in the form of Ali Bahadur) was no longer available, not to mention his own calculations of the inevitability of British supremacy following the signing of the Treaty of Bassein by the Maratha *peshwa* in late December of 1802.

The sanctimonious condemnation leveled at Anupgiri over the centuries contrasts sharply with the fact that all the major actors in north Indian affairs, including the British, sought alliance with him. Clearly,

to Anupgiri's Bundelkhandi *jaidad* (the right to collect revenues for the maintenance of troops) of twenty-two lakh rupees. See section below "Theatres of empire."

28 Sarkar, *Fall of the Mughal Empire*, vol. III, pp. 190–191. Sarkar's dim view of Anupgiri also reflects, it should be noted, the Marathi and Persian sources upon which much of his magnum opus is based, which were written from the perspective of Anupgiri's employers who sought to manipulate the *gosain* but were themselves manipulated by him.

29 Bhalla, "The Gosain Brothers," 135.

30 There was a history of bad blood between Shinde's lineage and that of Anupgiri: three decades before, while in the service of Safdar Jang, Rajendragiri's battle plan against Ahmad Khan Bangash had been leaked to the Afghan by Jayappa Shinde, Mahadji's brother. This betrayal cost the lives of an entire contingent of *gosain*s. See Srivastava, *The First Two Nawabs of Awadh*, p. 187.

Anupgiri and his men had much to offer a potential ally. One characteristic that recommended the *gosain* was the high quality of his horse and foot and their willingness to take inordinate risks in battle. This fact emerges time and again in Roy's blow-by-blow account of the exploits of Rajendragiri and his disciples: in 1751, when the *gosain*s came to the relief of the besieged Safdar Jang at Allahabad and set out on daily raids mounted on "excellent mares" to cause havoc in the Afghan camps; in 1753, again in the service of Safdar Jang, when Rajendragiri and his men repeatedly launched themselves into "the fire-vomiting" Mughal artillery in Delhi to engage the enemy in hand-to-hand combat; in 1759 when Anupgiri and Umraogiri mounted a surprise night attack that devastated a large, predatory Maratha encampment in Rohilkhand; again in 1764 when, in the service of Jawahir Singh, Anupgiri led a band of guerrilla fighters armed to the teeth into Delhi so that they could mount a covering artillery fire under which his cavalry could enter the city.[31] When the *gosain*s fought surprise attacks at close quarters and at night they were successful – so successful that rumors circulated about their magical invincibility.[32] By contrast, when they were involved in contests that pitted massive armies arrayed against each other on an open plain in the light of day, they fared poorly – in part because allied armies were as likely as not to engage in treacherous behavior when the *gosain*s were in the picture. Prominent examples of the latter include Rajendragiri's defeat by Afghan forces at Chilkiya in 1752, Anupgiri's defeat by Hindupat at Tindwari in Bundelkhand in 1762, and again Anupgiri's failure to break through the English lines at Buxar in 1764.[33]

  Whether on horseback or on foot, *gosain*s were employed to best advantage as guerrilla soldiers and in small, surprise early morning raids over city walls and into enemy encampments. As I have suggested in chapter 2, this kind of military service conformed well to the slave culture implicit in Saiva warrior asceticism, where hundreds and even thousands of men would be inculcated from youth in the complete submission to and incorporation in the social world of the *akhara*, at the head of which stood the master/commander.[34] Another feature Anupgiri brought to bear in attracting allies was what British officials would deride

---

[31] Sarkar (Roy), *History of the Dasnami Naga Sanyasis*, pp. 127–128, 156–157, 171–172; Srivastava, *First Two Nawabs of Awadh*, p. 235.

[32] For example, Srivastava, *First Two Nawabs of Awadh*, p. 235.

[33] Sarker (Roy), *History of the Dasnami Naga Sanyasis*, pp. 133–136, 161–162, 164–165. It would appear that Anupgiri was aware of the tactical deficiency of his forces, since he would engage in the 1790s with a European adventurer, John Meiselbach, to train his infantry according to European drill. I return to this point below.

[34] An ethic of servitude was not restricted to *gosain*s and *naga*s; it is evident in the *ghulam-shahi* ("imperial slave") component of the Durrani Afghan army in the eighteenth century. See Gommans, "Indian Warfare" 270–273.

as "intrigue." In this he shared an important characteristic of his six-teenth and seventeenth-century predecessors, the *yogi* lords described in chapter 2. Anupgiri possessed a seemingly endless supply of intelligence and his abilities as a diplomat, go-between, and a negotiator of payments to avoid military confrontation were proverbial; as such, he was emblem-atic of the class of men described by Kolff that constituted the grease between the cumbersome gears of the alliance-seeking states.[35] He was employed repeatedly in this regard by Shuja in overtures to Shinde in the early 1770s, and by Najaf in negotiations with various Jat clans and Jaipur in the late 1770s and early 1780s. By the mid-1780s, following Najaf's death, he began bringing these talents to the fore as a free agent in and around Delhi, eventually facilitating Shinde's own ascendancy with the Mughal emperor. Anupgiri's ready access to intelligence is not surpris-ing since he was, as a *gosain*, institutionally tied to a web of Dasnami institutions that crisscrossed the subcontinent – a glimpse of the depth and breadth of which, for Bihar and eastern Uttar Pradesh, can be had from Francis Buchanan's extensive surveys of those territories in the early nineteenth century.[36] As Cohn, Kolff, and Bayly have all noted, the infor-mation web possessed by ascetics had proved useful in facilitating trade and banking in the seventeenth and eighteenth centuries, so that some of the most influential trader-financiers of the Gangetic north by 1780 were *gosains* with soldiering connections.[37] Significantly, *gosain* traders

---

[35] These were talents that he perfected in Najaf Khan's service, which served him well in the treacherous political and diplomatic landscape of the Delhi–Agra–Jaipur triangle in the late 1770s and early 1780s. See, e.g. Sarkar (and Roy), *History of the Dasnami Naga Sanyasis*, pp. 193–206. See also D. H. A. Kolff, "The End of an Ancien Régime: Colonial War in India, 1798–1818," in J. A. de Moor and H. L. Wesseling (eds.), *Impe-rialism and War: Essays on Colonial Wars in Asia and Africa* (Leiden 1989), esp. pp. 45–46; for comparisons to Europe, see the discussion in Gommans, "Indian Warfare," 279–280.

[36] See, for example, *An Account of the Districts of Bihar and Patna*, vol. I, pp. 57–262; *An Account of the District of Shahabad, 1812–1813* (Patna 1934, reprint New Delhi 1986), pp. 51–151; and "An Account of the Northern Part of the District of Gorakhpur, 1812," MSS Eur.D.91–92, OIOC, fols. 139–345. Given the dates for the Shahabad account, the true dates for Gorakhpur are probably 1813–1814.

[37] The relevant arguments here are well known: Bernard Cohn, "The Role of the Gosains in the Economy of Eighteenth and Nineteenth Century Upper India," *Indian Economic and Social History Review* 1, 4 (1964): 175–183, notes that the privileged status of *gosains* and their command of subcontinental pilgrimage routes enabled them to extend and diversify their institutional savings into urban landownership, money-lending, and trade in luxury goods in urban centers throughout the north. Dirk Kolff, "Sanyasi Trader-Soldiers," *Indian Economic and Social History Review* 8, 2 (1971): 213–220, extends Cohn's argument to suggest that the monastic-business networks were also effective in supporting *naga* soldiering. Bayly (*Rulers, Townsmen and Bazaars*, esp. pp. 125–144) building on these arguments, emphasizes the importance of military-trader ascetic orders in facilitating commercial and financial links between the increasingly regional political economies of the eighteenth century. See also the discussion in Das Gupta, *Fakir and Sannyasi Uprisings*, pp. 24–27.

in the eighteenth century were perceived as a "neutral" or non-aligned group that served to maintain the subcontinental flow of capital despite the emergence of the regional polities that were inheriting the mantle of Mughal rule. Indeed, so adept were *gosains* in commerce, and so far-reaching their intelligence, that even Warren Hastings relied upon them in attempting to massage trading connections with Tibetans in central Asia in the 1780s.[38]

Gosain military entrepreneurship on the imperial frontier

Nagas [are] a description of rogues who from going quite naked[,] close shaved and well rubbed with oil are so slippery that no one can seize them while they force their way with a dagger pointed at both ends and held by the middle.
                                                    – Francis Buchanan, 1808[39]

An excellent picture of Anupgiri's operational style can be glimpsed from Bristowe's letters to Hastings and the Calcutta Secret Committee in 1775–1776, a period when the *gosains* were, largely as a result of Bristowe's influence in Lucknow, being maneuvered out of the nawab's service. Shuja had died early in 1775 and Asaf was under greater obligation to the British resident and troops than his father had been. In 1775 the *gosains* captured much of western Bundelkhand from the Marathas, from Kalpi (just southwest of Kanpur across the Jamuna) to as far as Jhansi, yielding about eleven lakh rupees of revenue. Since they already were obliged to the nawab for a large portion of Doab revenues, this latter conquest raised the total responsibility of the *gosains* to the treasury to somewhere between twenty-five and twenty-seven lakh rupees (one lakh equals one hundred thousand), which the nawab would reduce in early 1776 to eighteen lakh in lieu of payment of troops. In August of 1775 Anupgiri made an overture to Hastings through Bristowe, seeking an alliance and diplomatic protection. During an interview at that time between Bristowe and Anupgiri's *vakil* or legal representative, the *gosain* probed the possible British response if he were to become an independent force – particularly whether the Company would afford political insulation from the nawab. In response to pointed questioning, the *vakil* informed Bristowe that "his master consider'd himself independent and, as he has a large body of men of his own cast under his

---

[38] Sushobhan C. Sarkar, "A Note on Puran Giri Gosain," *Bengal Past & Present* 43 (Apr.–Jun. 1932): 83–87; see also Jonathan Duncan, "An Account of Two Fakeers, with their Portraits," *Asiatic Researches* 5 (1808): 45–46.
[39] Buchanan's Dinajpur Account, in Martin, *Eastern India*, vol. II, p. 517.

command . . . his excellency [the nawab] could not of himself reduce him."[40]

By October, Anupgiri had taken to discountenancing altogether the authority of passports issued by the nawab for travel through the Doab districts, and instead respected only those written by Najaf Khan; again Anupgiri (through his *vakil*) made renewed representations of friendship to Bristowe, which Bristowe rebuffed in short order. Not surprisingly, Anupgiri avoided Lucknow and Faizabad; Umraogiri, by contrast, paid Bristowe a personal visit in Faizabad and repeated the overtures of alliance that his younger brother had made in August. Umraogiri's own statements, paraphrased by Bristowe, are revealing: "[Umraogiri] desired me not to look upon him as upon the other officers of the nabob's government for he was no *Motteseddy* [clerk, bureaucrat] but a soldier . . . [H]e considered himself obliged to his sword for everything he held." By this time, the *gosains* had about 10,000 horse and 9,000 foot in their pay; more importantly, they were making preparations to bolster those numbers, fortify their positions, and win over the local notables in their districts to their cause. According to Bristowe, they were "daily collecting together ammunition, entertaining new troops, using their best endeavors to attach the Rana of Goad, the Rajas of Bundlecund and all the petty Rajas in the neighbourhood to their interest." The means by which they were attaching the local "petty rajas" to their interest was by demanding very low rents or no rent at all from the fall harvests, a tactic which Bristowe felt would surely produce positive results for the *gosains*. By December they were storing ammunition in forts in Bundelkhand, particularly Moth, their childhood home in the time of their guru, Rajendragiri.[41]

By February of 1776, Bristowe was lamenting the fact that the nawab had not dismissed the *gosains* earlier and put loyal men in charge of the revenues of their districts – though precisely how the nawab would have gone about this task is difficult to imagine given the general disarray of his forces at the time. In any event, Bristowe feared that "the *rubby* [*rabi*, or winter-spring] harvest will be collected by the Gofseynes and not a single rupee [will] come into the nabob's treasury." At this point the nawab, now encamped at Etawah in a show of force, agreed to reduce the revenue demand to eighteen lakh rupees instead of twenty-seven, allowing only slightly more than half of the *gosains*' claim that they had advanced fully seventeen lakh rupees to the troops under their charge. Bristowe

---

[40] Bristowe to the Board, letters received 24 Jul. 1775 (undated), 11 Sep. 1775 (dated 22 Aug. 1775), 8 Jan. 1776 (dated 13 Dec. 1775), and 8 Apr. 1776 (dated 1 Mar. 1776), BSMC.

[41] See Bristowe to the Board, letters received 8 Nov. 1775 (dated 11 Oct. 1775) and 8 Jan. 1776 (dated 13 Dec. 1775), BSMC.

also noted, importantly, that "the army of the Gofseynes is near Jansy, [and] They have on the spot not above seven or eight hundred horse and troop" – a significant reduction from the nineteen thousand cavalry and foot soldiers in the *gosains'* employ only six months earlier. The whereabouts of the remainder of their troops becomes clear in Bristowe's next major correspondence on the subject of the *gosains*, dated 1 March: the resident reported that not only had they paid to date only the meager sum of one lakh rupees to the treasury, but their "agents" had occupied the many small forts that dotted the region and refused to relinquish them despite orders to that effect by the nawab and despite Anupgiri and Umraogiri's attendance on the nawab at the time. Once the *rabi* revenues were collected (but not paid into the treasury), the *gosains* withdrew all their troops and artillery, and treasure, from the Bundelkhand forts and made preparations to assemble at a location unknown. Bristowe speculated that Etawah was their destination and had heard a rumor that 5,000 were at a place called "Akary"; he observed that, in fact, 1,500 soldiers joined the brothers at Etawah in the previous week and that they were armed and ready for action in case of a pre-emptory attack by the nawab himself.[42]

By early April Anupgiri dispensed with the charade of loyalty to the young nawab: he abandoned his Bundelkhand and Doab districts and openly joined forces with Najaf Khan who was laying siege to the Jat fortress at Dig near Bharatpur. With him he took "near nine thousand men of the *Seneass* [*sanyasi*] and other Hindoo casts." Bristowe would opine, characteristically, that "Nudjif Cawn will have little to boast of, from the acquisition of the Gossaine, who has never served a prince whom he did not betray." (Contrary to Bristowe's opinion, Anupgiri would remain loyal to Najaf up to the time of the Persian adventurer's death in 1782.) Meanwhile, Umraogiri was still encamped near the nawab at Etawah, and had with him between 3,000 and 4,000 men; they would soon follow Anupgiri. Together with Anupgiri's force, then, there were according to Bristowe's intelligence at maximum 13,000 men under the *gosain* banner. By late May it was clear to Bristowe that Anupgiri was using the revenues he had collected from his lately abandoned districts to cement his relationship with the cash-poor Najaf Khan, whose troops were rebellious for want of pay. In exchange, Najaf granted Anupgiri "certain lands" in the vicinity of Agra yielding twelve lakh rupees. In mid June, Bristowe reported that "The Gossaynes may have about twenty thousand men with him, out of whom about four thousand are cavalry,

[42] Bristowe to the Board, letters received 7 Feb. 1776 (dated 26 Jan. 1776) and 8 Apr. 1776 (dated 1 Mar. 1776), BSMC.

six thousand *sinassies* armed with nothing but spears and *tulwars* [swords], and the rest matchlockmen."[43]

There are two main points of interest in the above chronology. First, note should be taken of the varying strength of the *gosains*' forces between late 1775 and mid-1776. They begin with about 19,000 troops, most of whom they employ to collect the *rabi* revenue in their Doab and Bundelkhand districts, keeping less than 1,000 men for their personal guard. Then, as soon as the collections are complete, around late March, the troops begin to withdraw from the districts and reassemble; by early April Anupgiri sets off with 9,000 men "of the Seneass and other Hindoo casts;" Umraogiri has with him only 3,000 or 4,000. By mid June, however, their force is back up to about 20,000 again, 6,000 of whom are "poorly" armed *sanyasis*. What is interesting about these figures is (a) that they vary so markedly around harvest schedules, reflecting no doubt the high degree of permeability between soldiering and cultivation noted by Kolff;[44] and (b) that they seem to suggest that not all the men under Anupgiri and Umraogiri's command were *sanyasis* as such. This emerges with particular clarity in the remark by Bristowe that Anupgiri had set off for Dig with 9,000 men of "the Seneass and other Hindoo casts."

Second, emphasis should be placed on the language that Umraogiri used to describe himself at this time, which held for Anupgiri as well, namely, that "he was no Motteseddy but a soldier" and that "he considered himself obliged to his sword for everything he held." Increasingly in the eighteenth century the multiple strands of state service in India were bound to, or at least expressed in terms of, what were becoming closed caste identities – e.g., as *Brahman, Khattri, Rajput*, or *Kayastha* (the upper-case first letters are intended to suggest the increasingly closed, caste-bound nature of these identities). Umraogiri's assertion suggests that the *gosains* understood themselves to be not simply above bureaucratic service, but consciously and avowedly beyond simple caste categorization. To be a soldiering *gosain* was to be dependent on the sword only – akin to Sikh and Maratha identity in the early eighteenth century, or Afghan and Rajput identity in the sixteenth century.[45] The *khalsa* Sikh

---

[43] Bristowe to the Board, letters received 22 Apr. 1776 (dated 9 Apr. 1776), 13 Jun. 1776 (dated 30 May 1776), and 8 Jul. 1776 (dated 10 Jun. 1776), BSMC.

[44] Kolff, *Naukar, Rajput and Sepoy*, esp. pp. 3–17.

[45] An important point here is that while individuals seem to have been able to adopt the mantles "Afghan" or "Rajput" or "Maratha" (and the religious culture that went with those identities) with relative ease in the period before about 1700, after that date such terms gained political potency because they invoked increasingly elite, closed, military professional identities that could only be reproduced biologically. In addition to Kolff, *Naukar, Rajput and Sepoy*, see Gommans, *The Rise of the Indo-Afghan Empire*, and Gordon, *The Marathas*.

commitment to the symbol of the sword as a core component of community identity from 1699 onward is suggestive in this regard.[46] Not unlike the institutionalization of arms in the *Nanakpanth*, the continuation of *gosain* military culture that generated this supra-caste identity was cemented not by biological lineage and kin loyalty, but by the necessarily non-biological, corporate culture of the ascetic order. When Anupgiri and Umraogiri were sold as children to Rajendragiri, they were stripped of their Brahman coil, and ushered into a fluid, ambiguous – and symbolically dangerous – world beyond status, a world that prized only military ability, subcontinental mobility, and abject loyalty.

The *gosain* who would be king

From 1789 to 1802 Anupgiri was allied to the Maratha adventurer, Ali Bahadur. During that time they would devote themselves fully to the conquest of Bundelkhand. In addition to being the place where Anupgiri began his military-ascetic career, Bundelkhand was home to the Rajput descendants of Chhatrasal, who had thrown off the Mughal yoke and established, with Maratha aid, Bundela Rajput independence in the early eighteenth century.[47] As a result of Maratha assistance, Chhatrasal is said to have made over fully one-third of the province (the western portion including Jhansi, Moth, and Kalpi) to Maratha overlords. Over the course of the century, and during the 1770s and 1780s in particular, infighting between the various Rajput clans that descended from Chhatrasal, and between the various Maratha clans descended from Baji Rao's generals who exercised a claim on Bundelkhand revenues, and between the Marathas and the Bundelas generally, rendered Bundelkhand one of the most fractured provinces of the subcontinent (and given subcontinental politics in this period, this says a great deal). The peak of this infighting occurred in 1784, when nearly all the main Rajput lineage groups were arrayed into two parties and faced each other at the battle of Gathyaura (three miles east of Chhatrapur). In Bundeli folklore this moment is often referred to as the *Mahabharata* of Bundelkhand, and is said to have been

[46] W. H. McLeod, *The Evolution of the Sikh Community* (Delhi 1975), p. 13, observes that for Guru Gobind Singh (d. 1708) "the characteristic name of God was *sarab-loh*, the 'All-Steel'," and it is no accident that in the preparation for Sikh baptism the baptismal water is stirred with a two-edged sword. See also the many references to the sword in *Textual Sources for the Study of Sikhism*, ed. W. H. McLeod (Manchester 1984); and, more generally, Lorenzen, "Warrior Ascetics," for a theorization of the genesis of the Sikh *khalsa* or "army of the pure" in the seventeenth century as a phase of armed asceticism in Indian history.

[47] A concise summary is given in "Papers Relative to Bundelkhand," Add.MS 13,591 (Manuscripts Reading Room, British Library, London), fols. 1a–9a.

so ferocious as to have deprived the province of most of its brave warriors. A Rajput commander named Arjun Singh would emerge victorious in that contest. But despite that victory, and despite the fact that the province was pitted with gullies and ravines and dotted with massive fortresses set on rugged hillocks, most notably those of Jhansi in the west and Kalinjar in the east, the way was now open for the major powers – namely, the Marathas and the English – to make serious inroads into Bundelkhand. With Anupgiri and Ali Bahadur's entry into the province in 1790, it appeared the Maratha *peshwa* was making his move.

Anupgiri had faced the Rajput clans of Bundelkhand once before in his career, in 1762 when, while in the service of Shuja, he was soundly defeated by the forces united under Hindupat and chased out of the province. For a brief time in the 1770s he gained control of a large portion of western Bundelkhand, but this was wrested from him by Maratha overlords. Anupgiri's reentry into Bundelkhand with Ali Bahadur in 1790 brought him into direct conflict, for the second time, with the Bundela Rajput chieftains of that province. His second try was more successful than the first: in 1792 he defeated the pride of the Bundelas in Bundelkhand, Arjun Singh, the guardian of Bhakta Singh (a descendant of Chhatrasal) and commanding general of his army.[48] The victory was all the more significant in that it was Arjun Singh who had commanded the army under Hindupat (and Ghuman Singh) which had handed Anupgiri his inglorious defeat in 1762.

For Anupgiri the victory against Arjun Singh was more than strategically important: it was the moment that enabled him (and others) to begin referring to himself as "maharaja." This is reflected in the bardic poetry describing Anupgiri and his victory in 1792. The battle against Arjun Singh was commemorated in verse by Padmakar (the nom de plume of Pyarelal Bhatt), who would become in later years a well-known *rasika* poet of Bundelkhand, Mathura–Vrindaban, and eastern Rajasthan.[49] The epic poem he composed after the battle, entitled *Himmatbahadur Virdavali* (roughly translatable as "ode to the bravery of Himmat Bahadur"), was

---

[48] Bhagvandin, the editor of *Himmatbahadur Virdavali*, claims (p. xxxi) that Arjun Singh was a *panwar rajput*, which could mean that he was a member of the dominant *panwar* lineage centered in Ujjain and Malwa and heir to what Kolff calls the Rajput "great tradition", or that he belonged to the less prestigious *panwar* subgrouping within the extended Bundela clan. See Kolff, *Naukar, Rajput and Sepoy*, pp. 59, 121. The latter seems more likely, given that Arjun Singh's father was born and raised in northern Bundelkhand (Bhagvandin, in *Himmatbahadur Virdavali*, p. xxxi). In either case, the ethnographic marker would have signified a proud military heritage.

[49] On the *rasika*, or "school of sweet devotion," genre, see Bhagwati Prasad Sinha, *Ram Bhakti men Rasika Sampraday* [The Rasika Community in Ram Worship] (Balrampur 1957); and Philip Lutgendorf, *The Life of a Text: Performing the Ramcaritmanas of Tulsidas* (Berkeley 1991), pp. 310–321.

Padmakar's first major work and praised Anupgiri as a universal world conqueror or *chakravartin*:

Himmat Bahadur is a great king, incomparable in his excellent benevolence.
He is generous, brave, and compassionate, [but] to his amassed enemies he is death itself.

· · · · ·

He scorches his humbled enemies in their jungle hideaways.
He touches the poor with long-armed compassion during religious sacrifices.
He gives endowments to support dharma, and is the clothing that covers Hindu shame.
He is the embodiment of radiant splendor, but an insatiable demon when his anger is provoked

· · · · ·

He is as true to his word as Harishchandra, [and] is ever the source of bliss.
He is the enemy of sadness, constantly engaged in sacrificial rites.
The lamp of his own sect blazes radiantly, [he is] the most valiant protector of the earth.

· · · · ·

To the class of poets he is like the sun to the lotus, [and] is full of benign moral conduct.
He is extremely knowledgeable, [and] always puts forth a serene countenance.

· · · · ·

When he sees the needy he is compassionate, when destroying evil he is merciless.

· · · · ·

He is a remarkable horseman and an unsurpassed archer.
He chants Siva *bhajan*s with such excellence and equanimity – no one can compare.
Himmat Bahadur is a powerful king, his army's presence immediately destroys his foe.
His occupation is world conquest, he is notorious in the lands of his enemies.

· · · · ·

Now I'll sing of an army that all the *thakur*s [Rajputs] have heard of.
Near the massive Ajaygarh fort, united they are fearsome.
Whence the conch shell is blown, [can be seen] his mighty sword.
The incessant beat of the kettledrum scatters his enemies like so many snorting pigs.[50]

That Padmakar would compose this royal panegyric for a *gosain*, a class of person long vilified by the Bundela Rajputs, was all the more remarkable in light of the fact that, prior to joining Anupgiri's entourage

---

[50] *Himmatbahadur Virdavali*, pp. 2–8 (selections from vv. 3–50).

in 1792, the poet had served in the court of Anupgiri's Rajput opponent, Arjun Singh.[51] Bhagvandin, the modern editor of the poem, found this to be a particularly bitter pill to swallow. Steeped in the patriotic Hinduism that colored Hindi literary study in the first half of the twentieth century, Bhagvandin was at a loss to explain Padmakar's shift in loyalties, especially considering the many noble qualities that recommended Arjun Singh. His lengthy introduction concludes with the lament that Padmakar had not chosen to commemorate the Rajput's earlier victory against Anupgiri in 1762. His point-by-point comparison between the Rajput and the *gosain* is instructive:

1 – Arjun Singh was a Kshatriya, and a true Kshatriya. Himmat Bahadur was the son of a *Sanadhya* brahman beggar and the disciple of a thieving *gosain*. 2 – Arjun was a Kshatriya who was completely devoted to Kshatriya patriotism. Himmat Bahadur was a brave brahman and a *gosain* devotee of Siva who served the foreigner and the irreligious *yavana* [Muslim]. 3 – Arjun Singh never begged the assistance of anyone, he always fought with his own personal strength and helped others. Himmat Bahadur always sought the aid of others. 4 – Himmat Bahadur fought with his own self interest in mind, he wanted to establish his own state come what may. The villages and territories that Arjun Singh won in battle he always offered to his ward [Bhakta Singh], and if he had wanted he could have established a state at any time. 5 – Even on his deathbed Himmat Bahadur was engaged in trickery and deceit, which for a man of courage and honor is a great sin. One hears nothing of this sort concerning Arjun Singh. 6 – Himmat Bahadur was a kind of traitor to his country. Arjun Singh was innocent of this treachery. Indeed, because he fought against a traitor we can speak of him as a lover of his country. As a result of all these points, the name of Arjun Singh is accorded such great respect that Himmat Bahadur's name pales in comparison.[52]

Clearly, for those who knew of him by the early twentieth century, Anupgiri was something of an anachronism. Yet, because he was celebrated by a poet who would himself be held up as a rising star in the Hindi literary pantheon, Anupgiri could not be swept completely under the rug. He remained a problem, an occasionally recurring headache for those who would shape the patriotic Hindu nationalism that was crystallizing in north Indian literary and religious culture. There are additional indications of this. For example, for Sitaram, a retired Bihar government official who would go on to write an important history of Ayodhya in the 1920s, Anupgiri – as "Raja Himmat Bahadur Goshain" – was significant mainly for having ordered some of his *naga*s to kidnap a young *khattri* damsel of the town so that Shuja might satisfy his lustful urges upon her, thus sparking a Hindu rebellion among the *khattri* elite that was only quelled with the intervention of Shuja's mother.[53] Regardless

---

[51] Bhagvandin, introduction to *Himmatbahadur Virdavali*, p. v.   [52] *Ibid.*, xxxvi.
[53] Sitaram, *Ayodhya ka Itihas* (Prayag 1932), pp. 157–158. I have not come across any other mention of this event.

of its authenticity, the story is not all that surprising: as we will see from the following chapter, Anupgiri and Umraogiri had "many women" (see the following chapter) and their *gosain* entourages (described by early nineteenth-century British officials as "households") did include numerous female sexual slaves. What is remarkable is the communalist nature of the story, which seems to have had more to do with the politics of the early 1900s than any such event itself. In this, it is reminiscent of the sectarian memory of Thaneswar in 1567, recounted in chapter 1.

But I digress. Padmakar's decision to attach himself to Anupgiri's rising star in 1792 was based, no doubt, on hard-headed political calculations: Arjun Singh was no more, defeated and killed in battle (by the hand of Anupgiri himself, according to the poet's telling); the *gosain* was the most powerful military patron in the general vicinity. It is significant that Padmakar did not attach himself to Ali Bahadur instead. One reason must have been that Anupgiri was born in Bundelkhand. Another may have been that Ali Bahadur was probably a Muslim (despite being the grandson of the former *peshwa*, Bajirao I),[54] though it is hard to say to what degree he paid attention to such matters. He did refer to himself as a "nawab", which tended to indicate at least a leaning toward a more "Islamicate" culture if not Islam itself.[55] If so, he may not have been perceived as a likely patron for the "*vir-rasika*" style of commemorative verse that Padmakar was peddling. Whatever the outcome of such speculation, Padmakar's action was not only a recognition that Anupgiri was the real power in the province, but that Rajput supremacy in the region was at an end, humbled by a lowly *gosain*.[56] (As we shall see in chapter 5, Anupgiri and his *gosain* sensibilities may have offered additional attraction.)

---

[54] Given the fluidity on the ground when it came to religious identity in the eighteenth century, one should not read too much into the fact that his name was Ali. His father was the fifth son of Bajirao, named "Shamsher" Bahadur (b. 1734; "*shamsher*" is a Persian term, meaning sword); his mother was Mastani, a Muslim. When Bajirao brought her into the "royal" household, the fact of her religious identity (or at least background) caused a scandal. See R. D. Palsokar, *Bajirao I: An Outstanding Cavalry General* (New Delhi 1995), p. 53.

[55] "Islamicate" refers "not directly to the religion, Islam, itself, but to the social and cultural complex historically associated with Islam and the Muslims, both among Muslims themselves and even when found among non-Muslims." Marshall G. S. Hodgson, *Venture of Islam: Conscience and History in a World Civilization*, vol. I, (Chicago 1974), p. 59.

[56] Indeed, according to an independent Bundelkhandi telling (related in Bhagvandin, *Himmatbahadur Virdavali*, pp. xxxi–xxxii), the end of Arjun Singh's dominance had been predicted by a *sadhu* whom Arjun Singh used to wait upon in his youth, who prophesied that the Rajput would rise to great fame and win three important battles, only to be killed in the fourth (the battle against Anupgiri) by a member of Arjun Singh's clan. The contrast with Padmakar's assertion that Anupgiri himself killed Arjun Singh is significant insofar as it suggests that united Rajput dominance in Bundelkhand was under strain well prior to Anupgiri's arrival in 1790.

Emboldened by the victory against Arjun Singh, if not the praises heaped upon him by the likes of Padmakar, and enriched by the newly acquired revenues of a major portion of Bundelkhand, Anupgiri began to make alterations in his military capabilities that were commensurate with his newly acquired vision of himself as maharaja. Most notably, soon after 1792 he engaged the services of a European adventurer by the name of John Mieselbach.[57] By the turn of the century, Mieselbach was commanding approximately 6,000 of Anupgiri's footsoldiers and, in conformity with the *gosain*'s wishes, training them according to European infantry drill – adding to the general British apprehension at the time that "The emigration of Europeans to the Military service of the Native princes is become very frequent and if not checked may produce very serious consequences in the improvement of their discipline."[58] By 1800, Anupgiri had under his command approximately 10,000 men,

[57] Some sources identify Mieselbach as recently arrived Dutch soldier of fortune and nephew of the chief of the Dutch Chinsurah Factory, one Mr. Heining (see "Papers Relative to Bundelkhand," fol. 5b; and "Correspondence of Thomas Brooke," fol. 205f); other sources identify him as a Dane (most notably, Bhalla, "The Gosain Brothers," 136). This latter impression is probably based on the fact that he retired to the Danish settlement at Serampore after 1807 and died there in 1819. Hence W. R. Pogson, *History of the Boondelas* (Calcutta 1828, reprint New Delhi 1974), p. 126, erroneously quotes Mieselbach's obituary in the *Government Gazette* (Calcutta, 28 Oct. 1819) to the effect that Mieselbach was a Dane. (Bhalla also cites the *Government Gazette* obituary, but does not misquote it.) The notice in the *Government Gazette*, in fact, makes no mention of Mieselbach's nationality, but does note that "the Danish flag was hoisted half mast high on the occasion" of his death. According to "Papers Relative to Bundelkhand" (fol. 5b) and "Correspondence of Thomas Brooke" (fol. 205f), Mieselbach signed on with Anupgiri and Ali Bahadur in 1792–1793, just after the battle against Arjun Singh, to assist in the subsequent siege of Kalinjar. Mieselbach's career path is further confused by the assertion in the *Government Gazette* that he was in the service of Anupgiri for eighteen years. Mieselbach remained in Anupgiri's employ until 1804, the year of the *gosain*'s death; if the *Government Gazette*'s (admittedly loose) assertion is to believed, he entered Anupgiri's service in 1786 – when Anupgiri was involved in intrigues in Delhi. However, the earliest mention of Mieselbach that I have seen is in official Company correspondences of 1795, according to which the adventurer and four other Europeans (two of whom, named Arnott and Bellasis, were said to have been in Company employ) entered Bundelkhand in March to seek their fortunes in the service of Indian princes (see C. W. Malet, Resident at Poona, to John Shore, Gov-Gen., no. 4 of 17 Apr. [dated 25 Mar. 1795], Bengal Political Consultations (BPC), OIOC; and W. Palmer, resident with Scindia, to Shore, no. 18 of 12 Jun. 1795 [dated 28 May 1795], BPC). They first appeared to join with the Bundela Rajputs of Kalinjar, led by Dhokub Singh; however, they soon found themselves completely outnumbered and surrounded by Ali Bahadur's men. Mieselbach, not unwisely, decided to switch sides (G. T. Cherry, Resident at Lucknow, to Shore, no. 16 of 21 Sep. 1795 [dated 10 Sep. 1795], BPC). The fate of Bellasis and the other three men is unknown, but it is likely they followed suit. This, then, appears to be the route by which Mieselbach eventually came to Anupgiri's attention.

[58] Palmer to Shore, no. 18 of 12 Jun. 1795 (dated 28 May 1795), BPC. According to one observer ("Papers Relative to Bundelkhand," fol. 96f), however, this fear was misplaced with regard to Mieselbach: "For some years past one battalion has been placed under the charge of Mr. Misselbeck, but has not yet attained any great degree of discipline."

4,000 of whom were "Nangas of the tribe of Sunnasee, 1500 Chundelas [Rajputs], and the remainder Hindoostanees."[59] In other words, Rajputs from one of the main rival clan lineages in the region were willing to serve under Anupgiri's standard. Also significant is the term "Hindoostanee," which referred to a more general and diverse peasant base.[60] By 1803 the Rajput force under his command had swollen to nearly 4,000 cavalry, "said to be very superior in equipment to the cavalry generally maintained by the native princes of India." In addition, he possessed "three Battalions of infantry, disciplined and armed in the European manner, under the command of Colonel Meeselback and of a considerable number of irregular infantry [presumably *nagas*] carrying matchlocks and otherwise seriously armed." The opinion of the political agent who provided these estimates, Graeme Mercer, was that "these troops constitute the most effective force at present existing in Bundlecund."[61] What Anupgiri had achieved in terms of Bundelkhandi political culture with the defection of Padmakar in 1792, he would achieve in military-cultural terms with the increasingly successful recruitment of Bundelkhandi (if not Bundela) Rajputs and peasants in the following decade.

But did Anupgiri in the mid-1790s really believe himself to be a king, a *chakravartin* in the classical Indo-Persian mold, as Maharaja Himmat Bahadur Anupgiri Gosain? The following sections, outlining the mechanics of his alliance with the British and their entry into the politics of Bundelkhand, throw some doubt on the extent to which he committed himself fully to such visions of royal grandeur despite Padmakar's high-flying rhetoric. Even in the mid-1790s, much prior to British involvement, there are strong indications that Anupgiri's pretensions to kingship were simply that: a conscious pretending. Following his defeat of Arjun Singh, Anupgiri and Ali Bahadur commenced the piecemeal settlement of the province, ostensibly on behalf of the *peshwa*. This involved the bringing to heel of the numerous petty and not-so-petty Rajput chieftains of the province, which, as the decade progressed, seemed to be an endless task – symbolized by Ali Bahadur's lengthy (and ultimately unsuccessful) siege of the fortress at Kalinjar by the turn of the century, and complicated by constant raids against their combined forces. As early as the mid-1790s, rumors began to swirl in Bundelkhand that "Himmut Buhadoor instigated these depredations [of local Rajput chieftains against Ali Bahadur's forces], in order to secure his own power, which he apprehended would

---

[59] "Papers Relative to Bundelkhand," fols. 95b–96f.
[60] See the discussion of polity and peasantry in Kolff, *Naukar, Rajput and Sepoy*, esp. p. 27.
[61] G. Mercer to Edmonstone, Shahpore, no. 9 of 3 Mar. 1804 (dated 5 Sep. 1803), BSPC. The description of Anupgiri's troop strength also comes from this letter.

be terminated by the establishment of tranquillity [sic]: for while he commanded the troops, his sway was absolute, and that of Ulee Buhadoor nominal; and it is probable that the dread of the Peeshwa alone deterred him from usurping the government of the province."[62] It appears that Anupgiri had not deemed it politic to abandon the tested methods of military entrepreneurship.

Theatres of empire

On the 14 August 1802, Ali Bahadur died, "afflicted with a dropsy" while engaged in the siege of Kalinjar.[63] If there had been any doubts about Anupgiri's stature as the main player on the ground in Bundelkhand up to this point, this event removed them. Later British estimates put his force at this time to be "a body of eight or ten thousand Nauguh or matchlock and rocket-men of a peculiar tribe generally known in the northern provinces of India."[64] Ali Bahadur left behind a brother, Ghani Bahadur, and two sons – Shamsher Bahadur (mentioned in the above quotation), a youth of sixteen years, at the time resident with his mother in Poona, and Zulfikar Ali Bahadur, a child of two years, at Kalinjar with his mother. Ghani Bahadur, realizing that he held a preeminent position among Marathas in Bundelkhand with the death of his brother, so long as his brother's elder son remained in Poona, immediately placed the two-year-old Zulfikar Ali on the throne and declared himself regent. To confirm the coronation of the child-nawab (who was held on the lap of his uncle during the ceremony) on 23 August, the assembled nobles offered *nazars* (gifts in cash) of varying amounts; significantly, Anupgiri presented eleven gold coins – nearly double that presented by Ghani Bahadur himself. In so doing, Anupgiri sent a message to all concerned: first, that he considered himself the main figure of authority in the province (and was acknowledged as such by his main rival and friend, Ghani Bahadur[65]); and second, that while he may have sanctioned Ghani Bahadur's action, he understood Zulfikar Ali's status to be independently legitimate according to the announcement made at the last moment by Begum Chanda Bhani, the mother of the young child, that "as soon as the

---

[62] Pogson, *History of the Boondelas*, p. 121 n. 105.

[63] Wm. Scott, Resident at Lucknow, to N. B. Edmonstone, secretary to Government, Secret, Political, and Foreign Departments, no. 26 of 16 Sep. 1802 (dated 26 Aug. 1802), BPC.

[64] John Baillie to Mercer, no. 319 of 7 Mar. 1805 (dated 13 Aug. 1804), BSPC.

[65] The amicable relations that prevailed between Anupgiri and Ghani Bahadur is reflected in a letter of late August 1803 from Anupgiri to Ahmuty, no. 15B of 3 Mar. 1804 (undated, but received 26 Aug. 1803), BSPC.

eldest son [Shamsher Bahadur] of the late Nawaub should arrive from Poona he should be placed upon the *Musnud*."[66]

Not surprisingly, few in Bundelkhand or beyond the province trusted Ghani Bahadur's intentions – least of all his nephew, Shamsher Bahadur, who set off early in the following year, with the *peshwa*'s blessing, for Kalinjar. Meanwhile Anupgiri, in January of 1803, instructed Mieselbach to probe the possibility of opening negotiations with the British through Richard Ahmuty, the Collector at Allahabad.[67] Intelligence reached Anupgiri in June of that year that in tandem with Shamsher's approach, Daulatrao Shinde was plotting an ambitious joining of forces with Jaswant Rao Holkar and Raghuji Bhonsle so as to mount a series of pre-emptive strikes against the Company in the Gangetic Plain, using Bundelkhand as a staging ground. If successful, such a combination would have dramatically changed the scope of the coming Anglo-Maratha war, essentially opening up a third and much more damaging theatre of operations all-too-close to the heart of British supply lines at Allahabad. Anupgiri promptly instructed Mieselbach to forward his intelligence to Ahmuty, who immediately passed it on to Calcutta.[68] In early

---

[66] "Translation of a paper of intelligence from the camp of Zoolfekaur Ally Khan son of the late Nawaub Ally Behaudur, dated the 24 and 25 of Rubbee us Sauni, corresponding with the 24th and 25th of August 1802," no. 28 of 16 Sep. 1802, BPC. My interpretation of this event differs substantially from that of Bhalla, "The Gosain Brothers," 133–134, who (citing the same source) felt that Anupgiri conspired with Ghani Bahadur in placing the child on the throne. Rather, I would argue that Anupgiri was hedging his bets, waiting to learn of the intentions of the *peshwa* and to see whether Shamsher Bahadur would depart for Bundelkhand so as to stake his claim. The passage cited above continues thus, in case there is any doubt about Anupgiri's intentions: "The Rajah replied [to the statement by the Begum Chanda Bhani] that since, were the Musnud to continue vacant, the military and civil affairs would get into confusion, he consented to the measure of placing Zoolfekar Ally on the Musnud, until his eldest brother should arrive from Poona, who would then assume the reins of Government."

[67] Meiselback to Ahmuty, no. 160 of 22 Jun. 1803 (dated 1 Jun. 1803), BSPC. Mieselbach notes Anupgiri's concern in this letter that nearly six months had passed since his earlier communication with Ahmuty and the Governor General, which would place the original contact in January.

[68] In Mieselbach's words: "While I was setting [sic] with the Rajah an express by couple of Jassoos arrived from Dowlut Row Sindia's camp with a letter for the Rajah and one for Gunnee Behadur. The contents of which was as follows: That Dowlut Row, Holkar, and Nagpore Rajah all combined together that they will have an army about 200,000 horsemen, and 12 brigades to face the English Army, and Nizam's now at Deccan, and that he had sent off about 5,000 pindarrahs and 3,000 horsemen with six battalions: Jasseby to stay with the Bhow to be in readiness in that Quarter, and also had wrote to General Peron to combine with the Seiks and that the Rajah and Gunnee to be in readiness in this part should the war be proclaimed, so that it is his wish to face and attack the English from all Quarters. I asked the Rajah if I might write to you on this subject, his answer to me was that I might do as I please, but not in his name; I asked him for the copy of the letter he had received but he declined giving it fearing it might be sent by the English to Dowlut Row Scindia." Meiselback to Ahmuty, no. 160 of

July, Shamsher Bahadur arrived at Kalinjar, supported by 5,000 horse in the service of Holkar; on the morning of 23 August the young nawab made his move, attacking and plundering Ghani Bahadur's camp, and seizing him and his family. At about the same time he demanded, as a show of submission, a payment of 9,000 rupees from Anupgiri. The *gosain* refused, and held his ground from a nearby encampment in plain view.[69]

Shamsher Bahadur's aggressive tactics in dealing with his own uncle, whose poisoning he ordered in due course,[70] in combination with the reported approach of Maratha troops in the form of *pindari*s (cavalry units known for ruthless pillaging and rapine) from the south and west, seems to have convinced Anupgiri that his most secure future lay with the British. He commenced negotiations with them in earnest. For their part, the British recognized that Anupgiri's intelligence had proven particularly valuable in confirming suspicions that had arisen in the Calcutta council regarding Daulatrao Shinde's intentions in north India, and had enabled them to take crucial preventive diplomatic and strategic measures;[71] more importantly, Wellesley and Lord Lake deemed the benefits of acquiring the de facto control over Bundelkhand (a portion of which had been granted to them on paper by the Treaty of Bassein) and depriving that province from the Marathas to be too advantageous an opportunity to let slip by. Wellesley instructed Ahmuty (representing the Governor

22 Jun. 1803 (dated 1 Jun. 1803), BSPC. He would add in a letter to Ahmuty the following day, 2 Jun. 1803 (no. 161 of 22 Jun. 1803, BSPC), that "5,000 pindaries with 3,000 Horsemen are ordered to join Himmut Bahadur, and Gunnee Behadur is commanded by Durram Row Pundit to begin to make depredations into the Company's dominions." For the lay of the land in 1803, see Sarkar, *Fall of the Mughal Empire*, vol. IV, pp. 221, 235.

69 William Scott, resident at Lucknow, to Edmonstone, no. 45 of 22 Sep. 1803 (dated 27 Aug. 1803), BSPC; "Translation of a paper of intelligence from Kalinjer dated the 4th of Jemmadi ul Awul 1218 Hij. corresponding with the 23rd of August 1803," no. 46 of 22 Sep. 1803, BSPC. For Shamsher's arrival, see Ahmuty to Edmonstone, no. 25 of 28 Jul. 1803 (dated 11 Jul. 1803), BSPC.

70 See Pogson, *A History of the Boondelas*, p. 123.

71 See, for example, Edmonstone to Colonel Collins, resident with Shinde, no. 163 of 22 Jun. 1803 (dated 18 Jun. 1803), BSPC. An intriguing measure of the precise value of that particular item of intelligence to British strategic designs during the middle months of 1803 is afforded by correspondence between Mieselbach and Governor General Barlow five years later, following the announcement that the pension of the Dutch adventurer had been set at a paltry 300 rupees per month. In a breathtakingly long letter to Barlow, dated 4 Jun. 1807 (no. 7 of 19 Jun. 1807, BPC), Mieselbach lamented the amount, compared it unfavorably to remunerations whilst in Anupgiri's employ, and enumerated the many considerable services he had rendered to the Company, first and most important among which was the intelligence that he transmitted in June of 1803 regarding the amassing of Maratha troops. Barlow promptly issued his opinion, no. 11 of 19 Jun. 1807, that Mieselbach's service was indeed unusually remarkable and hence he was due a revised pension of 1,000 rupees per month.

General) and Graeme Mercer (who represented the Commander-in-Chief, Lord Lake) to come to terms with Anupgiri regarding a mutually agreeable arrangement for the "transfer" of Bundelkhand to British control, with the understanding that the *gosain* and his troops would aid in the "settlement" of the province. It quickly emerged in negotiations with Anupgiri, whom the British were careful to address henceforth as either Raja or Maharaja Himmat Bahadur and whose principal representative throughout this phase was Colonel Mieselbach, that his main objects were threefold: (1) the granting of a very large Bundelkhandi *jaidad*, or the right to collect revenues for the maintenance of troops, the longevity of which was contingent upon the duration of military operations against "refractory" Bundela and Maratha warlords in the province; (2) the eventual grant of a *jagir* in the Ganga–Jamuna Doab in the vicinity of Sivarajpur on the south bank of the Ganga above Kanpur; and (3) the release of his brother Umraogiri from the confinement he had been subjected to as a result of his entanglement in the Vizier Ali conspiracy of 1799.[72]

The second and third points were readily complied with; the first, which the British ultimately did agree to, was a matter of some revealing discussion and subsequent contention, the details of which are worth recapitulating. During preliminary negotiations with Ahmuty and Mercer, the suggestion was made that, rather than have Anupgiri support the troops on his *jaidad*, the Company pay them directly, and that any temporary land grant in Bundelkhand be made to the *gosain* for the private and personal maintenance of him and his family. Not surprisingly, Mieselbach – on Anupgiri's behalf – rejected this suggestion on the grounds that "the Rajah would consider this proposal as a wish on the part of Government speedily to dismiss his troops, and to annihilate his own influence and power in the province."[73] The suggestion was withdrawn and the *jaidad* granted; a formal agreement was drawn up on 4 September 1803,[74] so that British troops could legally enter the province to join forces with Anupgiri's men, thus commencing the piecemeal "conquest" of the province. The task that confronted them was essentially two-fold: on the one hand, to deal with the Maratha warlords in the province, particularly Shamsher Bahadur, preferably by coming to some formal treaty arrangement, but, failing that, to overcome them by brute force; and, on the other hand, to subjugate the various and sundry Bundela chieftains and *kiladars* (fortress-commanders) who had to date resisted

[72] Edmonstone to Mercer, no. 2 of 3 Mar. 1804 (dated 22 Jul. 1803), BSPC.
[73] G. Mercer to Edmonstone, Shahpore, no. 9 of 3 Mar. 1804 (dated 5 Sep. 1803), BSPC.
[74] The terms are spelled out in a *wajib al-arz* (protocols guiding the treaty) of that date, no. 11 of 3 Mar. 1804, BSPC.

the *gosain*'s authority. Anupgiri assured them that all this would be readily accomplished. His *jaidad*, meanwhile, included fairly well-accessible estates (*mahals*) to the west and east of the Ken River in eastern Bundelkhand producing about twenty lakh rupees, slightly more than half of which had formerly been granted to him by Ali Bahadur.[75]

Joint military operations seemed to get off to a positive start, with Ahmuty recommending a thirteen-gun salute to honor Anupgiri upon his arrival on 16 September in the quickly erected British encampment at Teroa.[76] Ahmuty estimated at this time that "About four thousand horse and 8,000 foot have accompanied Himmat Behadur exclusive of the three battalions [about 1500 infantry] under Mr. Meesselback with 25 pieces of ordnance of different calibres" – the increased numbers reflecting Anupgiri's burgeoning troop responsibility under the new and improved *jaidad*. However, it very soon became apparent – especially to Colonel Powell, commanding British forces in Bundelkhand – that Anupgiri neither maintained a sufficient force in the field nor was he overly anxious to engage the enemy, despite repeated assurances from the *gosain* to Powell of his ability to deal expeditiously with the recalcitrant warlords in the province. Powell concluded that Anupgiri was "a crafty old Hindoo" and was propagating the view that the British detachment in Bundelkhand was little more than "a tool in his hands to execute whatever objects he may have in view."[77] Ahmuty, meanwhile, had been compelled through illness in early October to take a recuperative leave from the province and could therefore no longer act as a check on the *gosain* (one almost suspects Anupgiri's occult hand here); he would be replaced in early November by Mercer's protégé, Lieutenant (soon promoted to Captain) John Baillie, representing Lord Lake.[78] Anupgiri took advantage of the temporary absence of any political check on his authority to further curtail the size and operational range of his forces. Consequently Powell complained in late October "that a much higher degree of importance had been attached to the force and military abilities of the Rajah, than they are either of them, entitled to."

---

[75] The exact value of the *jaidad* would be a matter of contention, with estimates ranging from eighteen to twenty-two lakh rupees. See esp. no. 103 of 17 May 1804, BSPC, a schedule of the *mahals* and their contested values drawn up by Captain John Baillie.

[76] Ahmuty to Mercer, no. 17 of 3 Mar. 1804 (dated 15 Sep. 1803), BSPC.

[77] Powell to Mercer, no. 60 of 3 Mar. 1804 (dated 15 Oct. 1803), BSPC.

[78] Ahmuty to Mercer, no. 28 of 3 Mar. 1804 (dated 28 Sep. 1803); and Ahmuty to Mercer, no. 30 of 3 Mar. 1804 (dated 5 Oct. 1803), BSPC. In the first letter, from Banda, Ahmuty informs Mercer (who is near Agra with Lake) of his illness and begs to be allowed to return to Allahabad; in the second, written from Allahabad, Ahmuty informs him of the increased fever and his decision to return to that city of his own accord. For a different explanation of Ahmuty's illness, grounded in Saiva sorcery, see Buchanan's Gorakhpur account, in Martin, *Eastern India*, vol. II, p. 493. On Baillie's appointment, see Mercer to Bailie, no. 79 of 3 Mar. 1804 (dated 20 Oct. 1803), BSPC.

Despite Anupgiri's boasts of cutting Shamsher Bahadur's forces to pieces at his leisure with a mere 1,500 men, Powell claimed to have "the most undoubted proof of his real sentiments being the very opposite to those he professed, [namely,] that he would never have dared with his whole united force to have met Shumshere."[79] Powell also reported that the people of Bundelkhand preferred the British to the *gosain*: "As one instance of the confidence which the natives already testify towards the English, I shall only mention that the ryotts and zemindars of the Rajah's own villages come to sollicit [sic] me for safe guards for protection against the Rajah's people, although he himself is present."[80] The British colonel would also lose no opportunity in apprising Mercer of Anupgiri's true troop strength, which he estimated (in late October 1803) at no more than 3,000 or at most 4,000 horse, and between 1,000 and 1,500 foot (under Mieselbach's command)[81] – a far cry from the 12,000 men, both horse and foot (exclusive, it will be recalled, of Mieselbach's battalions, said to be attending the *gosain* alone in mid-September).

Baillie, soon after his arrival in the province, agreed substantially with Powell's assessment of Anupgiri's delaying tactics.[82] By April of 1804 he suspected that the *gosain* "has not now a single man more than he had under Allee Buhadur" when his revenue assignment was only worth twelve lakh rupees.[83] Baillie elaborated in an official letter to Mercer in early June, just two days after Anupgiri's death: "I could never induce him to submit a muster roll of his forces, nor could I form a correct estimate of their number, from the circumstance of a large proportion of them being constantly employed in the collection of the revenue of his Jaidad, but I have now reason to be convinced that the number of his cavalry has never exceeded two thousand five hundred and that these with the three battalions of infantry of 1500 men commanded by Colonel Meisilback and occasional levies of matchlockmen employed in the collections have uniformly constituted the whole of the rajah's force."[84] A month later, in early July, having "obtained particular muster rolls of the troops, cavalry

---

[79] Powell to Mercer, no. 85 of 3 Mar. 1804 (dated 22 Oct. 1803), BSPC.

[80] Powell to Major Armstrong (with Lake at Agra), no. 75 of 3 Mar. 1804 (dated 18 Oct. 1803), BSPC. In a letter to Mercer the previous day, no. 76 of 3 Mar. 1804, BSPC, he had noted that "they one and all refuse to have any kind of settlement transacted through the medium of the Rajah."

[81] Powell to Mercer, no. 85 of 3 Mar. 1804 (dated 22 Oct. 1803), BSPC. Powell's open disdain for Anupgiri would earn him (Powell) a formal censure from Wellesley (Edmonstone to Powell, no. 88 of 3 Mar. 1804 [dated 16 Nov. 1803], BSPC).

[82] His assessment of Anupgiri's intentions can be seen in Baillie to Mercer, paragraph 8 of no. 126 of 3 Mar. 1804 (dated 18 Nov. 1803), BSPC.

[83] Private letter from Baillie to Mercer, included as no. 109 of 17 May 1804 (dated 5 Apr. 1804), BSPC.

[84] Baillie to Mercer, no. 234 of 21 Jun. 1804 (dated 6 Jun. 1804), BSPC.

and infantry in the service of the Rajah with accounts of the collections of Revenue in the several districts of the Jaidad and of the disbursements and balances due to the troops," Baillie concluded that "the whole of the military establishment mentioned by the late Rajah Himmut Behadur consisting of cavalry, artillery and infantry, regular and irregular, including the battalions of Colonel Meiselbach and the Garrisons of forty eight forts, amounts in number to nine thousand eight hundred and fifty men, of which two thousand six hundred are denominated "mounted cavalry," fifteen hundred, regular infantry under the command of Colonel Meiselbach and the remainder Golandazes or matchlockmen."[85]

Baillie's "volume of accusations against the Rajah"[86] stemmed in part from disagreements over the exact revenue value of the *jaidad* – Baillie insisting that it was worth fully twenty-two lakh rupees, Anupgiri assessing it at eighteen lakh and demanding an adjustment of two lakh more.[87] To exacerbate matters, Baillie learned from Mieselbach that Anupgiri was in fact squeezing twenty-four lakh rupees out of his *jaidad*, and that "the districts which he set apart for the Company could never be collected without the whole of the force in the country being employed in it during the Government of Allee Buhadur."[88] Baillie added, however, a more serious charge, namely, that while Anupgiri put up a facade of enmity and aggression against the Bundela Rajputs, he secretly colluded with them to prolong the military operations in the province, thereby extending the term of his *jaidad* collections: "The Boondelahs are not so submissive, because they have the Rajah behind the curtain to support them,

[85] Baillie to Mercer, no. 237 of 9 Aug. 1804 (dated 9 Jul. 1804), BSPC. Baillie noted also that approximately a quarter of the *jaidad* had been assigned (illegally, from the official point of view) in the form of *jagir*s "as a provision for his brother Rajah Omrao Geer, for his nephews the sons of Omrao Geer and for others of his principal Sirdars." Since these monies were being spent on excessive "household expenses" and therefore ran counter to the mandate of the treaty (especially when it came to the *jagir* for Umraogiri), which stipulated that the *jaidad* was to be strictly applied to the maintenance of troops, Baillie recommended the immediate resumption of that portion of the revenue assignment. There is no hint in this official communication that these *jagir* assignments might have bolstered Anupgiri's overall troop strength, though it seems likely that they would have done.

[86] Private letter from Baillie to Mercer, included as no. 109 of 17 May 1804 (dated 5 Apr. 1804), BSPC.

[87] Baillie to Mercer, no. 102 of 17 May 1804 (dated 23 Mar. 1804), BSPC.

[88] Private letter from Baillie to Mercer, no. 109 of 17 May 1804 (dated 5 Apr. 1804), BSPC. Baillie adds that Anupgiri, to add insult to injury, "went on collecting in the districts which he assigned to us." According to Baillie, when Mieselbach had informed Ahmuty of these sundry details, presumably before the latter's illness removed him from the province, Ahmuty's reply was, "We must please the Rajah until we get rid of the Nawab [Shamsher Bahadur]." This introduces the possibility that Ahmuty was colluding with Anupgiri in some loose manner, and that he had departed the province under the cover of fever so as to escape the glare of Powell's discomfiting inquiries.

tho' he is obliged to disavow his support and sometimes even to attack them." It is not entirely surprising, then, that in early June, just before Anupgiri's timely demise, Company troops in the field accidentally fired upon *gosain* cavalry during a routine nighttime march, supposing them to be the enemy.[89]

Anupgiri's influence over the Bundelas affords yet another vantage point from which to discern the complex military alignments in which *gosain*s (and the British) specialized. When Anupgiri had signed the treaty with Wellesley in early September 1803, a large contingent of *naga*s (between 2,000 and 3,000 men) formerly serving in Ali Bahadur's forces had chosen to sign on with Shamsher Bahadur's army, suggesting a division of loyalties among *gosain*s. After Shamsher had capitulated to British power in October of 1803, those *naga*s had then joined forces with the Bundela chief, Raja Ram, one of the main fonts of resistance to British power in Bundelkhand, and later still entered into the service of the commanders of the forts of Kalinjar and Ajaigarh, themselves besieged by Anupgiri's own forces.[90] Despite the appearance of hostility between Anupgiri's forces and these renegade *naga* battalions, it is likely that this was simply part and parcel with Anupgiri's technique of having a foot in many boats at once. What better way to prolong hostilities – and the collection of *jaidad* revenues – than by controlling a large share of the pieces on the Bundelkhandi chessboard? As if to confirm this point, the "disaffected" *naga*s made repeated overtures to Baillie through both Shamsher Bahadur and Kanchangiri, Anupgiri's senior *chela*/commandant, between November of 1803 and August of 1804. In late August – well after Anupgiri's death – Baillie finally decided that it would be politic to take one large contingent of about 2,000 *naga*s up on their offer: he advanced their *sardar*s (commanders) a small payment through Kanchangiri, placed them under the command of Mieselbach, and sent them off to defend against predatory raids by their former paymaster Raja Ram and other Bundelas in the vicinity of Ajaigarh, Kalinjar, and, later, in the ravines near Banda. According to Mieselbach, "the Gosayns conducted themselves very gallantly."[91] These men would remain in British service for nearly seventeen months, until early February of 1806, when Baillie would make up their arrears in pay (to the tune of just under 110,000 rupees, substantially less than the twelve lakh or 1.2 million proposed by Kanchangiri on their behalf) in exchange for "an

[89] W. D. Fawcett to J. Gerard, no. 93 of 21 Jun. 1804 (dated 1 Jun. 1804), BSPC.
[90] Baillie to Mercer, no. 319 of 7 Mar. 1805 (dated 13 Aug. 1804), BSPC.
[91] The quote is from Meeselback to Baillie, Camp Thakoora, no. 340 of 7 Mar. 1805 (dated 12 Dec. 1804), BSPC; see also Baillie to Mercer, no. 339 of 7 Mar. 1805 (dated 13 Dec. 1804).

obligation upon their part, not to join the Boondelas, nor to appear as an armed body in this province, on any future occasion." In the meantime, their numbers had swollen to 3,279 men. Baillie, who ordered a muster on 1 February 1806 to ascertain their exact number, chided Kanchangiri for "having improperly increased the number of the naugas, during my absence from the province [for much of 1805], by inviting several bodies of this class of men from distant parts of the country, and secretly enrolling them in the division of naugas."[92]

For their part Wellesley and Lord Lake had, as early as October 1803, come to the same conclusion as Baillie and Powell regarding Anupgiri. They determined that given the *gosain*'s intrigues and the more public failure on his part to raise the requisite number of troops, it would be better to simply renegotiate the treaty agreement of the previous month and "resume" the *jaidad*, granting him instead the *jagir* at Sivarajpur.[93] Though Baillie seemed to get some indication that such proceedings would not be altogether offensive to Anupgiri, he deemed it politic to bide his time until the *gosain*'s duplicity and inaction were openly known to all and the military conditions in the province were more favorable.[94]

---

[92] This brings to mind Francis Buchanan's observation in Bihar five years later (see the introduction to this chapter) that most of the *naga*s in Bihar had decamped the province to serve in the "armies of the Rajas beyond the Yamuna." For the details of the muster and dismissal from British service of these *naga*s, see Baillie to Edmonstone, no. 37 of 13 Feb. 1806 (dated 3 Feb. 1806), BSPC. The muster roll affords some interesting details: the *naga* battalions described themselves as "Joona Akarah" and "Annunda Akarah"; the top ranking cavalry commanders (eight from the *anand akhara* and four from the *juna akhara*) were called "Srimunthoo" (from the honorific *sri* plus *math* [this term does not lend itself to easy translation: *math* can refer to the ascetic order in an abstract sense, or to the physical structure that houses ascetics; since these were highly mobile *naga*s, the more abstract connotation is called for; thus a *srimathu* may be taken to signify a *svami*, one who embodies the very essence of the order]), each receiving 150 rupees per month; lower-ranking commanders were called "Muhuntoe" or "Mohuntee" (from *mahant*, or guru/abbot), receiving anything from twenty to sixty rupees per month. The *anand akhara* possessed twenty-eight *mahanti* cavalry officers earning sixty rupees per month and 120 earning twenty rupees per month; the *juna akhara* possessed twelve and forty-seven respectively.

[93] Mercer to Ahmuty, para. 6 of no. 44 of 3 Mar. 1804 (dated 8 Oct. 1803), BSPC.

[94] Baillie to Mercer, para. 8 of no. 109 of 3 Mar. 1804 (dated 9 Nov. 1803), and no. 176 of 3 Mar. 1804 (dated 14 Dec. 1803), BSPC. In the December letter, for example, he notes: "his [Anupgiri's] conduct upon this occasion has added to the many proofs which I possess; and which have been submitted to His Excellency the Commander in Chief as the grounds of my entire conviction, that exclusively of the assistance in the department of supply which the presence of the Rajah has afforded, and of the services of Colonel Meiselback at present in the southern districts of Boondelcund, our connexion with this chieftain will in no degree secure to us the beneficial effects which might have been justly expected from the favourable terms which were originally granted to him.

"His failure on the present occasion however, will furnish an additional instrument of the success of my negociation hereafter for the relinquishment of his Jaidad, and I shall not fail to apply it in the manner but calculated to accomplish His Excellency's views."

Mercer encouraged his protégé in this regard, observing candidly that "My friend Himmut has certainly taken care of himself, and the sooner he is looked after the better; whenever you think it advisable to notice his laxity in the service, and deficiency of troops publicly, a letter to the purport you formerly mentioned will be sent by the Commander in Chief [Lord Lake]; but His Excellency says, that it would not be right for him to write it without some public grounds."[95] Before Baillie could put any of these plans into action, however, he was stopped short on 2 June 1804 by news of Anupgiri's failing health. Sensing time to be short, Baillie rushed to Anupgiri's side for a final interview. He would recall later that day that the *gosain*'s "faculties and powers of utterance are almost entirely exhausted[;] . . . on the occasion of my visiting him this morning, he made an exertion for the purpose of requesting *my protection of his infant son* which I thought would have proved fatal."[96] Anupgiri died the very next day, 3 June 1804.[97] By that time, or just afterwards, his brother Umraogiri had swept into camp; he immediately deputed two of his *chela*s with fifty horsemen to conduct Anupgiri's body to the banks of the Ganga for interment at Sivarajpur, "agreeably to the directions of the deceased."[98]

It is at this stage that Baillie came into his own and earned, as they say, the "approbation of His Excellency the Most Noble the Governor General." His description of the sequence of events is revealing:

5.   . . . as *the solemn declaration of the Rajah to me on the day before his death left no doubt of his intention of bequeathing all his property and rights to his only son*, an infant now in camp[,] and the avowed inclination of the several sirdars pointed to this boy as the only heir of his father's property, and successor in the command of the troops whose rights they were disposed to acknowledge, I considered it to be indispensably [sic] to the important object of preventing tumult and disorder in the camp, to evince my own acknowledgement of those rights by a formal act

---

[95] Private letter from Mercer to Baillie, included as no. 108 of 17 May 1804 (dated 30 Mar. 1804), BSPC.

[96] Baillie to Mercer, no. 137 of 5 Jul. 1804 (dated 2 Jun. 1804), BSPC. This letter is catalogued out of order, and should precede no. 232 of 21 Jun. 1804. Emphasis added.

[97] What caused Anupgiri's death is not entirely clear. Baillie does not discuss the question. That he may have been the victim of an assassination plot is certainly possible. When discussing Anupgiri with some descendants, who will remain anonymous, it was quietly alleged, first, that he had been killed by the British; others later alleged that he had been poisoned by one of his women.

[98] Baillie to Mercer, no. 232 of 21 Jun. 1804 (dated 4 Jun. 1804), BSPC. In this letter Baillie makes reference to a private letter to Mercer of 3 June, which unfortunately is not included in the consultations volume. Given the events that immediately transpired and Umraogiri's later accusations about Baillie and Kanchangiri's manipulations (see the next chapter), this is probably a very revealing letter, which probably explains its absence in the proceedings.

and declaration vesting the command of the *Rosala* [cavalry] on Rajah Nerinder Geer [the child] till the pleasure of Government should be known.

6.   I proceeded accordingly to the camp of the late Rajah this morning and having summon'd Rajah Omrao Geer and all the principal sirdars to his tent, I placed the boy upon his father's musnud and directed all the chiefs to make the customary presents and acknowledgements of his authority which were offered unanimously and with the greatest readiness and satisfaction by all, in my presence excepting Rajah Omrao Geer who departed from the tent with some appearance of displeasure.

7.   The general character of Rajah Omrao Geer [Umraogiri] and the limited influence which he possesses over the troops of his deceased brother, give me no ground to apprehend any ill effect from his dissatisfaction at the measure which I was induced to adopt and I have every reason to hope that my endeavors to prevent any new commotion or disturbance in the country upon this critical and arduous occasion, will prove to be completely successful and that no material difficulty will occur in the accomplishment of any objects which His Excellency the Commander in Chief or the supreme Government may have in view respecting the Rajah's Jaidad.[99]

In sum, Baillie performed precisely the same role in the usurpation of authority upon Anupgiri's death that Anupgiri had performed at the death of his old ally, Ali Bahadur, in 1802. The fact that the tool in each coronation drama was a two-year-old child only underlines the symmetry of the occasions. Baillie was probably aware of the parallel, since he had been active now in Bundelkhand for almost seven months and had very quickly upon his arrival there comprehended the political and military lay of the land. Baillie's main source of intelligence on the factions within the *gosain*'s entourage was Colonel John Mieselbach,[100] the European adventurer that Anupgiri had engaged in 1795 and entrusted with the most sensitive mission in the *gosain*'s career – the negotiations for alliance with the British in Bundelkhand.

One may ask, however, who played the role of Ghani Bahadur, the scheming uncle of the child nawab in 1802 who had appointed himself regent, during the upheaval in the *gosain*'s camp in June of 1804. The answer becomes apparent in subsequent correspondences: perched firmly between the child rajah Narindragiri and the British agent, John Baillie, was the *gosain*, Kanchangiri, Anupgiri's most able and trusted *chela*, who would later manage Anupgiri's estate on behalf of the child. Not surprisingly, Baillie describes him as a "well behaved person" who "is said to

---

[99]   Baillie to Mercer, no. 232 of 21 Jun. 1804 (dated 4 Jun. 1804), BSPC. Emphasis added. One need only compare the italicized portion of this extract with that in the previous paragraph to appreciate Baillie's remarkably dexterous powers of interpretation in the service of Company interests.

[100]   Baillie to Mercer, para. 5 of no. 234 of 21 Jun. 1804 (dated 6 Jun. 1804), BSPC.

possess considerable wealth"; moreover, he was "the principal manager of the late Rajah's affairs and the person to whom the care of his property was uniformly entrusted."[101] Kanchangiri also happened to have a reputation for ruthless efficiency when it came to collecting revenue from recalcitrant *zamindar*s. Three years earlier, he had attracted the notice of the British garrison in Allahabad by pursuing a Brahman landlord (who had reneged on a debt to Anupgiri) into Awadh, capturing him and his children, burning the house in which he was hiding and killing several women and children therein.[102] After Anupgiri's death, Kanchangiri figured prominently in subsequent discussions over the resumption of the *jaidad* and the relocation of Narindragiri and the *naga* corps to the *jagir* near Kanpur in March 1806. More immediately, however, there was still the pressing matter of paying Anupgiri's troops; Kanchangiri proved instrumental in guaranteeing that the various captains formerly in Anupgiri's service, who controlled the many forts and collected revenue in the *jaidad mahal*s, in fact, directed that revenue not into their own pockets but to the rank and file soldiery. And regarding that soldiery, particularly Anupgiri's cavalry, Baillie would experience a remarkable change of heart, observing that though admittedly few in number, "they are far superior in appearance to any troops of this description which I have seen, in the country [Bundelkhand], and that under the superintendance of an European officer, they would be found of the highest utility in any situation in which their services might be required."[103]

Within three days of Anupgiri's death, Baillie's coup was complete. He reported to Mercer that,

whatever may have been the principles or motives by which the conduct of the late Rajah was guided, and the objects to which the services of his troops were directed during his life time, I have not observed the smallest trace of disaffection or disorder in his camp since his death, and on the contrary, the conduct and appearance of all his relations, principal sirdars, and troops have been such as to inspire me with the fullest confidence in their attachment to the British Government, and in their ready submission and obedience to its will and commands.[104]

Anupgiri's "widow" replied to Baillie's letter of condolence by stating that "His [Anupgiri's] children, his relations, his servants and his troops who have been supported during a period of sixty years by troves of his

---

[101] Baillie to Mercer, no. 72 of 5 Jul. 1804 (dated 21 Jun. 1804), BSPC.

[102] Lt. Col. A. Kyd to Col. W. Scott, no. 71 of 24 Jun. 1802 (dated 23 Jul. 1802 [sic., should be 1801]), BSPC.

[103] Baillie to Mercer, no. 234 of 21 Jun. 1804 (dated 6 Jun. 1804), BSPC. As we shall see in the next chapter, Baillie would toy with the idea of retaining some 500 cavalrymen for his personal guard in 1806. His superiors in Calcutta quashed the idea.

[104] *Ibid.*

money are now the faithful servants of the British Government and ready to obey their commands."[105] This was not hyperbole: Anupgiri's *naga* and non-*naga* horse and foot, under the command of Kanchangiri and Mieselbach respectively, continued to serve the Company as irregulars (similar to James Skinner's "yellow boys") until the end of February 1806 in the work of subjugating the province.[106] Some were anxious to remain in British service after that date: as early as late June 1804, while Baillie was beginning to probe the question of resuming the *jaidad* and taking direct control of Bundelkhand – and less than three weeks after Anupgiri's demise – several of the commanding officers among the *gosain*s intimated to him "their earnest desire of being admitted into the immediate service of the British Government on any terms which may be granted to them."[107]

Guru, *chela*, and empire

Surveying the trajectory of Anupgiri's career from the mid-1760s onward, particularly following his defeat against Company arms at Buxar in 1764, one can begin to discern a pattern: Anupgiri preferred (even under Shuja and Asaf ud-Daulah) the political and military topography of the western and southwestern edge of the Jamuna–Ganga region, from Delhi in the north to Bundelkhand in the south. The reason for this is clear: as the territorial fringe between Company and Maratha spheres of influence, the western Doab and Bundelkhand represented the last vestige of fluid *ancien régime* politics between relatively weak states dependent as much on intrigue, military entrepreneurship, and constantly shifting alliances as on brute force.[108] As that fringe shrank, as Anupgiri found himself

---

[105] The widow of Rajah Himmat Bahadur to Baillie, no. 235 of 21 Jun. 1804 (received 6 Jun. 1804), BSPC. I put "widow" in quotes because the question of her marriage to Anupgiri – and *gosain* marriages in general – was contentious, and not simply for later British observers seeking to unravel the hermeneutic tangle of Anupgiri's "family." I explore this issue in detail in the following chapter.

[106] Baillie to Edmonstone, no. 98 of 13 Mar. 1806 (dated 28 Feb. 1806), with enclosed letters from Narindragiri and Kanchangiri to Baillie, nos. 99 and 100 of 13 Mar. 1806 respectively (both dated 27 Feb. 1806), BSPC.

[107] Baillie to Mercer, Banda, no. 72 of 5 Jul. 1804 (dated 21 Jun. 1804), BSPC. It is not known to what degree *gosain*s were taken into Company service, though it is not difficult to see the advantages it afforded aging warriors. Mieselbach sought on a number of occasions (and usually successfully) to have his wounded men enrolled on the "invalid thana" lists. See, e.g. Baillie to Edmonstone, no. 8 of 26 Feb. 1807 (dated 14 Feb. 1807), BPC; and J.Richardson to Edmonstone, no. 32 of 4 Jan. 1808 (dated 18 Dec. 1807), BPC; see also Seema Alavi, "The Company Army and Rural Society: The Invalid Thana, 1780–1830," *Modern Asian Studies* 27,1 (1993): 147–178, and Alavi, *The Sepoys and the Company*.

[108] On that world see Kolff, "The End of an Ancien Régime."

increasingly hemmed in on all sides, he was impelled toward the conclusion that he must opt for one or the other major power with which he and those close to him, *gosain*s, would be most likely to thrive – or at least survive. The timing of his overtures to and alliance with the British from January to September 1803 suggest that a major factor in his decision-making was the Treaty of Bassein, signed on the last day of 1802, between the Governor General and the *peshwa*. From Anupgiri's perspective, the significance of that treaty was that the *peshwa* had become a British vassal and could no longer hold sway over the Maratha warlord lineages. This meant that Anupgiri could no longer seek the protection of the office of the *peshwa* (via his sons and grandsons) when threatened by the likes of Shinde, whether Mahadji or Daulatrao. Add to this Shamsher Bahadur's aggressive posturing in Bundelkhand and his reliance on Holkar's horse in entering the province and arresting his uncle in the latter half of 1802, and one can easily perceive Anupgiri's apprehensions about the future if he continued to look to the southwest.

The alliance with the British was doubly advantageous for Anupgiri: it gave him full control over a massive *jaidad* – nearly twice that which had obtained under Ali Bahadur, much of which he would apparently not direct toward the maintenance of troops – *and* a future *jagir* near Sivarajpur, where his family, retainers, and adherents could (theoretically) live out their lives in relative independence and autonomy. That it took over five years after Anupgiri's demise for that latter eventuality to come to pass, and not without significant wavering on the part of Kanchangiri, his charge Narindragiri, and their adherents, suggests that it was anything but an easy decision.[109] In any event, Anupgiri's death in 1804 threatened the entire fragile arrangement; hence Baillie's haste in rushing to the *gosain*'s bedside, and his baldly aggressive interpretation of the *gosain*'s dying wish for the "protection of his infant son" as an intention to bequeath "all his property and rights to his only son."

Baillie was particularly keen to certify the ascension of Narindragiri (and Kanchangiri) as the new leader of Anupgiri's army because of the imminent arrival of Umraogiri on the scene. Umraogiri's evident displeasure at Narindragiri's coronation ceremony suggests that he either had not had time to discuss these matters with Anupgiri, or that he disagreed completely with his political-cultural calculations vis-à-vis the British. Certainly he was the senior *chela* of Rajendragiri, as his elevation by Safdar Jang to the office of commander of the *gosain* forces after his master's death in 1753 made clear.[110] In any event, he wished to assert himself as the true and rightful heir to the mantle of his and his brother's guru,

---

[109] See, e.g. the extensive correspondences included as enclosures in J. Wauchope to J. Adams, no. 85 of 4 Jul. 1815 (dated 18 May 1815), BPC.
[110] Srivastava, *First Two Nawabs of Awadh*, p. 236.

Rajendragiri. By 1799 Umraogiri had even taken to identifying himself as "Rajendragiri Gosain," thus symbolically subordinating Anupgiri to himself in the process.[111] We do not know Anupgiri's feelings on the matter, though a ballad by the bard, Man Kavi, current in Bundelkhand from the early 1790s suggests that part of Anupgiri's rise to prominence there included, in a Saiva sectarian context, the assertion that he and not Umraogiri was the disciple chosen to lead the *akhara*. Man Kavi's poem, entitled *Anupaprakash* (The Splendor of Anupa[giri]), covers much of the same panegyrical ground as Padmakar's *Himmatbahadur Virdavali*, but is different in one important respect: it gives a guru genealogy at the outset, along with a marvelous vignette that explained and recorded the decision of Rajendragiri to take up arms. Umraogiri is conspicuous by his absence in the genealogy. The vignette that accompanies the genealogy confirms that this was no ordinary lapse on the part of the poet. As will be recalled from an earlier recounting of the tale (see the introduction to this book), the young Rajendragiri was guarding the entrance to a cave in which *his* guru, Dhyangiri, was absorbed in deep meditation. While thus engaged, Rajendragiri dutifully barred entrance to an unfamiliar figure, who turned out to be the divine apparition of Narayangiri, the guru of Dhyangiri's guru (in other words, Rajendragiri's great-grand-guru). Impressed with Rajendragiri's guru-devotion, Narayangiri granted a boon to the young ascetic. Rajendragiri responded: "Maharaj, my wish is that I will one day be a great king and that everyone will obey my orders." Narayangiri granted this wish and said, "henceforth, you and the *chela*s you embrace will rule from generation to generation."[112] Apparently those *chela*s did not include Umraogiri.

It is possible that Umraogiri's displeasure was grounded in a less self-interested complaint: the elevation to the *masnad* of the two-year-old Narindragiri on the basis of that child's blood relation to Anupgiri contradicted established practice (not to mention the prophesy of Dhyangiri, noted above), whereby the mantle of authority in the order is passed over the generations from guru to *chela*. Significantly, however, Umraogiri's attempt to oppose the elevation of the child Narindragiri seems to have met with no support among Anupgiri's followers. Baillie, it will be recalled, reported on 4 June 1804 that all but Umraogiri seemed content to accept the investiture of the two-year-old Narindragiri as maharaja, and that "the limited influence which he [Umraogiri] possesses over

---

[111] See, in particular, correspondences concerning his role in the Vizier Ali plot: G. H. Barlow, secretary to Government, to Samuel Davis, Magistrate of Benares, no. 3 of 13 May 1799 (undated), no. 11 of 3 Jun. 1799 (dated 28 May 1799), and, most notably, J. H. Craig to D. Vanderheyden, no. 7 of 20 Aug. 1799 (undated), Bengal Separate and Secret Consultations (stored with BSPC), where reference is made to "Raja Rajinder Gheer Ghossein, more usually known by the name of Rajah Omrau Gheer."

[112] Lala Bahadur Bhatt, 1870 prose rendering of Man Kavi, "Anupa Prakasa," fol. 1.

the troops of his deceased brother, give [sic] me no ground to apprehend any ill effect from his dissatisfaction."[113] This episode suggests that the assembled followers of Anupgiri either had no idea of the machinations taking place beneath the surface, or, conversely, understood only too well what Kanchangiri and Baillie, with Mieselbach's assistance, had engineered and viewed Umraogiri's arrival as an unwelcome attempt to undermine the coup. A letter from Anupgiri's "widow" to Baillie soon after the *gosain*'s death confirms this estimate and suggests that she too had a more than an innocent role in the drama: "the accounts which I have since received of your kindness to my infant son and to the *adopted son* of my late husband[,] Kower Kunchun Geer[,] both from their own letters and the statements of Sundur Lall and Adjudeea Purshad [the *gosain*'s *vakils*] have recalled me to the shore of tranquility and have afforded consolation to my mind."[114]

Given the foregoing paragraphs, is it possible to conclude that, in offering up the child, Narindragiri, as a prince-in-waiting, Anupgiri was balancing the political desire of the imperial state for natural-born heirs, on the one hand, with the *gosain* norms of guru-*chela* succession, on the other? Perhaps, but it is difficult to know precisely what Anupgiri intended at the moment of his death. Certainly we can perceive in the five years it took to settle down to their *jagir* in Rasdhan an unwillingness on the part of *gosain*s to disarm and become "neither vagrants nor plunderers but fixed inhabitants [who] quietly employ themselves in their religious function" – i.e., to accommodate themselves to the non-martial, ascetic religiosity held up as exemplary in Warren Hastings' proclamation three decades earlier.[115] Indeed, Anupgiri's commitment to the continuation of military ascetic culture may have been hinted at in the very name of

[113] Baillie to Mercer, no. 232 of 21 Jun. 1804 (dated 4 Jun. 1804), BSPC.

[114] The widow of Rajah Himmat Bahadur to Baillie, no. 235 of 21 Jun. 1804 (received 6 Jun. 1804), BSPC. Emphasis added. The events surrounding the transfer of Anupgiri's heirs to the *jagir* near Kanpur, and the travails of his family there over the next four decades, give some indication that the begum, while she played along, was soon weary of the drama. The examination of the fate of the *gosain*s near Sivarajpur – and in Rasdhan in particular – over the next four decades is the subject of the following chapter. A feature of the discussions worth noting here, however, is how British officials involved adjudged the merits of various claims according to the standard of a "biological family." Different officials would attach different legal weight to whether an individual was the actual biological offspring or "adopted" (i.e., a *chela*, though the *chela*s were soon careful to describe themselves legally as "adopted" children), favoring the former in disputes. By the 1840s, when officials were adjudicating the inheritance of the estate after Narindragiri's death, legitimacy as natural-born heirs depended on whether both parents were of the same religion. In all of this can be seen the further refinements of political and biological legitimacy according to official convenience that would evolve into the contentious "Doctrine of Lapse."

[115] See nos. 5 and 6 of 21 Jan. 1773, FDSP.

the place to which he sought to retire, and the actual site of Umraogiri's retirement: *Sivarajpur* – the place of the rule of Siva. What is certain is that at the end of his life Anupgiri was caught between two worlds and struggled to reconcile each with the other, if not to ensure his own survival (which by 1804 had become moot in any case), then the survival of the people closest to him and the ascetic culture of arms in which they thrived.[116]

The problem of the armed ascetic, while certainly an emblematic feature of the *ancien régime* – though not unproblematically so – was solved by hook and by crook by the British in Bundelkhand in the early nineteenth century.[117] As this chapter makes clear, Anupgiri's dealings with the British were laden with irony. But the deepest irony of all is that the *gosains* of the late eighteenth century resembled no community so much as the men of the East India Company – with their subcontinental trade networks, their fluidly cohesive identity, their considerable talent for intrigue and penchant for subterfuge, their substantial financial wherewithal, and their military adaptability (including an ability to recruit widely) – perched on the edge of subcontinental dominance. So familiar in 1800, they became each other's antithesis in the century to follow – to the extent that after 1880 the armed ascetic symbolized patriotic resistance to foreign imperialism until Gandhi crafted a non-violent asceticism as part of a "civilizational" critique of the West.[118]

---

[116] Of course, anyone who has read Thomas Broughton's description of Kamptagiri's arrival at Daulatrao Shinde's camp with 1,500 armed *naga*s in 1809 (*Letters Written in a Mahratta Camp* [London 1813], p. 129) will know that many of Anupgiri's followers were unwilling to give up the life of military entrepreneurship and settle down on the *jagir* at Rasdhan. Kamptagiri was a disciple of Kanchangiri, who himself would for a short time (with Narindragiri and the Begum in tow) seek service beyond the Company's dominions. But that, along with the travails of the family/disciples in Rasdhan, including the participation of *gosains* in the revolt of 1857, are the subjects of the following chapter.

[117] By hook and by crook, but not once and for all: significantly, another, perhaps more coherently articulated (or at least more coherently remembered, given the importance of state-building for historical documentation and national memory) armed asceticism had begun to take political and territorial shape in the late 1790s in the Punjab (another important north Indian buffer region, in a game with greater stakes) under Ranjit Singh. The British would not have to deal with Sikh *khalsa* military culture until the 1830s, and the solution to the problem that that martial identity posed for British Indian empire, for better of for worse, was to be found in the encouragement and cooptation of Sikh *khalsa* ideals into the culture of imperial arms. See McLeod, *Evolution of the Sikh Community*; cf. Richard Fox, *Lions of the Punjab: Culture in the Making* (Berkeley 1985).

[118] Gandhi's non-violent asceticism was, in part, a response to the decadence that he perceived in the early twentieth-century military *akhara*s; and the assertion of non-violence was a subtle way of retaining the trump card of violence. See the discussion in chapter 6.

What factors contributed to Anupgiri's effectiveness as a military entrepreneur? I have suggested here that Anupgiri's identity as a *gosain* (which, in fact, connoted freedom from status, keeping in mind Umraogiri's ejaculation that "he was no Motteseddy but a soldier" and that "he considered himself obliged to his sword for everything he held") conferred upon him key advantages in negotiating the treacherous political landscape of the late eighteenth century. First, it gave him access to a ready supply of trained and disciplined troops from a wide recruitment area – much wider than was usually available to the average *jamadar* in the north Indian military labor market – which he would gradually augment with more diverse Rajput and Hindustani numbers. Second, as a *gosain* he was connected to an institutional Dasnami network that could, if called upon, provide much in the way of useful political intelligence. Third, and perhaps most importantly, as an ascetic in pursuit of political power he was almost expected to behave in a shamelessly duplicitous manner (see chapter 5 for more discussion along these lines). And as any student of late eighteenth-century empire in India knows, shameless duplicity was the best way to get ahead.

Being a soldiering *gosain* in the eighteenth century did not confer simply a freedom from the burdens of status, it conferred elasticity of identity. Anupgiri deployed this ambiguous asceticism to full advantage, so that none of his eighteenth-century contemporaries could pin him down. Whenever he was between a rock and a hard place, he would offer to abandon all his wealth and weapons and retire to the banks of the Ganga and engage in prayer and meditation. For example, in 1785, when Anupgiri was at odds with Mahadji Shinde, J. W. Anderson (the British agent at Shinde's camp) reported:

Mahajee Sindia's suspicions of Himmut Behadre having been raised to a great height, He was yesterday induced to station parties of horse over his tents as a guard upon him. Himmet Behadre went immediately to the Durbar with a very small retinue, instead of the numerous armed attendants, with which he used of late to be accompanied, and after declaring to Sindia that he was determined to reliquish all worldly pursuits, and attach himself in future to the observances of religious duties he presented him with all the sunnuds he holds for his several possessions. Sindia after pausing a while returned the sunnuds and declared he had no other view in stationing of the horsemen round his tent, than to try his fidelity which he had now afforded him so ample a proof.[119]

Despite his claims to the contrary, however, Anupgiri was anything but otherworldly. The British seem to have understood this – or perhaps they

---

[119] J. W. Anderson to Hastings, Sindia's camp at Muttrah, dated 10 May (recorded in progs. 26 May 1785), BSMC.

were simply less susceptible, given their status as relative outsiders, to the ascetic aura that surrounded him and the elasticity of identity it conferred. Indeed, Anupgiri himself may have sensed their insensitivity to his political idiom, and consequently decided to fall back on the simpler rhetoric of kingship and biology as a basis for political legitimacy in his dealings with them. In any case, the British were only too willing to grant him a sedentary retirement on the serene banks of the Ganga, to nudge him and his men toward the idealized, otherworldly *sanyasi* lifestyle evoked in Hastings' proclamation of 1773. Indologists wedded to the categorical separation of the Indian renouncer and the man-in-the-world – and to the fundamental individuality of the former and absence thereof in the latter – will protest that Anupgiri was not a true *sanyasi* renouncer and, hence, that his worldliness should not be seen as theoretically problematic.[120] In part, I agree: Anupgiri was not a typical ascetic. He certainly did not abandon the world for the life of a "world renouncer." Rather, he was abandoned by one world, that of his family – for reasons that are forever lost to us – and cast into another, the world of ascetic soldiering. But he was an important kind of ascetic nevertheless and there were many who were much like him,[121] whether or not their actions were emblematic of individualistic ascetic agency in a world riven by caste and driven by *dharma*.

---

[120] See Louis Dumont, "World Renunciation in Indian Religions," *Contributions to Indian Sociology* 4 (1960): 33–62; later published as appendix B to Dumont, *Homo Hierarchicus: The Caste System and Its Implications*, trans. Mark Sainsbury, revised edn (Chicago 1980), pp. 267–286.

[121] It is impossible to say how many. Certainly he was not the first orphan to be "adopted" and to become widely known for his activities on the margins of a monastic order. See Pinch, "History, Devotion, and the Search for Nabhadas of Galta."

4   Begums and ranis in Rasdhan

Sexual relations can be conceived of as a kind of combat, and eroticism as a contest and perverse behavior.

– Vatsyayana, *Kamasutra*, II.7.1[1]

Rasdhan, 1999

Rasdhan is a quiet village set amid a stately ruin. The crumbling vestiges of its troubled past include a *garhi* or fort surrounded by a moat, one wall of a *haveli* or mansion, a Sitala *mandir*, and a *baithak* or pavilion for watching the sunset. In better condition is the gracious tank on the outskirts of the village adjacent to the Sitala *mandir*, as well as a small and still active *masjid* (mosque) and a *gosaiyan mandir*, both in the village proper. Dotted about, in the village courtyards and fields and amid the ruins, are graves – some are *samadhi*s of *gosain*s, and others are *mazar*s of Muslim notables. In the fort itself is a grave that some say contains Kale Saiyid, a Muslim, while others say it contains Gosain Baba, a Hindu. Amidst these vague and contradictory reminders of a bygone era, the residents of Rasdhan go about their daily tasks, working their fields, tending their livestock, pursuing their trades.

In the fields near the *baithak*, Kailash and I met Sarmanpuri, or "Dadda" as he is known to his friends and family. Dadda is a peasant-farmer, sixty-five years old. He tends his land with the help of sons, brothers, and nephews. He immediately dropped what he was doing to show us around. Though he was by no means the richest man in the village, he was respected and well loved. At the same time, there were hints that his forthright personality rubbed some people the wrong way.

---

[1] *The Complete Kama Sutra*, trans. Alain Daniélou (Rochester, VT, 1994), p. 159. In this instance, I prefer the Daniélou to the Doniger and Kakar translation (cf. *Kamasutra*, trans. Wendy Doniger and Sudhir Kakar [New York 2002], p. 56): "They say that sex is a form of quarreling, because the very essence of desire is argument, and its character is perverse." It is estimated that Vatsyayana composed the text in the third century of the Common Era (see Doniger, "Introduction" to *Kamasutra*, p. xi).

He proudly pointed out the sights, and took pleasure in the knowledge that his lineage was tied to the history of the place – indeed, that his lineage *was* the history of the place, the history of *"gosain raj,"* or *gosain* rule, as the villagers put it. He showed us the grass-covered *samadhi*s of Sankargiri and Sundargiri, adjacent to the *baithak*. These men, Dadda's ancestors, had managed the fort and estate lands a generation or two after the maharaja, Narindragiri, had died in 1840. As we headed back into the village, we passed the crumbling wall of the *haveli* which, Dadda told us, belonged to the begum. By this time we had attracted small entourage, sons and nephews mostly, eager to enjoy the impromptu holiday from Dadda's fields. A small grave behind the wall, inside what was the *haveli*, suggested that it had become a kind of *dargah*, or shrine-tomb. The grave contained the remains of the Begum's body. They spoke of her in under-tones, as *rakhain*, a kept woman, or worse. They did not know her name, so I hazarded a guess – and suggested that she was the mother of Narindra-giri. This bit of information seemed to surprise them, and though I have known it (or thought I knew it) for several years it continues to surprise me.

The Begum is a problem for the *gosain*s of Rasdhan, a thorn in the side of their memory. The problem is not simply that she was a woman, nor necessarily that she was a kept woman. The problem is that she was Muslim, or that she is remembered as such. As a Muslim, she does not fit into the *gosain* past, or what the *gosain* past has become in late twentieth-century India. Yet they know she is somehow central to the story of Rasdhan, to the story of Anupgiri and Narindragiri, to the story of *gosain*s. Her grave and their graves, her house and their houses, her land and their land, are all too close together for it to be otherwise. They act surprised when I tell them she was Narindragiri's mother, but no doubt they have heard it before, from their Muslim neighbors.

The Begum of Rasdhan is an indelible question mark, like the grave of Kale Saiyyid/Gosain Baba in the fort – allegedly Muslim but vaguely Hindu. She is the mirror-image of *gosain*s themselves, allegedly Hindu but vaguely Muslim.

In May of 1809, a full three years after the termination of *gosain* ser-vice under the British in Bundelkhand, Narindragiri settled in Rasdhan. It would prove a troubled refuge. As we shall see toward the conclu-sion of this chapter, even the decision to migrate to Rasdhan was a tor-tured one, and the first decades of *gosain* "retirement" were anything but retiring. Between 1808 and 1841 a series of disputes arose among the extended *gosain* "family" descending from Anupgiri and Umraogiri. Though these disputes were, on the surface, concerned with inheritance rights and pensions, at their core was the status of women and children among *gosain*s. The closing act of these disputes, with which this chapter begins, occurred in 1841, when the British reclaimed, or to use the official terminology, "resumed," the Rasdhan estate, citing both financial mismanagement and family illegitimacy. As a result of this act, the *gosain*s of Rasdhan, Narindragiri's heirs and followers, were left with little more than small pensions. It is not surprising, then, that many of Rasdhan's *gosain*s, complaining that their "*ilaqa* [realm] had been taken away from them for many years past," joined in the popular rebellion that followed in the wake of the Sepoy Mutiny of 1857.[2] So deep was their resentment of all symbols of British authority that they took a leading part in the famous "Cawnpore Massacre" of the men, women, and children from General Wheeler's entrenchment as they tried to board boats after the abortive truce with the Nana Saheb.

Hinted at in historical legend concerning Anupgiri and Umraogiri's childhood "adoption," and confirmed in the pages that follow on the travails of *gosain*s in Rasdhan, is that some (and perhaps many) children were purchased into the *akhara*s. As noted in chapter 2, ascetic slaving was not peculiar to the chaotic, war-torn transition from Mughal to British rule. Abu'l Fazl, the late sixteenth-century chronicler of Akbar's reign, hinted at this when he observed of the *yogi* and *sanyasi* combatants at Thaneswar in 1567 that "the asceticism of most of these men arises from the world's having turned its back on them, and not from their having become cold-hearted to the world."[3] Children purchased into the *akhara*s experienced a kind of compulsory renunciation, the stripping away of biologically determined kinship, however nascent, and the gradual adjustment to a new identity. This lent new meaning to the term *chela* (disciple), not to mention *gosain* (master of emotion), and *naga* (naked). The experience in Bundelkhand suggests that enslavement in the *akhara* offered unusual opportunities for individual advancement in the shifting terrain of the late-Mughal world; and the experience at Rasdhan suggests that the corporate bonds forged in the *akhara* were more than simply martial. Clearly there was – in some measure – life after "social death."[4]

---

[2] "Narrative of Events at Cawnpore by Nanukchund," trans. Doulut Pershad, no. 727, Home Miscellaneous Proceedings, OIOC, fol. xix (863 of entire MS), detailing events of Monday, 22 June 1857, at Budruka. For *gosain* involvement during the course of the rebellion around Kanpur, see also fols. vi, viii, x–xii, xix, xxiv–xxvi, xxix–xxxi. Prominent among the *gosain* rebels were Lalpuri Gosain, who rode an elephant with a flag (vi); and Kal Indargiri Gosain, "a budmash [hooligan] of Rusdhan" (xxxiv), also described as "a disciple of the Rusdhanwalahs, who had thrown off the yoke of the Raj Ranee" (xxxi). We meet Kal Indargiri later in this essay.

[3] *Akbar Nama*, vol. II, pp. 423–424.

[4] Cf. Orlando Patterson, *Slavery and Social Death* (Cambridge, MA, 1982). On the problem of slavery in South Asian anthropology and history, see Chatterjee, *Gender, Slavery, and*

But it was an uncertain life, made less secure (as we shall see) by the increasingly rigid morality of the Company state.

The records pertaining to Rasdhan are additionally important because they shed light on the women who were linked to soldiering *gosain*s in the late eighteenth, early nineteenth centuries. We have glimpsed some of these women in earlier chapters. Indeed they appear at crucial moments: during the slaying of Anand Kur at Thaneswar in 1567, during the concocted coronation of Narindragiri at Banda in 1804. But they recede too quickly from sight. In Rasdhan between 1809 and 1841 we are afforded a more detailed, quotidian view – though even here they tend to emerge in moments of crisis. Some of these women were described as slaves, some as prostitutes. Some, who were usually described as "concubines" in the official correspondence, emerge as independent women of means and power. These women chose to describe themselves as begums and ranis – no doubt in a bid to secure a position in an age that frowned, increasingly, on public sexuality. As we shall see, some women seemed to traverse all these roles in a single lifetime.[5]

Though women appear in the records in greater numbers during and after the shift to Rasdhan, they are occasionally visible prior to 1808. There is even a suggestion that the decision to retire to Rasdhan was connected to a prominent woman in Anupgiri's company, a woman described as his "wife" in British records. "Rusadhaw" was "the place [Anupgiri] originally came to when he took protection" in 1787 from the wrath of Mahadji Shinde. In the following year, Anupgiri's "family" was reportedly ensconced in the village, now rendered in Company intelligence reports as "Rudjahaun."[6] In 1789 Anupgiri had departed, but his "wife" remained in the village with considerable moveable property including a large number of "elephants and other animals."[7] The fact that a woman served as Anupgiri's representative in charge of his property

---

Law in Colonial India, pp. 1–31. Also illuminating is Chatterjee, "A Slave's Quest for Selfhood in Eighteenth-Century Hindustan," *Indian Economic and Social History Review* 37, 1 (2000): 53–86.

[5] This was not as unusual as it may seem; see Indrani Chatterjee and Sumit Guha, "Slave-Queen, Waif-Prince: Slavery and Social Capital in Eighteenth-Century India," *Indian Economic and Social History Review* 36, 2 (1999): 165–186.

[6] This spelling suggests that the village name is derived from Persian for "retreat" or "refuge." The prefix "*rad*" means rejection, and "*jahan*" means world.

[7] The terms family and wife are put in quotation marks given the fact that the *gosain* entourage also included purchased children, sexual-slaves, and prostitutes. It is likely that the "family" referred to in Company correspondence referred to this wider community as a whole, and not to some normative, two-parent nuclear family subset thereof. Similarly, the term "wife" probably referred to the senior-most female member of the *gosain* entourage, whether or not there had been some formal ceremony or marriage contract that bound her to Anupgiri or Umraogiri. The first reference to Anupgiri's family occurs in a letter from Lt. Col. Harper to Governor General Macpherson, received 5 Apr.

is significant, since Anupgiri had no shortage of *chela*-lieutenants who could have performed such functions. If nothing else, it suggests that she possessed both power and status, and is more evidence, if it is needed, of the considerable scope for female political aspirations in the eighteenth century.[8] Women who circulated among *gosain*s before 1804 seemed to possess some independence and power; as I suggest below, the powerful among them revolved in an oscillating orbit with their *gosain* partners. The reduction of "Rasdhaniya *gosain*s" to the status of mere pensioners in 1841 was a double blow for these women, since it rendered them and their female heirs wholly dependent on *gosain*s – it made them "their" women. The presence of women at Rasdhan, moreover – whether as sex-slaves, courtesan-*tawaif*s, or wife-begum/ranis – may be taken by some to signify the degree to which soldiering *gosain*s had drifted from their institutional and ideological moorings in the remembered lineage of the ancient ascetic master-sage, Shankaracharya. As we shall see in this chapter, such a strategic understanding underpinned British attitudes as officials sought to domesticate *gosain*s via their pension and inheritance claims after 1808. But the following chapter will make evident that sexuality and asceticism were not necessarily contradictory practices in the context of *gosain* military entrepreneurship.

This chapter begins, as noted, with the "resumption" of the Rasdhan *jagir* by the British in 1841, and the series of official "discoveries" that animated that decision. I then turn to events in the 1810s: first to inheritance disputes involving the descendants of Kanchangiri (d. 1808), who was Anupgiri's senior *chela* in the 1790s and early 1800s, and Umraogiri (d. 1809), Anupgiri's elder brother; then to the series of controversies

---

(dated 28 Mar.) 1786, BSPC. Umraogiri's family is first mentioned in a letter from Ives to Cornwallis, received 5 May (dated 26 Apr.) 1788, BSPC. For references to "Rusadhaw," see postscript to a letter from Harper to Macpherson, received 3 Oct. (dated 9 Sep.) 1787, BSPC. "Rudjahaun" is mentioned in letters from Ives to Cornwallis, received 27 Jun. (dated 14 Jun.) 1788, BSPC, received 12 Aug. (dated 30 Jul.); Cornwallis to Ives, received 2 Sep. (dated 31 Aug.); and Ives to Cornwallis, received 9 Sep. (dated 25 Aug.) 1789, BSPC. In the last letter Ives noted he complied with Asaf's order to seize Anupgiri's property, but not without pointing out that "a very considerable expence will be incurred on account of the food of the elephants and other animals which is estimated at 300 rupees per diem."

8 See Rosalind O'Hanlon's introduction to Tarabai Shinde, *A Comparison between Women and Men*, ed. Rosalind O'Hanlon (Delhi 1994), pp. 47–53, for discussion and a survey of other evidence. O'Hanlon notes (p. 47) that Shinde "has her own clear sense of a vanished Indian warrior and courtly culture, where some women at least had commanded power and wealth on their own terms." As Shinde put it (pp. 47–48 and 99), "People in those days [prior to the nineteenth century] used to yield to three kinds of will: of women, of children, and of kings. But in today's circumstances there's only one, and that's rulers. Children can still be willful about things too. But women can't get their way anymore, I don't see how they can."

that marked Narindragiri's slow migration to and coming of age in Rasdhan between 1806 and 1814. In each case, the claims forwarded by
the various parties reveal new details about the inner workings of *gosain*
military entrepreneurship and corporate identity in the eighteenth and
early nineteenth centuries. They also reveal, *inter alia*, the way religion
and respectability was deployed by the British to manage and recon-
stitute the non-biological corporatism of *gosain*s into discrete family
lineages.

An important backdrop to these transformations is the hardening of
British-Indian civil law in the nineteenth century. It is difficult to know the
degree to which officials dealing with disputes in Rasdhan made recourse
to the body of information and case law concerning ascetics that was
being amassed in Company-controlled territories far from Rasdhan during the first decades of the nineteenth century. Judging from the tenor
of their letters, examined in detail below, it would appear that prior to
1841 the legal tangles produced by Rasdhan and related disputes represented virgin territory for most officials. Nevertheless, there is evidence
that similar kinds of controversies were erupting in other parts of India,
and that officials were arriving at a normative understanding of asceticism and the problem of the "Ghurbaree Gosawee" (*gharbari gosain*), or
"householder" *gosain*, in order to deal with their inheritance disputes.
In 1825 John Warden of Bombay Presidency directed inquiries concerning marriage and inheritance customs to representative members of the
"several thousand Gosawees of the first rank" who periodically visited
the source of the Godavari River at Nasik.[9] He reported that "They at
first received the proposal to disclose the laws of their order to the public
authorities with the greatest hauteur; when, however, it was explained to
them that the measure was only adopted to enable Government to decide
upon civil suits in which their brethren were parties, they relented, and
cheerfully imparted what was solicited." Warden was confident that since
"the motive for giving the information at all was to benefit themselves, it
is not likely that they have practised deceit to the prejudice of their own
rights." Nevertheless, he had the information cross-checked: "The same
question was frequently put in two or three different shapes, and an air
of consistency pervades the whole, which could not perhaps have been
effected by falsehood, even if it had been an object to have kept us in
ignorance."

---

[9] Warden's report was included as an appendix to Arthur Steele, *Summary of the Law and
Custom of Hindoo Castes within the Dekhun Provinces Subject to the Presidency of Bombay,
Chiefly Affecting Civil Suits* (Bombay? 1827; new edn, London 1868; reprint Delhi 1986,
as *The Hindu Castes, their Law, Religion and Customs*), pp. 444–446. I am grateful to Sumit
Guha for bringing this reference to my attention.

The information collected by Warden was not unlike that which concerned caste Hindus: most notably, "a Gosawee is not permitted to marry other than a Gosawunee; if he do so, his marriage is not annulled, but his wife is not acknowledged as a Gosawunee." In addition, "a man of the Geeree sect . . . cannot marry a woman of his own sect, but may select a wife from any of the remaining nine." There were additional provisions in case of abandonment, adultery, and divorce. Nowhere in Warden's notes, however, is the status of the children produced by a non-permissible union discussed – and this was the pivotal issue in Rasdhan. Indeed, the fact that Warden's informants held that non-permissible unions were "not annulled" suggests that the children of those unions may not have been deemed "illegitimate" by *gosain*s themselves, and consequently may not have experienced the loss of inheritance rights that they did eventually experience under British-Indian law. The language of permissibility noted by Warden did, however, leave considerable room for legal maneuver, and British officials seem to have taken full advantage of that room to plot a course toward a "doctrine of lapse" for *gosain*s in 1841, whether or not Warden's notes were availed of in the process. As for the descendants of Anupgiri and company, their first explicit acknowledgment of a normative marriage code approximating the one described by Warden occurs in 1841, when a "respectable" member of the "Goosaeen family at Banda" is asked for information on marriage customs in his community. Should we conclude from this that Anupgiri and Umraogiri and their followers somehow failed to live up to *gosain* standards on the question of marriage? It is difficult to say. What is clear, however, is that a model of asceticism that required a moral distinction between married and unmarried was slowly taking shape among *gosain*s in the early nineteenth century. Whether or not this was simply an ideological-*cum*-epistemological import from an Enlightenment, Christian Europe written onto the blank slate of Indian culture is a question that will be taken up in due course.

Sex, death, and children

On 11 January 1840 Narindragiri Gosain died. The son and heir of Anupgiri Gosain, Narindragiri had settled in Rasdhan in 1809 at the age of nine, following the death of his manager Kanchangiri.[10] Narindragiri's death occasioned an official inquiry into the *gosain* legacy at Rasdhan,

---

[10] The detailed correspondence concerning Narindragiri's decision is contained in the following Bengal Political Consultations (BPC): nos. 29–30 of 24 Oct. and no. 70 of 26 Dec. 1808; and nos. 26–33 of 16 Jan., 100–105 of 30 Jan., 32 of 11 Feb., 16–20 of 13 Mar., 15–18 of 27 Mar., 13 of 24 Jun., and 41–42 of 5 Sep. 1809.

and contributed to an evolving Company understanding of Hindu asceticism throughout the Gangetic north. His death brought into the open a contest for the mantle of maharaja and *jagirdar* on the part of three male claimants, each of whom was a front for his respective mother. The first claimant was an adopted son, Kalindargiri, aged seven – "a chela [disciple] supported by the Ranee or widow of the late Raja [Narindragiri] and apparently in possession." Next came Padam Indargiri, also aged seven and "son of a Mussulman concubine" named Roopun. And third was Jai Indargiri, aged ten, "son of Lallun, a prostitute." (In other letters she is named as "Lullan," and described as a "Mahomedan concubine.") Each of the boys claimed to be Narindragiri's son – the first, as "adopted," the other two as "natural-born." An appendix to this chapter provides a table of these and other *gosain* relationships.

After lengthy deliberation with officials at all levels, the Lieutenant-Governor of the North Western Provinces came to a decision on the 12 May 1841, declaring the "Jageer of late Narinder Gir to have lapsed to Government by failure of legitimate issue." In other words, the Company-state declared the *jagir* of the territory of Sikandra Bilaspur (of which Rasdhan was the administrative and geographic center) to no longer exist, thereby terminating the royal status of the *gosain* descendants of Anupgiri. This decision was, as its language suggests, part of an evolving official posture with respect to "princely" succession that emerged full-blown in 1848 as the notorious "Doctrine of Lapse," which in turn was largely responsible for transforming the military mutiny of 1857 into the north Indian rebellion of 1857–1858. The internal logic that justified this act was the mismanagement of the *jagir* by Narindragiri, but officials noted as well as "the unsuitableness of such grants to our system of Government and the injurious effects they exercise on the prosperity of the people."[11] The British did not sweep aside all *gosain* claims in Rasdhan, however. In place of the *jagir*, pensions equivalent to the net cash proceeds of Sikandra Bilaspur minus 20 percent for management costs, and adjusted over a period of fourteen years to repay creditors, were settled on three recipients. Importantly, the claim of the first son, the "adopted" *chela* Kalindargiri, was rejected outright. Instead, his adoptive mother, the "Raj Ranee" and widow of Narindragiri, would receive one-third of

---

[11] J. Thomason, secretary to the Government of the North West Provinces, to T. H. Maddock, secretary to the Government of India, Revenue Department, Fort William, no. 23 of 15 Mar. (dated 24 Feb. 1841), Foreign Department, Political Proceedings (FDPP), NAI. See also Maddock to Thomason, no. 28 of 15 Mar. 1841, expressing concern for the "adopted" son, and the summary statement in no. 81 of 11 Jul. 1845. The ages of the children and additional details of the families are given in no. 24 of 15 Mar. 1841, cited in greater detail in the discussion below.

the pension for the remainder of her life. The remaining two-thirds would be divided between the two natural-born sons, Padam Indargiri and Jai Indargiri, despite their status as "illegitimate" offspring. Upon the death of the Rani, her pension would be divided equally and absorbed into the pensions of the two natural-born sons, whose rights would be regarded as hereditary – that is, transferable to their natural-born sons in succession. The *chela*, Kalindargiri, would have to fend for himself.[12] Thus, a *jagir* that had been earning nearly Rs. 110,000 per year was reduced, in the first fourteen years after the declaration of the Lapse, to three pensions of 6,000 rupees per year each. "*Gosain* raj" in Rasdhan had come to an end. From this point on, Rasdhan would be subject to the police and courts and revenue administration of British India.

The contest for the mantle of Narindragiri in 1840–1841 brought renewed official scrutiny to the lives of the Rasdhan *gosain*s, and to the increasingly anomalous legal status of "their" women (as wives, concubines, prostitutes, and slaves) and children (as sons, daughters, *chela*s, and slaves). In other words, the case became an opportunity for British officials to inspect the dirty laundry of the *gosain*s – or to inspect laundry that only appeared dirty according to a new doctrine of cleanliness. The first revelation emerged in the context of the claim brought forward by the natural-born children of Narindragiri, who were declared "illegitimate" due to the status of their mothers as "Mahomedan concubines." In the course of the investigation into the propriety of their claim, the fact emerged that Narindragiri himself was an "illegitimate" son of Himmat Bahadur (Anupgiri). This occasioned some official hand-wringing in 1840, since the subsequent investigation revealed that though his mother was "called by Colonel Baillie the Ranee or Begum, . . . she was not his regularly espoused wife."[13] Further complicating matters was the fact that the Rani/Begum turned out not to be Hindu but Muslim: thus the claim of the two natural-born sons in 1840 *appeared to be* "precisely similar to that of their father, the late Raja [Narindragiri] who was also the offspring of a Mahomedan concubine." But appearances could be deceiving, as the discussion below concerning Umraogiri's opinion of Narindragiri's accession demonstrates. Also complicating matters was the fact that the Board of Revenue was in favor of the succession of the natural-born sons;

---

[12] This individual was prominent amongst those who would take up arms against the British sixteen years later. According to "Narrative of Events at Cawnpore," fols. xxx–xxxi, "Kalindurgir, a disciple of the Rusdhanwalahs, who had thrown off the yoke of the Raj Ranee, joined the Nana's standard, and got a zemindar named Raja Bhao to join him." For a list of the Rasdhaniya *gosain*s who were in league with Kalindargiri, see fol. xii.

[13] Thomason to Maddock, no. 23 of 15 Mar. 1841, par. 3, FDPP.

the members of the Board, at least, were not put off by the prospect of a "mixed" Hindu-Muslim marriage. Their enlightened position may have been due in part to the expert advice of the Persian linguist, ethnographer, and folklorist, Henry Miers Elliot, who served as secretary to the Board, and who noted in writing with respect to the Rasdhan case that "it appears to be a custom prevalent among the Mahrattas for children of mixed blood to inherit the property of their ancestors."[14]

Elliot's opinion notwithstanding, the official determination that the *chela*'s (Kalindargiri's) claim was "inadmissible" was a particularly important measure from the point of view of the British-Indian state. In 1845 William Sleeman, who had risen in official circles as a result of his campaign against *thagi* (or thuggee), would summarize the Rasdhan affair to discern its legal implications insofar as it offered precedent for future cases:

it appears that the right of a cheyla, or adopted son, to succeed to the grant enjoyed by his adoptive father, has not been recognized by Government. Gosaens in Bundelkhand, and elsewhere, entered the army and engaged extensively in trade, and amassed much wealth and attained high rank. This relieved them from the rigid rules of the monastic order, by which they are bound while they have no office but the priesthood, and no property but the endowments of temples; to such office and property no son can succeed. If the priest has a son, he must become adopted by the rules of the order before he can succeed; and then he succeeds in virtue of the adoption, and not the birth. The order levels all castes, and a Hindoo of any caste can become a Gosaen; but they cannot marry according to the rules of the order, and the only difference between the women with whom he cohabits is in their caste. All sons succeed to lay property accumulated in trade, or in any service but that of the church. The office in which Himmut Bahadoor served our Government was a secular one, the command of a military force; and the grant he received, or his son received, became lay property to which a son very properly succeeded.[15]

Underlying Sleeman's observations is an Enlightenment understanding of religion and, by extension, monasticism, according to which the

---

[14] H. M. Elliot, Secretary to the Sudder Board of Revenue, North West Provinces, Allahabad, to Thomason, no. 24 of 15 Mar. 1841 (dated 1 May 1840), par. 6, FDPP. In addition to his massive translation work embodied in his and Dowson's eight-volume *History of India as Told by Its Own Historians*, Elliot also authored *Memoirs on the History, Folk-lore, and Distribution of the Races of the North Western Provinces of India*, 2 vols., ed. John Beames (London 1869, reprint 1985 under a changed title); the material in these volumes was originally compiled in the 1840s and intended as a supplement to Horace Hayman Wilson, *Glossary of Judicial and Revenue Terms and of Useful Words Occurring in Official Documents Relating to the Administration of British India* (London 1855, reprint Delhi 1968).

[15] W. H. Sleeman, Agent to the Governor General in Bundelkhand, to F. Currie, secretary to the Government of India, Fort William, no. 81 of 11 Jul. 1845 (dated Jhansee, 27 Jun. 1845), FDPP.

*gosain*s of Rasdhan (and soldiering *gosain*s generally) failed to pass muster. Sleeman defined the *gosain*s of Rasdhan as formerly religious but presently secular beings, and identified cohabitation with and sexual reproduction through females (along with the accumulation of wealth, and power, through trade and warfare) as a significant symptom of the transformation from one state of being to the other. For observers closer to the scene, sexual activity (and, tied to it, the definition of marriage and the possibility of offspring) was even more crucial to the particular status of *gosain*s. Sexual activity and the welter of bio-legal entities that emerged out of it served as both agent and marker of the shift from religious to secular. Hugh Rose, the deputy collector at Cawnpore who was on the ground at Rasdhan soon after the death of Narindargiri, reported in March of 1840 that "Goossains are enjoined celibacy, but if they deviate from that rule they cease, I presume, to be Goossains and their children may succeed like those of other people. The prohibition is against their having children, not against their children inheriting."[16]

Rose's opinion on the question of *gosain* celibacy, not to mention the legal status of children, legitimate or not, relative to inheritance, was of such import that his superiors called for more information. The conduit of that information, S. Fraser, the political agent in Bundelkhand, headquartered at Jhansi, decided to ask "the most respectable [member] of the Goosaeen family at Banda," for his opinion. This individual, Jagatgiri Gosain, heir and successor to the *gaddi* (seat) of Kanchangiri, provided a written statement clarifying the issue of celibacy and offspring. Fraser summarized "the most principal fact to be deduced from" Jagatgiri's statement as follows: "there is an established custom of marriage amongst the Goosaeens which alone constitutes legitimacy and that other connections are considered irregular and open to objection."[17] Unfortunately the details of that marriage custom are not described – not in Jagatgiri's statement, nor in Fraser's gloss. But it bears marked similarities to the normative code described by John Warden of Bombay Presidency in 1827, noted earlier. Jagatgiri's statement began with ascetic discipleship. He noted that "Sunkur Acharij [Shankaracharya] had 4 Chelas," whom he lists, along with their respective *chela*s, in tabular fashion (I have provided conventional, modern spellings in brackets where appropriate):

[16] H. Rose to R. Lowther, Commissioner, Allahabad, no. 24 of 15 Mar. 1841 (dated 16 Mar. 1840), par. 9, FDPP.

[17] S. Fraser to J. Thomason, no. 25 of 15 Mar. 1841 (dated 5 Dec. 1840), par. 4, FDPP. The statement by Jagatgiri [Juggutgir] which follows was included as an enclosure to this letter.

1. Bulbuder, Surop acharij who had 2 Chelas
   1. Teerut [Tirtha]
   2. Usram [Asrama]
2. Pudum acharij, had 2 Chelas
   1. Bun [Vana]
   2. Arun [Aranya]
3. Naralotuk acharij, had 3 Chelas
   1. Gir [Giri] (20 Castes)
   2. Parbut [Parvata]
   3. Saugur [Sagara]
4. Purhur Roodhur acharij, had 3 Chelas
   1. Sirsotee [Sarasvati]
   2. Bherutee [Bharati]
   3. Purree [Puri] (28 Castes)

Immediately apparent in the above enumeration is that the names of the ten *chela*s of Shankaracharya's four *chela*s correspond to the ten names (*das-nam*) of the Dasnamis,[18] suggesting (if there was any doubt) that the soldiering *gosain*s descending from Rajendragiri understood themselves as members of that wider ascetic community. Following this enumeration, Jagatgiri then noted that "Gosaeens are prohibited from marrying into their own caste, nevertheless some in ignorance neglect this." The implication of this statement is that *gosain*s were not subject to a blanket prohibition against marriage, but simply enjoined to conduct marriage with women from other castes. The parenthetical phrases "20 Castes" and "28 Castes" after Gir and Purree appear, in this context, to indicate the number of castes from which women were considered marriageable for *gosain*s with these suffixes attached to their names – which, as it happened, were the suffixes used by martial Dasnamis. Jagatgiri formalizes his assertion of the legality of *gosain* marriage and offspring inheritance in a later passage:

Amongst Gosaeens, and especially in our family, it is a custom that so long as a child survive, born of a wife regularly married, a Chela cannot be heir, but if there be no legitimate child [the *chela*] becomes heir. *This is authorized by the Shastras;* indeed Raja Himmut Buhadoor had many Chelas, but Raja Nurindurgir was preferred to them, although Rajah OomraoGir, his Chela, was alive and Ootumgir and Rajgir are now surviving nevertheless the son succeeded, the Chelas receiving a suitable allowance for their support.[19]

---

[18] For contending explanations of these names in Dasnami tradition, see Ghurye, *Indian Sadhus*, pp. 82–85; and Giri, *Society and Sannyasin*, p. 16. The delineation of descent from Shankaracharya was also a feature of Warden's 1827 note, but he included it in reference to unmarried "Gosawees". See Steele, *Summary of the Law and Custom of Hindoo Castes*, pp. 433–434.

[19] Emphasis added. See below for discussion of the assertion that Umraogiri was Anupgiri's *chela*. While it may reflect Jagatgiri's own maneuvering – in placing Umraogiri one step

We should resist the urge to treat this as a bald, on-the-spot invention of tradition on the part of Jagatgiri. As noted earlier, independent evidence suggests that *gosain* families had existed for some time, and that sexual reproduction of offspring did, in fact, change the way they were perceived by Dasnamis and in the wider community. Between 1810 and 1814 the ever-perceptive surgeon-surveyor, Francis Buchanan, noted considerable controversy surrounding the status of Dasnamis who had married and had children in what is now Bihar and eastern Uttar Pradesh. While many Dasnamis adhered to a code of sexual renunciation, others numbering well into the hundreds (and possibly thousands) in each district had "been unable to resist the allurements of the sex."[20] Buchanan's remarks on Purnea District in north Bihar are particularly relevant:

Many of the Dasnami Sannyasis of this district have not been able to resist marriage, and their ten divisions have become exactly analogous to the Gotras of the Brahmans, no person marrying a girl of the same denomination with that of his father. These persons, on account of their yielding to the temptations of the flesh, are called *Sang-Yogis* [joined-*yogi*s], but they call themselves Sannyasis, Gosaings, Atithi, and even Fakirs, which is a *Moslem*[21] title.

The Sang-Yogis are said by some to owe their origin to a pupil of Sangkaracharya, who could not resist the flesh, and married; but those whom I have consulted know nothing of their history. Some of them cultivate the ground by means of servants; but they all beg, and some have charity land, and the number of those whom they guide is very great. They admit of concubines (*Samodhs* [from Skt., *sammoda*, "great delight, pleasure"?]). The Pandits say that they have no learning, but it is evident that the sacred order [celibate Dasnamis] views the Sang-Yogis with considerable jealousy; and these fellows have indeed the impudence to bestow their blessing on the Brahmans, to which those here quietly submit, but those from Bengal cannot well restrain their indignation.[22]

It would appear, then, that the soldiering *gosain*s of Rasdhan who cohabited with women and produced offspring through them had plenty of company in Gangetic north India. If Jagatgiri was guilty of any misrepresentation, perhaps it was in his attempt to endow *gosain* marriage and

---

down on the ladder of descent, Jagatgiri raised his own position vis-à-vis Umraogiri's descendants, many of whom were still living – it probably was a function of the fact that his guru was Kanchangiri.

[20] Buchanan, *Account of the Districts of Bihar and Patna*, vol. I, pp. 89–92, see also pp. 369–371. The quote refers to Dasnamis in the town of Gaya. For similar passages in other districts, see *Account of the District of Shahabad*, p. 219 (for the quote here), p. 53 (for Arrah), p. 73 (for Ekwari); *An Account of the District of Bhagalpur in 1810–1811* (Patna 1939), pp. 274–275; and Buchanan's account of Gorakhpur excerpted at length in Martin, *History, Antiquities, Topography, and Statistics of Eastern India*, vol. II, pp. 476–477.

[21] According to Buchanan, *Account of the District of Bhagalpur*, p. 210, "all religious mendicants, Hindu and Moslem, here as well as in Puraniya, are called Fakirs and Padres."

[22] Buchanan, *Account of the District of Purnea in 1809–1810* (Patna 1928, reprint New Delhi 1986), pp. 269–270.

inheritance practices with the aura of ancient tradition, as evident in his vague assertion that "this is authorized by the Shastras." While the *shastras* (generic shorthand for the Brahmanical ethico-legal corpus known as *dharmashastra*) do not contradict his specific assertion, neither do they support it. They do, however, view the very prospect of *sanyasi* sexuality as a dangerous abomination, an understanding that is supported by a close reading of hagiographical accounts of Shankaracharya.[23] The *shastric* and hagiographic prohibition of sexuality is reminiscent of Deputy Collector Rose's on-the-spot opinion offered soon after Narindragiri's death: "The prohibition is against their having children, not against their children inheriting." The key difference is that while Rose was describing a prohibition on the production on offspring, the *shastras* prohibit *sanyasi* sexuality pure and simple. It is easy to confuse the two issues – after all, no sex means no sexually produced children. One can easily imagine Rose and other Company officials interpreting sexuality as sexual reproduction since the claims to inherit Narindragiri's estate and title turned on the question of legitimate birthright.

At the same time, it is important not to overstate the role of British understandings. Rasdhan did not represent the first time controversy had erupted over celibacy and the problem of sexuality among ascetics. It is even possible that Jagatgiri (and married *gosains* generally) looked to earlier controversies for quasi-legal guidance. That the issue had emerged prior to 1841 among Dasnamis is evident from Buchanan's accounts of Bihar, not to mention John Warden's interviews in 1825, noted earlier; and the fact that Warden spoke with *gosains* during the periodic festival at Nasik suggests that his interlocutors were soldiering *gosains*. The question of sex and marriage had emerged in the eighteenth century as well, among Vaishnava ascetics enmeshed in arenas of power. Two well-known cases from the 1730s concerned, first, the Ramanandi *mahant* (superior, abbot) of Galta (on the outskirts of Jaipur) and, second, the Nimbarka *mahant* of Vrindavan, both of whom were pressured into marriage at the urging of Maharaja Jaisingh II (r. 1700–1743). There were important differences between these two cases and the *gosains* of Rasdhan, not least of

---

[23] The early seventeenth-century *Yatidharmasangraha* by Visvesvara Saraswati, for example, warns of "dire consequences on him who after becoming a sannyasin has sexual intercourse." The offender "becomes a worm in ordure for 60,000 years, passes through the lives of a rat, a vulture, a dog, a donkey, a pig, a tree without flowers and fruit, a goblin and then he is born as a *candala*" (an outcaste, "untouchable", or "scavenger"). See *Vayupurana* quoted in *Yatidharmasangraha*, p. 108, cited in Kane, *History of Dharmasastra*, vol. II, part 2, p. 952. Other passages are equally explicit in enjoining total abandonment of sex. For the dangers of sexuality in fourteenth-century Shankara hagiography, see Madhava-Vidyaranya, *Sankara-dig-vijaya*; chs. 9 and 10 in particular. I discuss the Shankara hagiography in greater detail in chapter 5, below.

which was sectarian. Nevertheless, the controversies generated considerable correspondence and, presumably, legal opinions from Jaisingh's court, increasingly overtaken by Brahmans from Maharashtra by way of Banaras. It is worth noting, as well, that *gosain* agents of Anupgiri (and occasionally Anupgiri himself) were present in Jaipur later in the century and must have been aware of the controversy surrounding the issue.[24] And as we shall see in the conclusion to this chapter, there is additional, more voyeuristic evidence that women and sexuality were problems for – and proximate to – armed ascetics in the eighteenth century in what is now southern Rajasthan.

Political sensitivity about ascetic sexuality, marriage, and religious legitimacy was a reflection of locally constituted social and ideological realities, which preceded the rise of British-Indian law and came face to face with it. In Rasdhan the social and ideological realities included the sharp disparity between the indeterminate status of the women who orbited *gosain*s, and the remarkable amount of economic and political power they seemed to exercise among *gosain*s – so much so that it may be said that *gosain*s were just as often in orbit around "their" women. As Jagatgiri's statement suggests, quite a few women had come into what may be termed an "oscillating orbit" with *gosain*s in recent generations, possibly (it may be argued) as a result of the material success of *gosain* arms under Umraogiri and Anupgiri during the second half of the eighteenth century (but it is worth remembering, as noted in the following chapter, that there were other perfectly good reasons for the presence of women among *gosain*s). The key passages occur after Jagatgiri's enumeration of Shankaracharya's *chela*s:

The particulars of Rajah Indurgir are as follows; he had many Chelas, but it is only necessary to specify two.–

Rajah Oomrao Gir had many women[;] many had no families[,] 6 had families.–

1. Kutrunee woman, 2 sons _____	1. Gungagir Raja Dilawar Jung
	2. Raja Rajgir.
2. a Ghosau _____	1 son. Ootumgir.
3. a Goojureen _____	1 son Hunsrajgir.
4. a Moosulmanee _____	1 son Gungbaksh

---

[24] On Jaisingh II and the *mahant* of Galta, see Horstmann, "The Ramanandis of Galta," pp. 160–165; on the *mahant* of Vrindavan, see Catherine Clémentin-Ojha, *Le Trident au Palais: Une Cabale Anti-Vishnuite dans un Royaume Hindou à l'Époque Coloniale* (Paris 1999). I am grateful to Professor Horstmann for directing me to these titles. What is not clear is whether women were present among Ramanandis and Nimbarakas, and whether sexuality was an issue among them, *prior to* Jaisingh's efforts to discipline the orders.

5. a woman caste not known, 2 sons_____   1. Jeetgir Juggut Bahadur.
                                                       2. Jewungir
6. (no details)
   Unoopgir Raja Himmut Buhadoor had many women of whom the particulars of two are known.
1. a Rajpooteen, who had no sons.–
2. a Begum, 1 son Nurindurgir. . . .

With respect to Narindragiri, Jagatgiri added:

The particulars of Raja Nurindur Gir's story are these; he had many women but only two were regularly married to him, one is dead, one alive, but neither had families.–
   A Rajpooteen had a daughter who was brought up in a mussulman family. She was taken by the Raja and called Roopa Begum.– This woman had one son called Puddum Indurgir and a daughter Hurhur Bharjub.
   Lallun, a prostitute who had a son Jy Indurgir.
   These 3 children were all brought up by a Brahmin nurse.

By Jagatgiri's account, then, while women had not been worth mentioning with respect to Rajendragiri's era (prior to 1753), they were a significant part of *gosain* existence in the generations that followed. Put differently, while Shankaracharya and Rajendragiri "had many Chelas," Anupgiri, Umraogiri, and Narindragiri "had many women." They came from a variety of backgrounds and included a Rajpooteen [*Rajputin*], a Rajpooteen who was brought up as a Muslim, a Goojureen [*Gujarin*], a Kutrunee [*Khatrin*], a Moosulmanee [Muslim], a Begum, a prostitute, and two of unknown description. Some of these women bore children and consequently merited more detail in Jagatgiri's account. Most were thought of, apparently, as concubines or mistresses. Significantly, only when he gets to Narindragiri's generation does Jagatgiri refer to marriage, viz., "he had many women but only two were regularly married to him."

Slave-sons, slave-mothers

Jagatgiri should not be seen as a dispassionate observer in all this. He had at one time represented himself as a natural-born son of Kanchangiri, and he had expert personal knowledge of the travails of birth and legitimacy and the unpredictable power of women. In 1815, seven years after Kanchangiri's death, Jagatgiri (who was still a "minor") and three older *chelas* (identified as "adopted sons") petitioned the British for pensions. They noted that Captain Baillie had promised Kanchangiri a pension of 2,000 rupees per month in 1806 for his services in the Company resumption of Anupgiri's *jaidad*, but that their guru's sudden demise in 1808 shortly after returning to Company-controlled territory had prevented him from formally taking it up. They had for some years after his death lived "on the bounty" of Narindragiri in Rasdhan, but by 1815 that bounty no longer appeared as bountiful (see section "Coming of age in Rasdhan," below). Consequently, having fallen on hard times, they requested that the proposed Rs. 2,000 be divided into *five* separate pensions. Jagatgiri was to receive the largest share, Rs. 775, with Kamptagiri receiving Rs. 325, and Madhogiri and Mahendragiri each receiving Rs. 300. In addition, they asked that Mukundgiri, the five-year-old "natural-born" son of one Ramgiri – the senior "adopted" *chela* who had died just prior to Kanchangiri's own death – also be awarded Rs. 300 per month.[25] The *chela*s argued that Jagatgiri be given the greatest amount on grounds that he was the only natural-born son of Kanchangiri among them and that the maintenance of his mother (then residing in Banda) and two other "widows" of Kanchangiri would be paid out of his pension. (It was subsequently agreed that Jagatgiri only provide for the maintenance of his mother, Cheman Kuar, and that the other two widows, Chehtee Begum and Man Kuar, receive token sums of Rs. 30 and 20 respectively.) Kamptagiri's share, which was slightly larger than the other two *chela*s, reflected the fact that "he was the senior adopted son alive, and [had] a wife and two children to support; whereas all the others were unmarried."

The Superintendent of Political Affairs in Bundelkhand, John Wauchope, had all but cemented this arrangement when Chehtee Begum (also known as "Aqila" Begum) exploded on the scene from Agra and objected vociferously. Her revelations, together with the new information subsequently solicited from the *chela*s, shed substantial new light on the complex dynamics of relations between *gosain*s and "their" women. It is best to quote Wauchope as he struggled to make sense of the shifting sands of Kanchangiri's family:

[25] Wauchope, Superintendent of Political Affairs, Bundelkhand, to Adam, no. 85 of 4 Jul. 1815 (dated Bandah, 18 May 1815); and nos. 14 and 15 of 16 Dec. 1815 (dated 2 Dec. and 15 and 28 Nov. 1815), BPC. The amounts proposed varied slightly, depending on the details of disbursement and whether Mukundgiri was to be included in the pension. Concerning Mukundgiri, the *chela*s explained (in no. 15 of 16 Dec. 1815) that Ramgiri, Mukundgiri's father, had "had a dispute with his father [Kanchangiri], in consequence of which he separated from him and went to reside in the Rajah of Jytpoor's country; that Kunchun Geer, before his death, sent for him in order to be reconciled to him, and that Ram Geer was actually on his way to obey this summons, when he died [–] an event which took place about six months before Kooar Kunchun Geer's demise." Some of the details of the pension proceedings were later copied into nos. 102–105 of 3 Jan. 1834, FDPP, to provide information in a later inquiry.

The lawful wife of Kooar Kunchun Geer died several years before himself[,] and his female dependents [sic] who now claim a provision are

1st. Chehtee Beegum a Moosulmanee concubine

2nd. Chemun Kooar the mother of Kooar Juggut Geer, and

3rd. Mawn Kooar.

Chehtee Beegum is allowed by all the Chelahs, or adopted sons, to have been admitted to all the privileges of a wife by Kooar Kunchun Geer, to have received on the occasion of Kunchun Geer's death (she being then with the Rajah's troops in Dowlut Row Scindeah's country) a *khillut* [robe] of condolence from Maharajah Dowlut Row Scindeah, and also to have succeeded, by the Kooar's [Kanchangiri's] express desire, to the principal part of his personal property . . .

Chehtee Begum[,] on her arrival, would not hear of this portion [of the pension allotted to her, namely, Rs. 30] and refused to accept less than 400 Rupees per mensem.[26]

Much to the discomfiture of the *chela*s, Chehtee Begum produced one or two other bombshells. Most importantly, she informed Wauchope that Jagatgiri was not the "real" son of Kanchangiri, but was adopted when a child of four months. The *chela*s admitted this, but insisted that Jagatgiri was "formally pronounced by Kooar Kunchun Geer on his death to be his sole heir, '*Guddhee Nesheen*,'" or "incumbent to the throne." Chehtee Begum allowed that this was the case, but insisted in turn "that the management of Juggut Geer was delegated by Kunchun Geer to her." Moreover, she "produced a deed to this effect, signed by Kooar Kunchun Geer, dated four years before his death, and having all the appearance of authenticity, by which Kunchun Geer makes over to her all his personal property, as well as the guardianship of the minor Juggut Geer." Four individuals, three of whom had died, witnessed this deed. The fourth was Ayodhya Prasad, "who held a responsible situation in the service of Rajah Himmat Behadoor, and afterwards in that of Kunchun Geer, and he testifies to the authenticity of the deed." Chehtee Begum also informed Wauchope that the other "widows" – Cheman Kuar, the "mother" of Jagatgiri, and Man Kuar – were "only slave girls in the family of the late Kunchun Geer, on a very trifling allowance." The *chela*s conceded that this was so. The final "misrepresentation" that was exposed by Chehtee Begum concerned Mukundgiri, the supposed "real son" of the late Ramgiri. "It appears," wrote Wauchope, chagrined, "that he was adopted, when an infant, by the widow of Ram Geer, shortly after her husband's death."

In fact, Chehtee Begum's allegations appear to have been slightly more serious than Wauchope was willing to admit in an official correspondence.

[26] Wauchope to Adam, no. 38 of 15 Apr. 1816 (dated Bandah, 31 Mar. 1816), BPC.

A review of the relevant Persian documents that occurred over a century later revealed that Chehtee Begum claimed in addition that Kamptagiri, Madhogiri, Mahendragiri, and Mukundgiri were "mere slaves purchased with her own money and that they worked as her slaves in Kanchan Gir's lifetime." Moreover, Jagatgiri was "a slave purchased for a hundred rupees when he was only three or four months old," and that "she had adopted him with the consent of her husband." Jagatgiri's "mother" Cheman Kuar was, in fact only "a slave girl" who had been "engaged as a wet nurse for Jagat Gir." Man Kuar, likewise, "was another slave girl . . . who was childless."[27] There are two reasons Wauchope may have wished to suppress this information in his letters. One is that he may have been embarrassed at not having learned of Chehtee Begum's scandalous information prior to arriving at his plan of disbursement for the pension. The other, and to my mind more likely scenario, is that the facts that were emerging as a result of her explosive entry on the scene shed too much light on Kanchangiri's activities in 1804, particularly with respect to his and Baillie's staging of Narindragiri's succession (more on which below).

In any event, Wauchope recognized the force of Chehtee Begum's claim and the "favor in which [she] was evidently held by Kooar Kunchun Geer." It certainly could not have hurt her case that the *chela*s did not dispute her charges with any degree of force or legal imagination. However, though Wauchope and his superiors supported her claim, they still felt that Jagatgiri should be considered "the representative of the family" even though it was clear he was not a natural-born son to Kanchangiri. Their inclination here was, admittedly, in keeping with Kanchangiri's wishes regarding Jagatgiri as *gaddi nishin*, but it clearly contrasted with the succession of Narindragiri to Anupgiri's *gaddi*, not to mention later doctrines of male primogeniture and lapse. In any case, there followed a month-long deliberation over a recalculated division of Kanchangiri's pension in light of Chehtee Begum's new information. The pension agreed upon for Chehtee Begum was significantly lower than the Rs. 400 she had originally demanded, but it still cut severely into the pensions of Jagatgiri and Mukundgiri. Meanwhile, the sums allotted to Madhogiri, Mahendragiri, and Kamptagiri remained unchanged:

[27] "Note on Reversions to Jagat Gir's Allowance," dated 19 Apr. 1933, enclosed in "Genealogical Tables of Gushain Family," formerly F.14/1933 of Bundelkhand and Baghelkhand Agency Files, now archived as R/2/449/15, Indian States Residency Records (ISRR), OIOC. The "Note" summarizes the Persian documents in the Central India Agency office, Indore. Judging by the tenor of the cover letter to these documents, the information concerning Jagatgiri's birth were still well-guarded secrets in 1933, over a century later.

Kooar Juggut Geer in perpetuity 625
Chehtee Begum to revert on her lapse to Juggut Geer 250
Kooar Kampta Geer in perpetuity 325
" Madho " " 300
" Muhinder " " 300
Mukind Geer the adopted son of Soan Koar the widow of Ram Geer, a hereditary
   provision 200

Rs. 2000

At first glance this may seem a victory for Chehtee Begum. After all,
she had originally been allocated a pittance of Rs. 30 in the original plan
of disbursement. Now she was to receive Rs. 250 monthly until her death,
which would only occur twenty-six years later, in 1842.[28] A significant
feature of Chehtee Begum's pension, however, was that it would "revert
on her lapse" to Jagatgiri. In plain English, the Rs. 250 that she had
received monthly was subsumed upon her death into Jagatgiri's pension,
which grew accordingly to Rs. 875. For a woman who had, in her own
words, "purchased" Jagatgiri "for a hundred rupees when he was only
three or four months old," this must have appeared galling. To the son,
by contrast, the pension and status conferred upon him by the British
would seem, as he came of age, little more than a confirmation of what
was owed him by rights. Possibly he and his *chela* brothers resented the
imputation that they were mere slaves, and in this sense they may have
savored the fact that the British conferral of status upon them brought
the Begum down a peg or two, or three. In any case, Jagatgiri would evolve
into "the most respectable [member] of the Goosaeen family at Banda" by
the 1840s, and would be called upon to offer his opinion regarding *gosain*
custom and tradition by political agents. Chehtee Begum, meanwhile,
would do all she could in her remaining years to frustrate attempts by the
*chela*s of Kanchangiri (her former "slaves") and their "slave girl" wives
to extend their pensions by "adopting" new *chela*s.[29]

---

[28] For the date of Chehtee Begum's death, see "Pension of Jagat Gir," Board's Collection
no. 196,345 (F/4/2719), OIOC, enclosing a letter from R. Hamilton to G. F. Edmonstone, secretary to the Governor General, AGG for Central India, extract of 7 Nov. 1856
(dated Indore, 20 Oct. 1856), Fort William Foreign Consultations.

[29] "The Humble Petition of Ranee Taje Koonwur," no. 105 of 3 Jan. 1834 (undated but
probably 1828), FDPP, in which the widow of Madhogiri (d. 1827) sought to defend
the claim of her late husband's *chela*, "Rodrindrurgeer." Chehtee Begum is here referred
to as "Aqila Begum." According to W. H. MacNaughten, secretary to Government, to
N. C. Hamilton, secretary to the Lieutenant-Governor of the North Western Provinces,
no. 26 of 15 Mar. 1841, Agra (dated 25 Sep. 1837), FDPP, the timely adoption of the son
of Madhogiri was not proved. The pension technically lapsed to Government, though
a small amount was given to the natural-born daughter for her life with a provision for
the maintenance of the mother, Taj Kuar.

It may seem odd, considering his biography, that Jagatgiri, when called upon by Fraser in 1841 for an opinion on the legitimacy of Narindargiri's heirs, would assert a *gosain* tradition of marriage and biological legitimacy bolstered by reference to Shankaracharya and the *shastra*s. Certainly elements of it strike this twenty-first-century observer as something of an invention, concocted to lend a Brahmanical pedigree to *gosain* practices that may have become widespread only in the eighteenth century. Several points must be kept firmly in mind in order to understand his puzzling position. First, though not necessarily most importantly, he was a well-wisher of the British. He had benefited enormously from Wauchope's decision-making in 1816, despite the determined attempts by Chehtee Begum to derail his elevation. Second, and perhaps more importantly, Jagatgiri thought of himself as Kanchangiri's son and *chela* and heir. Kanchangiri would only be a dim memory for him, since he died in 1808 when Jagatgiri was a mere child, older than Mukundgiri, but probably not too much younger than Narindragiri. He probably perceived a filial debt to his guru. Third, he certainly owed a debt to his *chela* brothers – or, given the difference in age, uncles – namely, Kamptagiri, Mahendragiri, and Madhogiri. They had promoted him as a "natural-born" son of Kanchangiri – possibly in order to mimic the successful accession of Narindragiri – and though the gambit ultimately failed, he still rose to primacy among the heirs. Probably they would have apprised him of all that occurred at the death of Anupgiri, and their own guru's role in manipulating the accession so as to favor the British takeover. Now, in 1840, the legitimacy of that accession, Narindragiri's accession, was being called into question. We can easily imagine that he felt an urgent call to defend its legitimacy, and thereby the good name of not only his guru-father but also himself. Hence the inheritance by "adopted" *chela*s as well as natural-born sons must be made to appear in conformity with *gosain* tradition. Working backwards he would have deduced that for natural-born offspring to be legitimate in the eyes of his patrons, the British, the parents must be married, and for the parents' marriage to be legitimate, the marriage must be legal according to Hindu law – i.e., *dharmashastra*. Seen in this light, it is likely that Jagatgiri was attempting to substantiate as longstanding and legal a device that had been adopted for reasons of political expediency by John Baillie and Kanchangiri in 1804, namely, the succession to Anupgiri's *gaddi* of the infant Narindragiri, *as a natural-born son* (more on this vexed issue in a moment).

At the same time, Jagatgiri was able to hedge his bet: *chela*s could be considered legitimate heirs if, and only if, there were no natural-born children. Recall his exact phrase: "Amongst Gosaeens, and especially in our family, it is a custom that so long as a child survive, born of a wife regularly married, a Chela cannot be heir, but if there be no legitimate child [the *chela*] becomes heir." Once his claim to succeed as a "natural-born son" was exposed, he was able to fall back on the fact that as a *chela* he could still occupy the position of *gaddi nishin* bestowed upon him by Kanchangiri. The fact that Kanchangiri did, in fact, put him forward in this manner, thus overlooking his senior *chela*s, speaks volumes, since it suggests that he was using Jagatgiri to repeat the charade that he and Baillie had enacted (possibly with Anupgiri's connivance) by installing Narindragiri in 1804. According to the *chela*s, Jagatgiri was installed on the throne in 1808, when Kanchangiri was on his deathbed. This date was not disputed by Chehtee Begum. But the very fact of the infant Jagatgiri's adoption/purchase, not to mention the fact of the deed produced by Chehtee Begum attesting to her guardianship of Jagatgiri, suggests that Kanchangiri had long been contemplating the possibility of a similar maneuver on the occasion of his own demise. He needed not only a child to be paraded as a natural-born son, but a widow to pretend to act as mother and dowager. The date of the deed is certainly suggestive of this, falling as it does in the same year as Anupgiri's death. In fact, it is possible that Kanchangiri's more senior *chela*s – and even Jagatgiri himself – were unaware of the subterfuge, and believed Jagatgiri to be the "real" son of Kanchangiri, until the arrival of the furious Chehtee Begum from Agra.

Umraogiri's nine wives

If Chehtee Begum exploded a few bombshells in 1816, Jagatgiri had one of his own to detonate in 1841. He informed Fraser that there were serious doubts as to whether Narindragiri was, in fact, either a natural-born or "adopted" son of Anupgiri. The infant's status had been seriously questioned from the start by Umraogiri, who alleged that Anupgiri's Begum, Chait Kuar, had produced a child out of thin air. As Jagatgiri described it,

> it is not known whether he [Narindragiri] was born of her or not; because the Begum went to Lucknow having obtained permission from Himmut Buhadoor and from thence she wrote that a son was born to her but none of the family would eat with Nurindurgir, and considered it improper, and even to this day, Raja Oomraogir [Umraogiri] and his family have this objection believing him [sic: not] to be the Begum's son but no body can speak with certainty on this subject.[30]

This was an extremely serious revelation and may well have played some role in the decision to declare the *jagir* "lapsed" in 1841 – despite the

---

[30] Enclosed in S. Fraser to J. Thomason, no. 25 of 15 Mar. 1841 (dated 5 Dec. 1840), FDPP.

official references to mismanagement of the estate, Narindragiri's debt, and lack of "legitimate" male issue. Most certainly it was an added factor in Umraogiri's public refusal to accept Baillie's installation of the child on Anupgiri's *masnad* (seat) in 1804, and his immediate departure "from the tent with some appearance of displeasure."[31] The implication is, as Jagatgiri tells it, that had Narindragiri been natural-born, Umraogiri would have raised no objection to the succession – lending credence, of course, to Jagatgiri's claim regarding the succession rights of natural-born sons of "a wife regularly married."

But Umraogiri recalled the episode differently, and had additional reasons for rejecting the staged coronation of Narindragiri. From his perspective, by placing Narindragiri on the *masnad*, Baillie and Kanchangiri were ignoring his claim as senior *chela* of Rajendragiri. According to this view, even if Narindragiri had been the natural-born son of Anupgiri, that still did not endow him with superior rights to inherit the *gaddi*. What counted were seniority and the intentions of the deceased. And as far as Umraogiri was concerned, not only was he, Umraogiri, the senior *chela* of their common guru, he was Anupgiri's intended successor to Rajendragiri's *masnad*. No doubt he had made these points to Baillie in 1804, upon Anupgiri's death, only to be rebuffed. He rehearsed them two years later in a lengthy petition to Wellesley:

The late Muha Rajah Anoop Geer Himmut Buhadur and myself were full brothers. On the death [in 1753] of Muha Rajah Rajinder Geer, my spiritual preceptor, I received from the late Nawab Sufdur Jung a Khellaut [*khilat*, or robe of honor] investing me with the government and in concert with my Brother and the adherents and dependants of my family, I proceeded to arrange and regulate the affairs of the Province. My brother, in the spirit of our mutual harmony and friendship, adopted my eldest son, and for a period of twenty years, continued to conduct the administration of public affairs, allowing me a jaidad of two lacks of rupees for the maintenance of myself and attendants while, I being relieved from the weight of all worldly concerns, passed my time on the banks of the Ganges in the full and undisturbed exercise of my religious duties. My brother continued in the province of Bundelcund for fifteen years, during which time he manifested every degree of attachment and devotion to the British Government. It is now two years since he sent for me in haste in his last illness; and *committing into my hands his ring and his chelah Kunchun Geer*, resigned his soul to his creator. With these facts all the chiefs and Rajahs of Bundlecund are acquainted but is probable that Captain Baillie, who had the charge of the affairs of that Province, was not fully apprized of them. While I was engaged in mourning for the death of my late brother, the above mentioned chelah, in concert with the other officers of the Government, availing himself of my absence, by various pretexts carried Captain Baillie to his

---

[31] Baillie to Mercer, no. 232 of 21 Jun. 1804 (dated 4 Jun. 1804), BSPC. See the previous chapter for a detailed discussion of this scene.

House and persuaded him to place on the Musnud a child of five years of age born of a Musselman woman in my brother's family. The Chelah considering my presence in the Province to be extremely hostile to his views, procured thro' Captain Baillie, a letter later addressed to me by his Excellency Lord Lake advising me to withdraw from all interference in the management of public affairs and to retire to some place within the company's dominions when an adequate provision would be assigned by the British Government for the support of myself and my followers. On the receipt of his Lordship's letter I immediately proceeded to the Headquarters of the army at Cawnpore.[32]

Several points in Umraogiri's petition are significant, but none more so than his assertion that Anupgiri had identified him, on his deathbed, as the new guru to his *chela*s. He did this, allegedly, both in symbol and in fact, by presenting Umraogiri with his ring *and* his senior *chela*, Kanchangiri. Kanchangiri possessed a self-understanding, however, that did not include obeisance to Umraogiri. This was evident in his maneuvering vis-à-vis Baillie and Narindragiri, but also in the recollection of his *chela* Jagatgiri, nearly four decades later, that Umraogiri was a *chela* of Anupgiri – thus placing Kanchangiri and Umraogiri on equal footing. Significantly, Jagatgiri's statement also included mention of the fact that both Umraogiri and Anupgiri were originally *chela*s of Rajendragiri, as did Umraogiri's petition. Umraogiri claimed that he had been certified as the senior *chela* by virtue of Safdar Jang's conferral of a *khilat* upon him at the death of their guru, Rajendragiri, and that he eventually handed power over to Anupgiri so that he, Umraogiri, could be "relieved from the weight of all worldly concerns" and pass "time on the banks of the Ganges in the full and undisturbed exercise of my religious duties." It is difficult to know Anupgiri's view on these matters. It is possible that his extraordinary success in Bundelkhand elevated himself in his own mind to a new level of autonomy, whether or not he fully subscribed to the monarchical model that his court poet, Padmakar, was peddling – and that he tended to adopt when dealing with the British.

Regardless of what Anupgiri intended, Umraogiri derided the coronation charade that Kanchangiri and Baillie had concocted – mostly because it weakened his hold on what he regarded as his *akhara*, as senior surviving *chela* of Rajendragiri. But he did as Baillie and Lake requested and retired to Company territory – to Kanpur or, more precisely, to nearby Sivrajpur, his settlement on the south bank of the Ganga – and he meddled no more in Anupgiri's affairs. Finally, after considerable delay, the new agent, John Richardson, in consultation with Baillie arrived at a

---

[32] "Translation of an Arzee from Omrao Geer," no. 83 of 2 Apr. 1807 (received 1 Nov. 1806), BPC. Emphasis added.

monthly pension of Rs. 1,000 as a reward for his good behavior.[33] They noted that Umraogiri's five sons, who had performed significant military services in Bundelkhand in their own right, had already been rewarded with pensions of Rs. 400 each. Umraogiri shifted to Banaras in early 1808 and, in the words of one of his *chela*s, "left this transitory world, and traveled to the world of eternity" in mid-January of 1809.[34]

Umraogiri's death sparked a new round of correspondences on the part of his *chela*s, who were concerned his pension be continued to his dependants. This necessitated, in turn, official clarification on the exact dimensions of Umraogiri's immediate family network, independent of the five sons already receiving pensions. According to the eldest of these, Gangagiri (alias "Dilawar Jang"), who prayed that Government would "give some support to his [Umraogiri's] dependants that their wages may continue as before," the deceased "left nine females and one son as determined [sic] who remained near him in his lifetime." In addition, there were "about forty or fifty *uteet*s[,] brothers adopted[,] besides other servants." Richardson divided the nine females into two groups, "four legal widows" and "five concubines." For the former, he suggested monthly pensions of Rs. 50 each, for a total of Rs. 200. The latter – "three of whom are Mussulman women, and two Hindoos" – did not merit any consideration in his view.[35] From later genealogical tables compiled in the early 1930s it is evident that each of the four women deemed a legal widow by Richardson (with the assistance of Gangagiri) was a mother to four of the five sons that had received independent pensions: thus, Shitab Kuar was mother to Jagat Bahadur, Rani Kumla mother to Uttam Gir, Bibi Mitteh mother to Ganga Baksh, and Chumpa Kuar mother to Ganga Gir (alias Dilawar Jang).[36] This coincidence raises the likelihood that

[33] Nos. 5 and 6 of 25 Aug. 1809, BPC.

[34] For Umraogiri's move to Banaras, no. 32 of 18 Apr. 1808, BPC; and "Translation of a petition from Koar Jeewungeer the second son of the late Rajah Omerow Geer," no. 62 of 20 Feb. 1809, BPC, for the quote. The exact date of Umraogiri's death, 12 January 1809, is known from Table I of "Genealogical Tables of Gushain Family," R/2/449/15, ISRR, entitled "Genealogical Table showing the distribution of the pension of Rs. 1000 per mensem granted in perpetuity to Raja Umrao Gir, brother to Maharaja Anup Gir Himmat Bahadur (Goshain)." The political agent for Bundelkhand, J. Richardson, was the first Company official to learn of Umraogiri's death, in the petition cited here.

[35] These pension deliberations are outlined in nos. 32–35 of 6 May 1809, BPC. Gangagiri provided a list of the distinct households, enclosed in these proceedings, but it is rendered in extremely sketchy form and is, consequently, of little use.

[36] This is arrived at by comparing two "Genealogical Tables" enclosed in R/2/449/15, ISRR: Table I, concerning Umraogiri, cited above, and Table II, "Genealogical Table showing the distribution of the pension of Rs. 2,000 per mensem granted to 5 sons of the family of Raja Umrao Gir, in consideration of their being the nephews of Maharaja Anup Gir Himmat Bahadur."

Richardson's estimation of their status as "legal widows" was a function, in large part, of the fact that their sons had proven themselves militarily or politically in Bundelkhand and were now recipients of sizable pensions. In other words, which of Umraogiri's nine women were to be deemed "wives" in official hindsight depended on the existence of high-achieving sons already receiving pensions in the present. Richardson also noted that "there is still unprovided for one son called Hunse Raje Geer, 14 or 15 years of age," and recommended that he receive Rs. 400 per month. The remaining Rs. 400 was awarded to Jiwangiri, who had just been summoned back by Umraogiri to Company territory from his post in Jaipur, only to learn of his father's demise (more on this momentarily).

An interesting and possibly revealing footnote to these proceedings concerned the youngest son, "Hunse Raje Geer," or Hansrajgiri. In a June 1809 letter requesting that he temporarily receive his pension in Banaras rather than Banda, in Bundelkhand, Hansrajgiri noted that his appointment as successor to Umraogiri was confirmed by "*the arbitrators*" who "*seated me in his place.*"[37] This is an evocative phrase. The arbitrators to whom Hansrajgiri referred were probably the members of a *Dasnami panchayat* or arbitration council appointed to certify succession and inheritance and, when necessary, to adjudicate disputes. Based on records from a 1798 case, Bernard Cohn suggested that Banaras had in place a permanent Dasnami *panchayat* – this is not surprising, considering the plethora of Dasnami *maths* in that city – and it was probably the same *panchayat* that adjudicated Hansrajgiri's succession in 1809.[38] Since there was no dispute between Umraogiri's seven sons, each now having received a monthly pension of Rs. 400, it would appear that the

---

[37] No. 6 of 22 Aug. 1809, BPC.

[38] Cohn, "The Role of Gosains in the Economy," 177–178. Cohn cites the *Sadr Diwani Adalat* Proceedings, Calcutta High Court Record Office, 30 May 1798, pp. 11–17, 29, and 8 Aug. 1798, p. 45. In the 1798 case, the *panchayat* divided the *mahant*'s personal property among the *chela*s. The relative amounts reflected the standing of each *chela* in relation to the *mahant* – so that the senior-most received the greatest share but also the responsibility of performing the death rites and erecting a fitting *samadhi* monument. The dispute erupted when the *chela* who had served as a traveling agent alleged that the senior *chela* had manipulated the division of property by virtue of his position and his uninterrupted access to the guru. This is not unlike Umraogiri's claim, cited above, that Kanchangiri took advantage of his absence "while I was engaged in mourning for the death of my late brother," and convinced Baillie to place Narindragiri on the *masnad*. The plaintiff in the Banaras case likewise claimed that the defendant took advantage of the fact that he "remained at home as treasurer at the *math*" while he, the plaintiff, "traveled throughout Bengal transacting commercial dealings." The defendant "kept the keys to the treasure box, and knew where the property was kept, as well as keeping the ledgers, day book, and the book containing the outstanding debts, and it was through this knowledge of his that he was able to get a larger share of the property of their *guru*."

panchayat was simply following ceremonial practice in certifying Hansrajgiri as successor to Umraogiri. The significance of this act is that it occurred at all, because it suggests that at least one of Umraogiri's heirs (and possibly Umraogiri himself) recognized the importance of Dasnami institutional authority in these matters. That it was not Gangagiri (alias Dilawar Jang) or any of the other older sons/*chela*s who was installed on Umraogiri's *gaddi* is also noteworthy, since it conforms to the separate pensions awarded them for their autonomous service in Bundelkhand. Here it is useful to recall Umraogiri's earlier words: "My brother [Anupgiri], in the spirit of our mutual harmony and friendship, *adopted my eldest son*, and for a period of twenty years, continued to conduct the administration of public affairs." This is apparently a reference to Gangagiri, a.k.a. Dilawar Jang, but it would appear that several others connected to Umraogiri made their military careers in the service of Anupgiri. Meanwhile, and perhaps in exchange, Anupgiri provided his brother "a jaidad of two lacks of rupees" so that he might be "relieved from the weight of all worldly concerns" and pass his time "on the banks of the Ganges in the full and undisturbed exercise of my religious duties." It was during those later years, on the banks of the Ganga, that one of Umraogiri's women gave birth to Hansrajgiri who, too young to take part in Anupgiri's Bundelkhand escapades, "remained near him [Umraogiri] in his lifetime."

Coming of age in Rasdhan, 1809–1814

Much else was transpiring in the summer of 1809, while Hansrajgiri was seating himself on the *gaddi* of Umraogiri. Not least of all, in May of that year Narindragiri, the heir to Anupgiri Gosain, was arriving in Rasdhan. Over three years had passed since the resumption of the Bundelkhandi *jaidad* and the termination of *gosain* military service under the British. Not surprisingly, the migration from military entrepreneurship in Bundelkhand to retirement in Rasdhan was a torturous one. Kanchangiri had decided in September of 1806 that rather than proceed immediately to the *jagir* in Rasdhan, the *gosain*s should instead seek military employment with Daulatrao Shinde at Gwalior.[39] He took Narindragiri and Anupgiri's widow with him. The decision to temporarily forego retirement at Rasdhan seems to have been precipitated in part by a delay in the delivery of the official Company *sanad* (title) granting Narindragiri the *jagir*, and in part by the insistence that the *gosain* cavalry be entirely disbanded so that "British Law [might] prevail in the Rajah's jaggeer in the same

[39] Baillie to Edmonstone, Banda, no. 7 of 16 Oct. (dated 30 Sep. 1806), BSPC.

manner as in all other parts of the Company's dominions."[40] So instead the *gosain*s opted for continued military employment, and Shinde's offer of nine lakhs-worth of *jaidad* revenues from the vicinity of Moth, their old headquarters in the days of Rajendragiri in the 1740s, was too good to pass up. But there were complications: the revenues of Moth were claimed by the *subadar* of Jhansi, who wrote repeatedly to Baillie on the subject and who ultimately had his way on the matter. Nevertheless, the *gosain*s remained with Shinde through 1808 while they explored various other opportunities.[41] After Kanchangiri's death in early October of that year, Narindragiri (or rather, his new manager, Goman Singh) indicated his desire to proceed to Rasdhan and reopened negotiations with the British agent, now in the form of Baillie's successor, John Richardson. However, as before, a major sticking point was the desire of the *gosain*s to proceed to Rasdhan with their full military establishment, including troops, weapons and, especially, heavy artillery. The question was resolved in mid-May of 1809, when the *gosain*s stored their guns and military stores at Sirsah and proceeded to Rasdhan.[42]

In the midst of their perambulations, however, dissension began to grow among Kanchangiri's *gosain* ranks. Indeed hints of this could be seen as early as 1806 in the months leading up to their departure from Bundelkhand. In May of that year, during the wait for the delivery of the Company *sanad* confirming the *jagir* at Rasdhan, and amid rumors that their forces were to be disbanded, a group of *gosain*s at Tindwari, eight miles northeast of Banda, decided to take matters into their own hands. Baillie "received authentic intelligence of preparations in the fortress of Tinwaree by Cooar Gunput Geer, for the defence and maintenance of that fortress in opposition to his master's [Kanchangiri's] command, and

---

[40] On the delay of the *sanad*, which did not arrive until 10 May, see Baillie to Edmonstone, no. 61 of 15 May 1806 (dated 4 May 1806), BSPC. Baillie had instructed Kanchangiri to disband the *gosain*s in late February (see no. 97 of 13 Mar. 1806, BSPC); he had originally hoped to retain some 500 *gosain* cavalrymen in British service, but this was countermanded by order of Government (no. 97 of 13 Mar. 1806 [dated 25 Feb. 1806], cf. no. 9 of 16 Oct. 1806 [dated 30 Sep. 1806]). Concerning the preeminence of British law in Rasdhan, see Edmonstone to Baillie, no. 7 of 29 May 1806 (dated 27 May 1806), BSPC.

[41] Baillie to Edmonstone (with intelligence from the *subadar* of Jhansi), no. 49 of 8 Jan. 1807 (dated 23 Dec. 1806); Baillie to Edmonstone (with enclosures 2–4), no. 1 of 26 Feb. 1807 (dated 10 Feb. 1807); and "Translation of a letter from Subadar of Jhansi," no. 23 of 9 Jul. 1807 (undated), BPC.

[42] Erskine, acting resident in Bundelkhand, to Edmonstone, no. 29 of 24 Oct. 1808 (dated 7 Oct. 1808); "Translation of an *arzee* from Nurinder Geer," no. 30 of 24 Oct. 1808 (received 4 Apr. 1808); Richardson to Edmonstone, no. 26 of 16 Jan. 1809 (dated 29 Dec. 1808); Edmonstone to Richardson, no. 33 of 16 Jan. 1809 (dated 16 Jan. 1809); Richardson to Edmonstone, no. 16 of 13 Mar. 1809 (dated 24 Feb. 1809); Richardson to Edmonstone, no. 13 of 24 Jun. 1809 (dated 8 Jun. 1809), BPC.

to the engagements contracted with me; several pieces of heavy cannon had been mounted on the walls of the fort, and around the town; the inhabitants of which had abandoned their dwellings."[43] Kanchangiri immediately brought Ganpatgiri to heel and suppressed as well a similar expression of discontent closer to hand – at the very fortress of Sumonee in front of which Baillie was then encamped.

While he was alive, Kanchangiri had been able to keep a lid on such momentary eruptions. His death in October 1808 inaugurated a new, more deeply divisive phase for the *gosain* army. In November, while the new manager Goman Singh (who was apparently not a *gosain*, and was appointed with the blessings of Baillie) was trying to usher the young *gosain*-raja toward Rasdhan, two of Kanchangiri's *chela*s, Madhogiri and Ramgiri, sought to hamper his every move – even to the point of offering to bribe the *subadar* of Gwalior for assistance in blocking the route. According to one report Shinde also began to involve himself in this new round of *gosain* intrigue and conspired to install Ramgiri as manager in place of Goman Singh.[44] The latter managed to prevail in that instance, but matters again came to a head in June of 1809, after Narindragiri had arrived in Rasdhan. This time, however, it was clear that women were also key players behind the scenes. According to Richardson, "the women belonging to the late Rajah Himmutt Bahaudur and the wife of the young Rajah himself (a child) . . . refuse to go across the Jumnah or to join the young Rajah at Rusdan." Meanwhile, Ganpatgiri (aforementioned from the 1806 affair at Tindwari) appeared at Banda to register a complaint against Goman Singh who, he alleged, "has the young Rajah under controul [sic], and maintains an entire ascendancy over him."[45] In April and again in August of 1810, Narindragiri (now twelve years of age) leveled a series of accusations of his own against Ganpatgiri and several other *gosain*s, whom he referred to as "atteats" (from Sanskrit *atithi*, a short-term guest and, as Francis Buchanan noted in Bihar [see above], one of several terms *gosain*s used to describe themselves), and one Thakurprasad Pandit (referred to in the correspondence as "Cashmerian" or Kashmiri): not only had these men taken the elder Rani (his mother) and young Rani (his wife) to Kanpur and incited them against him, they obstructed his movements about the *jagir*, stole his animals and property, dismissed his officers, appropriated the revenues of the estate, made false representations to the military authorities at Kanpur,

[43] Baillie to Edmonstone, no. 61 of 15 May 1806 (dated 4 May 1806), BSPC.
[44] R. Close, Acting Resident with Sindiah, to Richardson, no. 31 of 16 Jan. 1809 (dated 29 Nov. 1808); Delamain, Commanding the post at Koonch, to Richardson, no. 29 of 16 Jan. 1809 (dated 22 Nov. 1808), BPC.
[45] Richardson to Edmonstone, no. 13 of 24 Jun. 1809 (dated 8 Jun. 1809), BPC.

misled the District Magistrate, and entangled his manager Goman Singh in the district court with frivolous lawsuits. Narindragiri did not blame his mother for this, but rather vowed that that he was "ready to make a provision for the Ranee, equal to my means, and according to what she received, during the life time of my father."[46]

Richardson wrote to the Rani on 9 August 1810 requesting her presence in Banda so that he might assist in untangling her affairs. By now Narindragiri and his retinue, including Goman Singh, were parked in Banda awaiting Richardson's decisions on their fate. The Rani's reply arrived on Richardson's desk on 20 October.[47] She was apprehensive "on account of the evil disposition of Gomaun Sing" and his influence over Richardson, and asked for more clarity with respect to the latter's intentions before she would proceed to Banda. More importantly, she stated that she was deeply in debt to "the Mahajuns [bankers] of Cawnpore" and that "without discharging these sums, my moving from thence [would] be very difficult." Richardson was, as the Rani feared, inclined toward Narindragiri and Goman Singh's point of view. He even suspected, based largely on "the report of the respectable native chiefs of Bundelkhund, and the statement of the old servants of the deceased Rajah," that "this woman, calling herself 'the Rannee' of the Rajah Himmut Bahadur . . . who is now leagued with the atteets, and in Cawnpore, was never married to the said deceased Rajah; but like many other concubines, was in his service; but that she is certainly an atteet."[48] Richardson nevertheless felt that Ganpatgiri, who had in the meantime died, "was the great cause of these disputes," whereas the other *atiths* were, "from every account . . . merely the servants of the deceased Rajah Himmut Bahadur." He recommended that the Rani be separated from

---

[46] "Proceedings of Mr. John Richardson," no. 151 of 28 Dec. 1810 (dated 12 Apr. 1810), BPC. This contains four long documents: (1) "Letter from the Rajah Nerinder Gier," received 12 Apr. 1810, and (for the quote), (2) "Translation of a letter from the Rajah Nerinder Geer," received 16 Apr. 1810, (3) "Proceedings of Mr. John Richardson Agent to the Governor General in Bundlelkhund, the 9th of August 1810," and (4) "Proceedings of Mr. John Richardson Agent to the Governor General in Bundelkhund under date the 20th of October 1810." According to Narindragiri (and Goman Singh who, no doubt, had a hand in writing the first two documents), the main instigators were: "Gunput Gier, the chelah of Doorgah Gier, and Shew Gier, the chelah of Achel Gier, and Takoor Purshaud, the son of Soonder Laul of the Cashmerian Cast who was in the time of my father Dewan."

[47] "Proceedings of Mr. John Richardson Agent to the Governor General in Bundelkhund under date the 20th of October 1810," BPC (see the previous footnote).

[48] This assertion, that the Rani "is certainly an atteet," is an interesting one given the contradictory evidence from the revelations of 1840 and 1841. If the Rani had presented herself in this way, one could speculate that this was an attempt on her part to cement her legal status (recalling Warden's note of 1827 and the stipulation that permissible *gosain* marriages were between male and female *gosain*s).

their nefarious influences and that a pension of Rs. 100 per month be bestowed upon her. As for the young wife of Narindragiri, Richardson ordered that the magistrate of Kanpur "should cause the young Rajah's wife to be taken to and deposited in his [Narindragiri's] house."

In early March Richardson received reports that the "the Atteets and the old Ranee," still in Kanpur, were making preparations to decamp to Banaras with Narindragiri's wife. He immediately asked Russell, the magistrate of Kanpur, to intervene and suggested to Narindragiri in the meantime that he depute a confidential person to attend the magistrate and assist in the avoidance of bloodshed. Narindragiri chose two household servants, "Nonny Geer and Shaikh Noor Ally," who departed with a retinue immediately for Kanpur. Russell reported in late March that the Rani, faced with his and Richardson's intervention on the side of Narindragiri and Goman Singh, had resolved "to throw herself under the immediate protection of the Rajah, by accompanying his wife to Rasdaun." Narindragiri had anticipated such a contingency and instructed his men on the spot to accede to this request should it be forthcoming. After some negotiations, the Rani's "clamorous" creditors were satisfied with a Rs. 5,000 advance from Narindragiri. By early April of 1811 the two Ranis were settled in Rasdhan and Richardson had confirmed Goman Singh in the management of Narindragiri's affairs.[49]

For a brief moment, all seemed well. But six months later Goman Singh died, sparking off a new round of intrigue. Narindragiri appointed Goman Singh's widow manager, with the actual duties to be carried out by her late husband's clerk, one "Oodyeraje" [Udayraj]. Richardson was alarmed on two counts: "a woman cannot with propriety be the young Rajah's manager," and Udayraj did not appear to possess sufficient fidelity for such "an important trust."[50] Consequently in February of 1812 he nominated Ayodhya Prasad as the child-raja's manager, with the assistance of Waj ud-din Khan. Both were old and trusted servants of Anupgiri. Their overtures to Narindragiri were rebuffed, however. Ayodhya Prasad reported in late May that a new circle had formed around the child-raja; some of the names were familiar, others were new: "Hunsraje Geer [confirmed as Umraogiri's heir in 1809], Noonee Geer [deputed to Kanpur by Narindragiri in March of 1811 to deal with the Rani], Tage ud Deen, and Tackoorpurshaud [the "Casmirian"] would not permit the Nawab Wudju ud Deen Khan to exercise the authority of manager, or to get possession of any of the Rajah's papers." To make matters worse, these men had "possession of the Rajah's seal" and were "writing whatever they

---

[49] See the letters between Richardson and Russell during March and April, enclosed in Richardson to Edmonstone, no. 66 of 3 May 1811 (dated 14 Apr. 1811), BPC.
[50] Richardson to Edmonstone, no. 41 of 25 Jan. 1812 (dated 11 Jan. 1812), BPC.

chose, in the Rajah's name, and putting his seal to the same." Meanwhile, Narindragiri had accused Goman Singh's widow and her man Udayraj of embezzlement; he then declared himself, though only thirteen years of age, "capable of judging of what is beneficial or otherwise to my affairs and able to manage my own concerns." After all, he observed, "The people who managed a country producing 20 Lacks of Rupees per annum and commanded 15,000 Horse and Foot are all, except two or three that are dead, still with me." However, if the British Government insisted upon the appointment of a manager, then Narindragiri preferred Noonee Geer, "who is the son of my uncle" (presumably in reference to Umraogiri). Faced with these options, Richardson reluctantly felt it "better that the Rajah be left to himself."[51]

Predictably Narindragiri's affairs worsened in the coming months. The confusion was compounded by the arrival of a new political agent in Banda, John Wauchope, and a new district magistrate in Kanpur, J. Ryley, toward the end of 1812. Another new figure appears in the correspondence during this phase, namely, "the Rajah's grandmother," sometimes referred to as "the Begum." (Narindragiri refers in a later letter to two additional women, "Jamdakhanum" and "Sahibjan", as "the women of the family of Maharajah".[52] It is likely that one of these was the "grandmother", and that she was an elder wife of Anupgiri.) In mid-July of 1812 Narindragiri had bestowed upon his grandmother the incomes from two villages, Hatuman and Mahmudpur, suggesting that she had only recently arrived in Rasdhan.[53] In March or April of 1813, this individual joined forces with Taj ud-din Bakshi (described as "the tutor"), Sohan Lal, Nonigiri, "and other of the Atteets his dependants," against Thakurprasad "Cashmeree," whom they accused of seducing the young Raja "into every species of profligacy and immorality."[54] Taking the administration

---

[51] Richardson to Edmonstone, no. 35 of 25 Sep. 1812 (dated 7 Sep. 1812), BPC; and "Proceedings of Mr. J. Richardson Acting Agent to the Governor General under date the 2nd September 1812," no. 36 of 25 Sep. 1812, BPC.

[52] "Translation of a letter from Rajah Nerender Geer Himmat Bahadur to the Superintendent of Political Affairs in Bundelcund ," no. 24 of 20 May 1814 (no date), BPC.

[53] "Translation of a letter from the Grand Mother of Rajah Nerinder Geer," no. 33 of 17 Sep. 1813 and "Translation of the copy of a grant enclosed in a letter from Rajah Nerinder Geer," no. 34 of 17 Sep. 1813, BPC. The *sanad* is dated 8 Rajab 1227, which corresponds to 17 Jul. 1812. Some questions immediately jump to mind: Was the grandmother, in fact, a senior wife of Anupgiri? It seems likely. Meanwhile, the Rani is nowhere to be seen during this phase. Has she left Rasdhan temporarily? As we shall see, she returns in 1814.

[54] Wauchope to J. Ryley, Magistrate of Zillah Cawnpore, no. 14 of 18 Jun. 1813 (undated), BPC; this is also recorded as no. 28 of 26 Jun. 1813, Bengal Judicial Department, Criminal Consultations (BJCC), OIOC, London. The other "atteets" named in the chargesheet drafted by Wauchope are: "Nonee Geer, Sheo Gheer, Kedar Geer, Moje Geer, Muttra Geer, Nehal Geer, Nyne Geer, Imrut Geer, Davee Geer, [and] Bussunt Geer."

of the *jagir* into their own hands, the grandmother and company expelled Thakurprasad from Rasdhan, confined Narindragiri to his rooms, and seized his seal. Ryley's attempts to intervene and make contact with Narindragiri via the *thanadar* (police superintendent) of nearby Rajpur were initially rebuffed by Taj ud-din and Sohan Lal, who insisted that only the agent at Banda had jurisdiction over the affairs of Rasdhan. A second, more forceful visit to Rasdhan by the *thanadar* in unison with an official from Wauchope's office, one Amir Ali, on 14 May, revealed new cracks in the insurgency. After some preliminary attempts by the conspirators to once again rebuff the visitors, some servants appeared and stated that "the Begum" had ordered "the Atteats" to guard the rooms of the palace in which Narindragiri was confined. A few hours later, one Phulgiri attended by Hawanchalgiri (described as "a relation of the Rajah's") came forward to state that

Nonee Geer and others, Atteets, had confined the Rajah in the Mebj Mehleh and had taken up their abode within the fort for the last six weeks and that in disobedience to the orders of the Agent to the Governor General and the Magistrate, they persisted in a continuance of their improper behaviour and that during the last two days they had prevented the Rajah from taking his usual meals and his servants from shaving, and that the Begum had been presented by them with 1,000 Rupees in cash, and a village in Jageer, to consent to take upon herself the responsibility of their transactions.

Later, in the evening, one of the sepoys who accompanied the *thanadar* was perceived by Narindragiri "from the top of the wall." The young raja yelled down that he wished to speak to the sepoy's master. The *thanadar* was immediately summoned and the two held an extended interview, during the course of which Narindragiri "called out that he had been in a state of confinement for the last six weeks, requesting him to give immediate information to me [Ryley] of this outrage, and also to state that the Begum was grossly reviled." The *thanadar* returned to the village *kachehri* (courthouse) and was then informed that the Begum herself was approaching. Ignoring the *thanadar*'s polite remonstrance that protocol required him to wait upon her at her leisure, the Begum came forward and denounced as "very improper" the refusal to allow the *thanadar* to deliver the magistrate's letter and declared as well that "the quarrels and dissentions which existed between the Cashmeries and the Atteets would be the ruin of her Family." In response he asked her to "use her influence with the Atteets to desist from such outrageous conduct," and then proceeded back to Rajpur.[55]

[55] For the visit of the *thanadar* to Rasdhan, see Ryley to G. Dowdeswell, chief secretary to Government, no. 48 of 5 Jun. 1813 (dated 21 May 1813), BJCC.

Despite the Begum's assurances, however, matters soon took a more serious turn. Nonigiri and Sivgiri, who seemed briefly to repent of their earlier involvement in the uprising, reported to the *thanadar* that after his departure some of the *gosain* conspirators had burst into Narindragiri's rooms fully armed and demanded that he write immediately to the Governor General's agent at Banda: were they to be "severely punished . . . they would not suffer the Rajah to outlive their disgrace." On 1 June Ryley received an urgent message from Phulgiri informing him that a subset of the conspirators, including "Tajuddin, Mooja Gueer, Kedar Gueer, Imrut Gueer, Muttra Gueer and other Atteets[,] forcibly took away Rajah Nerinder Gueer from Rasdan upon an elephant and carried him across the Jumna." Once it was clear that they were not proceeding directly to Banda to wait upon Wauchope, Ryley suggested sending a battalion of sepoys in pursuit. Meanwhile, Wauchope, who was on tour, alerted the resident with Shinde as well as several local chieftains, "requesting them to use their utmost means to seize the perpetrators of this outrageous act of violence, and to obtain the rescue of the Rajah."[56] Perhaps aware that the net was closing in on them, the conspirators decided to repair to Banda with Narindragiri in tow and make the best of it. They arrived there on the 11 June and informed Wauchope's deputy, R. T. Glyn, who had not yet been fully apprised of the situation by either Ryley or Wauchope, "that [Narindragiri] crossed the Jumnah on a hunting excursion, and that Mouj Gueer, Khador Gueer and others not permitting him to return, insisted upon his proceeding to Banda, to lay the state of his affairs before the Agent."[57] Wauchope's return to Banda on the 24 June put a stop to the charade, however. He quickly ordered the arrest of Taj ud-din and four *gosain*s, including Nonigiri, and dispatched them on two elephants under the guard of twenty sepoys to be tried by Ryley in Kanpur. Twelve others, including Hansrajgiri, Sivgiri, and Sohan Lal, were ordered to pay Rs. 200 each security against attending the court in Kanpur. Their more lenient treatment reflected the fact that Narindragiri had voluntarily withdrawn charges against them. Finally, Wauchope was pleased to announce that Narindragiri had nominated the respected Waj ud-din Khan as manager. "[I]f the Rajah will allow himself to be regulated by this person, I have no doubt that he will reform from that course of profligacy and extravagance into which, I have every reason to believe, he has been led by the influence and example of Thakoorpershaud Cashmeeree."[58]

---

[56] Ryley to Dowdeswell, no. 62 of 12 Jun. 1813 (dated 1 Jun. 1813) and Ryley to Wauchope, no. 65 of 12 Jun. 1813 (dated 2 Jun. 1813), BJCC; Wauchope to Ryley, no. 16 of 18 Jun. 1813 (dated 5 Jun. 1813), BPC.

[57] Glyn to Ryley, no. 30 of 26 Jun. 1813 (dated 11 Jun. 1813), BJCC.

[58] Wauchope to Ryley, no. 38 of 17 Jul. 1813 (dated 29 Jun. 1813), BPC.

Again, all seemed well in Rasdhan. On 7 October sentences were meted out in the Kanpur court: Taj ud-din, Nonigiri, Sivgiri, Kedargiri, Mojgiri, Mathuragiri, Nainigiri, Nehalgiri, and Debigiri, and were found guilty by Ryley of "resistance to the process and contempt to the authority" of the district court and were fined accordingly. The first three were ordered to pay Rs. 500, the next four Rs. 200, and the last two Rs. 100. Since Sohan Lal had attended the court when ordered to do so in the first instance, Ryley recommended his pardon. On the following day, the Governor General in Calcutta ordered that the *jagir*, which had been temporarily "attached" by government in June due to news of the kidnapping affair, be restored to Narindragiri.[59] Remarkably, Wauchope seems to have allowed Thakurprasad to remain in Narindragiri's service, despite having warned him in June "of the heavy responsibility which would attach to him if the conduct ascribed to him proved true" – and despite the fact that no less a figure than the trusted Waj ud-din Khan had confirmed that "the Rajah's health and morals had suffered to a lamentable degree from the vicious courses into which he had been plunged by" the Kashmiri.[60] Waj ud-din Khan died soon after his appointment as manager however, which may have had something to do with the resurrection of Thakurprasad's fortunes (though the records are unusually silent on this point).[61] In any case, it did not take long for controversy to once again erupt in Rasdhan. In late February of 1814 several *atith*s led by Nonigiri and Kedargiri, who had been fined for contempt of court the previous October, "approached the door of the apartment of the women of Rajah Nerinder Geer." According to a petition that they filed with W. Tippet, acting magistrate in Kanpur, in March, the *atith*s "had gone to make their obeisance at the door of the Ranee Sahib, their mistress," but "Thakoor Purshad, Azzeez oollah and other Cashmerians had stationed sentries at the doors who prevented them." The *atith*s had then been forcibly ejected from the village. They claimed further that "7 sentries were stationed at the door of the Muhul, [and] that Bhujjun Lall the Ranee's servant had been for two days confined under sentries and removed and that the Ranee had in consequence passed two days in bewailing and lamentation." Tippet received two letters purportedly from the Rani "(vizt. Ranee Chiet Kooar

[59] Dowdeswell to J. E. Colebrooke and J. Deane, Board of Commissioners in the Ceded and Conquered Provinces, no. 25 of 8 Oct. 1813 (dated 25 Sep. 1813), and Adam to Wauchope, no. 26 of 8 Oct. 1813, BPC.

[60] Wauchope to Ryley, no. 14 of 18 Jun. 1813 (undated), BPC.

[61] For the year of Waj ud-din Khan's death, see M. Ainslee, Agent to the Governor General in Bundelkhund, to Macnaghten, secretary to Government, no. 45 of 21 Jun. 1833 (dated 3 Jun. 1833), Fort William Political Consultations (hereafter FWPC), extracted in "Resumption of the Jagheer of the late Wujjie ood Deen Khan," no. 58833, Board's Collection (1834/35), OIOC.

the wife of Rajah Anoop Geer Himmut Behadur)" essentially confirming the petition of Nonigiri and Kedargiri: "the malice of the Cashmerians had proceeded to such a height that her existence was a burthen to her and she was in fear of both her honor and her life begging that a chupprassie [clerk, peon] might be sent [from Kanpur] to protect her honor." Tippet resolved to write to Narindragiri to urge him to take steps "to secure the peace and comfort of the Ranee and the other ladies."[62]

In mid-April the complainants, namely, Taj ud-din, Nonigiri, Kedargiri, Sohan Lal, several other *atith*s, and a *vakil* (lawyer) on behalf of Rani Chait Kuar, appeared before Wauchope in Banda. They complained, first, of the indignities being suffered by the Rani "at the instigation of Azeez Oollah and Thakoor Purshaud two Cashmereans in the Rajah's service," and second, of the dismissal of the former group from the provision "to which they conceive their connection and services with the late Rajah Himmut Behadur entitle them." In the meantime Wauchope had received from Narindragiri's grandmother "repeated complaints of the ill usage she receives from her grandson, which, in common with the other members of the late Rajah's family she attributed to the baneful influence the Cashmereans have obtained over the Rajah's mind." Like Tippet, Wauchope took it upon himself to write to the young raja to offer a friendly "remonstrance," especially "in consideration of the serious distress and privation to which I understand Ranee Chyte Kooar is now exposed." But given that Government (in the form of his predecessor, Richardson) had, in 1812, declared Narindragiri "competent to conduct his own affairs," he did not feel "authorized to interfere in rescuing him from the course of profligacy and extravagance into which I am credibly informed his association with the Cashmereans has lately plunged him."[63]

A month later, in May 1814, Wauchope received Narindragiri's reply. It was electric. After rehearsing the travails of the previous year, including his detention and kidnapping by Nonigiri, Taj ud-din, Sohan Lal and the other *atith*s, he alleged that "the rogues wrote improper letters against me in the names of Chyt Coar, and Jamdakhanum, and Sahibjan, the women of the family of Maharajah [Anupgiri] (who is in heaven) and having affixed the seal of these weak women, presented them to [Mr. Tippet] the acting Magistrate." He defended Thakurprasad and Azizullah, and insisted that "without my orders they cannot expend a cowree." As for the Rani and the other women of his family, he was explicit:

[62] "Translation of Proceedings held by Mr. Tippet acting Magistrate of Cawnpore under date the 16th of March 1814," enclosed in Tippet to Wauchope, no. 26 of 13 May 1814 (dated 11 Mar. 1814), BPC.
[63] Wauchope to Adam, no. 25 of 13 May 1814 (dated 15 Apr. 1814), BPC.

The weak women desire that the aforementioned rogues shall again be employed. The hundred Rupees fixed by the Governor General in Council to Chyt Coar is paid monthly, even one or two hundred Rupees extra from time to time for cloths etc. and the other women according to custom get what is proper and are regularly paid.

The above women are inimical to me in desiring the rogues to be restored, to this effect they have written improper letters and falsely related acts that are unworthy [of] the dignity of my family to the acting Magistrate, and to the presence [Wauchope]. They are wholly unworthy of credit for what opportunity has Uzeez Oollah and others to carry off and dispose of money and jewels or why should I suffer it? On account of the death of Moharajah [Anupgiri] (who is in heaven) during my minority, I am well acquainted with the world, and require no one [to] point out what is my own interest, and every one is well disposed towards me.[64]

Wauchope did not, it seems, draft a reply. Narindragiri and Thakurprasad were left to their own devices. A petition from Rani Chait Kuar eighteen years later, in December of 1832, confirms that matters remained where they stood in 1814. In addition to reporting her distressed condition and the ruinous state of her followers, especially Nonigiri and Sohan Lal, she complained that the managers had conspired to give over to moneylenders many of the villages constituting the *jagir* so as to satisfy the steep debt into which Narindragiri had plummeted.[65]

Just over seven years later, Narindragiri would die. At the time of his death he was about forty or forty-one years of age.

Gosain tawaif

This journey back in time, beginning with Narindragiri's tumultuous death in 1840 and ending with his coming of age in Rasdhan between 1809 and 1814, has brought us into the *gosain* household. Once inside, it becomes clear that women were central actors in *gosain* politics – both in internal maneuvering vis-à-vis other *gosain* factions, and with respect to the mechanics of succession under British patronage. The history of

---

[64] "Translation of a letter from Rajah Nerender Geer Himmat Bahadur to the Superintendent of Political Affairs in Bundelcund ," no. 24 of 20 May 1814 (no date), BPC.

[65] W. H. Macnaghten to Swinton, Chief Secretary, no. 5 of 21 Jan. 1833 (dated 25 Dec. 1832), FWPC, extracted in no. 60007, Boards Collection (1834/35), OIOC. According to the petition, which was received in December of 1832, the Rani complained that Narindragiri, "having associated with the lower class of people contrary to usage of the family . . . expended considerable sums of money and consequently he has become involved into debt to the amount of 3 Lacks of rupees exclusive of interest, the Mahajuns [bankers] have induced the Rajah through their leagues with the officers newly appointed to mortgage to them his villages for the money lent to him, and they separately collect the revenue of the same."

gosain settlement in Rasdhan (and Banaras and Banda) suggests that
there were significant numbers of women in *gosain* retinues, and some of
these women were remarkably influential. Two, in particular, stand out,
based on the foregoing discussion: Chehtee Begum a.k.a. Akila Begum,
in Kanchangiri's establishment, who exploded onto the scene in Banda
in 1808 to demand a recalibrated pension for Kanchangiri's heirs; and
Narindragiri's "mother," Chait Kuar, who in the late 1790s produced
a "son" of uncertain pedigree under mysterious circumstances while on
leave from Anupgiri's camp. A third woman who is more mysterious but
clearly influential was Narindragiri's "grandmother," also known as "the
Begum" (named either Sahibjan or Jamdakhanum). She appeared on the
scene in 1812 and sided with the old "ateets" against the Kashmiris and
Narindragiri. Given Narindragiri's cryptic comment in 1814 about the
"women of the family of the Maharaja," it seems likely that this was one
of Anupgiri's older wives.

It is difficult to get a firm handle on the women who entered into oscillating orbit with *gosain*s. They constantly reinvented themselves to suit the
moment – not unlike their *gosain* partners. The powerful deemed themselves – and, for the most part, were taken to be – ranis or begums, terms
that connote means and status. Many more, however, were described in
official correspondence as "concubines," "prostitutes," and "slaves" –
terms that approximated the Hindustani *tawaif*, *randi*, and *bandi*, respectively. These should not be thought of as fixed statuses. Narindragiri's
mother, Chait Kuar, was alleged by the children of her rivals to have begun
life as "a Mahomedan concubine named Kamraur."[66] John Richardson,
Baillie's successor as agent in Bundelkhand, believed her to also be an
atith. Like so many in the eighteenth and early nineteenth centuries, her
origins were ambiguous. One could easily imagine a situation whereby
a girl could be purchased as a slave, eventually gain service as one of
several "prostitutes" or "concubines" in a military entourage, produce
a son or otherwise gain influence and means, and gradually achieve
status and seniority as senior "wife." This is no more unusual than a
purchased slave boy gradually gaining the status of *chela* and son, and
eventually claiming the *gaddi* as *mahant*, as was the case with Jagatgiri (not to mention Umraogiri and Anupgiri and probably many others). On the other hand, it is possible that a woman might enter the
service of a successful commander like Anupgiri, having already established her reputation as high-status *tawaif* – a term that is often translated as "courtesan" but connotes a much broader range of cultural

---

[66] H. Rose, Deputy Collector Cawnpore District, to R. Lowther, Commissioner of
Allahabad, no. 24 of 15 Mar. 1841 (dated Cawnpore, 10 Mar. 1840), FDPP.

accomplishments. In this case she would enter the military establishment on her own terms, and bring a considerable retinue with her, according to a negotiated contract of so many rupees per month plus incidental expenses for the upkeep of her own musical entourage and household connections.[67] As such, she was a kind of commander in her own right and could be expected to behave haughtily to slaves (male or female) that she considered "beneath" her. This scenario may well have approximated Chehtee Begum's situation in 1808, when Jagatgiri and his older and more seasoned *chela*/brothers tried to take advantage of the relative ignorance of the new Company rulers to cement a higher status for themselves and usurp her position as senior "wife."

Even if a woman were a highly accomplished *tawaif* in eighteenth-century north India, it is entirely possible that, like many *gosain*s, she had been an orphan early in life.[68] She may well have been "adopted" into a *tawaif* "*gharana*" or circle in the same way that Anupgiri and Umraogiri and countless others were introduced into the *gosain akhara* – as young children who, as fate would have it, were abandoned or sold by their parents, or otherwise cut off from them, and cast adrift in an uncertain world. Indeed, the term *gharana*, which derives from *ghar*, or household/home, is analogous in many ways to *akhara* insofar as it constituted a corporate body composed of people whose identity was shaped not by biological ties but shared professional understanding, practical expertise, and behavioral style. For the young boys who became *naga*s, that meant understanding of and practice in the arts of war, particularly close-quarter combat, and a specific way of presenting themselves as predator-warriors

---

[67] For an excellent example of two such arrangements executed in late eighteenth-century Kanpur, see Hasan Shah, *The Nautch Girl*, trans. Qurratulain Hyder (New Delhi 1993), pp. 31–33. The original title of this Persian tale was *Nashtar*, or "Surgeon's Knife." Usually described as an "autobiographical novel," Hasan Shah is said to have written *Nashtar* in 1790; it was subsequently translated into Urdu by Sajjad Hussain Kasmandavi in 1893. The story describes the tragedy of a love affair between Hasan Shah, head *munshi* to one "Ming Sahib," and Khanum Jan, a young woman brought up in a "band of camp followers who sang and danced for English officers of the East India Company" (p. vii).

[68] Beyond the work of Indrani Chatterjee and Sumit Guha, cited earlier, the historical literature on courtesans in late medieval, early modern India is limited – more so when one tries to connect nineteenth and twentieth-century developments to earlier periods. See, for example, Moti Chandra, *The World of Courtesans* (Delhi 1973). New studies are emerging, however: Veena Talwar Oldenburg, "Lifestyle as Resistance: The Case of the Courtesans of Lucknow," in V. Graff (ed.), *Lucknow: Memories of a City* (Delhi 1997), pp. 136–154, provides a useful portrait of the continued autonomy, if not agency, of north Indian courtesans in a world that has become decidedly more patriarchal. Durba Ghosh, "Colonial Companions: Bibis, Begums, and Concubines of the British in North India, 1760–1830" (Ph.D. dissertation, University of California, Berkeley, 2000), uses Bengal court records concerning inheritance to situate north Indian courtesans in the transition to British rule; see chapters 2, "Residing with Begums," and 3, "Lives of Contrast."

hardened by life on the edge. Their professional identity entailed expert use of the tools of war – the cudgel, stone, dagger, sword, spear, lance, disk, bow and arrow, and increasingly as the seventeenth century became the eighteenth, musket and "rocket." With luck, and experience, they could one day aspire to be *gosain* commanders. Girls that were absorbed into a *tawaif gharana* likewise came to possess and partake in a corporate identity forged out of a shared understanding, expertise, and style. Theirs was a close-quarter, hand-to-hand combat of a different kind, steeped in the art of entertainment, the theatre of love, and the craft of sex. Among their tools of war were the crystalline voice, the coquettish glance, the heaving bosom, the rhythmic foot, the eloquent hand, and the coupling embrace. As Mahlaq Bai Chanda, the famous Hyderabadi *tawaif*, put it,

> "The sly glance is more murderous than arrow or sword;
> It has shed the blood of many a lover."[69]

By elevating co-religionist marriage and family-based production of offspring as the basis for legal respectability during the early nineteenth century, the British successfully marginalized both the *tawaif gharana* and the *gosain akhara*.[70] In so doing, they severely restricted the degree to which *gosain*s and *tawaif*s could wield their respective weapons in the pursuit of material and political gain. Some would carve out new identities for themselves, as "respectable" representatives of the *gosain* household. It is hard to know for certain what became of the others – those who were on the losing side of pension disputes – though we do know that many, such as Kalindargiri in 1857, would choose open rebellion.

Embedded in the British apprehension, and domestication, of *gosain* households was, as I have suggested above, an understanding of asceticism that allowed no room for sexuality, soldiering, slaving, the acquisition of material wealth (including slaves), and the production of offspring. For the British, asceticism meant monasticism, and therefore meant quiet, celibate, sedentary worship. As Warren Hastings put it in 1773, when banning armed *sanyasi*s and *fakir*s from the province of Bengal, acceptable *sanyasi*s were restricted to those "fixed inhabitants" who "quietly employ themselves in their religious function,"[71] i.e., worshipping a distant, inscrutable, yet loving God. As it happened, and as Hastings

---

[69] Trans. Syed Sirajuddin in Susie Tharu and K. Lalita (eds.), *Women Writing in India*, vol. I (New York 1991), p. 122.

[70] Seen from the vantage point of the Presidency centers, the British concern for sexual respectability was as much a repudiation of the mixed-race marriages of early Company officials as it was an attack on the seductive late-Mughal decadence in which *gosain*s and early Company officials (and countless others) were immersed. See Ghosh, "Colonial Companions," 276–291.

[71] No. 5 of 21 Jan. 1773, FDSP.

noted, there were plenty of individuals on the ground in Bengal and elsewhere who, as *bhakta*s and *sadhu*s (devotees), not to mention *pujari*s and *purohit*s (temple officiates and priests), approximated that Enlightenment definition of religion and its monastic corollary. The religious and literary culture in which these figures were immersed reveals, moreover, a deep discomfort with the political exploits and lavish lifestyles of warlord ascetics. The *sant-bhakti* verse of Tulsidas and Kabir are particularly relevant in this regard, given their prominence in the development of early modern and modern Hindu religious culture. As I note at the outset of the next chapter, a sentiment attributed to the fifteenth-century Kabir (but probably composed in the seventeenth or even eighteenth century) lampooned armed *yogi*s as "false *siddha*s, lovers of *maya* . . . They shame their profession by wearing gold. They collect stallions and mares, acquire villages, and go about as millionaires."[72] Likewise, the early seventeenth-century Tulsidas, also considered in the following chapter, had nothing but contempt for the stock figure of the self-centered ascetic – the "*tapasi*," or one who practices *tapas*, or austerities, to gain power – who, in his view, is a "master of deceipt," "scheming and guileful," and "hypocritical."[73]

The rising intolerance for "political *yogi*s" was, significantly, part of a larger shift in religious culture: as David White has observed, in his study of *siddha* traditions in medieval India, the term "*yogi*" or "*jogi*" has long been associated with a suspect tantra subculture, replete with "black magic, sorcery, sexual perversion, and subversion of alimentary prohibitions," and has been a target of orthodox and devotionalist Hindu ire for about the last eight centuries.[74] Some taste of this is can be found in the negative understandings of *sanyasi* sexuality as institutionally corrosive, noted earlier, in *dharmashastra* and Shankaracharya hagiography. By the late eighteenth century, I would argue, these combined critiques created a religio-cultural context in which Company policy-makers such as Hastings and Sleeman could operate with relative confidence and freedom – and as is well known, *dharmashastra* offered a particularly rich source from which Company officials drew for the derivation, or rather, *divination*, of British-Indian law. But the British, while clearly instrumental in the decline of the *gosain* power in Rasdhan, not to mention the popularization of orthodox Brahmanical attitudes generally (and especially via the Law), should not be seen as the primary authors of cultural and religious

---

[72] Translated most recently by Lorenzen in "Warrior Ascetics in Indian History," 61, who questions the attribution to Kabir and suggests a later, post 1526 date for composition.

[73] *Sri Ramacharitamanasa* (Gorakhpur 1968), 135–150 (ch. 160, d. 160, ch. 162). See Pinch, "History, Devotion, and The Search for Nabhadas of Galta," esp. 392, for more discussion.

[74] White, *The Alchemical Body*, pp. 8–9. It appears, then, that British apprehensions about "political sadhus" that I describe in *Peasants and Monks in British India*, pp. 4–9, had a long pedigree.

change in modern India. This is another way of saying that we should not confuse the court with society, though the former clearly reflects shifts occurring in the latter – and, to a lesser degree, vice versa. Nor should we rely overly on court records to construct arguments about cultural change. To do so grants far too much agency to the British as *colonizers*.[75] What is clear from the recounting of early modern religious culture in this work is that a deep distrust of armed ascetics – and of non-monastic ascetics generally – was in the air, and that a measure of that distrust had to do with vague concerns about unbridled sexuality. The British shared that distrust and, indeed, did much to popularize it; but they did not invent it.

*Yogi*s fighting

This brings us to an unusual painting held in the National Museum in Delhi (figure 8). I first came across this painting in the mid-1980s, in a "coffee-table" book depicting India's immense variety of "holy men".[76] As is typical with books of this sort, there was not much in the way of descriptive information. The caption simply read, "War among the Sadhus. Courtesy of the National Museum, New Delhi." No artist, no date, no place. The painting was set amid colorful photographs, and some paintings, of picturesque ash-besmeared *sadhus*, many of whom were engaged in a variety of painful austerities. There were, of course, plenty of the obligatory images of the unruly men of the *naga akhara*s (see chapter 6), marching naked to the Ganga to immerse themselves in the cold water during the *kumbha mela*. Coffee-table books such as this capitalize on the stark juxtaposition of the "other-worldliness" of Indian asceticism and the in-your-face power of Indian ascetics. For photojournalists, these mysterious men offer a glimpse of an ancient, autochthonous Indian past surviving in the present, untouched by the dualist West, whether Muslim, Christian, or modern. Partly for this reason, the painting was a puzzle. Whereas most of the other images had a consciously crafted timeless quality about them, this one had conflict and change – and history – woven into its very fabric.

The painting merits close inspection: The central figure is an aging warrior about to draw his sword. Fury is etched upon his face. A distraught old woman tries to restrain him. Racing toward the old warrior from the left are two younger men, swords raised. They are being restrained as well, but by men who look much like them. Meanwhile, on the right side

---

[75] This, too, is too large a topic to deal with fully, but see Pinch, "Same Difference in India and Europe"; and Nicholas Dirks, *Castes of Mind: Colonialism and the Making of Modern India* (Princeton 2001), esp. the coda, for a response.

[76] Ramesh Bedi and Rajesh Bedi, *Sadhus: The Holy Men of India* (New Delhi 1991), p. 53.

Figure 8. "*Yogis* fighting." By Gangaram, second quarter of the eighteenth century. Held in the National Museum, New Delhi, acc. no. 63.1801. Reproduced with permission.

of the painting, a young boy holding a bow, with arrows tucked in his waistband, dashes toward the combatants, in hopes of intervening. It is a curious scene. In the flash of a moment, perhaps as a result of a misspoken word or a perceived affront, harmony has given way to fracture. The anger on some faces and despair on others are suggestive of an earlier time of friendship, even love. Only one person is unperturbed. In the foreground a placid young woman observes the unfolding skirmish while tending a crying newborn. A young boy by her side also looks on, but with an expression of horror on his face. She, by contrast, seems utterly unconcerned. Indeed, she almost appears to relish the collapse of the social world around her. This is a hint, perhaps, about the nature of the conflict, namely, that it somehow revolves around her.

In 2002 I finally managed to see and photograph the painting. The Keeper-in-Charge at the National Museum, Dr. Daljeet Khare, provided more information. The painting was called "*Yogis* Fighting," the artist was Gangaram of Mewar (southern Rajasthan), and the painting dated from the second quarter of the eighteenth century. It was originally part of the Sri Motichand Khajanchi Collection, which was acquired by the National Museum in the 1960s.[77] Beyond this, nothing is known for certain about the work. Even the title, "Yogis Fighting," is speculative, and derived solely from the fact that the combatants, with the exception of the aging chieftain, are naked save for their loincloths and weapon-harnesses, and some appear smeared with ash. Paired with it, however, was another painting by Gangaram, "Flagellation in the Harem." This image, according to the 1960 catalogue of the collection, features "four female attendants in the pavilion, their faces expressing pity or perverse pleasure. In the foreground two stern women are engaged in the act of flagellation. The one to the left has raised the whip to strike the victim whose face is contorted with pain and fear. Her hands are tied with a rope held by another woman. A second woman, also with her hands tied behind, is crying for mercy." Based on this, the authors of the catalogue concluded that "Gangaram was not only very partial to sadistic subjects, but he depicted them with an emphasis on ugly reality which he cynically enlivened by clever caricature . . . Whether he painted such themes out of sadistic delight, cynicism, or out of a reforming zeal, or whether he catered to the perverted tastes of his patron, we do not know."

Even though it was produced a full half century before the events described in this chapter, Gangaram's work is a useful endpoint for our consideration of the fate of armed *gosain*s in north India during the

[77] Karl Khandalvala, Moti Chandra, and Pramod Chandra, *Miniature Painting: A Catalogue of the Exhibition of the Sri Motichand Khajanchi Collection* (New Delhi 1960), p. 61.

transition to British rule – and especially the role of women and children in that transition. Like messages in a bottle, they force the reader to journey across time, to confront unmediated images of the eighteenth-century past. As was all-too-apparent to the artist, armed ascetics and "their" women and children were significant features of the eighteenth-century north Indian world – as was harsh corporal punishment for female slaves. Whether or not "*Yogis* Fighting" and "Flagellation in the Harem" were imaginary scenes or depicted actual events in Mewar from the early eighteenth century,[78] they each may be seen as an expression of reformist indignation, a commentary on the social evils (and secret sexuality) presumed to be lurking within distinct corporate bodies that were coming into close proximity with each other in the eighteenth century: the *gosain akhara*s and the *tawaif gharana*s.

Appendix I: Descendants of Rajendragiri Gosain

Men	+	Women	→	Children/*chela*s
Narindragiri [d. 1840]	+	"Raj Rani"	→	Kalindargiri ["adopted"; 1857 insurgent]
	+	Roopun	→	Padam Indargiri
	+	Lallun	→	Jai Indargiri
Umraogiri [d. 1809]	+	Shitab Kuar	→	Jagat Bahadur
	+	Rani Kumla	→	Uttamgiri
	+	Bibi Mitteh	→	Ganga Baksh
	+	Chumpa Kuar	→	Gangagiri [a.k.a. "Dilawar Jang"]
	+	"five concubines" [3 Muslim, 2 Hindu]		
Kanchangiri [d. 1808]	+	Earlier "lawful wife", deceased		
	+	Chehtee Begum [a.k.a. Aqila Begum]	→	"adopted"/purchased: Kamptagiri Madhogiri Mahendragiri Ramgiri → Mukundgiri

[78] It is possible that the scenes are imaginary *and* real at the same time, that they reflect a loose amalgam of rumor and fact deriving from a local scandal, not unlike the salacious depictions of the tragic affair between Elokeshi and the *mahant* of Tarakeswar in Kalighat painting over a century later. See Pratapaditya Pal and Vidya Dehejia, *From Merchants to Emperors: British Artists and India, 1757–1930* (Ithaca 1986), pp. 171–176.

Men	+	Women	→	Children/*chela*s
	+	Cheman Kuar	→	Jagatgiri ["adopted"/purchased]
	+	Man Kuar		
Anupgiri [d. 1804]	+	Rani Chait Kuar [a.k.a. Kamraur]	→	Narindragiri ["adopted"/ purchased]
	+	Jamdhakhanum?		
	+	Sahibjan?		
				Kanchangiri [*chela*]
Rajendragiri [d. 1753]				Anupgiri [*chela*, "adopted"/purchased] Umraogiri [*chela*, "adopted"/purchased]

5   Shakti bhakti

Secretly Kaula, outwardly Saiva, and Vaisnava among men.
                              – from *Kularnava Tantra, c.* 1400[1]

The fifteenth-century poet Kabir was so disgusted with the spectacle of
armed ascetics that he is said to have penned the following verse:

> Never have I seen such *yogi*s, brother.
> They wander mindless and negligent, proclaiming the way of *Mahadeva*
> [Siva].
> For this they are called great *mahant*s.
> To markets and bazaars they peddle their meditation – false *siddha*s,
> lovers of *maya*.
> When did Dattatreya attack a fort? When did Sukadeva join with
> gunners?
> When did Narada fire a musket? When did Vyasadeva sound a battle
> cry?
> These numbskulls make war.
> Are they ascetics or archers? They profess detachment, but greed is their
> mind's resolve.
> They shame their profession by wearing gold.
> They collect stallions and mares, acquire villages, and go about as
> millionaires.[2]

As David Lorenzen has pointed out, the mention of muskets and gunners
suggests that the poem was composed well after Kabir's death (Lorenzen
suggests a sixteenth-century provenance) and subsequently attributed to
the poet. Such attribution was common practice with Kabir followers;

---

[1] *Kularnava Tantra*, ed. Taranatha Vidyaratna with an introduction by Arthur Avalon (Sir
John Woodroffe) (Madras 1965, reprint Delhi 1975), 11.83, cited in David Gordon
White, *Kiss of the Yogini: 'Tantric Sex' in its South Asian Contexts* (Chicago 2003), p. 310
no. 133. A common version of the aphorism is, according to White, "Outwardly Vedic,
a Saiva at home, secretly a Sakta."

[2] *Kabir-bijak*, ed. Shukdev Singh (Allahabad 1972), p. 103 (r. 69). This verse is cited in
Farquhar, "The Fighting Ascetics of India," 439; Ghosh, *Sanyasi and Fakir Raiders in
Bengal*, p. 13; and Lorenzen, "Warrior Ascetics in Indian History," 61, who begins his
essay with it. I have altered slightly the English rendering by Lorenzen.

and the poem does lampoon *yogi*s in a way that Kabir would have liked. Given the history of soldiering ascetics that is detailed in the foregoing chapters, the verse could easily have been composed as late as 1804 – and perhaps even later.

The significance of the poem is that it reflects – regardless of when it was composed – a wide religious condemnation of false religion, and false *yogi*s in particular, that was gaining momentum in northern India, especially after 1500. This was not an exclusively Muslim or Hindu condemnation in the conventional sense of those religious terms, in the same way that Kabir was neither conventionally Muslim nor Hindu. Born into a Muslim community of Banarasi weavers, his poems about the all-pervading presence of God, the futility of ritual, the falseness of formality, and the corruptions of orthodoxy were composed for anyone within earshot of his perch on the steps that led to the Ganga. Kabir did not think of himself as Hindu or Muslim, since, in his view, God was neither Hindu nor Muslim – neither Ram nor Rahim. For him, the only difference that mattered was the difference between those who loved God and those who pretended to love God – and even worse were those who pretended to be gods. For Kabir and the *bhakta*s (God-lovers), *sadhu*s (anchorites), and *sant*s (truth-tellers) who followed in his considerable wake, immortality could not be had via ritual expertise, privileged textual knowledge (such as was peddled by the many *maulvi*s and *pandit*s who lined the streets of Banaras), or as a by-product of caste prerogative. They held that there was only one route to immortality: through *bhakti*, the rapturous and captivating love of God.

This was not simply an argument about style. It reflected a profound disagreement about the very nature of God: and whether men could legitimately aspire to be gods. As such, it reflected deep disagreement about religious truth. Nor was it entirely new: *bhakti* was not simply a product of the late medieval, early modern era, any more than Christian love was invented out of whole cloth during the Protestant Reformation. But, like love in the West, it took on new political meanings and gained a wider purchase among both the ordinary and the elite in cities and towns across northern India after about 1500.

The growing popular appeal of *bhakti* after 1500 paralleled, paradoxically, the expanding military and political power of armed *akhara*s across northern India. In fact, the opprobrium heaped upon *yogi*s, armed or otherwise, by pious God-fearing/loving men like the author of the Kabir verse cited above, may have been a function of the growing visibility of men like Anupgiri and Umraogiri, and the *gosain*s and *naga*s they commanded. The increased volubility of the devotional critique, to our ears at least, may be the result of the analytical normalization of devotional belief in a distant, all-pervasive, and loving God as "religion" in the Enlightenment epistemology of the Western academy. It is also due, to a large extent, to the fact that major Indian rulers were allying themselves – either explicitly or implicitly – with the symbols, structures, and proponents of this devotional belief to shore up their claims to political legitimacy. This book began with a glimpse of one such dynastic lineage, the Kachwahas of Amer–Jaipur, who allied themselves after about 1500 with the Ramanandis of Galta. An important endpoint in this process is Warren Hastings' ban on wandering *sanyasi*s and *fakir*s, the armed "vagrants" whose raids into Bengal posed an implicit and explicit threat to the modernizing agrarian-revenue state the Company was trying to create in the late eighteenth century. It will be recalled that Hastings made an exception for those ascetics who were "fixed inhabitants," who "quietly employ themselves in their religious function," prominent among whom were (again) Ramanandis – who, by the early eighteenth century, had carved out for themselves a position as the main institutional guardians of *bhakti* in northern India.

The world of religious devotion is readily available to the historian, largely because it is so closely bound up with the history of the early modern state – in both Europe and India.[3] (Nevertheless, the world of religious devotion should not be reduced to the history of the early modern state.) Gaining access to the world of the early modern *yogi* and his dispersed heirs is more difficult. In part this is because *yogi*s were not given to expressing themselves in verse. They were the medium, as well as the message; they were not the messengers. As we shall see, they emerge only as a negative imprint in devotional literature, much as the popular agrarian "cults" of early modern Europe or the Americas only emerge as negative imprints in Catholic Inquisition records. In addition, their religion ran counter to the prevailing winds of trans-regional state formation in India since the sixteenth century. Unruly, hardy ascetics who inhabited and seemed to thrive in the rugged frontier – whether desert, mountain, forest, or jungle – were a constant and worrying reminder to the emperor and his subordinate (or insubordinate) nobility that they were not totally in charge in the sixteenth and seventeenth centuries. They were an implicit threat to the theoretical universal sovereignty of the monarch.[4] This endowed them with a strong gravitational pull. Even

---

[3] The literature on Europe is vast, but see, e.g. Roberto Bizzocchi, "Church, Religion, and State in the Early Modern Period," trans. Barbara Dooley, *Journal of Modern History*, 67, Supplement: "The Origins of the State in Italy, 1300–1600" (December 1995): 152–165.

[4] And sometimes not so implicit: Abu'l Fazl asked, in his prologue to a description of the duties of the Imperial Treasurer, "If a house or a quarter cannot be administered without the sanctions of hope and fear of a sagacious ruler, how can the tumult of this world-nest

when they were drawn into the orbit of the local or imperial monarch, it was in the form of a combustible alliance: neither could fully trust the other. If the threat posed for the state was implicit prior to the eighteenth century, it was explicit thereafter. Unruly, hardy ascetics and their apparent claim to sovereignty over the frontier, particularly if that frontier occasionally spilled into the settled agrarian countryside as part of a sacred landscape, could not be tolerated by the modernizing regimes of the eighteenth century, whether European or Indian. Once again, the endpoint to that historical narrative is Hastings' Company suppression of the "*Sanyasi* and *Fakir* Rebellion" in Bengal.

But every story has an epilogue, and the epilogue to the suppression of armed ascetics in Bengal is the apotheosis of armed asceticism in Bundelkhand. Anupgiri and Umraogiri, among the most powerful warlords of the eighteenth century, recognized that the Company regime could not be beaten. Their response was to join it, to become servants of the Company, beginning with failed attempts in the mid-1770s. As I have suggested above, in chapter 3, there was, in the predatory, corporate culture of the Company-*raj*, an ethic that appealed to them. Perhaps there was more than flowery Persian rhetoric at work in Anupgiri's 1786 exclamation that "I have a firm system of obedience and attachment from eternity with the Hon'ble Gentlemen and I am bred by their house."[5] But in maneuvering to join forces with the Company, they – and those around Anupgiri especially – molded themselves into something that they were not: an extended Indian princely family. This process may have begun as early as the 1780s in Vrindaban and was certainly well underway in the 1790s in Bundelkhand, long before the alliance with Lord Wellesley was hammered out in 1803. But it was nudged along by an army of British officials and agents, beginning, most crucially, with John Baillie in 1804 and ending with William Sleeman in the 1840s. Though it bought them some time, not to mention a small *jagir* centered on Rasdhan, in the end the princely attire did not suit them. They had been better off wearing no clothes.

The main thrust of this chapter is to describe and give shape to the *bhakti* critique of unbridled asceticism since about 1500, particularly as

---

of hornets be silenced save by the authority of a viceregent of Almighty power? How, in such a case can the property, lives, honour, and religion of the people be protected, *notwithstanding that some recluses have imagined that this can be supernaturally accomplished,* but a well-ordered adminstration has never been effected without the aid of sovereign monarchs." *A' in-i-Akbari*, vol. II, p. 55 (emphasis added).
[5] "Copy of a letter from Maha Rajah Anoopgheer Himmut Bahader to Serferage ud doula Colonel Harper afsud Jung," received Lucknow, 27 Mar. 1786, enclosed in a letter from Lt. Col. Harper to John Macpherson, received 5 Apr. 1786 (dated Lucknow, 28 Mar. 1786), BSPC.

it concerns the military *akharas*. A related goal is to describe the ways in which devotional piety aided in the constellation of modern Hindu and Muslim religious understandings – and how those new understandings redefined the religious map of Rasdhan and other places connected to Anupgiri and Umraogiri in the nineteenth and twentieth centuries. I begin, however, with a closer look at the pre-*bhakti* Saiva religious culture that hovered about Anupgiri and Umraogiri, particularly given the numerous women that were in their midst. This closer look is more than warranted, not simply because women were (in British eyes) an important mark against their religious status as *gosains*, but because it is difficult if not impossible to understand the animus of the devotional critique that followed minus a fuller appreciation of what constituted religion in an earlier form. In any case, as the aphorism that opens this chapter suggests, it always pays to delve a little deeper.

The view from Clan Mountain

In making sense of the situation in Rasdhan, British officials presumed that military service and the wealth – and women – that accrued from it were responsible for moving *gosains* from a religious to a secular station in the eighteenth century. As William Sleeman put it (see the previous chapter), "Gosaens in Bundelkhand, and elsewhere, entered the army and engaged extensively in trade, and amassed much wealth and attained high rank." This, in turn, "relieved them from the rigid rules of the monastic order." H. Rose understood the issue in terms of sexuality, but the end result was the same: "Goossains are enjoined celibacy, but if they deviate from that rule they cease, I presume, to be Goossains . . ." For many British observers, "temptations of the flesh" lured heretofore celibate *gosains* into what were, in effect, marriages – whether or not those marriages were cemented in ritual and sanctioned by law.

There may be some truth to the above formulations. Indeed, the notion that women and sex posed a problem for Saiva asceticism is, at one level, supported by Dasnami tradition. The remembered founder of the Dasnami order, Shankaracharya, is said to have come dangerously close to losing himself to a life of sensual, sexual pleasure. This occurred as a result of a debate with Ubhaya Bharati, who asserted that the great sage could not claim to be a true *gyani* or "fully realized being" without knowledge of *kusumastra-shastra*, "the art and science of sexual desire."[6]

---

[6] Madhava-Vidyaranya, *Shankara-dig-vijaya*, p. 117. I have altered the translation of the term *kusumastra-shastra*, which is translated by Tapasyananda as "the science and the art of love between the sexes." I prefer "sexual desire" or even the term he often employs

Realizing that he was "on the horns of a dilemma," Shankara resolved
to enter the just-deceased body of a king, Amaruka, who was renowned
for "having more than a hundred wives of exquisite beauty." To calm his
disciples' fears, Shankara assured them that "the continence of one who
knows the Yogic practice of Vajroli will remain unbroken. So even if I
indulge in the enjoyment of sex-love with this body, no evil will result
from it."[7] (*Vajroli* is the *hathayoga* technique of urethral suction during
sexual intercourse, about which I will have more to say.) After securing
his own body in a remote mountain cave, Shankara metempsychosically
entered the body of Amaruka and took up his study of sex. To quote his
fifteenth-century hagiographer, Vidyaranya:

In clean and cool crystalline halls he engaged himself continuously in all forms of
amorous indulgences with these charming and responsive women – in playing at
dice with them, offering various forms of sexual indulgences as wager; in drinking wine in golden cups from their hands and making them drink the same; in
impressing kisses on their faces having half closed eyes, emitting fragrant breaths
and speaking honeyed words; and in holding their bare bodies in tight embrace
forgetting everything else in the thrill of concentrated joy. Serving well the bodies
of these women – their bosoms, his teachers in the study of sex-love – he, standing
as a witness in the king's body, observed closely all the centres and expressions
of amorous gratification.

for *kama*, "sex-love." Tapasyananda later notes (p. 123, n.1) that "there are many who
object to the subject matter of this chapter [ch. 10, 'Acquirement of Knowledge of Sex-
Love'], because it depicts Sankaracharya in the midst of women . . . As the subject
matter has been dealt with by a great sage like Vidyaranya, we have given almost a full
translation." The present discussion relies upon ch. 10 as well as pp. 115–122 of the
previous chapter. Mandana, one of Shankara's stoutest opponents, is described (p. 86)
as "the great householder" and "confirmed follower of Vedic ritualism." Ubhaya-bharati,
"who was as handsome as she was learned," is described (p. 92) as "none other than
Saraswati embodied in a human body."

7 *Vajroli* refers to the yogic technique of retaining one's seminal fluid while locked in the
amorous embrace of a passionate woman. Shankara's *chelas* reminded the sage about the
example of Matsyendra, who had fallen into a similar trap only to be rescued by his *chela*,
Gorakh. The example of Matsyendra is significant, in part because Vidyaranya's text was
directed at the *yogis* who claimed descent from Gorakh, as Gorakhnath. In the words of
Padmapada (p. 119), Shankara's anxious disciple, "in days of yore, a great Yogi named
Matsyendra, entrusting his own body to his disciple Goraksha, entered into the body of
a dead king and thereby got access into his palace. While the Yogi thus reigned as the
king, prosperity attended that kingdom. Timely rain brought down bounteous harvests.
Observing all this, it occurred to his ministers that some great soul must have entered
into the dead body of the king. So they advised his consorts to use all their amorous
skill to keep the king completely absorbed in love sports, so that he might not leave the
body. The king got so immersed in the emotional display of these women, their amorous
advances, soft laughter, sweet songs and lovely dances – that he forgot everything about
Samadhi and spiritual matters, and behaved exactly like a sensuous man." Eventually, to
make a long story short, Gorakh had to assume the disguise of a dance instructor and
save his guru from his baser self.

So expert did Shankara-Amaruka become in the art and science of sex that he authored a commentary on Vatsyayana's *Kamasutra*. Meanwhile, Shankara's *chela*s grew anxious, particularly after their *guru* overstayed his own deadline of a month in Amaruka's harem. They decided to disguise themselves as musicians and gain entry into the palace, where "they saw their teacher surrounded by a bevy of beauties like the moon thronged by the stars." Shankara, who "looked in the present setting like the very embodiment of Kamadeva, the god of love," ordered them to perform. In song they begged the sage to not forget his *chela*s, his teachings, and his original mission, and they implored him to return to his original body. He did so, and rejoined as well the debate with Ubhaya Bharati that had occasioned his exploration of sex in the first place, urging her in a famous speech not to confuse the body with the self: "For the body is just an object to you like a pot [and] the senses are only instruments of the self, just as a sickle is of a farmer." The point of the episode was to show that sexual pleasure afforded but "a shadow, a perversion" of the true bliss that is acquired through knowledge, *gyan*. On a practical level, the moral of the story is that sex was a fatal distraction, even for a *sanyasi* skilled in *vajroli*. Shankara claimed such sexpertise, as it were, but he still needed the timely intervention of his *chela*s to be brought back "to the realisation of his duties."

This controversial story about Shankara's dangerous dabbling in a world of sensual delight would seem to support the interpretative stance adopted by British officials seeking to explain the "secularizing" signif- icance of women among *gosain*s. Sex and Saiva asceticism, Shankara's hagiographer seems to be saying, do not mix. Despite the apparent com- monsensical quality of this formulation, I would argue that it is a partial view, based on a partial understanding of what constituted the full range of *gosain* belief and practice in early modern India. It only seems com- monsensical to us because of our own predispositions with regard to reli- gion. If we probe deeper, a different logic begins to emerge. The notes of Francis Buchanan offer some useful clues for a place to start. As noted in the previous chapter, Buchanan encountered many *gosain*s – including many 'married' *gosain*s, or *sang-yogi*s – while surveying Bihar in the early nineteenth century. South Bihar was of particular interest, both because of the numerous *gosain*s there, married and unmarried, as well as the powerful Bodh Gaya *math* (monastery) to which many, if not most, of the unmarried *gosain*s in the region belonged. By this time it was clear to Buchanan that *gosain*s, who also referred to themselves as Dasnamis, were the most influential of the many religious "guides" dispersed throughout the towns and villages of Bihar, particularly among the lower castes.[8] The

---

[8] Buchanan, *Account of the Districts of Bihar and Patna*, vol. I, pp. 89–92, 369–371.

chief, or *mahant*, of the Bodh Gaya *math* at the time of Buchanan's visit was Balakgiri. Balakgiri's predecessor, Ramatgiri (d. 1806), "lived to a very great age, was very intimate with the European Gentlemen at Gaya, and was a man of considerable learning." Balakgiri, by contrast, struck Buchanan as an ignorant charlatan:

[He] is not a man of learning, and he thinks it decent to smear his face with ashes, but in no other respect has he anything ascetic in his appearance. His equipage is showy, his attendants numerous, and his dress very rich (Shals and *kinkhap*). In place of having his hair like a mop, which is the usual fashion of the sect, he wears a fine plait of hair (I presume not the growth of his own head) wrapt round so as to form a large turban.

Buchanan was more favorably disposed toward another one of Ramatgiri's *chela*s, Saryugiri, "a plain, unaffected man" of "very high" character, "by far the most learned person in the vicinity of Gaya." According to Buchanan, "many pretend that he was intended for the succession [to the *gaddi*] and was set aside by the influence of Raja Mitrajit of Tikari, the chief Zemindar of the district." Saryugiri had instituted a claim for 200,000 rupees against Balakgiri which, by the time of Buchanan's visit, had "hitherto failed of success."

The details of that succession dispute need not detain us. Buchanan would later learn that despite Saryugiri's Dasnami respectability, he indulged in some puzzling practices. This revelation occurred toward the end of Buchanan's survey of religious education in south Bihar, just prior to his discussion of astrology and medicine:

The only other part of what can be called divinity [in the region] although it may more properly be called magic, is the science of Agam, or of the Tantras. It is taught only by one person, Saryugiri of Buddha-Gaya, whom I have formerly had occasion to mention. He instructs his pupils chiefly in the Syamarahasya and Tararahasya, both belonging to the Virbhav, or that form of worship which is accompanied by drinking spirits, eating flesh, fish and parched grain, and copulation. It seems very strange that such impure indulgences should be taught by a man, who, from being of the order of Sannyasis, should have abandoned the sex and all worldly enjoyment. Many of the order are no doubt frail [i.e., they had succumbed to "the temptations of the flesh"]; but I certainly should have expected that the only man of learning that I have met belonging to it, would have abstained from the profession of openly teaching doctrines so directly opposite to its rules. He also teaches the Tantrapradip, which explains the doctrines of both the Pasubhav and Virbhav.[9]

Saryugiri was, it would appear, a *tantrika* – one who is expert in tantra. The term tantra can mean many things, including "ritual framework" and "treatise." But the details of Buchanan's passage, together with the

---

[9] Buchanan, *Account of the Districts of Bihar and Patna*, vol. I, p. 301.

references to *virbhav*, *pasubhav*, *Syamarahasya*, and *Tararahasya*, suggests that Saryugiri was involved in what David Gordon White has described as the "mainstream" or "hard-core" practices centered on corporeal fluid transactions that give tantra its historical specificity, and not the later abstractions that are more properly understood as a kind of orthoprax, high-caste "Tantrism."[10] At the center of these hardcore practices is a ravenous gang of female demigods known as the *yogini*s. Theologically, the *yogini*s are subordinate to – and, importantly, possessed within themselves the "clan fluid" (*kula-dravyam*) of – Bhairava in union with his consort, the variously named Goddess (*devi* or *shakti*). But their dangerous manipulability makes the *yogini*s the pivot of hardcore tantra practice. When worshipped with alcohol, blood offerings, and animal (or human) sacrifice, the *yogini*s manifest themselves as "ravishing young women" who can, if handled properly, reward their human devotees with the clan fluid and the powers that that fluid conferred – including the *yogini*s' own power of flight. Not surprisingly, the extraordinary powers, fearsome appearance, and bloodthirsty nature of the *yogini*s make them dangerous beings with which to interact – even in their deceptively beautiful human form. Hence those *tantrika* adepts who are brave enough, and skilled enough, to approach and interact with them are deemed *vira*, or "virile hero," or *siddha*, "perfected being."

The origins of hardcore tantra practices are to be found, White argues, in a *kaula* (from *kula*, "circle" or "clan") cult that ranged across the subcontinent from the ninth through twelfth centuries, but was particularly successful in central India, especially what is now northern Madhya Pradesh and southern Uttar Pradesh – in other words, in the region we know as Bundelkhand. *Kaula* gatherings were often widely known "secret" affairs that would occur in a variety of remote locations – in

---

[10] White, *Kiss of the Yogini*, pp. 7–26, 14–16 (on *tantrism*). As White notes on pp. 14–15: "Whereas the sexual content of Kaula practice had the production of a sacramentally transformative ritual substance (*dravyam*) as its principal goal, later Tantric sexual practice came to be grounded in a theory of transformative aesthetics, in which the experience of orgasm effected a breakthrough from 'contracted' self-consciousness to an expansive 'god-consciousness,' in which the entire universe came to be experienced as 'Self.' The exegetical syntheses of these thinkers, arguably the greatest metaphysical writings of the entire medieval period in South Asia, have become the basis for the 'soft-core' practice of the great majority of high-caste Hindu Tantric practitioners of the Indian subcontinent. But these practices do not constitute the Tantric mainstream so much as a Tantric orthopraxy whose practices shade into those of orthoprax brahmanic ritual . . . This type of practice, comprised of highly elaborate, semanticized rites, has prevailed among elite Indian practitioners, whose numbers, in comparison to those of what I am calling the Tantric mainstream, are relatively insignificant." The best known of these "tantristic" texts is *Tantraloka of Abhinavagupta with Commentary by Rajanaka Jayaratha*, ed. Mukund Ram Shastri, 12 vols. (Allahabad 1918–1938, reprint with introduction and notes by R. C. Dwivedi and Navjivan Rastogi, 8 vols. (Delhi 1987).

or near a cremation ground, in a field, or on a "Clan Mountain" (*kula-parvat*). These settings provided, according to White, the original "tantric sex scenario":

At these gatherings the Yoginis would descend from the sky to meet their male consorts awaiting them on the ground. These Yoginis' flight was fueled by the human and animal flesh that was their diet; however the Siddhas or Viras, by virtue of their own practice, were able to offer the Yoginis a more subtle and powerful energy source. This was their semen (*virya*), the distilled essence of their own bodily constituents. The Yoginis, gratified by such offerings, would offer their form of grace to the Siddhas or Viras. Instead of devouring them, they would offer them a counterprestation of their own sexual discharge [*raj* or *rajas*], something these male partners would have been as needful of as the Yoginis were of male semen.[11]

A *vira* could ingest the sexual discharge – the "clan fluid" – of the *yogini*s in three ways. The first two were straightforward: he could collect the sexual discharge in a basin and drink it, or he could engage in oral sex with the *yogini*. Either practice was known as *rajpan*.[12] The third method was the most difficult, but potentially most rewarding: the *vira* could ingest the sexual fluid of the *yogini* by engaging in a form of genital sex called *vajroli mudra*, mentioned above in the context of Shankara. *Vajroli mudra* enabled the *vira* to literally drink or "resorb" the *yogini*'s sexual discharge through the eye of his penis. Leaving aside the contested issue of whether *hathayoga* techniques describing urethral suction are, in fact, physiologically possible,[13] *vajroli mudra* and its variants (including *khechari mudra*) normally – in a non-tantra context – involved the post-ejaculate redirection of the *yogi*'s own semen upwards to his cranial vault, "even when embraced by a young and passionate woman."[14] If performed correctly, this redirection upwards of one's own semen was said to confer long life and even victory over death. Engaging in *vajroli mudra* with a *yogini* was more difficult, since the *vira* would have to exchange his semen for her fluid. But the reward was immense: the entry of the *kula-dravyam* into his cranial vault produced a result that was exponentially more powerful than were he simply depositing his own semen there.

Though he interpreted it as "carnal intercourse" with the devil, the Italian traveler Pietro Della Valle learned of such practices among the *yogi*s he encountered near Ahmedabad in the 1620s. These *yogi*s venerated "certain immortal, spiritual and invisible women to the number of forty,

---

[11] White, *Kiss of the Yogini*, pp. 10–11.   [12] On *rajpan*, see *ibid.*, pp. 99–102.
[13] See White, *Kiss of the Yogini*, p. 295 n. 88; also useful is the discussion in Mircea Eliade, *Yoga: Immortality and Freedom*, trans. W. Trask, 2nd edn (Princeton 1969), pp. 227–273.
[14] See, e.g. Svatmarama, *Hathayogapradipika*, pp. 52–54. On *khechari mudra*, see vv. III. 32–44.

known to them, and distinguished by forms and names, and through their supernatural operations." Interaction and, ultimately, sexual intercourse with these immortal, invisible women produced remarkable effects:

... the yogi who, by lengthy spiritual exercises, can succeed in having an apparition of any one of these women, who predicts the future to him, and favours him with the power to effect other wonders, is esteemed by them as having reached the level of great perfection. But most of all he is revered if he is received as a husband and the woman has carnal intercourse with him, for after that he remains excluded from any dealings with all the other women of the world. This is the highest level he can achieve; and then he is also called a man of the spirit, and accounted to have a nature more than human, with the promise of a thousand marvelous things, which for brevity I shall leave out.[15]

His careful use of the passive voice suggests that Della Valle did not credit these stories. And like Sleeman, Rose, and Buchanan two centuries later, he had a hard time digesting the information about ascetic sexuality given his assumptions about legitimate asceticism as monastic celibacy. Though he was told that *yogi*s "do not marry, and they profess strict chastity, at least in appearance," he nevertheless added that "it is known that in secret many of them behave basely when given the chance."

Was Saryugiri – whose *tantrika* practices would seem to run up against Dasnami proscriptions concerning sex, or, as Buchanan would put it, "copulation" – also simply behaving basely when given the chance? Unlike the subjects of Della Valle's observations, Saryugiri was not just any wandering *yogi*. He was a Dasnami, and – more importantly – he was the intended (and possibly the legitimate) heir, albeit dislodged by a rival, to the *gaddi* of the Bodh Gaya *math*. So some resolution of the contradictory Dasnami and tantra trajectories is in order. A closer consideration of Shankara's own paradigmatic experimentation with sex on the one hand, and Buchanan's reference to Saryugiri's employment of "parched grain" on the other, reveals some common ground. As noted earlier, the commonsensical conclusion to be drawn from Shankara's brush with sex and sensuality – from the point of view of Shankara's *chela*s – is that women are to be avoided. But Shankara himself held that sex with beautiful women is fine so long as you let it (semen, that is) get to your head: and *vajroli mudra* was the way to get it there – so that "no evil will result from it." What does Buchanan's "parched grain" have to do with all this? The Hindi/Sanskrit term for parched grain is *mudra*. But this is only one of several more abstract, euphemistic meanings, including "aphrodisiac." White argues, however, that the primary meaning of *mudra*, in the context of tantra, is "seal" – and that it refers to the hermetic seal that encircles the penis

---

[15] Della Valle, *The Pilgrim*, p. 240.

when it is in the vagina's embrace. This seal, in turn, is crucial to maintain the vacuum that the *yogi* needs in order to reabsorb, via his urethra, his ejaculated semen or, preferably, the *yogini*'s sexual discharge. Hence the technical translation of the term *vajroli mudra* often reads "the seal of the place of the male organ."[16] What Buchanan translated as "parched grain" was, then, a veiled reference to *vajroli mudra* – which is not entirely surprising given the adjacent reference to "copulation."

If nothing else, Saryugiri's example suggests that tantra may have represented a fluid substratum of practice for *gosain*s in early nineteenth-century Bihar. A corollary is that women and sexuality, far from representing threats to *gosain* asceticism, may have been crucial to it. Is this speculation also applicable to Rasdhan, and to the *gosain*s of Bundelkhand? The fact that Anupgiri and company hailed from the region that is generally regarded as the epicenter of the medieval *kaula* cult is not, I believe, without significance. Hence such speculation is more than warranted, and I detail additional supporting clues below. A hardcore tantra substratum would certainly help to understand, if not explain, the remarkable agency of women surrounding Anupgiri and his heirs. It is also worth noting that hardcore tantra involving *hathayoga* practices may have afforded particularly useful advantages to soldiering *gosain*s: the successful performance of *khechari mudra* with any female, whether *yogini* or human, served to not only conquer death, old age, and disease, but was said to also counteract poisons and ward off sleep, hunger, thirst, confusion, and, most importantly, weapons.[17]

There are several suggestive clues to the presence of a tantra water table beneath the Dasnami *gosain* landscape in Bundelkhand and, later, Rasdhan. The first has to do with the names of two villages connected to Anupgiri, namely, Rasdhan and Kulapahar. Depending on how one wished to translate it, "Rasdhan" could mean either "the source of beauty" (*ras* = beauty, *dhan* = source) or "rice paddy juice" (*ras* = juice, *dhan* = rice paddy). The former definition would sit well with the impression gleaned from Company correspondence, noted in the previous chapter, that Anupgiri's connection to the village originated with the women that were in his entourage. These same Company sources also revealed several versions of the village name, including the evocative "Rudjahaun" (or Radjahan). In Persian, *rad-jahan* may be interpreted as "retreat [*rad*] (from) the world [*jahan*]." Another possible reading, however, based on a pronunciation of the "dj" consonant in early Company writing as a hard "j", would be "Raj-jahan" – a name that would translate as "the

---

[16] White, *Kiss of the Yogini*, pp. 81–82.
[17] Svatmarama, *Hathayogapradipika*, vv. III.32–44.

world deriving from *raj*" (female ejaculate) or "the world of *raj*." This pronunciation is, in fact, supported by the early twentieth-century editor of Padmakar's *Himmatbahadur Virdavali*, Bhagvandin, who observed that the mid-eighteenth-century pronunciation of the village name was "Rajdhan."[18] This version can only be translated as "the source of *raj*."

If Rasdhan/Rajdhan is replete with provocative ambiguity, Kulapahar's meaning is thoroughly straightforward. It will be recalled from chapter 3 that the village was Anupgiri's birthplace – or, rather, the village said by his early twentieth-century descendants to be his birthplace.[19] The association with Kulapahar was more than twentieth-century invention. While negotiating the details of *gosain* retirement to Rasdhan in 1806, Narindragiri described the village as "the residence and place of nativity of my ancestors" and requested it in "jaigeer to my Brother Kooar Kunchun Geer."[20] The meaning of the term *kula-pahar* is identical to that of *kula-parvat*, or "clan mountain," a generic term referring to a prescribed site for the "secret" enactment of *Kaula* tantra rites. Anupgiri's Kulapahar is located in what is now Mahoba District (formerly the southwest corner of Hamirpur District), in the hill tracts of central Bundelkhand just on the Uttar Pradesh side of the border with Madhya Pradesh, midway between the towns of Mahoba and Panwari. The Hamirpur District Gazetteer from 1909 makes no reference to the birth of Anupgiri – or Himmat Bahadur, as most of the gazetteers tend to refer to him. This is not altogether surprising, since the author of the gazetteer also reports that "the place has only risen to importance since it came into British possession."[21] Bhagvandin, who relayed the birthplace detail, received his

---

[18] Bhagvandin, 'Introduction' to Padmakar, *Himmatbahadur Virdavali*, p. xxi.

[19] *Ibid.*, p. xix. The *gosain* descendants of Umraogiri continue to regard Kulapahar as their anscestor's birthplace.

[20] Rajah Nerinder Geer to Baillie, received 30 Sep. 1806, enclosure no. 4 (continued) of Wauchope to Adams, Bandah, no. 85 of 4 Jul. 1815 (dated 18 May 1815), BPC. Since Narindragiri was still very young at this time, it is likely that the actual letter was dictated by his manager, Kanchangiri.

[21] *Hamirpur: A Gazetteer*, vol. xxii of the District Gazetteers of the United Provinces of Agra and Oudh, comp. and ed. D. L. Drake-Brockman (Allahabad 1909), p. 189. The author also notes that "the name Kulpahar is said to be derived from those of the united villages of Kulhua and Paharia, on which the town now stands." Unfortunately, though he later adds that "as regards the early history of Kulpahar [*tahsil*, or administrative block] there are many village and other traditions relating to the occupation of villages by Kols, Gonds, Lodhis, Parihars and Chandels," he does not transmit any of them. A later gazetteer for the district, published in 1988, repeats the two villages supposition but adds an interesting detail: "Earlier the place was known as Kolhupara, but in the beginning of the 18th century the people began to call it Kulpahar." He describes as well "an isolated octagonal structure on a small mound" near a large shrine-dotted tank known as Garha Tal located south of the village and said to have been constructed by the Bundela Rajas. "It [the octagonal structure] must once have been very beautiful and is still picturesque, though in ruins." *Uttar Pradesh District Gazetteers: Hamirpur*, comp. and ed. Balwant Singh, (Lucknow and Allahabad 1988), p. 271. Sadly, I was unable to see the village during either of my visits to the region.

information from interviews with *gosain* descendants in Banda, Banaras, and perhaps even in Rasdhan/Rajdhan and elsewhere; he added that Anupgiri and Umraogiri's father was a "*Sanadhya* Brahman" who died in the children's infancy. According to nineteenth-century British attempts to categorize them, *Sanadhya*s were a mid-level group of "cultivator" Brahmans prominent throughout the Doab (the rich agricultural region bounded by the Ganga and the Jamuna) and Bundelkhand who claimed membership in the more prominent "pure" *Kanaujia* Brahman lineage.[22] It is possible that this detail about the *gosains*' Brahman pedigree reflected an attempt by later *gosains* to lay claim to a high status. This, however, would not explain the link to Kulapahar. Like Rasdhan/Rajdhan, it is suggestive of a tantra strand amid *gosain* religious understandings.

The late eighteenth-century poet Padmakar provides additional clues. Padmakar was, it turns out, a devotee of the goddess Tara, a form of *shakti* (supernatural energy), a consort of Siva beloved by *tantrikas* of all stripes.[23] Among the many services he had performed for Arjun Singh, his Rajput employer prior to joining Anupgiri's entourage, was the blessing of his sword with thousands of incantations to the goddess Chandi, another manifestation of *shakti* often associated with violence, devastation, and weaponry.[24] If Anupgiri also had an air of tantra about him, as I am suggesting here, this would help to explain the poet's willingness to join the *gosain*'s entourage in the early 1790s.[25] Padmakar's decision to employ a poetic style known as "*vir-rasmay*" (lit., hero-flavored) to describe Anupgiri's exploits (hence the subtitle "*Virdavali*") thus may have held a double meaning – referring to Anupgiri as both a conquering hero-king on the battlefield as well as a *tantrika vira* off it. That conveying the latter meaning was part of Padmakar's agenda is evident in introductory verses that describe Anupgiri as a "passionate demon god,"

---

[22] Elliot, *Memoirs of the History, Folklore, and Distribution on the Races*, vol. i, pp. 94–95, 146–149, 320, 336–337.

[23] Bhagvandin, 'Introduction' to Padmakar, *Himmatbahadur Virdavali*, p. xv.

[24] *Ibid.*, p. xxxiv. On Chandi or Candika, *Classical Hindu Mythology: A Reader in the Sanskrit Puranas*, ed. C. Dimmitt and J. A. B. van Buitenen (Philadelphia 1978), pp. 220, 225. The following ode to the goddess from the Siva Purana (quoted on p. 220) captures the sentiment best: "Smeared with the mire of demon blood and fat, ablaze with rays, May your sword be auspicious! O Candika, we bow to you!"

[25] It may be recalled that prior to joining Anupgiri in the early 1790s, Padmakar served as the court poet to Arjun Singh, the Rajput general in command of Bakht Singh's forces. To later, more nationalist-minded authors, such as Bhagvandin, Padmakar's choice was puzzling – after all, Arjun Singh was a proud Rajput, a Kshatriya, whereas Anupgiri was a lowly thieving *gosain*, entirely without caste. Indeed, Bhagvandin viewed Padmakar's decision as treasonous, since Anupgiri would eventually invite the British into Bundelkhand and prove instrumental in their eventual capture of Delhi. But if Padmakar were himself a Tara devotee, the prospect of joining Anupgiri's entourage would have presented no ideological difficulties whatsoever.

"thirsting to give pleasure," "deep like the ocean," "fierce like Rudra," yet "refined and sophisticated," and "expert in the sixty-four arts."[26]

Most compelling, however, is the religious iconography associated with Anupgiri, in life and in death. The first is an image of the goddess Ganga who, according to Shah K. S. Gupta, the proprietor of the Shah-ji *mandir* in Vrindaban, was the *gosain*'s "special deity" or *ishta-devta*. Today Gupta's massive Krishna temple occupies the structure that was Anupgiri's fortified headquarters during the 1770s and 1780s (see the introduction). Anupgiri's Ganga stands in a corner of the main shrine in the Shah-ji *mandir*, as part of a constellation of images that surround and are subordinate to Krishna – the main object of worship in Vrindaban generally. In the eighteenth century, by contrast, she stood on a lavish canopied dais and occupied the place of prominence in Anupgiri's *darbar*.

The significance of Ganga is manifold. At the level of popular theology, Ganga is symbolic of all women as mother-nurturers who provide life-giving fluids. To quote White:

The identification in South Asia of rivers with goddesses, or of goddesses with rivers, is so ancient and common as to be overlooked in terms of its intrinsic meaning. From the very beginning, first in Vedic traditions of Sarasvati (the Sarasvati River) and later in the Epic and Puranic Ganga (the Ganges River), goddesses are identified with flows of nurturing, vivifying fluids. More than this, every goddess, every river, is in some way a replica, a 'hologram,' of the great riverine goddess, Ganga, whose flow from heaven is present in every localized goddess of flowing water . . . Just as local traditions throughout India identify this or that temple tank or stream with the 'mother' stream, Ma Ganga, or claim that an underground passage connects said water source with the Ganges, so, too, every local or minor goddess is recognized to be a manifestation of the great Goddess. In all cases, every individual case of a river/goddess replicates 'hologrammatically,' the Mother/Goddess as the fluid source of all life. By extension, because all women are potential mothers . . .; every woman also replicates the great Goddess as mother. This also means that a woman's sexual and menstrual fluids are as potent and dangerous as those of the Goddess, and are in fact the *same* as those of the Goddess, whose fluids flow through every woman, indeed every female creature that can be construed as a 'mother.'[27]

---

[26] Padmakar, *Himmatbahadur Virdavali*, vv. 4–7, p. 2. According to Vatsyayana, "the sixty-four arts" may be understood on two levels. On the one hand, it can refer to a range of accomplishments that any cultured individual should possess – singing, telling jokes and riddles, understanding foreign languages, dice, etiquette, knowledge of omens (but also some less innocuous skills, such as the art of impersonation and disguise). On the other hand, the "sixty-four arts" can refer to the techniques of love-making. See *Kamasutra*, trans. Doniger and Kakar, pp. 14–15 (i.3.15), 39–42 (ii.21–31).
[27] White, *Kiss of the Yogini*, pp. 32–33.

In focusing his attentions on Ganga, then, Anupgiri may have been invoking a hydraulic understanding of the world, at the center of which were women/mothers/goddesses in possession of vital fluids. One can picture Anupgiri watching from his balcony as an array of *nachani*s (known to British observers as "nautch girls" or "dancing girls") performed amidst a lamp-lit garden bisected into four quadrants by narrow channels of water; directly below him, and also facing the garden from an open terrace, stood Ganga on her dais, also watching. The evening's entertainment would conclude – as all such evenings did – with the warlord selecting one of the women as his sexual partner for the night. Were her movements and gestures deemed by Anupgiri to have been animated by Ganga or, more likely, one of her attendant *yogini*s? In joining with her on his latticed terrace overlooking the Jamuna, was Anupgiri gaining access to powerful clan fluids? Or was he simply behaving as any other successful military entrepreneur might have done in the late eighteenth century, and simply enjoying the fruits of his labors on and off the battlefield? Knowing this requires evidence of a more intimate nature than is generally available to the historian. But given the circumstances, and the religious symbolism that swirled about him, such a speculation is not at all unwarranted.

Ganga's presence was appropriate for another reason, leaving aside the question of tantra. As noted above, Anupgiri's headquarters during the 1770s and 1780s was in Vrindaban, on the banks of the Jamuna. By bringing Ganga to the Jamuna, Anupgiri was producing a microcosm of the *sangam* (riverine confluence) at Prayag (Allahabad), hundreds of miles downstream, a site of no small significance for soldiering *gosain*s. The Prayag *sangam* was, after all, the place where Anupgiri's guru, Rajendragiri, mounted his attacks on the *Bangash* Afghans who were besieging the Allahabad fort in 1751, thereby gaining the favor of (and two-and-a-half decades of lucrative *gosain* service with) the nawabs of Awadh (and, by extension, the Mughal emperor, Shah Alam). The lands that were awarded the *gosain*s to maintain their troops in *nawabi* service were situated, moreover, in the rich plain that is fed by the annual floods of the Ganga and Jamuna, a tract known as the Doab or "two waters." Vrindaban is situated on the western edge of that tract.

The rich imagery that surrounded Anupgiri at Vrindaban, while he was in his prime and manipulating politics along the Delhi–Agra axis, struck a variety of religious and geo-political chords. It is said that "Himmatgir" is entombed in his palace at Vrindaban, at the base of a corner wall that faces the river, in a small Krishna temple that has seen fairly recent renovations (see the introduction). The *samadhi* marker bears the symbols that one would expect of revival *bhakti* Hinduism, including a conch shell,

a mace, a lotus flower, a crescent moon, an open book, a banner streaming from a flagpole, a medallion, a spiral, all of which surround a pair
of footprints. There is, however, another site, in Kalwara village on the
outskirts of Banda, which is claimed to be Anupgiri's final resting place
(see also the conclusion to chapter 6). To my mind, this seems a more
likely candidate for Anupgiri's *samadhi*: first and foremost, it is closer
to the scene of his death, described in chapter 3. The decrepitude of
the site leaves a more powerful impression than its Vrindaban rival. Neither this site nor Vrindaban, however, conform to John Baillie's assertion
in 1804 that Anupgiri's body was taken by his brother Umraogiri to be
interred at Sivrajpur, west of Kanpur on the south bank of the Ganga (see
chapter 3).[28] All that remains of the structure that housed Anupgiri's
samadhi at Kalwara is a crumbling archway reminiscent of the stately
ruins in Rasdhan. A few feet away is an "image" of Bhairava, Siva of
the cremation ground. In some ways it is a fitting reminder of Anupgiri's
humble beginnings. The "image" is a stark one: a stone roughly the shape
and size of a human skull and marked with vermillion paste. The place-
ment suggests that Bhairava stands guard over Anupgiri's *samadhi*, in
the same way that Rajendragiri stood guard over his guru's deathless
trance.

There are even indications that the tantra-*shakta* constellation of meanings retained their appeal for *gosain*s well after Anupgiri's passing. On
the outskirts of Rasdhan/Rajdhan, near a large tank constructed in the
early nineteenth century, stands a small temple dedicated to Sitala, "the
goddess of smallpox." Judging by its location, style, the materials used
to construct it, and its condition relative to nearby structures, it would
appear to have been built slightly after the construction of the fort and the
begum's *haveli* – in other words, in the early or mid-nineteenth century.
Sitala is one of the many names for the goddess-consort of Siva; she is
especially propitiated in times of disease, dislocation, and scarcity. The
image is ensconced in the wall of the temple; facing it and situated in the
middle of the chamber is a Siva *lingam* (phallus) surrounded by a *yoni*
(vaginal opening). Off to one side and facing the *lingam/yoni* in a kneeling
position is Nandi, Siva's bull. The temple is said to have been constructed
by Narindragiri. Today, despite evidence of some continued worship at
the temple, it shows signs of neglect, suggesting that it is no longer a center of the village's religious life. If tantra had once been central to *gosain*
martial asceticism, it had clearly been usurped by other, and as we shall
see, more modern religious understandings.

---

[28] Though there is a *samadhi* at Sivrajpur, it has been renovated very recently by the *sanyasi*
in attendance. It probably contains the remains of Umraogiri.

Good *sadhu*s, bad *sadhu*s

The view of Anupgiri's life from atop Clan Mountain raises the possibility that women and sexuality did not necessarily enter *gosain* military entourages from the margins of ascetic practice, as the ideologically corrosive spoils of war. Rather, as the vessels for the transmission of clan fluid, women may well have resided at the core of *gosain* asceticism – as the font from which all military success and political power, and war booty, flowed. This is another reminder that asceticism for *gosain*s was not first and foremost a means to a liberated consciousness or a blissful, loving union with a distant and inscrutable God; rather it was a path to power, a way of becoming a god-man. As such, *gosain*s were both subjects and objects in their own understanding. They moved from the margins to the center: being worshippers, they became the worshipped. This brand of practice, this approach to religion, was not without controversy in medieval and early modern India – primarily because it challenged what came to be prevailing understandings of God and, therefore, appropriate ascetic behavior in relation to God. The most vociferous critics after 1400 came from a *bhakti* or devotionalist perspective that saw God as a thing apart – a distant, inscrutable, all-powerful, yet loving being whose lasting intervention in the world occurred at a discrete moment in the far distant past. That being was increasingly conceived, in northern India, as either Ram or Krishna, avatars of Vishnu; hence the form that *bhakti* took was often described as *Vaishnava*, of or relating to Vishnu.[29] Indeed, the persistence, and even revival, of *kaula* tantra esoterica amidst the increasingly dominant Vaishnava *bhakti* religious culture in north India after about 1400 provided the context for the aphorism that begins this chapter, "Secretly Kaula, outwardly Saiva, and Vaisnava among men."

For their part, *bhakti* reformers were adamant in their disdain for *yogi*s who claimed special powers by virtue of their hathayogic and/or tantric prowess. The *bhakti* literature is rife with examples of puffed up *yogi*s who are deflated and sent packing by humble, God-loving *sadhu*s. One of the best known of these stories concerns the founder of the Galta lineage near Jaipur, Paihari Krishndas, whose defeat of the shape-shifting Taranath is recounted in the introduction to this book. Paihari Krishndas' monastic descendants at Galta, and the ethic of devotional servitude (*dasya*) they cultivated, would be central to the political culture of the Amer–Jaipur state from the sixteenth century onward. From the *bhakti* perspective,

---

[29] On the *bhakti* poets and their understanding of religion, see J. S. Hawley and Mark Juergensmeyer, *Songs of the Saints of India* (New York 1988), and *The Sants: Studies in a Devotional Tradition of India*, ed. Karine Schomer and W. H. McLeod (Delhi 1987).

a loving alliance between ascetic and sovereign, immersed together in humble devotion to Ram or Krishna, could be productive of great things. Wrongly constituted, however, it was susceptible to great mischief. If the sovereign was too easily taken in, or if the ascetic had an evil heart full of ulterior motives, civilization itself could be undermined. Such was the message of Tulsidas, who flourished in Banaras in the late sixteenth and early seventeenth centuries, at the height of Mughal eclecticism under Akbar and Jahangir. A power-hungry ascetic and a gullible prince play central roles in the prologue to Tulsidas' version of the life and times of Ram, the *Ramcharitmanas*, a text that was often described as the Bible of north India by nineteenth-century British missionaries.[30]

A central concern for Tulsidas was the evil of unbridled asceticism fueled by unconstrained *tapas* (or heat/power-generating austerities). The epitome of such asceticism was manifest in the person of Ravan, the ten-headed demon-king of Lanka who achieved his power through perfected sacrifice and austerity. Condemning Ravan to death at the hands of Ram in the concluding sections was not enough for Tulsidas: He opened the first book of the epic, concerning Ram's childhood (*Balakanda*), with a lengthy prologue detailing the travails of Pratapabhanu, a king who lived many generations earlier.[31] The purpose of this prologue is to show how Pratapabhanu, a good and just king, was ruined by a vengeful, deceitful forest-dwelling ascetic – a false ascetic, since he was, in fact, a prince in disguise. This ascetic-prince is given the name "Tapas" by Tulsidas. He manages, through a spiraling series of duplicitous acts, to bring about the ruin of Pratapabhanu and his kingdom. He is also indirectly responsible for Pratapabhanu's rebirth as Ravan generations later. Throughout this portion of the text, Tapas is referred to as a "master of deceit" (ch. 160), as "scheming and guileful" (d. 160), and as "hypocritical" (ch. 162). Meanwhile, the king, completely taken in by Tapas' professions of humility, praises him in unwittingly ironic terms: "Wise mystics like yourself, free from all self-conceit, habitually conceal their personality. Their highest good they find in the adoption of lowly guise. That is why saints and scripture proclaim that the perfectly destitute are dear to *Hari* [Vishnu]. Mendicants like yourself, without money or home, raise doubts in the minds of Brahma and Siva. But whatever you may be, I reverence your feet; now, master, be gracious to me" (ch. 161). Tulsidas then offered his own commentary on the spectacle:

---

[30] See Pinch, "*Bhakti* and the British Empire."

[31] For verse translations, see W. Douglas P. Hill, *The Holy Lake of the Acts of Rama: An English Translation of Tulsi Das's Ramcaritamanasa* (Oxford 1952), pp. 72–81, which I have relied on for the prose in this paragraph; for the Hindi verse, see Tulsidas, *Sri Ramcharitamanasa*, pp. 135–150.

The more the ascetic spoke of his detachment, the greater grew the king's belief in him. When the hypocritical ascetic saw that the king had submitted thought, word and deed to his influence, he said, 'Brother, my name is *Ekatanu* [One-body].' At the word the king bowed his head and said again, 'Explain to me, as to your own dear servant, the meaning of that name' (ch. 162). 'In the beginning [answered Tapas], when the world was created, I was born, and since that time I have worn no other body; that is why I am called One-body (d. 162). My son, marvel not in your heart; *tap* [short for Tapas] renders all easy of attainment. By the power of *tap* Brahma creates the world; by the power of *tap* Vishnu preserves it; by the power of *tap* Sambhu destroys it; there is nothing in the world that cannot be accomplished by *tap*.'

Hints at a more positive, pre-modern understanding of *tapas* is to be found in the much earlier telling of Ram's tale by Valmiki in Sanskrit, namely, in the *Ramayana*.[32] There is, significantly, no mention in Valmiki's *Ramayana* of King Pratapabhanu and his downfall at the hands of the evil Tapas. To understand *tapas* in the *Ramayana* the reader must turn to a lengthy digression in Valmiki's *Balakanda* which is concerned with explaining the development of (and the troubled relationship between) two important characters – Vasistha and Visvamitra, the former the adviser and guru to both Rama and Dasrath (Ram's father), the latter the military guru to Ram and his brother Lakshman.[33] Long before the days of Ram, according to Valmiki, a great king named Visvamitra wandered the earth looking for people to conquer, when he came upon the lovely *ashram* of the sage Vasistha. After receiving the hospitality of Vasistha, Visvamitra tried to steal the sage's magical, wish-fulfilling cow. The cow, not wishing to be abandoned by the sage, produced a host of armies. A battle ensued, resulting in the utter destruction of the monarch Visvamitra and his family. Dejected, Visvamitra made his way to the Himalayas where he performed great austerities (again, *tapas*) and was granted a boon by Siva. He chose weapons; the battle with Vasistha thus recommenced – but still the sage, by virtue of his inner power as a Brahman, was too powerful. In Visvamitra's own dejected phrasing: "The power of the Kshatriyas is no power at all. Only the power of a brahman's energy is power indeed. All my weapons have been destroyed by a single brahman's staff." So Visvamitra chose to undertake even greater *tapas*, to become a truly powerful Brahman – and at this he succeeded, to the astonishment of many.[34] And it was as a Brahman ascetic sage that Visvamitra much later presented Rama with his own

---

[32] See, e.g. Anna N. Subramanian, *The Concept of Tapas in Valmiki Ramayana* (Madras 1977).

[33] *The Ramayana of Valmiki*, vol. I, Balakanda, trans. R. P. Goldman (Princeton 1984), pp. 220–232 (*sargas* 50–56), pp. 246–247 (*sarga* 64), and pp. 175–177 (*sarga* 26).

[34] *Ramayana of Valmiki*, Balakanda, pp. 229–231 (*sarga* 55.23 for the quote).

arsenal of weapons, after the God-prince had slain the demon-goddess, Taraka, who tormented the people of the region. Hence, while a superficial point of the section is to underline the true source of Vasistha's power, his Brahmanness, the final irony (and the true import of the tale) is that Brahmanness is not ultimately beyond the reach of a non-Brahman: Visvamitra, after amazing austerities (again, *tapas*), literally transforms himself into a Brahman, and is confirmed as such by none other than Vasistha.

For Tulsidas, the claim that "*tap* renders all easy of attainment . . . There is nothing in the world that cannot be accomplished by *tap*," was palpably untrue, so much so that he puts those words into the mouth of the scheming Tapas so as to emphasize their false quality. Not so for Valmiki, who saw *tapas* as the only route to personal transformation, and even corporeal transfiguration. Valmiki's story of Visvamitra's quest for power and respect occurs late in the Balakanda, after Ram journey's with Visvamitra to Mithila. By contrast, Tulsidas tells of the travails of Pratapabhanu quite early in the *Ramcharitmanas* text. But nevertheless both events are said to have transpired ages before the life and times of Ram on earth, and serve to explain the unique traits of key characters (Visvamitra in Valmiki, Ravan in Tulsidas). Valmiki's description of the original Visvamitra as a frustrated monarch encountering an ascetic sage, Vasistha, in the forest, further underscores the parallel between the two episodes and leads to the conclusion that Tulsidas was giving a pointedly different reading of *tapas*. Not unexpectedly, there is no description in Tulsidas' *Ramcharitmanas* of Visvamitra's *tapas*-induced metamorphosis in the distant past: he is simply described as a "great enlightened hermit" who "lived in a forest" where he "practised *Jap* (muttering of sacred formulas) and *Yoga* (contemplation) and performed sacrifices."[35] Tulsidas does not use the term *tapas* here, but chooses instead the term *yoga* – which the Gita Press editors dutifully translate as "contemplation." In a slightly later verse (*d.* 209) Visvamitra bestows upon Ram "every kind of weapon" (*ayudh sarb samarpi*). But there is no explanation as to how Visvamitra came by the weapons in the first place. And not surprisingly: one should not be both ascetic and archer.

There is further indication in a later scene from the Balakanda section of the *Ramcharitmanas* that the poet was not only aiming barbs at untamed *tapas* but at its all-too-visible practitioners, namely, armed

---

[35] *Sri Ramacharitamanasa*, ch. 206.1–2, p. 144 (for both the Hindi and English). Hill, *Holy Lake*, p. 94, translates the passage (which he identifies as ch. 204) as "The great and wise sage Viswamitra dwelt in the forest, deeming it a holy retreat, and there he prayed and sacrificed and practised austerities." His use of the term "austerities" is probably informed by the Valmiki *Ramayana*, however. See his note on Viswamitra on p. 537.

Saiva ascetics. This occurs during the famous "breaking of Siva's bow" vignette, during which Ram wins the hand of Sita, the fair princess of Janakpur. After Ram has broken the bow – much to the consternation of the assemblage of rival princes but to the delight of Sita – the great sage Parshuram appears. Though Parshuram is generally thought of as a ferocious, Kshatriya-hating Brahman, Tulsidas depicts him in terms typical of unruly Saiva asceticism.

A coat of ashes looked most charming on his fair body; his broad forehead was adorned with a *Tripundra* [three horizontal lines of sandal paste indicating loyalty to Siva]. Having matted locks on the head, his handsome moonlike face was a bit reddened with anger; with knitted brows and eyes inflamed with passion, his natural look gave one the impression that he was enraged. He had well-built shoulders like those of a bull and a broad chest and long arms; he was adorned with a beautiful sacred thread, rosary and deerskin. With an anchorite's covering about his loins and a pair of quivers fastened by his side, he held a bow and arrows in his hands and an axe upon his fair shoulder.[36]

Incensed at the breaking of Siva's bow, Parshuram flies into a rage. Gradually, despite much goading by Ram's younger brother, Lakshman, Parshuram comes to realize the divinity of Ram and hands over his own bow so that Ram may draw it. After praising Ram with such eulogistic phrases as "Glory to Him who takes away pride, ignorance, passion and delusion" (faults associated, it should be noted, with the evil Tapas who caused the downfall of Pratapabhanu), Parshuram "withdrew to the forest to practise penance."[37] The word that "penance" is translating here is "*tap*," short for *tapas*.

Tulsidas' aim in the Parshuram vignette is to subordinate ferocious Saiva asceticism to the devotional worship of Ram. Having done so, Tulsidas banishes the tapascetic to the margins. In the Valmiki *Ramayana*, by contrast, there is no such subordination and marginalization of Saivas in the Parshuram episode: Parshuram is certainly bested by Ram, and he does finally acknowledge that Ram is "the imperishable Slayer of Madhu, the lord of the Gods."[38] The difference is that Parshuram is not represented as a Saiva ascetic in Valmiki, but simply as a ferocious Kshatriya-hating Brahman whose appearance coincides with a set of inauspicious omens. He appears not out of anger at Ram for breaking Siva's bow, but to engage in a test of strength.

[36] *Sri Ramacharitamanasa, ch./do.* 268.2–4, p. 184. See also Frank Whaling, *The Rise of the Religious Significance of Rama* (Delhi 1980), p. 243, who makes particular note of the comparison to a Saiva ascetic.
[37] *Sri Ramcharitamanasa, ch./do.* 284.4, pp. 193–194.
[38] Whaling, *Rise of the Religious Significance of Rama*, p. 83. See also pp. 59–60. The Parshuram vignette occurs in the Balakanda, *sarga*s 73–75.

Though Tulsidas and Valmiki are remembered as the most important narrators of the story of Ram, they were not alone. Versions of the Ram story were composed with surprising regularity after Valmiki,[39] and they too reflect the emergence of *bhakti*-centric thinking and its implications for the tapascetic. The fourteenth or fifteenth-century *Adhyatma Ramayana* is a good example of this transition, since it is one of the first to assert that "sacrifices, giving, asceticism, and the study of the Vedas are of no avail without devotion to Rama" – in effect, doing for Ram what had already been done for Krishna.[40] Older versions, however, held closer to the Valmiki line on *tapas* – even if it meant celebrating Ram's arch-villain, Ravan. According to a Jaina version composed in Prakrit by Vimalasuri, for example, Ravan "is noble, learned, earns all his magical powers and weapons through austerities (*tapas*), and is a devotee of Jaina masters."[41]

Despite the pious expressions of concern evinced by Tulsidas and others, there remained plenty of ascetics in medieval and early modern India who chose not to yoke their *tapas*-oriented practices to an ideology of devotion to Ram. Such ascetics – whether described as *yogis*, *fakirs*, *sanyasis*, *tantrikas*, *siddhas*, *kapalikas*, or *naths* – are encountered at every turn in medieval literature and legend. They were also encountered in historical fact.[42] If we can rely on Abu'l Fazl and Badauni, they were even interacting with the Mughal emperor himself. What is remarkable is the degree to which Badauni's attitude toward *yogis* resembled that of Tulsidas. Indeed, it is hard to resist the speculation that Tulsidas' cautionary tale of Pratapabhanu and Tapas spoke in some way to Akbar and his flirtation with the world of Hindu asceticism. Bringing Tulsidas into the same analytical field as Badauni may raise a few twentieth-century eyebrows. But it is worth noting that Badauni himself, despite his disdain for Hindus (and perhaps because of this disdain), was charged by

---

[39] Paula Richman (ed.), *Many Ramayanas: The Diversity of a Narrative Tradition in South Asia*, (Berkeley 1991).

[40] *Adhyatmaramayana*, with the commentaries of Narottama, Ramavarman and Gopala Chakravarti, ed. Nagendranath Siddhantaratna (Calcutta 1935), III.10.21, cited in Whaling, *Rise of the Religious Significance of Rama*, p. 106.

[41] A. K. Ramanujan, "Three Hundred Ramayanas: Five Examples and Three Thoughts on Translation," in *Many Ramayanas*, p. 34. See also K. R. Chandra, *A Critical Study of Paumacariyam* (Vaishali 1970). In a separate note (p. 48, n. 5), Ramanujan observes that "through the practice of *tapas* – usually translated [as] 'austerities' or 'penances' – a sage builds up a reserve of spiritual power, often to the point where his potency poses a threat to the gods (notably Indra). Anger or lust, however, immediately negates this power; hence Indra's subsequent claim that by angering Gautama [a.k.a. Buddha] he was doing the gods a favor."

[42] See chapters 1 and 2 in particular; also useful here is White, *Alchemical Body*, esp. ch. 10.

the emperor Akbar to translate the Valmiki *Ramayana* into Persian.[43] In addition, both Tulsidas and Badauni were concerned with men who would be gods. The import of the *Ramcharitmanas* is that Ram was not simply a man, one of many avatars of Vishnu (as in Valmiki). Rather, Ram was himself identical with Vishnu, and all the other avatars were avatars of Ram as Vishnu.[44] Badauni's apposite concern was that Akbar was flirting with the idea that he was the image of God – and that he was the too-willing victim of those who would raise him to that height, or even higher. Abu'l Fazl was the first among these rogues, in Badauni's view, but there were many others: "Cheating, thieving Brahmans collected another set of one thousand and one names of 'His Majesty the Sun' [a reference to Akbar's proclivity to daily chant the 1001 names of the "Greater Luminary"], and told the Emperor that he was an incarnation, like Ram, Krishna, and other infidel kings; and though Lord of the world, he had assumed his shape, in order to play with the people of our planet."[45] Tulsidas, too, would have found this unacceptable.

Whether or not Akbar was, in fact, a target of Tulsidas' verse, later Vaishnavas were unambiguous in their belief that the poet had much of value to offer the emperor on the precise origins of miracles. Early eighteenth-century hagiography tells of a meeting between a generic Mughal sovereign – identified only as "*padshah*" (emperor) – and Tulsidas. The author of this tale is the Vrindaban-based Vaishnava poet Priyadas, and it occurs as part of his commentary on the *Bhaktamala*, the early seventeenth-century collection of hagiographical vignettes by Nabhadas.[46] (The *Bhaktamala* corpus, comprising the hagiographical verse of both Priyadas and Nabhadas along with subsequent commentaries, is second only to the *Ramcharitmanas* in the eyes of north Indian Vaishnavas.) According to Priyadas, the Mughal emperor had heard rumors about Tulsidas' ability to bring a dead man back to life, so he ordered one of his officials to invite the poet to Delhi to demonstrate

[43] Badauni, *Muntakhabu't Tawarikh*, vol. II, pp. 346–347, 378.
[44] The best discussion of this point is in Whaling, *Rise of the Religious Significance of Rama*, p. 109. As Whaling notes, Tulsidas' text is the heir to the *Adhyatmaramayana* on the avatar question.
[45] Badauni, *Muntakhabu't Tawarikh*, vol. II, p. 336.
[46] There are questions regarding the authenticity of the tale – though there is no doubt that Priyadas told it. For the story, see Sitaramsharan Bhagvan Prasad, *Goswami SriNabhaji krita SriBhaktamala Sri Priyadasji pranit Tika-Kavitta*, 7th edn (Lucknow 1993), *kavitta* 643–646, pp. 768–772. See also G. Pollet, "Early Evidence on Tulsidas and his Epic," *Orientalia Lovaniensia Periodica* 5 (1974): 157–162; and, cf. Pollet and others on general problems of authenticity and the evolving historical context of Tulsidas biographies, see Philip Lutgendorf, "The Quest for the Legendary Tulsidas," in W. M. Callewaert and R. Snell (eds.), *According to Tradition: Hagiographical Writing in India* (Wiesbaden 1994), pp. 65–85.

his abilities. Despite the anxieties of his many admirers in Banaras, Tulsidas accepted the invitation. Upon arrival in Delhi and being ordered by the emperor to perform the marvel (*karamat*), Tulsidas simply stated that "it's a lie, all I know is Ram" (*ka.* 644.4). Incensed, the emperor replied, "we'll see about this Ram fellow" (*ka.* 645.1), and threw the poet into prison. Tulsidas prayed for the intercession of his protector, Hanuman, and all at once an army of monkeys from all corners of the palace began wreaking havoc – "scratching eyes and noses," "tearing clothes off the emperor's women," and "heaving down bricks from the ramparts" (*ka.* 645.2–3). Finally, "caught in the ocean of despair," the emperor's eyes were opened and he realized that Tulsidas was the only one who could save him. He fell at the poet's feet and begged for mercy, only to be told to "enjoy the miracle for a little while longer" (*ka.* 646.1). The emperor, "drowning in shame, pleaded for protection," to which Tulsidas replied, "all you need do is pray to Ram" (*ka.* 646.2). When the emperor did so, the fury unleashed by Hanuman ceased.

There is more than Hindu–Muslim antipathy in the Mughal imprisonment of Tulsidas and the havoc unleashed on the imperial palace and its residents by Hanuman and his army of monkeys. Priyadas was hinting baldly at another, and probably far more important tension, between *bhakti* and *yoga*-tantra – and, more broadly, at what was increasingly perceived in northern India as a distinction between Religion and Magic. Priyadas' Tulsidas scoffed at the very idea of performing a marvel for the emperor not simply because "all I know is Ram" but because he did not dabble in the kind of marvel the emperor was interested in witnessing. Care must be taken here: belief in an all-powerful, distant, and loving God did not preclude an array of lesser supernatural agents – in Tulsidas' case, Hanuman – who could be called upon for aid in the mundane world (not unlike intercessory saints in late antique and medieval Christianity).[47] But such figures existed beyond the easy reach of mortals: they could be called upon, but their response was never guaranteed. They came out of a tender mercy for the supplicant, a mercy that was borne of appreciation for the supplicant's benign intent and sincere love for and submission to God. According to Priyadas, Tulsidas was exemplary in this regard, and so, in the end, was the Mughal emperor. Those who would claim supernormal abilities as a function of their own human effort – in other words, those who would claim to be gods – were, in the eyes of the newly pious,

---

[47] See especially Peter Brown, *The Cult of the Saints: Its Rise and Function in Latin Christianity* (Chicago 1981). As Bynum notes in *Holy Feast and Holy Fast*, p. 7, saints were "far too dangerous" to "be imitated in their full extravagance and power. Rather (so their admirers say), they should be loved, venerated, and meditated upon as moments in which the other that is God breaks through into the mundane world, saturating it with meaning."

whether *bhakta* or Muslim, simply tricksters. Hence Priyadas' need to deride such claims as "*jhuthi karamat*" – false marvels.

Hindu and Muslim

If Priyadas' story of the *padshah* and Tulsidas was a Vaishnava *bhakti* response to the legacy of Akbar's fascination with esoteric *yogis* and the mysteries of *hathayoga*, it may also be read as an early eighteenth-century Hindu response to Aurangzeb's legacy of temple desecration. The *padshah*'s eventual entreaty to Ram at the hands of Tulsidas (and Priyadas), and the symbolic conversion to Ram-*bhakti* that this implied, could be understood as an appeal to the new Mughal regime, post-Aurangzeb, to return to the tolerant eclecticism of Akbar – minus the magical *yogis*, of course. The date usually given for Priyadas' gloss to the *Bhaktamala* of Nabhadas is 1712, five years after the death of Aurangzeb. The text is generally understood to have marked the deepening institutionalization of Vaishnava religion in the political and religious economy of north India.[48] While his immediate concerns were questions of legitimacy among certain monastic lineages of Vaishnavas and the place of Siva and Saivas in the new Vaishnavism, Priyadas was aware of the challenges that recent Mughal sovereigns had posed for his co-religionists. Hence the concern expressed by Tulsidas' friends in Banaras when they learned he had plans to visit the emperor in Delhi. The challenges of political Islam were all-too-obvious by 1700: Aurangzeb's reign – and, to a lesser extent, the reign of his predecessor Shah Jahan – witnessed an upsurge in *Sharia* legalism, the banning of eclectic court rituals, renewed efforts at conversion, the pulling down of key temples and the desecration of their images, increased patronage of Muslim holy places and mosque-construction and repair, differential customs duties based on religio-ethnic identity, a renewed pilgrim tax, and the reimposition of the *jizya* – the poll tax on non-Muslims, abolished by Akbar a century earlier.[49]

The violence against and persecution of Hindus by Aurangzeb was not without a specific agenda, however. Leaving aside temples destroyed in the process of military conquest, the particular targets of Aurangzeb's wrath were large, public structures recently built or embellished by members of the nobility (such as, most famously, the Somnath temple in Gujarat, the Viswanath and Gopinath temples in Banaras, and the Kesav Rai temple in Mathura).[50] These structures were seen as challenges to

---

[48] Burghart, "Founding of the Ramanandi Sect," 121–139.
[49] See the summary discussion in Richards, *The Mughal Empire*, pp. 171–177.
[50] On the destruction of these temples, see Sharma, *Religious Policy*, 3rd edn, p. 172. On the broader problem of interpreting temple destruction, see *ibid.*, pp. 168–178. Required

Aurangzeb's revivalist Islam not because, as is so often presumed, they harbored religious rituals and meanings that were radically different and therefore monstrous and heretical, but because they celebrated and institutionalized the new brand of Hindu devotionalist belief that shared certain traits with its Islamic counterpart despite obvious differences. Most importantly, both conceived of God (with an upper-case G) as distant, inscrutable, all-powerful, but ultimately merciful and caring – not unlike that which the modern state would seek to become. Here it is useful to pay closer attention to Aurangzeb's own wording with respect to temple destruction. In 1659 he issued the following order, probably in the context of disputes over the ancient temples of Banaras: "It has been decided according to our canon law that long standing temples should not be demolished but no new temples be allowed to be built." A later order, probably issued in the early 1670s in response to the construction of a temple in Orissa, elaborated this principle into a policy: "Every temple built during the last ten or twelve years [in Orissa] should be demolished without delay." Officials were instructed, in addition, to "not allow the Hindus and infidels to repair their old temples."[51] In the interim Aurangzeb had learned to his dismay that "in the provinces of Thatta, Multan, and Benares, but especially in the latter, foolish Brahmans were in the habit of expounding from frivolous books in their schools, and that students and learners, Musulmans as well as Hindus, went there, even from long distances, led by a desire to become acquainted with the wicked sciences they taught." This news was reported to Aurangzeb on 9 April 1669 and led to his general order to "all the governors of provinces to destroy with a willing hand the schools and temples of the infidels" so as "to put an entire stop to the teaching and practising of idolatrous forms of worship."[52] Soon thereafter, the Viswanath temple in Banaras and the Kesav Rai temple of Mathura were "leveled with the ground."

What is often lost in this "clash of civilizations" is the steady hum of cultures in conversation. The point that begs emphasis here is that the dominant north Indian *bhakti* Hinduism that was being institutionalized in the seventeenth century articulated in religious form values that

---

reading is the two part series by Richard Eaton, "Temple Desecration in Pre-Modern India," *Frontline* (22 December 2000): 62–70, and "Temple Desecration and Indo-Muslim States," *Frontline* (5 January 2001): 70–77.

51 Sharma, *Religious Policy*, pp. 168–169.

52 Muhammad Saki Musta'idd Khan, *Ma-asir-i 'Alamgiri*, trans. Elliot and Dowson, *History of India*, vol. VII, p. 184. Eaton, "Temple Desecration and Indo-Muslim States," 74, notes that "We do not know what sort of teaching or 'false books' [Eaton favors a later translation by Jadunath Sarkar] were involved here, or why both Muslims and Hindus were attracted to them, though these are intriguing questions." I agree, though I am suggesting that we can speculate about the nature of those books.

many Muslims and non-Muslims, nobles as well as ordinary folk, found important and meaningful. These values included charity to the poor, ethical universalism, humility, social equality before God, and techniques of spiritual upliftment and enlightenment that kept in check the dangers of individual hubris.[53] Too often the desire to stamp out the monstrosity of "idolatry" is seen as the key factor that motivated Aurangzeb and other "temple destroyers." The term "idolatry" is rarely understood in terms of its rhetorical signification – it is rarely dissected, its entrails are rarely examined. More importantly, it obscures the fact that innumerable Muslims were drawn to the universe of religious meanings that resided beneath and within "idolatry," not to mention the fact that the gravitational pull felt by Muslims for seventeenth-century north Indian Hinduism was the major factor in stimulating Aurangzeb's blanket insistence on demolition. Indeed, that pull extended as far as Aurangzeb's own brother and main rival for the throne during the prolonged illness of Shah Jahan, prince Dara Shukoh. In addition to spending inordinate amounts of time in the company of Sufis, *yogi*s, Brahmans, and *sanyasi*s, Dara was said to favor the term *"Prabhu,"* a name of Krishna, to describe God, rather than Allah.[54] One important reason Aurangzeb singled out the Kesav Rai temple in Mathura is that its old wood railing had been replaced during Shah Jahan's reign, by Dara at his own expense. Was it simply, as Sri Ram Sharma argued, "an emblem of a Muslim's fall from grace"? Or was it a reminder of Dara's rising popularity, before he was executed by his brother, with the people over whom Mughals exercised their rule? In any event, Aurangzeb ordered it removed by the local Mughal *faujdar* (commander) in 1666.[55] Three years later the temple was destroyed outright.

The gradual decentralization of the Mughal Empire in the eighteenth century, following the death of Aurangzeb in 1707, meant that imperial orders to desecrate temples were a thing of the past. Whether or not the persecution of Hindus, or Hindu forms of worship, served to corrode the Mughal Empire from within, the declining power of successive Mughal emperors meant that they could ill afford to object to the concrete manifestation of religious consciousness among Hindu elites in the

---

[53] See Pinch, "History, Devotion, and the Search for Nabhadas of Galta."

[54] Muhammad Kazim, *Alamgir-Nama*, trans. Elliot and Dowson, *History of India*, vol. VII, p. 179.

[55] Sharma, *Religious Policy*, p. 170. Another important reason the Kesav Rai temple was troubling to Aurangzeb was that it was built by Bir Singh Bundela in the early 1600s, an ally of Jahangir and the murderer of Abu'l Fazl. The permission to build it was granted by Jahangir as a reward for that murder. See Khan, *Ma-asir-i 'Alamgiri*, trans. Elliot and Dowson, *History of India*, vol. VII, p. 184.

realm – particularly if those Hindu elites provided key economic, political, and military services. As a result, the eighteenth century witnessed an expansion of royal patronage for Vaishnava ascetics, poets, temples, and even the copying of sacred texts such as the *Bhaktamala* and the *Ramcharitmanas* in centers like Vrindaban, Mathura, Jaipur, Banaras, and Ayodhya.[56] Meanwhile, the unwillingness or inability of eighteenth-century Mughal sovereigns, not to mention Indo-Muslim rulers of the late Mughal "successor states" such as the nizams of Hyderabad or the nawabs of Awadh, to live up to the puritanical example set by Aurangzeb left many Muslim elites among the old "service gentry" feeling vulnerable, as though they belonged to a declining order. The reformist work of Muslim theologians such as Shah Wali 'Ullah (1703–1763) and his followers – who combated what they perceived as a "degenerate Islam" full of saints and shrine worship, false ritual, and local practices gleaned from the Hindu masses that surrounded them with a back-to-basics approach that resembled (and was influenced by) the teachings of the Arab theologian Muhammad ibn 'Abd al-Wahhab – reflected the anxieties of a community being slowly cut adrift in a world that cared little for its traditions of learning and its claims to privilege. The rise of British power did not check these trends, and indeed may have accelerated them. The classes that benefited most from Company rule in northern India were, first, mercantile and commercial elites and, second, lower-level professional literati (by the late nineteenth century, middle-level agriculturalists would be added to this list of imperial beneficiaries) – and they tended to be not just overwhelmingly Hindu, but overwhelmingly Vaishnava. And they expressed their religiosity in terms of the highly "aestheticized" or *rasika bhakti* that has now become the basis for mainstream Hindu understanding and iconic representation.

The wave of "orthoprax" devotional piety that swept across northern India in the wake of Tulsidas, Nabhadas, and Priyadas – not to mention Badauni, Aurangzeb, and Shah Wali 'Ullah – would eventually wash over the soil of Rasdhan. We know this from the topography of worship there. Three structures are especially noteworthy. The first two are Krishna temples, one in Rasdhan and the other in Budhouli, two kilometers distant.

---

[56] Lutgendorf, *Life of a Text*, p. 135: "From the limited evidence available, we may speculate that the early propagation and patronage of the Manas was primarily the work of sadhus and middle-class people – merchants and petty landowners – and that Tulsi's epic did not initially have a strong appeal for the religious and political elite. Beginning in the latter half of the eighteenth century, however, there was a great upsurge in the royal and aristocratic patronage of the Hindi epic, reflected in the collection and copying of manuscripts at courts such as Rewa, Dumrao, Tikamgarh, and especially Banaras and in the encouragement of oral expounders and the commissioning of written commentaries by the most influential among them."

The Rasdhan temple, located in the village proper (in contrast to the Sitala *mandir*, aforementioned, which is located on the outskirts of the village), is known as the "Gosaiyan" *mandir* and originally contained an image of Krishna known as Keshavdev; the image, which was made of gold and silver, was missing and had been stolen according to the *purohit* (priest) in charge. The Budhouli temple still contains its image of Krishna, however, known as Haridev. According to both *purohit*s, these two Krishna temples, along with one in Mathura and one in Jaipur, were built by "Himmatgir Bahadur." (Most *gosain*s in Rasdhan tend not to distinguish between Anupgiri and Narindragiri, and think of their past as "*gosain-raj*," or "*gosain*-rule," a better time when the writ of their forefathers ran wide. The Budhouli *purohit*, however, did possess a Hindi-language history of the region, *Kanpur ke Vidrohi*, which told of some of Himmatgir Bahadur's doings in Bundelkhand and the settlement of his heirs in Rasdhan.) The temple in Mathura alleged to have been built by "Himmatgir Bahadur" refers, certainly, to the Vrindaban temple situated at the base of Anupgiri's old palace wall, described earlier in this chapter (and in the introduction to this book); the *purohit* there claims that it too was built by "Himmatgir Bahadur."

The Budhouli *purohit*, Vijay Krishan Goswami, told an unusual story about the origins of the Krishna images in Budhouli and Rasdhan that purported to explain the original *gosain* connection to the area. The story begins at Dig, the palace adjacent to the stronghold of Bharatpur (near Mathura–Vrindaban), Lohargarh, the "iron fort." In the palace was one "Rani Sahiba," a wife of the maharaja, who was herself a Hindu *thakurin*. In the Bharatpur military establishment was a *gosain* commander by the name of Kalindargiri. During the 1775–1776 siege of Bharatpur by Najaf Khan, a siege in which (ironically) Anupgiri and Umraogiri took part, this Kalindargiri managed to hold the defenses of the palace – even though he commanded only 1,600 men and had six months worth of food. The Rani Sahiba, meanwhile, was concerned for her fate and the fate of her images of Krishna. She struck a bargain with Kalindargiri: he would protect her and her images of Krishna in exchange for half the estate (at that time, Bharatpur was among the wealthiest states in northern India). She double-crossed him, however. In retribution, the *gosain* loaded the images onto elephants and vowed to establish them in temples wherever they happened to stop. Haridev's chose Budhouli, while Keshavdev's favored Rasdhan. Goswami asserted that he had collected this information from the museum at Mathura many years ago. Regardless of its veracity, it does endow the region, and the *gosain*s who came to inhabit it, with an attractive *bhakti* pedigree – or a *bhakti* veneer, given the aura of *kaula* tantra that swirled about them in the eighteenth century. Kalindargiri, the

Rani Sahiba, the two Krishnas, and the plucky pachyderms all conspire to weave a devotionalist Rasdhan fabric over a tantric Rajdhan terrain.

The third structure that reflects the arrival of devotionalist piety in Rasdhan is not Hindu but Muslim, but it also involves a Rani Sahiba – or, more precisely, a "Raini Sahiba." This is the village *masjid*, located in what is now the Muslim quarter. A plaque above the courtyard attests to its having been constructed in AH 1271 (1854–1855) by one "Bibi Raini Sahiba, resident of Etawah." When asked about who she was, the resident *maulvi* said simply that "she stayed with the raja." (Beyond his earshot, other villagers offered a whispered agreement, but in harsher terms: she was *rakhain*, a "kept woman.") In any case, there were only two women that resided in the village and were connected to "the raja" who possessed sufficient means to have mounted such a construction project in the 1850s. One was Rani Chait Kuar, Anupgiri's widow, who was still alive in the early 1830s[57] and could, conceivably, have survived into the 1850s; the other was the "Raj Rani," Narindragiri's wife and, after 1841, widow. According to British officials seeking to untangle *gosain* pension claims in the 1840s, Rani Chait Kuar had begun life as a "Mohammedan concubine." We know less about the woman who became Narindragiri's wife, but given that many of the wives and concubines of *gosain*s were perceived as both Hindu and Muslim, depending on the circumstances, a similar logic could be applied to her. Rasdhaniyas today insist that the *mazar* inside the *haveli* wall contains the remains of the begum of "Himmatgiri," a *nom de guerre* that could refer to either Anupgiri or Narindragiri.[58]

While it would not have been out of character for either woman to have made recourse to a more formal expression of Islamic piety late in life, doing so suggests that the fluid boundaries between religious identities that marked the eighteenth century were definitely a thing of the past. But there is a nagging detail. The titles "Raini Sahiba" and "Rani Sahiba" are

---

[57] In 1832 "Ranee Chyte Koonwur" petitioned the Governor General complaining of Narindragiri's wasteful indebtedness, and of the poverty to which she and her adherents, including several *gosain*s, had been reduced. The petition, dated 1 Dec. 1832, is enclosed in a letter from W. H. Macnaughten, Secretary to the Governor General, to George Swinton, Chief Secretary to the Government, dated 25 Dec. 1832, and recorded as no. 6 of 21 Jan. 1833, BPC. These are later reproduced as para. 105 of Letter from Bengal to the Board (in London), 13 Mar. 1834. See Boards Collection, vol. 1519 (1834–1835), OIOC, London.

[58] Of course, it is also possible that the *mazar* contains the body of Anupgiri's elder wife who, as noted in the previous chapter, seems to have arrived in Rasdhan toward the end of 1812. She was referred to in the proceedings as Narindragiri's "grandmother" but by Narindragiri as one of "the women of the family of Maharajah [his 'father' Anupgiri] (who is in heaven)." One of these women was known, tantalizingly, as "Sahibjan," so it is possible that she was responsible for the construction of the *masjid*. Though, if this was Anupgiri's senior wife, she would have reached an extremely advanced age by 1854.

so close as to suggest the possibility that they were one and the same – that the Rani Sahiba, said to have once owned the Krishna images and who was, therefore, instrumental (albeit against her will) in the construction of two Hindu temples in Rasdhan and Budhouli, is identical with the Raini Sahiba who is credited with having constructed the *masjid* in Rasdhan in the 1850s. It is unlikely that the orthographic similarity is the product of a happy coincidence, even if the term "Rani Sahiba" was a generic compound title for a woman of status in the Indo-Persianate ("Urdu") culture of the eighteenth century. Whatever the truth of the matter, the similarity reflects the conundrum, for late twentieth-century Hindus and Muslims in Rasdhan and its environs, of ambiguous religious belonging – both with respect to the women who were joined in oscillating orbit with *gosain*s during their period of lucrative military entrepreneurship, and the *gosain*s themselves. The easy eclecticism of these eighteenth-century actors, who drew upon Hindu and Muslim – and British – symbolic codes with unconscious ease, appears to late twentieth-century eyes as nothing short of scandalous. If the geographic and orthographic proximity of Raini/Rani prods the villagers' subconscious sufficiently to produce some local discussion or even acknowledgment of the possibility that Raini is Rani, it is only in quiet conversation among old friends. In a time of conventional religious piety, and amid the politics and violence that erupt out of it, Raini/Rani is too explosive an identity: the axiom of essential of religious difference between Hindu and Muslim has structured too many lives, and too many neighborhoods, to allow for the implosion that a full reckoning with this memory would entail.

Umraogiri's men

If Rasdhan, Banda, and Vrindaban constitute the epilogue to the story of *gosain*s, Jhansi and Moth must be considered its prologue. Jhansi was Rajendragiri's headquarters in the 1730s when the two obscure infants, allegedly from Kulapahar, were adopted or acquired into the order. It was from Jhansi in the early 1740s that Rajendragiri first opposed Naru Sankar's Maratha incursions into Bundelkhand, when Umraogiri and Anupgiri would have been young boys. It is from Jhansi in 1744–1745 – as Umraogiri and Anupgiri were coming of age – that the *gosain*s were expelled eastwards to the stronghold in Moth, which Rajendragiri ulti- mately made his headquarters. And it was from Moth that Rajendragiri and his *chela*-commanders, amongst whom were now numbered the young warriors Umraogiri and Anupgiri, would make their way further east and north to Prayag (Allahabad) in 1751 and, ultimately, into Safdar Jang's *nawabi*-Mughal service.

There are still about thirty families of *gosain*s living in Jhansi, according to Sureshpuri Goswami, who numbers himself among them. Sureshpuri's family is well-off: he is an English Lecturer at Saraswati Inter-College in Jhansi, and his brother Vireshpuri is employed by Bharat Heavy Electricals Limited and lives in the new BHEL colony on the outskirts of town. Their wives, Sushila Devi and Savitri Devi, can trace their lineage back to Umraogiri's senior *chela*, Gangagiri (a.k.a. Dilawar Jang). Marriage into Gangagiri's lineage, for Sureshpuri and Vireshpuri, might be read as a kind of confirmation of status among Jhansi's respected *gosain* families. It is possible, however, that Sureshpuri and Vireshpuri's ancestors had an earlier marriage connection of sorts to Gangagiri. A lineage table from the 1930s showing the pensions received by the "adopted sons" of Umraogiri includes three individuals with the Dasnami suffix *puri*. This is in addition to the five main *chela*s described in the previous chapter.[59] Their names were Hamir Puri, Parichat Puri, and None Puri, and each is described in the genealogy as a "brother of No. 5's wife." The "no. 5" *chela* of Umraogiri, according to the table, was Rajgiri, Gangagiri's co-*chela* and subordinate. The considerably smaller pensions of the Puris suggest that they were much lower down on the chain of command than Rajgiri, their brother-in-law, and his co-*chela*s. If, in fact, Sureshpuri and Vireshpuri are descended from these men, their marriage into the lineage of Gangagiri (a.k.a. Dilawar Jang) is the expansion of an alliance that began in the late eighteenth century.

Behind the gated walls of the BHEL colony, Sureshpuri and Vireshpuri keep their most prized possession: a portrait of Umraogiri (figure 9, left). The portrait depicts Umraogiri mounted on a horse and wielding a sword. Beneath the painting is written, "C. in C. [Commander-in-Chief] Raja Umrao Giri." The painting is undated, but judging by the conventional military pose and the European style, it would appear to be a product of the late nineteenth or early twentieth century. A detail on Umraogiri's forehead confirms this speculation (see figure 9, right). Only at close range does one notice that the *tripundra*, the three white horizontal paste marks that Dasnamis typically employ to signify their Saiva loyalties, is intersected by a Vaishnava *tilak* – the sandalwood-paste parabola with a red dot at the base known as *urdhvapundra* that signifies allegiance to Vishnu via Lakshmi, his consort. This is a marked contrast to what appears to be an earlier portrait (figure 10) in the possession of the Mahanirvani Panchayati *akhara* in Daraganj, Allahabad. In this painting, which bears stylistic similarities to the painting of Anupgiri in the Himmatgir Temple in Vrindaban (see figure 1, introduction), Umraogiri sports only the

---

[59] Gangagiri, Jagat Bahadur, Ganga Baksh, Uttamgiri, and Rajgiri.

Figure 9. C. in C. Umraogiri and detail, artist and date unknown. Photographed by the author, courtesy of Sureshpuri Goswami, Jhansi.

tripundra – on his arms and torso. Those who commissioned the Jhansi work were not content, apparently, with a memory of Umraogiri that rendered him as a sectarian only of Siva. By the turn of the century, that would have reflected an understanding of him as only partially Hindu. The reconciliation of what were, at the level of the *akharas* at least, mutually antagonistic Saiva and Vaishnava symbols and meanings into a peaceful, systematic, Hindu whole was a hallmark of what came to be known as *sanatana dharma*, or "old time religion," in the late nineteenth and early twentieth centuries. The heavy lifting was done by scholar-activists in the wake of the "cow-protection" movement in religious centers in the Hindi belt, in towns like Banaras, Haridwar, and Allahabad.[60] For ordinary men and women seeking to take part in this new Hindu orthodoxy, all that was needed was the addition of a few strokes of paint on a portrait.

Three hours east of Jhansi is Bilhari, just across the border into Madhya Pradesh. Bilhari is the natal home of Sushila Devi and Savitri Devi.[61]

---

[60] By men like Jwala Prasad Mishra, Din Dayalu Sharma, and Madan Mohan Malaviya. See Lutgendorf, *Life of a Text*, pp. 360–370, who uses the characterization "old time religion"; and Kenneth Jones, *Socio-Religious Reform Movements in British India* (Cambridge 1989), pp. 77–82.

[61] For their genealogies, and that of many other branches descending from Umraogiri's *chela*s, see Table II of "Genealogical Tables of Gushain Family (1933)," R/2/449/15,

Figure 10. Umraogiri Gosain, artist and date unknown. Photographed by the author, with permission of Mahant Yogendragiri.

It is where the portrait came from. Sushila Devi's father is Jairamgiri, Savitri Devi's is Upendragiri. Jairamgiri and Upendragiri are brothers, the sons of Jankigiri. They occupy a large house along with their cousins Devigiri and Munna Raja, the sons of their uncle, Jankigiri's elder brother, Jagjitgiri (also known as Bhondu Raja). Jankigiri and Jagjitgiri were the sons of Daniapatgiri, so it stands to reason that he was the one who built the house; since then it has been subdivided into apartments to accommodate the generations that have followed. The architecture and furnishings reflect a British-Indian mix. While each of the apartments has a courtyard in the back with shrines, the large public room that faces the

ISRR, OIOC, London. According to the table, Jagjitgiri was the second son of Daniap-atgiri ("Kuar Dunyapat Gir"); Jankigiri was the fourth and youngest son.

street contains sofas and chairs and a coffee table. There is a comfortable air of bygone glory to the place. This is bolstered by the confident demeanor of Upendragiri (better known as the "Chikao Raja"), who styles himself "the head of the *gosain* family." Now in his eighties, Upendragiri had a reputation in earlier years as a great hunter and sportsman, and had even, according to his relatives, achieved some fame on the tennis courts. These were men who, in their youths, mixed easily with the British officials posted to their district, not to mention their wives. Such connections would have served them well under normal circumstances, save for the fact that their youth coincided with the closing act of the British Empire.

It seems odd that the descendants of Umraogiri's *chela*s should have prospered during the course of the nineteenth and early twentieth centuries, especially considering the relatively meager condition of Anupgiri's heirs. But it must be remembered that most, if not all, of Anupgiri's descendants – the Rasdhaniya *gosain*s – joined in the 1857 rebellion, especially in and around Kanpur. Those who were not killed in combat or executed after the British suppression of the uprising would have sought the safety of anonymity in the peasant countryside. Those who remained in Rasdhan have only begun to regain a foothold in the last fifty years or so, insofar as they have been able to convince the Government of India of their status as "freedom-fighters."[62] By contrast, most of the descendants of Umraogiri, whether via his *chela*s or his children, remained loyal to the British in 1857; the one exception was Kuar Devi Dayal, the grandson of Uttamgiri, who was executed at Banda in 1858.[63] One might even speculate that the identification of Umraogiri as "commander-in-chief" in the portrait reflects the falling fortunes of Anupgiri's descendants, especially in contrast to the relative prosperity of Umraogiri's men – especially after 1858.

The *gosain*s of Rasdhan and Bilhari share one thing in common, however. Being *gosain* means being Hindu: Saiva-Shakta habits are covered over with a proper Vaishnava veneer. So Jairamgiri and his cousins continue to venerate the weapons of Umraogiri and Anupgiri in front of a Siva-*lingam* shrine in the courtyard, but they do this during Dassehra and Divali – festivals associated not with Siva but with Vishnu. Even some of their names possess Vaishnava connotations that would have been less probable two centuries ago. For example, Jairamgiri, or "victory to Ram"-giri; and Janakigiri, which would be equivalent to "Sita"-giri (since Sita is

---

[62] When Kailash and I visited Rasdhan and Madaripur in November 1999 we were shown copies of letters that had been sent to Jawaharlal Nehru from Dadda's forebears, pleading their case.

[63] Table II of "Genealogical Tables of Gushain Family."

often referred to as Janaki, or the daughter of the land of Janak). Similarly the surname used by Sureshpuri and Vireshpuri, "Goswami" ("Lord of Cows"), is a reference to Krishna's tribe of cowherds, the *Yaduvamsh*. It is a title commonly associated with the Bengali Vaishnava followers of Chaitanya, such as Rupa Goswami, who, in search of Krishna's homeland, established themselves in Mathura–Vrindaban in the sixteenth and seventeenth centuries and made that region a center of early modern *bhakti*. Today terminological appropriation has led to the presumption that the term *gosain*, "complete control over emotions," is a corruption of *goswami*; but this etymological "fact" reflects, instead, the adoption of *goswami* by those who earlier had been described as *gosain* during the course of the nineteenth and twentieth centuries.

Being a proper Hindu in the twenty-first century also means consigning the Muslim admixtures of the eighteenth century to an irretrievable past. They are, at best, anomalies that cannot be explained – and are meant to be passed over quietly in polite company. Thus Jairamgiri expresses sincere puzzlement when he tells of a *mazar*, an apparently Muslim grave, in one of the interior rooms of his apartment. But – a sign, perhaps, that he is not willing or able to let the past die? – he does not try to conceal the grave. He readily shows it to me when I ask about any old graves or shrines in the neighborhood.

6   Indian *Sadhu*s

Sadhu means perfect, excellent, good, virtuous, pious, righteous.

K. K. Verma, 1955[1]

Prayag, 1954

Early on the morning of 3 February 1954, while Prime Minister Jawahar-lal Nehru and other dignitaries watched from their boats on the Ganga near Allahabad, the Prayag *maha-kumbha mela*, India's premier festival, descended into chaos. At the center of the commotion were armed *naga sadhu*s who tore into the throng of jostling, hapless onlookers. The crowd panicked; before long people were being crushed underfoot as tens of thousands sought escape. Over 800 lives were estimated to have been lost. A Government Inquiry Commission was quickly set up under the leadership of a prominent judge and legal scholar, Kamalakant Verma. Verma detailed, in his 130-page report, how the combination of poor administration, bad luck, and insensitivity on the part of many *sadhu*s in the *naga akhara*s – the armed ascetic bands that were the central spectacle of the festival – precipitated the explosion of violence and death so close to the *sangam*, the holy confluence of the Ganga and Yamuna rivers. In the course of its investigations the commission obtained the testimony of numerous witnesses, including Pandit Bishambhar Nath Pande, Chair-man of the Allahabad Municipal Board and a prominent local Congress Party official who was broadcasting from the festival for All-India Radio; D. C. Bhattacharya, a correspondent for the Calcutta daily *Amrita Bazar Patrika*; and Shanta Devi, Pande's wife, who attended the festival with her five-year-old daughter.[2]

[1] *Report of the Committee Appointed by the Uttar Pradesh Government to Enquire into the Mishap which Occurred in the Kumbha Mela at Prayaga on the 3rd February 1954* (Allahabad 1955), p. 106. (Hereafter, *1954 Kumbha Mela Report*).

[2] *Ibid.*, pp. 58–60 (for Bishambhar Nath Pande's testimony), p. 67 (Shanta Devi's testimony), and pp. 71–72 (Bhattacharya's testimony). On the attendance of the President

The worst of the violence and death occurred adjacent to and below the high ground of the Mahabir-ji (Hanuman) Temple. The temple was flanked by special routes to and from the *sangam* reserved for the processions of the *akharas*. Pande walked by this spot at 4:30 a.m., on his way to his broadcast station at the *sangam* tower, and "noticed that a very large number of people, who had already bathed, had taken up positions on both sides of the road reserved for the Akhara processions going to the Sangam and also on both sides of Mahabir Ji Temple Road by which the Akhara processions were to return from the Sangam." These people were positioned to get a good view of the *akhara* processions, but had consequently narrowed the width of the road. Pande "advised these people to move away and not to stay there because that might be dangerous for them if large crowds passed along those places. They did not listen to my advice."

About four hours later Bhattacharya, the *Amrita Bazar Patrika* correspondent, likewise positioned himself on the edge of the route near the temple, "in order to give a detailed report" for his paper. At around 9 a.m. the procession of the Mahanirvani Panchayati *akhara* came to a halt in from of him: "Two big elephants stood in my front on the route, one behind the other, leaving a gap of about fifty paces . . . I stood watching the paraphernalia of the Sadhus in their stately procession flanked by a vast crowd on either side. As far as my eye could reach, I saw only human heads." Finally the pressure of the crowd and the interminable delay convinced some of the onlookers to venture out into the procession route and attempt to cross between the two elephants. This was a mistake. Bhattarcharya recalled:

I remember having seen one or two Nagas alight from the back of an elephant, *trishul*s [tridents] in hand, and push back those who were about to break into the procession line. Some other Sadhus also joined the Nagas. The two elephants were still standing apart with a gap between them. Suddenly a person ventured forth and ran through the gap across the procession to its eastern flank where I and others like myself stood. This man breaking away from his line gave a fillip to others and so was quickly followed by a second, a third, a fourth and a fifth one and then a countless number that sallied forth upon us like streams in flood during the rains hurtling down the hill sides.

Bhattacharya was soon panicked by the crush of the crowd and began to fear for his life. Trapped in the "valley of death," his "feet struck against something on the ground. It felt like a human body. But how to look

and Prime Minister of India, the Chief Minister and Governor of Uttar Pradesh, and the Governor of the Punjab and Chief Minister of Madhya Pradesh, see pp. 79–80. Pande had been broadcasting a running commentary on the *kumbha* from a tower near the *sangam* for All-India Radio.

down? . . . It was fatal to bend or stoop . . . The wails and groans of the victims were lost in the tumult. The Sadhus shouted '*Jai*s' [victory], brandished tridents and waved flags as they marched on. Their *trishul*s rather frightened the people who stumbled and fell. Some Sadhus were found striking the persons who were near them."

Shanta Devi described the same scene, but from higher ground:

The Sadhus, instead of helping the distressed (men, women, and children) by allowing them to pass through their own *Shamiana* [tent], began to assault [them] indiscriminately . . . with their long *Chimtas* [long iron tongs]. My daughter first drew my attention and asked me as to why the Sadhus were beating the people with their *Chimtas*. Scores of people who wanted to ascend the slope fell in the ditch on account of the terror of these Sadhus. Then followed a general stampede and utter confusion. The pressure was forcing the people to tread over the bodies of the injured and the dead . . . The violence of the Sadhus sealed the only way of escape from death and injuries.

These and other witnesses made clear that the carnage would have been much less pronounced but for the behavior of the *naga sadhu*s in the procession. In the conclusion to his report, Kamalakanta Verma mounted an appeal to "anyone who purports to be a Sadhu" that "Sadhu means perfect, excellent, good, virtuous, pious, righteous." Verma quoted the poet Tulsidas, who likened the ideal *sadhu* to "the cotton-plant, whose produce is dry and white and thread-like. Though he suffers ill-usage [i.e., is spun and woven into cloth], he hides the faults of others [like clothing], and thus is worthy of reverence and wins honour in the world." In Verma's opinion:

those who want to be treated as Sadhus . . . should pause and ponder and should consider how far they come up to this standard. Is beating, with iron *Chimtas*, a poor exhausted pilgrim, who, pushed by relentless pressure from behind, is hurled across a roadway reserved for a procession of Sadhus, the act of a Sadhu? Is it right for a Sadhu only to insist on what he considers his rights, privileges and prerogatives, and to forget his duties? . . . My earnest request to the present generation of Sadhus is that they should put their house in order and should go back to their original noble role. As matters stand at present, the word 'Sadhu' has ceased to have its real significance and has become synonymous with the word 'beggar'.[3]

Had Verma's appeal been directed at the "domesticated," "house-holder" *gosain*s of Bilhari or Jhansi, or even Rasdhan – amongst whom Vaishnava *bhakti* had made some headway – it may have had an impact. But it is doubtful that the poetry of Tulsidas was an effective cudgel with

[3] *Ibid.*, pp. 106–107.

which to browbeat the *mahant*s and *naga*s that were involved in the mayhem. The men that came to a halt in front of the Mahabir-ji Temple on the
morning of the 3 February 1954, were members of the Mahanirvani Panchayati *akhara*, referred to in the report as the "Mahanirvani Akhara" or
the "Mahanirvani (Sanyasi) Akhara."[4] This and the other *akhara*s (Juna
and Niranjani) that were scheduled to process to the *sangam* that morning were Saiva *akhara*s. For these men, Tulsidas was the enemy: their
institutional memory was replete with pitched battles against the Vaishnava *akhara*s, often at the periodic festival gatherings in Hardwar, Nasik,
Ujjain, and Allahabad that are today known as *kumbha mela*s.[5] Indeed,
it is not clear that invoking Tulsidas would have had much impact for
*bairagi*s in the Vaishnava *akhara*s either. Insofar as they possess a role
model, it is Hanuman, the ferocious devotee of Sita-Ram, not the humble, soft-spoken sage of Banaras. As Lutgendorf and others have noted,
Hanuman has a broad appeal because he is a kind of Siva in disguise –
a paradigm of Vaishnava devotion perhaps, but first and foremost an
armed ascetic who will stop at nothing.[6] A Saiva ferocity – fueled by a
tantrik disregard for conventional morality – continues to lurk beneath
the surface of dualist devotionalism.

Sleeman, Bankim, and the Mahatma

For *naga sadhu*s, the *kumbha mela* disaster of 1954 was just another round
of violence during an event predicated on violence among men whose
profession was violence. If it was different, it was only because ordinary
householders had gotten in the way. The aftermath, however – the press
reports, the popular outrage, the official inquiry – woke these armed men
up to the fact that there was a thing called India and it was watching:
largely unbeknownst to themselves, the *akhara*s had taken on a significance beyond the sect. Likewise, the *kumbha* had become something
more than a periodic occasion for the *akhara*s to gather and act out their
sectarian rivalries. They and the *kumbha* had somehow become synonymous with that amorphous organism that is the nation. And indeed, it was
not only the Indian nation that was watching: the world would cultivate a
curious fascination for the *kumbha* and its martial *yogi*s as well. Ved Mehta
and Vikram Seth both published essays, decades apart, for *The New Yorker*

---

[4] *Ibid.*, pp. 53, 69.
[5] While skirmishes in the seventeenth and eighteenth centuries tended to favor the Saiva
ascetics, Vaishnavas seemed to gain an edge in the nineteenth century. See the discussion
in Pinch, "Soldier Monks."
[6] Philip Lutgendorf, "Monkey in the Middle: The Status of Hanuman in Popular
Hinduism," *Religion* 27 (Oct 1997): 311–332.

magazine that featured the mayhem of the 1954 *kumbha mela*, and the mysterious naked warrior *sadhu*s that were its centerpiece. Those essays would later form key chapters in their *magna opera*, Mehta's *Portrait of India* and Seth's *A Suitable Boy*. The naked, killer *yogi* still occupied a key place in Western imaginations, even if he had evolved considerably since the days of Ludovico di Varthema. But now those Western imaginations were also Indian.

The 1954 *kumbha mela* disaster reminds us, as well, that the *naga akhara*s had not been stamped out by the consolidation of British rule in the nineteenth century. Unlike his cousins in "Victoriental" imagination, namely, the murderous "thug" and the rapacious *pindari*, the *naga* lived on – but as a *sadhu*. This reflects a time of massive religious, social, and political change, to which sufficient justice cannot be done in the space allotted here. Some broad brush strokes will have to suffice. For every *gosain* trooper who was willing to become a hanger-on at Rasdhan or lucky enough to be rewarded with a pension at places like Bilhari, Banaras, or Banda, there were hundreds if not thousands who remained in the field continuing to search for armed employment. But with the extension of *Pax Britannica* across much of the Indian subcontinent, there was less and less armed employment to be had, even in Company armies.[7]

Opportunities in the armies of the princely states were also declining, burdened as those princes were by increasingly straitened finances and the disapproving gaze and guiding hand of the British resident. According to the mid-nineteenth-century official, William Sleeman, whom we met in chapter 4, the extension of British power had the demographic effect of expanding the ascetic orders in much the same way that it contributed to the rise of religiously inspired criminality, or "thuggee" (from *thagi*, crime). For J. Campbell Oman, an early twentieth-century interpreter of Indian asceticism for the British and American reading public and a great admirer of Sleeman, the logic of the transformation was straightforward: "the very excellence of the British organization, under which the soldiers' work was being efficiently carried out by one-tenth of the number of men formerly employed by the rival native rulers,

---

[7] Some may have even entered the Company army: according to *sepoy* (infantryman, from the Hindustani *sipahi*) Sitaram Pandey, for example, one of the soldiers who accompanied his uncle and himself during his journey from his village in Awadh to his enlistment near Agra, in 1814, was named Tillukdaree Gheer, or Tilakdarigiri. This fact stuck in his memory, no doubt, because they were attacked at night by a gang of "thugs" en route, and the man would have been strangled but for the intervention of Pandey's uncle. See *From Sepoy to Subadar: Being the Life and Adventures of a Native Officer of the Bengal Army Written and Related by Himself*, 3rd edn, trans. J. T. Norgate, ed. D. C. Phillot (Calcutta 1911), pp. 6–8.

was the cause of swelling very considerably the ranks of the religious mendicants."[8] Whatever the truth of Oman's assertion, Sleeman would certainly have possessed a deeper insight: many of the men in that free-wheeling, pre-British-Indian military labor market were already ascetics and had, on occasion, passed themselves off as "religious mendicants" when the circumstances warranted. Indeed, their penchant for dissimulation and anti-social behavior compelled Sleeman to distrust their ascetic pretensions altogether and classify them alongside "thugs" as perpetrators of yet another stripe of religiously inspired crime (I will return to this point).

The shifting demographics of asceticism in the early nineteenth century also saw – and in some ways produced – the emergence and regularization of the *kumbha mela* as a conventional religious fair for lay Hindus, the central spectacle of which was the march of the naked, armed, and dangerous *sadhu* armies – and not simply in Hardwar and Allahabad, but in Nasik and Ujjain as well. There is no question that these four locations (and others, like Vrindaban, sometimes regarded as a fifth *kumbha* city) had been sites of periodic – though ad hoc – gatherings of the *akhara*s, often in search of military employment, in the eighteenth and even seventeenth centuries.[9] The early nineteenth century, however, saw increased attempts on the part of the state to regulate these kinds of affairs.[10] And not just the British-Indian state: as a result of Vaishnava blood spilt by Saiva swords in 1789 at Nasik, a complaint would be registered on behalf of the *bairagi*s in the court of the *peshwa* in Pune, which would decide in 1813 to assign separate bathing areas to each order.[11] There is ample evidence, moreover, that this was the period that saw the emergence of a *kumbha* consciousness in Allahabad among those who stood to profit from

[8] J. Campbell Oman, *The Mystics, Ascetics, and Saints of India* (London 1903), pp. 101–102, citing Sleeman's *Rambles and Recollections of an Indian Official*. Oman also reported that Sleeman was "was fair-minded enough to recognize their good qualities as well as the service they could at that time render to the British Government by carrying a good report of it all over the country in their extensive wanderings through the remotest districts of the independent native States." But this was a Sleeman that had mellowed in his retirement. His view in younger days was, as we shall see, decidedly less sanguine.

[9] See, for example, the useful summary provided in Lochtefeld, "Vishva Hindu Parishad and the Roots of Hindu Militancy," 594–595.

[10] See Katherine Prior, "The British Administration of Hinduism in North India, 1780–1900," Cambridge University Ph.D. thesis, 1990.

[11] The evidence usually cited for this is a copperplate inscription, a copy of which was shown to one of G. S. Ghurye's associates by one Mahant Radhamohandas of Nasik. See Ghurye, *Indian Sadhus*, pp. 177–178. For reasons that are unclear, Ghurye reported the date of the Nasik battle as 1690, and the *peshwa* court decision as 1702, which is clearly impossible. Burghart, "Founding of the Ramanandi Sect," 137, n. 4, cites a reproduction of this inscription published in the Indian periodical *Jagriti* 10, 4 (1945): 896–897, which gives the 1789 and 1813 dates, respectively.

a much expanded and more regularly timed *mela*.[12] For their part, when they were not marching and occasionally fighting at these fairs, *naga*s sat in their *akhara* encampments and entertained visitors with their feats of austerity – usually for an unspoken fee. In a sense, the intensifying market competition for ever-greater feats of austerity ensured that *naga*s would live up to the image of the mysterious *yogi* that had settled in comfortable urban, middle-class imaginations – Indian as well as British – as a wild throwback to a pre-modern form of religious asceticism. Officials of the decennial census, beginning in the 1870s, tried to get reliable data on the actual numbers of, and sectarian distinctions between, such men, and decade after decade they cautioned against relying on the figures they arrived at: most ascetics were too itinerant or too distrusting of the state – or both – to be accurately counted.[13] It was clear, nonetheless, that there were tens of thousands of such men.

Insofar as periodic *akhara* gatherings had occurred prior to 1800 at such places as Nasik, Allahabad, and Hardwar, they had been occasions for the real display – and sometimes, as in 1751 at Allahabad, the real application – of military prowess, a display that both assumed and asserted substantial political power. As such, these gatherings evoked some of the characteristics of an "alternate public arena."[14] After 1800, via the *kumbha* and as a result of the gradual demilitarization of the Indian countryside, these gatherings evolved into religio-political theatre verging on caricature, closely supervised by imperial officials, and wholly removed from subcontinental politics. A description of "The Great Fair at Oojein [Ujjain]" in 1850, published in the 12 and 15 June editions of that year's *Delhi Gazette*, provides a telling glimpse of this changing scenario.[15] Responding to the threat of violence between *gosain*s and the much more powerful *bairagi*s during the main bathing day of the festival, local rulers solicited the armed assistance of two companies of the Gwalior infantry under the command of Captain A. F. Macpherson. Prior to the onset of the processions, Macpherson deployed his troops

[12] Kama MacLean, "Making the Colonial State Work for You: The Modern Beginnings of the Ancient Kumbh Mela in Allahabad," *Journal of Asian Studies* 62, 3 (2003): 873–905. Many of these issues were discussed at a recent gathering of the Kumbha Mela Group during the American Academy of Religion annual meeting (Toronto, 25 November 2002) panel no. A175, "The Kumbh Mela: When the Divine Meets the Mundane" (Mathieu Boisvert, panel organizer).

[13] Pinch, *Peasants and Monks in British India*, ch. 1, contains a preliminary discussion of some of these statistical issues.

[14] See Sandria Freitag, "Contesting in Public: Colonial Legacies and Contemporary Communalism," in David Ludden (ed.), *Contesting the Nation*. It should be noted, however, that Freitag is theorizing for a later period.

[15] "The Great Fair at Oojein," *Delhi Gazette*, 12 June 1850 (part 1) and 15 June 1850 (part 2).

throughout the city, on the bathing *ghat*s, and in temple balconies over-looking the river. He then endeavored to arbitrate the conflicting claims of the various orders for ceremonial precedence and eventually convinced the Saivas to conclude their military procession and ritual bathing in the morning well before the arrival of the much larger and more powerful Vaishnava armies. In case either party chose to later renege on the tim-ing of the processions, heavy guns were "posted to command the whole breadth of the stream," and a fenced barrier was constructed in the mid-dle of the shallow river "so as to form two separate pools" where the *bairagi*s and *gosain*s could bathe independent of each other. As a final pre-caution, 100 Brahmans were positioned between the two pools to assist the *naga*s in their ablutions, thereby (so went the reasoning) providing a sacred buffer of sorts between the two armies. Save for a potentially serious dispute over protocol between two Vaishnava battalions, which was quickly ironed over by Macpherson himself, the entire day passed without incident.

Macpherson, or those advising him, apparently felt that *naga* respect for the figure of the Brahman was so great as to prevent the two hostile *akhara*s from engaging in combat if they happened to be in the water at the same time. This may reflect a certain naiveté on the part of Macpher-son and company, though it is possible that some *naga*s had gained a greater respect for Brahmanical privilege in 1850 than Kanchangiri had possessed in 1801 (see chapter 3). Certainly Macpherson possessed a better opinion of *naga*s than Sleeman did. According to Sleeman, "Three-fourths of these religious mendicants, whether Hindoos or Muhammadans, rob and steal, and a very great portion of them murder their victims before they rob them . . . There is hardly any species of crime that is not throughout India perpetrated by men in the disguise of these religious mendicants; and almost all such mendicants are really men in disguise; for Hindoos of any caste can become Bairagis and Gosains; and Muhammadans of any grade can become Fakirs."[16] Indeed, Sleeman also alleged that ascetics were guilty of spreading seditious rumors and recom-mended their compulsory registration according to a strict Vagrant Act.[17]

---

[16] Sleeman, *A Report on the System of Megpunnaism or, The Murder of Indigent Parents for their Young Children (who are Sold as Slaves) as it Prevails in the Delhi Territories, and the Native States of Rajpootana, Ulwar, and Bhurtpore* (Calcutta 1839), p. 11. I am grateful to Sandria Freitag for suggesting this source.

[17] Sleeman's opinions were part and parcel of the ever-widening scope of colonial police power in the early nineteenth century, and the bandits and thugs that he sought to suppress were hold-overs of institutionalized violence from an era when the reach of the state was not nearly so total. See Stewart Gordon, "Scarf and Sword: Thugs, Marauders, and State-Formation in Eighteenth-Century Malwa," *Indian Economic and Social History Review* 6, 4 (1969): 403–429.

Such an act seems not to have been promulgated, though a bill was passed "for the punishment of Vagrants" in the towns of Madras, Bombay, and Calcutta. This legislation specifically targeted those "mendicants" who "shall seek to extort alms by offensively exhibiting any bodily ailment or deformity, or by any offensive or indecent practices, or by inflicting, or threatening to inflict, bodily injury on themselves . . ."[18] The testimony that led up to the promulgation of this law is especially revealing – in part because it suggests that increasing numbers of Saiva ascetics were wandering the streets of the prosperous capital cities of British India, but more for what it conveys about British attitudes concerning decency and gender. One Lieutenant Graham of Calcutta was particularly eloquent, having been confronted by the unsightly image of "a fuqeer of a sect common up the country" who was "stark naked as from his mother's womb":

Just before and immediately after encountering this disgusting apparition, I met several ladies, and other respectable females . . . I think I need not say anything more. I felt quite sickened at the thought of any of our ladies coming in contact with such indecency . . . Had I been in military costume I would have put him into the guard house at the fort gate.[19]

One doubts whether the Vagrant Act of 1840 was able to stem such grievous assaults on common decency, though it may have served to deaden the official nausea occasioned by the appearance of naked ascetics in the genteel Presidency centers.

The British were reminded of Sleeman's advice concerning the seditious potentialities of Indian asceticism during the 1857 Mutiny-Rebellion. As was widely reported afterwards, the onset of the mutiny phase in May had been preceded by such ominous signs as the circulation of a lotus flower from *sepoy* to *sepoy* through entire regimental units.[20] Reports gathered in the aftermath of revolt alleged that among those circulating rumors about the British designs on destroying Indian religion included a man, "ostensibly a fakeer," who wandered about "riding

---

[18] "Act no. XXII of 1840," passed 23 Nov. 1840, recorded in 8 Mar. 1841, Fort William Legislative Department Proceedings, OIOC, London. See Liet. Graham to Chief Magistrate McFarlane, 29 Apr. 1840, for the following quote. I am grateful to Kama MacLean for providing me with this material.

[19] I cannot leave this quote without drawing attention to the contrast between Graham's express feeling of powerlessness out of uniform and the powerful impression left by the ascetic's nakedness. The naked Indian makes the English policeman feel naked. Another letter in the same proceedings volume describes a missing "Chinaman," presumed to have been eaten by a local "fakeer."

[20] See, for example, Disraeli's speech to Parliament, 27 July 1857, partially reproduced in *1857 in India: Mutiny or War of Independence?* ed. Ainslee T. Embree (Boston 1963), pp. 11–12.

on an elephant with followers, and having with him horses and native carriages." This individual made "frequent visits" to the Meerut regiments that later began the revolt. He was ordered to leave the place, and eventually complied, but only after he "stayed some time in the Lines of the 20th Native Infantry."[21] Some of the ascetic rebels had more than symbolic and rumor-disseminating significance. As noted in chapter 4, many, if not most, of Anupgiri's heirs in Kanpur rose up in rebellion soon thereafter. The leader of the Kanpur *gosain*s was named Lalpuri Gosain, who, like the Meerut-based "fakeer," appeared during the hostilities mounted on an elephant with a military banner on display.[22]

It is not surprising then, given the participation of *gosain*s in 1857 and the centrality of *naga*s to the spectacle of the *kumbha mela*, that the figure of the armed ascetic became central in early Indian nationalist thinking. Foremost in this process are the rebel *santan* ("saints") who emerge in the late nineteenth-century fictionalization of the "*Sanyasi* and *Fakir* Rebellion" by the great Bengali writer and Government functionary, Bankim Chandra Chatterji. Many, if not most of the late eighteenth-century *sanyasi*s and *fakir*s who rose up in Bengal were, as I have suggested in chapter 2, all-too-real late-Mughal *yogi*s resentful of the Company intrusion into the countryside and what that meant for their practice of levying contributions from the villages along their routes. Bankim's imagined rebel in *Anandamath* was, by contrast, a modern patriot sprung organically from the soil for the express purpose of rescuing a golden age of Hindu glory from the clutches of foreign invaders, whether Christian or Muslim, European or Turk.[23] A passage from a recent translation of Bankim's in which Satya (Truth), the leader of the patriots, returns to the remote jungle hideout, evokes the imagined world of ascetic patriotism:

At a certain point a vast jungle touched the hill. The hill stood at the top; the highway at the bottom; and the jungle in between. A little noise mingled with the murmur of the trees. No one could know the nature of the noise. Satya walked in the direction of the murmur and entered the jungle. There he found rows of men seated amid the dark shadows of the trees. The men were tall, and armed. Here and there their polished equipment shone brightly in the moonlight that filtered through the openings between the branches. Two hundred men were sitting in perfect silence. Satya walked gently into their midst, and made a sign. No one rose and no one uttered a word. Past the files of men he walked, looking at each

---

[21] Testimony of Mr. Williams, a commissioner in the Meerut division, cited in J. W. Kaye, *A History of the Sepoy War in India, 1857–1858*, 2nd edn (London 1865), p. 566n.

[22] "Narrative of Events at Cawnpore," fol. 856.

[23] On the historical and biographical circumstances of Bankim's authorship, see Raychaudhuri, *Europe Reconsidered*, ch. 3.

face. He seemed to be searching for some one. At last he found the man he sought and touched his body by way of command. The man at once stood up. Satya took him aside.

This man was young, his face covered with a black beard and moustache. He was strong and handsome, dressed in yellow, the holy colour, his body anointed with sacramental sandal paste.

Later in the story, this youth describes his ascetic life path to a potential recruit: "We are all ascetics, you see. But our renunciation is only for this practice. When we have mastered all techniques, and attained our goal, we shall return to our homes for our duties as householders. We, too, have wives and children at home."[24] These were not men who had stripped themselves permanently of family ties, or had been shorn of those ties in infancy – who had suffered, intentionally or not, a "social death." Bankim's was a partial asceticism for the politically conscious upper class, the hardening *bhadralok* or "gentlefolk" of late nineteenth-century Bengal.

Bankim seems to have suffered official censure and professional set-backs for the anti-British views expressed in the original publication of *Anandamath*, and subsequent Bengali editions were cleansed of the more offending passages.[25] Regardless, young nationalists in the decades following *Anandamath* looked to the image of potent, political asceticism as refracted through Bankim's eyes. The most famous example of this is Aurobindo Ghosh, most notably his influential 1905 pamphlet, *Bhawani Mandir*, which drew explicitly on the religious and political imagery invoked and developed by Bankim, but also his wider literary and cultural writings between 1894 and 1908. Ghosh would begin an English translation of *Anandamath* in 1909, which would eventually be completed by his younger brother Barindra Kumar Ghosh.[26] *Bhawani Mandir* and *Anandamath* were eagerly consumed by revolutionary youth in Bengal and beyond at the turn of the century – and one suspects that it was the original, more radically anti-British version of *Anandamath* from

---

[24] Bankim Chandra Chatterji, *Anandamath*, trans. and adapted by B. K. Roy (New Delhi, 1992), pp. 33, 41.

[25] Raychaudhuri, *Europe Reconsidered*, pp. 117; some authors, e.g. Pinch, "Soldier Monks," have suggested that this was why the former Muslim rulers of Bengal were depicted as the enemy in later editions, but Raychaudhuri notes, p. 188, that "the relevant [anti-Muslim] passages occur in the first serialized version of the novel as well and hence cannot be dismissed as cautious afterthought."

[26] Bankim Chandra Chatterjee, *Anandamath*, translated by Sree Aurobindo and Sree Barindra Kumar Ghosh (Calcutta n.d.); see the foreword, pp. i–xii for a discussion by Girija Sankar Roy Chaudhuri of the importance of Bankim and *Anandamath* for Ghosh.

Bankim's magazine *Bangadarshan* that was secretly making the rounds.[27] Bankim's work spoke to women as well as men: the image of the militant female warrior ascetic emerges powerfully in *Anandamath*, with a prominent character, Shanti, a married woman, disguising herself as a male ascetic-warrior in order to secretly serve with her husband and his rebel companions. Rabindranath Tagore's niece, Sarala Debi Ghoshal, was galvanized by this to organize a physical culture campaign in which she exhorted the young men of Bengal to build up their muscles so as to better defend their women from British molestation. After her marriage in 1905, she was referred to as "Debi Chaudhurani" in an explicit appeal to the sense of male patriotic duty evoked in Bankim's work by the same name (*Debi Chaudhurani*, 1884, featuring another married woman warrior-patriot).[28] She was also instrumental in popularizing the slogan "Bande Mataram," the refrain of the *Anandamath* rebel anthem, which itself became the unofficial anthem of the Swadeshi Movement following Curzon's partition of Bengal in 1905.

Perhaps as a reflection of official apprehensions over what Bengal's nationalist style portended for all of India, or perhaps as an articulation of a more general "Sleemanesque" animus for Hindu ascetics, one Saiyyid Muhammad Tassaduq Hussain ("Head Constable, Police Lines, Saharanpur") published in 1913 an Urdu-language handbook that described the various ascetic orders and, in detailed line-drawings, examples of representative sectarian figures – including the distinctive sandalwood-paste sect marks.[29] (It is also possible that Hussain's handbook reflected the local memory of the powerful Saiva *gosain*s who used to control the reins of government in his posting. It will be recalled that the Mughal emperor himself had appointed Umraogiri as the *faujdar* or commander of Saharanpur in 1753, after the death of Rajendragiri.)

Official apprehensions about the seditious quality of Hindu asceticism were confirmed by Mohandas Gandhi. Despite Gandhi's non-violent principles, and his evident disgust for what he perceived as the travesty of the modern *akhara*s (see below), he welcomed the *naga sadhu*s

---

[27] To give some indication of its popularity, by 1906 an English translation by Nares Chandra Sen Gupta was in its fifth edition from Calcutta; a Telugu translation was published in 1907 in Madras.

[28] Radha Kumar, *The History of Doing: An Illustrated Account of Movements for Women's Rights and Feminism in India, 1800–1990* (New Delhi 1993), pp. 39–40. See also Tanika Sarkar, "Imagining Hindurashtra: The Hindu and the Muslim in Bankim Chandra's Writings," in David Ludden (ed.), *Contesting the Nation: Religion, Community, and the Politics of Democracy in India* (Philadelphia 1996), p. 171, for the anti-Muslim polemical strain in this and other works by Bankim.

[29] Saiyyid Muhammad Tassaduq Hussain, *Kitab-i Sadhu* (Sadhaura, Umballa District, 1913). On p. 5 it is noted that the work was sanctioned by Government Order No. 3232 of 1913. This rare document may be consulted at the OIOC, London.

who decided to attend the famous 1920 Congress meeting in Nagpur. In the grand narrative of the Indian nationalist movement, Nagpur was where Gandhi seized the reins of power from an older and, for the British, more palatable style of politician, men like Mohammed Ali Jinnah. If the news of Gandhi's ascendancy was unsettling, it was partly because of the kind of men that were attracted to him. According to an informant's report, "sadhus visited most of the villages and towns and the masses had a high regard for them, and thought a great deal of their instructions and preachings. When these Nagas took up non-cooperation, the scheme would spread like wild fire among the masses of India and eventually Government would be unable to control 33 crores of people and would have to give Swaraj." The tone of the report sounds almost gleefully expectant, which must have raised questions about the political appeal of these unruly ascetics, if not Gandhi himself. The informant added, ominously, that Gandhi urged the *nagas* to "visit the vicinities of cantonments and military stations and explain to the native soldiers the advisability of giving up their employments."[30] For British-Indian officials, watching nervously from what was becoming, increasingly, the British sidelines, this could only signal a repeat of 1857. After the Nagpur Congress, the intelligence branch of government would become increasingly concerned with the activity of people they termed "political sadhus."[31]

Some may be puzzled by the British apprehension of Gandhi, since his emergence seemed to signal an end to Bankim's model of political asceticism and the rise of a globally potent unarmed asceticism.[32] But, as historians and political scientists have amply demonstrated over the past four decades, who Gandhi thought he was and who people thought Gandhi was were two markedly different things; Gandhi recognized this, and may have even played along with it.[33] Another ascetic who attended the Nagpur Congress was the young Dasnami, Sahajanand Saraswati, the social reformer and future peasant leader who gravitated famously toward

[30] "Report of Sadhus taking part in non-cooperation," part 2, fol. 3, file no. 80 of 1921, Political Department, Special Section (PDSS), Bihar State Archives, Patna.

[31] The Index to PDSS files in the Bihar State Archives indicates numerous reports compiled on the subject of "political sadhus," especially between the years 1920–1935, when Gandhi dictated the terms of Indian politics. The term is employed in history sheets sent from R. S. F. Macrae, of the Bihar Police, to E. L. L. Howard, chief secretary to the Government of Bihar and Orissa, 3 Nov. 1921, and included as appendices in file no. 80 of 1921, part 2, fols. 8–20, PDSS.

[32] Though, to be sure, Gandhi was not always perceived by Indians to be non-violent.

[33] See Shahid Amin, "Gandhi as Mahatma," in R. Guha (ed.), *Subaltern Studies III: Writings on Indian History and Society* (Delhi 1984), pp. 1–61. On the global import of who Gandhi thought he was, see Lloyd and Susanne H. Rudolph, *The Modernity of Tradition: Political Development in India* (Chicago 1967), part 2; and Ashis Nandy, *The Intimate Enemy: Loss and the Recovery of Self Under Colonialism* (Delhi 1983).

Marx (and had, in the process, a bitter falling out with the Mahatma) in the 1930s. Sahajanand reported in his autobiography two decades later that it was Gandhi who drew him into nationalist politics, and that when Gandhi spoke at the Nagpur meeting it was as if Siva himself was holding forth, heaving "thunderbolts against the government."[34] Some would later argue that he used the popular veneration to cynically influence politics on behalf of the landed, capitalist interests in Congress (*pace* Sahajanand), or on behalf of Hindus everywhere – or some nefarious combination of both. The British had a different set of concerns: their apprehensions about Indian asceticism generally would be sharpened with the news that the "unGandhian" violence at Chauri Chaura in February 1922 had inspired a gang of twenty nationalist volunteers from Bihar, led by yet another *sadhu* with a banner, to proceed toward the scene of the carnage where, in their view, "Gandhi raj had been established."[35]

Gandhi's attitude toward the *akhara*s was identical to his attitude toward all Indians: if they wished to take part in his Non-cooperation Movement, it had to be on his terms. The banner-wielding *sadhu* at Chauri Chaura was emblematic of what Gandhi saw as the problem with Indian society, and human society, in the British imperial era: the willingness, indeed pathological eagerness, to resort to violence to redress a wrong. And just as Gandhi lectured everyone who would listen to him on the subject of the new moral compass that was needed to find a new national direction, he lectured *sadhu*s as well. In mid-January 1921 a particularly large number of Swaminarayani *sadhu*s (followers of the early nineteenth-century Swaminarayana, especially influential in Gujarat) appeared at a public meeting in the village of Vadtal in Kheda District. Gandhi had been invited to the village to suggest ways of resolving a dispute between *patidar*s (landlords) and *dharala* laborers that had communal overtones and had come to involve the *sadhu*s. According to the account that was soon published in Gandhi's newspaper, *Navjivan*, the Mahatma lost no time in addressing the *sadhu*s:

---

[34] Swami Sahajanand Saraswati, *Mera Jivan Sangharsh* (Bihta, Patna District, 1952), pp. 212–213, quoted in Walter Hauser, "Swami Sahajanand and the Politics of Social Reform, 1907–1950," *Indian Historical Review* 18, 1–2 (July 1991 and January 1992): 72. For another image of Gandhi as Siva, see the nationalist poster from Lahore entitled "Bharatuddhar" (Gandhi, the protector of India, *c.* 1930), no. 553, in *An Illustrated History of Modern India, 1600–1947*, ed. C. A. Bayly (Delhi 1990), pp. 392–393.

[35] Shahid Amin, *Event, Metaphor, Memory: Chauri Chaura, 1922–1992* (Delhi, Berkeley, 1995), p. 44.

I am very glad that so many sadhus have come to this meeting; because my message is not intended only for ordinary men and women, it is meant for all – and more so for the sadhus. When sadhus understand the meaning of non-co-operation and the reason why the people of the country have undertaken it, they will see that they cannot live as sadhus, cannot preserve the virtues of a sadhu unless they chant the *mantra* of non-co-operation.

Gandhi reminded the people of Vadtal that men of politics ["Kshatriyas"] and men of religion ["*sadhus*"] should intermingle but remain constantly aware of their *dharma* or duty: while the ideal *sadhu* "moves freely among them [Kshatriyas – by which Gandhi meant the local landowners, the *patidar*s]," he should not live "in too close association with them." He should seek "to enlighten them while remaining unattached like the lotus leaf."[36]

A separate account of Gandhi's Vadtal meeting, also published in *Navjivan*, depicts a slightly more acerbic and hectoring Gandhi. He opened his remarks with the same expression of delight that so many *sadhu*s were present, and that he was "always eager to meet sadhus." But he quickly shifted the tone by reporting that he had visited the 1916 Hardwar *kumbha mela* "in search of a sadhu who would gladden my heart," and that though he visited "all *akhada*s," he had been disappointed: "I see very little of the goodness of sadhus today. On the last day in Hardwar, I spent the whole night thinking what I could do so that sadhus in the country would be real sadhus." He ended up taking a strict dietary vow.[37] Similarly, in 1928 he cautioned against hoping "for too much from Jain and other sadhus and religious teachers . . . imposters have entered their fold and many sadhus spread irreligion or superstitions under the guise of religion."[38] His was not an isolated sentiment: increasing numbers of social reformers by the 1920s had soured on the Hindu ascetic and were inching toward the position of "Thuggee" Sleeman a century earlier, that those *sadhu*s who were not outright criminals were, for the most part, greedy scoundrels bent on satisfying their own wants and desires. Probably the most prolific critic on this score was Govindacharya Mishra,

---

[36] *The Collected Works of Mahatma Gandhi*, vol. xix (November 1920–April 1921), pp. 250, 255–256. See also *Navjivan*, 23 January 1921.

[37] From "K. G. Mashruvala's account of Gandhiji's tour [of Kheda District]," in *The Collected Works of Mahatma Gandhi*, vol. xix, p. 257. See vol. xiii, p. 164, for the nature of the vow.

[38] The *Collected Works of Mahatma Gandhi*, vol. xxxvii (July–October 1928), pp. 156–157; see also pp. 227–228 for more of the same. Gandhi also looked askance, with Sardar Patel, on the *Digambar* Jain tendency to wander naked into densely settled areas with no regard for the "minimum bounds of decency." See vol. xlvi (April–June 1931), p. 257.

author of *Sadhu Jivan* [The Life of the *Sadhu*s] (Calcutta, 1922–1923) and *Sadhu Samsar* [*Sadhu* Rebirth] (Calcutta, 1923). But such views were bubbling up from a variety of sources, including – perhaps most significantly, given its low social and political center of gravity – the "peasant-Kshatriya" reform movements in northern India during this period among, most prominently, Yadava, Kurmi, and Kusvaha Kshatriya farmers.[39]

This broad-based critique of the *sadhu* reflected the fact that many ordinary people were increasingly able to make recourse to a host of widely disseminated Vaishnava texts, and were beginning to decide for themselves what constituted religious truth and how to go about responding to it. Gandhi, though perhaps less ordinary, likewise drew much of his religious inspiration from the great Vaishnava poets of the sixteenth and seventeenth centuries, including, of course, Tulsidas. At the same time, he frowned upon the religious verse of the major *bhakti* reformers of his native Gujarat, especially Swaminarayana and Vallabhacharya. In a 1918 letter to Maganlal Gandhi, he wrote despairingly that these two "have robbed us of our manliness." A product of "this degenerate age of ours," their teachings were "all sentimentalism," incapable of making "one a man of true love." Gandhi preferred the verse of Tukaram and Ramdas, the rugged Marathi poet-saints of the seventeenth century – the century of the Maratha rebel-king Sivaji, remembered as a Hindu patriot chafing under Muslim domination. Their teachings and poetry provided "ample scope for manly striving."[40] Indeed, Ramdas was said to be Sivaji's guru, and much of his writings are in the form of political and religious advice he offered his princely charge. There is little doubt that Gandhi's advice to the *sadhu*s of Vadkal, that they should strive to be the aloof yet constant guardians of Kshatriya *dharma*, was based on his understanding of Ramdas' remembered example vis-à-vis the Maratha sovereign.

Many were curious as to why Gandhi did not himself become a *sadhu* or *sanyasi*. He was constantly asked this question; those who knew less about him, but were interested observers nonetheless, simply assumed that he was such a man – *pace* Winston Churchill's famously derisive description of the Mahatma as a "half-naked fakir." Gandhi usually answered those who pressed him to become a *sanyasi* with a discourse on the persistence of his own weaknesses and his inability to combat his own desires.[41]

---

[39] See Pinch *Peasants and Monks in British India*, esp. ch. 3.
[40] *Collected Works of Mahatma Gandhi*, vol. xiv (October 1917–July 1918), p. 504.
[41] See, e.g. vol. ix, (November 1920–April 1921), p. 257 (for the following quote); and vol. xxiii (March 1922–May 1924), p. 468.

My conscience did not approve of such a step then [at the 1916 Hardwar *kumbha mela*] and does not do so today. I am sure you will not believe that the reason for my not doing so is love of enjoyments. I am struggling to the best of my ability to conquer the desire for them. But in the very process of struggling, I see that I am not worthy of the ochre robe. I cannot say I always practise truth, non-violence and *brahmacarya* in action, speech and thought. Whether I want or no, I feel attachments and aversions, feel disturbed by desire; I try to control them with an effort of mind and succeed in repressing their physical manifestation. If I could practise them to perfection, I would be in possession today of all the supernatural powers they speak of; humble myself, the world would be at my feet and no one would ever want to laugh me out or treat me with contempt.

Despite Gandhi's protestations, however, it is difficult to resist the conclusion that he avoided becoming a *sanyasi* because to do so would have limited his moral and political appeal to Hindus only. Rather, he chose to stand in a space beyond Hindu asceticism: it was a vantage point, as well, that allowed him to serve as an object lesson for those *sadhus* and *sanyasi*s who had chosen to don their "ochre robes" without sufficient inner reflection or for the wrong reasons altogether. As such, his renunciation of renunciation was also a denunciation of renunciation. He knew perfectly well that he had achieved, through his leadership – and through his *satyagraha* and the often painful adherence to *ahimsa* that it demanded – a stature in Indian popular religious understanding that went well beyond that of a common *sadhu* or *sanyasi*. If this was not apparent to him before 1919, it was certainly so after that date with the increasing use of the term *mahatma* to describe him – a term that was usually reserved for only the most revered of *yogi*s, or for the ancient sages of the Vedic, epic past.

Mahatma. This term – and the popular veneration that went with it – may well have been Gandhi's undoing. Certainly he himself was unsettled by it, and frequently bristled at its use in his presence – especially in the early years. But there is ample evidence that, over time, Gandhi responded in kind. Most frequently commented upon were the extremities to which he pushed himself: his dietary regimen and especially the unusual manner, for many, in which he tested his sexual renunciation.[42] By the mid-1940s his experiments with truth were, for many observers, veering uncomfortably close to the *shakti*-tantra practices that swirled about Anupgiri and Umraogiri in the late eighteenth, early nineteenth centuries. Many people took this more yogic side of the Mahatma very seriously, and none more so than his assassin, Nathuram Godse. At his trial, Godse gave a long, passionate statement of his guilt and the reasons

---

[42] See Joseph Alter, *Gandhi's Body: Sex, Diet, and the Politics of Nationalism* (Philadelphia 2000).

that he must hang for it. Seeking to explain himself to the nation, he asserted:

My respect for the Mahatma's character is deep and deathless. It therefore gave me no pleasure to kill him. Indeed my feelings were like those of Arjuna [in the *Mahabharata*] when he killed 'Dronacharya,' his Guru at whose feet he had learnt the art of war. But the Guru had taken the side of the wicked Kauravas and for that reason [Arjuna] felt no compunction in punishing his revered Guru. Before doing so, however, he first threw an arrow at the feet of Dronacharya as a mark of respect for the guru: the second arrow he aimed at the chest of the Guru and finished him. My feelings toward Gandhi were similar. I hold him . . . in the highest respect and therefore on January 30, I bowed to him first, then at point blank range fired three successive shots and killed him.[43]

Godse admired Gandhi for, among other things, his insistence on the importance of religion in politics. But he held Gandhi personally responsible not only for the partition of the subcontinent, but for the emasculation of Hinduism. As long as Gandhi was alive, refusing to relinquish his stranglehold on politics and culture, India could not progress on the world stage. Therefore he had to be removed from the scene. There were many who found Godse's reasoning not only plausible but compelling. According to Justice G. D. Khosla, one of the three judges presiding at the trial, which was open to the public, there was not a dry eye in the house at the conclusion of Godse's lengthy statement.

The audience was visibly and audibly moved. There was a deep silence when he ceased speaking. Many women were in tears and men were coughing and searching for their handkerchiefs . . . It seemed to me that I was taking part in some kind of melodrama or in a scene out of a Hollywood feature film . . . I have, however, no doubt that had the audience of that day been constituted into a jury and entrusted with the task of deciding Godse's appeal, they would have brought in a verdict of 'not guilty' by an overwhelming majority.[44]

If nothing else, Gandhi's experiments, Godse's explanation, and Khosla's audience (or, rather, the audience in the courtroom over which Khosla, and Godse, presided), are all reminders that older understandings of the powers that a *yogi* possessed still had relevance in the twentieth century. For many, religion still signified more than the love of a distant God.

---

[43] "Godse's Statement," in *Gandhi Murder Trial: Official Account of the Trial of Godse, Apte, and Others for Murder and Conspiracy, with Verbatim Reports of Speeches by Godse and Savarkar*, special double issue of *The Word Quarterly* 1, 1 (Spring 1950): 61.

[44] G. D. Khosla, *The Murder of the Mahatma, and Other Cases from a Judge's Notebook* (London 1963, reprint Bombay 1965), p. 274. See also the insightful discussion in Ashis Nandy, "Final Encounter: The Politics of the Assassination of Gandhi," in Ashis Nandy, *At the Edge of Psychology: Essays in Politics and Culture* (Delhi 1980), pp. 70–98. Nandy discusses Godse's statement and Khosla's recollections on pp. 90–92.

Kalwara and Sivarajpur, 2002

According to the early twentieth-century author of the Banda District gazetteer, Himmat Bahadur's "tomb lay at Kalwara, about two miles from Banda." But, the author added cautiously, "hardly a vestige remains."[45] Nearly a century had passed since the publication of the Banda gazetteer. If a vestige hardly remained in 1909, was there likely to be any trace of the "tomb" today? There were other, more puzzling problems. First, I had already visited one shrine claiming to mark the site where Anupgiri had taken *samadhi*, namely, the Himmatgir Mandir in Vrindaban. Second, immediately after Anupgiri's death in June of 1804 John Baillie reported that he had "permitted two of the sons of Rajah Omrao Geer and a party of fifty horsemen to proceed with it [the body] across the Jumna, for the purpose of interment on the bank of the Ganges at Sewrajpore agreeably to the directions of the deceased."[46] A letter from Baillie two years later confirms that his belief was that Anupgiri was entombed at Sivarajpur.[47] The early twentieth-century gazetteer for Kanpur district makes no mention of any *samadhi* shrines at Sivarajpur (or Sheorajpur).[48] But Umraogiri had spent many years at this site. At the very least, his *samadhi* should have been there. It was clear that I had to visit both places to see for myself what had become of these *gosains*' bodies.

I had originally hoped to make this trip in February–March of 2001, so as to coincide with the first Prayag *kumbha mela* of the twenty-first century. The *mahant* of the Mahanirvani Panchayati *akhara* had invited me to stay in the *akhara* encampment during the festival and to witness the initiation of novitiate *naga sadhus* around which the armed parade marches occur – or perhaps to join in the initiation altogether (the wording was unclear: *mahant-ji* was enjoying *pan* when he issued the invitation). As it happened, events conspired to delay me until March of the following year, 2002. As luck would have it, March 2002 was not a good time to be wandering about the eastern Uttar Pradesh countryside asking questions about dead soldiering *gosains* and their interpenetrating Hindu–Muslim

---

[45] *Banda: A Gazetteer*, vol. XXI of the District Gazetteers of Agra and Oudh, comp. and ed. by D. L. Drake-Brockman (Allahabad 1909), p. 179.

[46] John Baillie to Graeme Mercer, 232 of 21 Jun. (dated 4 Jun. 1804, near Bhooraghur), BSPC.

[47] Baillie to Lt. Col. G. Prole, Banda, no. 3 of 10 Jul. 1806 (dated 19 Jun. 1806), BSPC: "a confidential servant of the late Rajah Himmut Behauder, named Ajodeea Purshad, was in the habit of attending me occasionally on the part of Kooar Kunchun Geer, but he has recently crossed the Jumna on a visit to the late Rajah's tomb at Seurajpoor and I have not heard of his return."

[48] *Cawnpore: A Gazetteer*, vol. 19 of the District Gazetteers of Agra and Oudh, compiled and edited by H. R. Nevill (Allahabad 1909).

lives: in February some train compartments full of Hindus returning from Ayodhya had been torched in Godhra, Gujarat, and this had been quickly followed by anti-Muslim violence throughout much of the state. Many observers had been shocked by the fact that the violence had even spread into the countryside – usually such calamities were restricted to urban centers, and poor localities in urban centers at that. The rapidity and precision with which the destruction was wrought suggested, for many, a well-placed organizational hand. Soon thereafter leading figures in the ruling Hindu nationalist party announced that a rally was to be held in Ayodhya in mid-March to once again demand construction of the Ram temple on the empty ground where the "Babari Masjid" once stood.[49] The entire eastern portion of the state was on tenterhooks. I was loath, however, to cancel the trip a second time, and in any case Kailash had caught the Anupgiri fever and had agreed to join me. If anyone could keep me out of trouble, it was Kailash Jha. And Abha, Kailash's wife, was comforted by the thought that Kailash would avoid undue risks with me in tow.

The train journey from Delhi to Allahabad was surreal: there were only five or six passengers in the entire bogey. This was the first time, in my experience, when a train had not been fully booked. Apparently rail travel had temporarily lost its allure. We spent the day in Allahabad renewing acquaintances at the local *akhara*s. By evening we were in Chitrakut, a popular Vaishnava tourist and pilgrimage destination more or less on the road to Banda. (Chitrakut was the wilderness in which Ram, Sita, and Laksman camped during their exile from Ayodhya. Once a forest – almost the equivalent of the playing fields of Krishna's Vrindaban – Chitrakut is now dotted with temples that mark various key episodes from their adventures.) We stayed in a *dharmasala* (an inn for pilgrims) that evening and the next morning made our way to Banda. We decided that perhaps it would be best to begin at the District Magistrate's office, since this was our first visit to Banda. The DM-*sahib* would know if there were any areas that we should avoid outright, and with luck he might know a little about the history of the place and be able to recommend additional sites to visit. While waiting on the veranda to be admitted into the DM's presence we chatted with a group of local journalists, all of whom shared the surname "Nigam." They immediately recognized the name Himmat Bahadur, but added that around Banda he is known as "Himmatgiri"; he was famous for being a chronic turncoat. Santosh

---

[49] The *masjid*, which dated from the early sixteenth century, had been torn down during a massive rally on 6 December 1992, an event which sparked its own wave of communal violence in the month that followed, especially in Bombay.

Nigam suggested that we meet the former postmaster of Banda, one Ehsan Awara, who still lives in the "Chhawani" section of town. He was, they assured us, the man who knew more than anyone about Himmatgiri – and about Banda's eighteenth-century past. They added that a structure not far from his house was known as the "Jangi Raja *ka mahal*" – or "the palace of the War Lord" – where Himmatgiri and his soldiers used to stay.

We all filed into the DM's office together. He assured us that we had already met the best-connected people in Banda (the extended Nigam family); after some probing discussion with the journalists about the mood of the city overnight, he sent us on our way with his blessing. We piled everyone into the Tata Sumo (the Indian equivalent of a Land Rover) that we had hired in Allahabad and headed toward Chhawani. Chhawani, it emerged during the drive, was the encampment reserved for Nawab Ali Bahadur and his allied forces. Fortunately Ahsan Awara was home. He is a spry, elderly gentleman with a ready smile and a playful glint in his eye. The journalists clearly had great affection for him, and it was not hard to see why: he seemed to embody the virtues of Banda. We spent the next hour exchanging information about Himmat Bahadur and his times. Awara's house, as it happened, was on the very site of Mieselbach's encampment, the *top-khana* or artillery and munitions ground. He showed us the "Jangi Raja *ka mahal*," or what remained of it: most, save the foundation and part of the first floor, had been torn down to make way for a modern four-storey structure. Finally, we asked whether there was any *samadhi* or tomb in the area. Awara smiled. Twenty-five years ago, when he had been a passenger on a bullock cart that was making its way through the village of Kalwara, not far from Banda, the driver had pointed to a crumbling wall and told him that it marked the *samadhi* of Himmatgiri.

We piled back into the Sumo, with Awara between me and the driver. As we reached the outskirts of Banda, the driver, following Awara's instructions, veered left onto a dirt track that was almost unnoticeable from the road. Soon we were winding our way into a small village. We pulled up next to an elevated section of the village, on top of which was the crumbling wall Awara had seen twenty-five years earlier. It resembled the ruins at Rasdhan. A few feet away was a simple stone image of Bhairava, described in the previous chapter. A villager approached and, when asked if there were any *gosains* about, replied in the negative but added that everyone remembered it as a *gosain* village. Near the Bhairava stone was a small, recently replastered temple. According to the villager, Bhairava used to occupy it, but recently an image of Kali had been installed. We examined the Bhairava stone. Its shape bore a vague resemblance to the upper portion of a human skull, minus the jawbone. Four vermillion marks were on what would be the right side of the cranium, indicating that someone still visited the spot and did *puja*.

After returning Awara-*sahib* to his house and exchanging addresses, we departed. Just before dusk we reached Rasdhan, where we enjoyed a happy reunion with Dadda and his family. We all slept under the stars in his courtyard, even though the air was thick with mosquitoes. The neighbors were showing a Bollywood film, and the soundtrack played loudly in the background. Around 3 a.m., a "tempo" – a three-wheeler used as a local bus-taxi service to ferry passengers between the several villages in the locality – roared into the courtyard. The tempo was owned by Dadda. The driver, Irfan, had developed a habit of coming home about this time every night, blind drunk. His arrivals had come to serve as a ritual entertainment for Dadda's two sons, who played all sorts of tricks on him. Irfan hurled threats at them while stumbling about the courtyard – at one point falling onto Kailash's *charpai* (stringed cot). They finally led him to his bed and he quickly began snoring. In the morning we chatted over tea. Dadda had had four sons, but two had died. The other two used to drive trucks, but the business is dominated by gangs – this is, after all, Phoolan Devi (the "Bandit Queen") country – so they got out of it. The family used some of its earnings to buy the tempo, and they hired Irfan, a friend, to drive it for them. We wandered about the village some more, taking a second look at many of the places we had visited in 1999. During that visit, the moat surrounding the *garhi* (fort) was high and we had been unable to cross. Now the water was low and the path was dry, so we ventured in. Dadda claimed that cannon balls were occasionally dug up now and then. Only a few walls with archways and plaster floral motifs were left. Most of the brickwork had been taken by villagers to build houses. However, we finally did get to see the grave of Kale Saiyyad – or Gosain Baba.

After a light meal with Dadda and his sons, we said our goodbyes and headed off in the direction of Sivarajpur. We had been through Sivarajpur once before, in 1999, but in our haste we had somehow failed to visit the nearby *ghat* on the Ganga, known locally (we now discovered) as Saraiya. Saraiya Ghat turned out to be a well-developed collection of temples – three dedicated to Siva and one to Sati – along with fine concrete steps leading down to the river, punctuated with large pier-like structures that jutted out into the water some distance. The temples had been built, we were told, in the late nineteenth century. There was also a *samadhi* over which was constructed a brick shelter, said to contain the *jivit* or living *samadhi* of one Taranath. Unfortunately the caretaker of the shrine, Swami Krishna Mohan Puri, had gone into Sivarajpur to tend to some business. We might find him at the shop of Ram Das Bania, the cloth merchant. The *samadhi* building was locked up. We drove back into town to see if we could find him at the cloth merchant. No such luck: he had come and gone. One of the shop owners informed us that the *samadhi* marker was recently restored: the original had been a simple dirt affair with white paint. Some of Swami-ji's friends and *chela*s had gotten together and arranged to have it properly tiled over during a prolonged absence. Swami-ji was well-educated, and spoke English. We would enjoy meeting him. After a cup of tea, we decided to head back to the *ghat*. As we arrived, an elderly saffron-robed figure began flagging us down from his bicycle. This was Swami Krishna Mohan Puri. He was just coming to look for us, having been informed that an American researcher and a gentleman from Delhi had come asking about the *samadhi*.

We parked the Sumo and followed Swami-ji to the *samadhi*. He motioned for us to wait at the entrance while he prepared the shrine. Finally, the space properly arranged, he gestured for us to enter. He was sweating, agitated. He said some people were trying to murder him, people who resented him for taking over the shrine. They suspected that he was going to try to take over the other temples. He stopped, and composed himself. Then, just as suddenly, he launched into a long narrative: This *gaddi*, or seat, belongs to the Juna *akhara*; it descends from the ancient Vedic *rishi* or sage, Dattatreya, through a *yogi* named Taranath, many hundreds of years ago. This is Taranath's *samadhi*. It is a place of great power. For example, nearby is a village called Tarapat. In that village lived a famous Brahman scholar, Gangadhar Diksit, who had a son, Vani Vilas. The son also wanted to be a great scholar, so he came to this *gaddi* and did *tapas*: Siva appeared and granted a boon. Vani Vilas asked to be victorious in debate at Kasi (Banaras). Siva was disgusted: "You can have anything in the world, yet this is what you request?!" He left without granting the boon. Vani Vilas did more *tapas*; Siva appeared again. Again the aspiring scholar asked to be victorious at debate in Kasi; again Siva refused. Finally, on the third try, Siva relented: "Fine, have it your way: let us go to Kasi." In Kasi the young scholar defeated all comers, including the chief guru of the Kasi *naresh*. The king himself, a great scholar, then came forward. Vani Vilas won that debate as well. Suddenly, he rose off the ground to a height of seven hands. The scholars of Kasi felt used, tricked: "This was a debate for men, not gods," they complained. Vani Vilas used the opportunity (as did Swami-ji) to deliver a disquisition on Hindu physics and the centrality of light – the engine of life. He concluded by asking the assembled scholars whether he should prove the importance of light by grabbing it and taking it away. They begged him not to. He responded: "Religion is the ability to control death," and then he demonstrated by restoring some dead fish and monkeys to life by directing light, the power of life. Finally, before departing, Vani Vilas repelled the Kasi *naresh* to Ramnagar, across the river where his palace still sits to this day.

It was getting late. I decided to pose the question directly: What about Umraogiri and Anupgiri Gosain, or Himmat Bahadur? Had he ever heard of them? (We had not mentioned any of these names during the afternoon, afraid that it might "queer the pitch" as it were.) Of course, he replied, they belonged to the Juna *akhara*. The temples were all built later. This place is the *gaddi* for the entire area. It also played a role in 1857. Jassa Singh of Unnao, Sati Prasad of Sivarajpur, and Mohan Rao Singh of Kotah were all followers of this *gaddi*. The saying was that when religion was in trouble, the revolution would start here. There was a battle here in 1857, the English approached from Bithaur on ships and fired cannons at the *ghat*. They never captured the rebel leaders. The English executed the wrong men, men who were disguised as the leaders. The real men lived out their lives, secretly, in Lucknow. The *gaddi* had lots of property. Much of it was stolen during Partition, in 1947 . . .

Swami-ji seemed to be grasping at straws, hoping to hit upon something – anything – that might interest two visitors from afar. We finally left, puzzled and tired. On the one hand, there was a *samadhi* at Sivarajpur; on the other, it seemed to be associated with the Juna *akhara*. The name Taranath suggested a Gorakhnathi–Kanphati connection, which was not unusual for the Juna *akhara*. The connection to Umraogiri and Anupgiri seemed tenuous, calculated to mollify us. Yet Umraogiri and his people had spent many years at or near this very spot, enjoying the gentle power of the Ganga as it flowed past. Nearly two centuries later, they are largely forgotten, absorbed into a formulaic past of an ancient *rishi*, a medieval *yogi*, and a modern Brahman.[50] Insofar as the place had political associations, they were only of the familiar kind, the punctuation marks of the Indian nation: the Mutiny-Rebellion of 1857 and Partition in 1947.

---

[50] A few days later, Swami-ji called me in Delhi with some vague connections about America's war in Afghanistan, thus adding the postmodern dimension of Terror to the layered significances of the *samadhi*.

Kailash's counterfactual and other conclusions

The unsettled political landscape of the eighteenth century[1] was the perfect breeding ground for warlords who did not fear death, who possessed the military skills, political dexterity, and charisma required to lead "masterless men." In these conditions, the warrior bands of wild *yogis* that had wandered the subcontinent for centuries matured into highly disciplined *gosain* armies. The most successful of these armies was the one led by Anupgiri and, occasionally, his brother Umraogiri. They brought particular skills to their warcraft, including a swarming guerilla technique, hardened bodies, high mobility, a love of intrigue, and little in the way of protective gear. Already possessed in the sixteenth century of sword, bow and arrow, *chakra*, and "rocks and stones" – not to mention an aura of invincibility – they would learn in the seventeenth and, especially, eighteenth centuries the use of musket, cannon, and the value of infantry – whether horse or foot. They would apply these skills *against* the British in late eighteenth-century Bengal, in what has come down to us, famously, as the "*Sanyasi* and *Fakir* Rebellion," and *for* the British in Bundelkhand after 1800. Because of the symbolic importance of armed ascetics in nationalist myth-history, the alliance of *gosain*s with Britons has struggled to find a place in the modern Indian historical narrative.

*Gosain*s were not the only armed ascetics to leave a mark on the north Indian labor market. *Bairagi*s to the west, especially in Jaipur, and Sikhs to the northwest, in the Punjab, were also becoming well known in this period. They were certainly well aware of one another, having shared certain practices and styles if not (by the eighteenth century, at any rate) religious understandings, and occasionally they met in battle. But whereas the Sikhs are well known to us, in part because they became emblematic of British Indian martial power in the late nineteenth century (one might say that they were fortunate enough to be defeated by the Bengal Army

---

[1] No matter how we try to sanitize the period with terms like "Mughal decentralization" and "successor states," it is difficult to ignore the chaos of that century, particularly its second half.

in the 1840s, just before it was going to need a new pool of military labor, in 1858), *bairagi*s and *gosain*s have remained, if anything (and despite their late-blooming nationalist notoriety as organic freedom fighters), a footnote to Indian history. Slowly, with the work of Monika Horstmann in particular, the *bairagi*s are coming into the light as the mainstay of Jaipuri power in the eighteenth century. The *gosain*s' importance for historians derives not simply from their opposition to British arms in Bengal between 1760 and 1800, but also (indeed, more) from the fact that at a crucial juncture in 1803 they made the extension of British arms up the Gangetic Plain from Bengal possible. I like to think of this fact as "Kailash's counterfactual," because on our travels together Kailash had a way of describing the alliance between armed ascetics and the British as a "what if" proposition that is gripping in its sharp simplicity: What if Anupgiri, since 1792 the de facto ruler of the suddenly very valuable real estate of Bundelkhand, had not turned his entrepreneurial eyes in 1803 toward Wellesley and the Company and away from his considerable Maratha connections gathering to the south and west? Indian history – indeed, world history – would look very different. Clearly the choices Anupgiri made mattered.

Having allied themselves with Anupgiri, Umraogiri, and their unruly *gosain*s, the British had to deal with them. One technique was suggested by Anupgiri himself, or at the very least those around him like the *vir-rasika* poet, Padmakar, who engaged in royal panegyrics to describe the warlord. The British used such pretensions to monarchical status to nudge the *gosain* descendants of Anupgiri and Umraogiri toward a quiet *jagir* in Kanpur District, headquartered in the sleepy village of Rasdhan, or toward lucrative pensions in towns and cities like Banda and Banaras. Once there, and especially in Rasdhan, the *gosain*s were domesticated into householders, and were over time consumed by fratricidal and connubial discord. Under the watchful eye and caring hand of a succession of governors general in Calcutta, political agents in Banda and Jhansi, local magistrates in Kanpur, and an army of *vakil*s, sepoys, *thanadar*s, and *chaprasi*s, the once-powerful corporate "family" of *gosain*s saw its power dissipate into a series of ever-multiplying and increasingly less distinguished lineages, each replete with numerous and expanding factions of bickering claimants. In short, by the early 1840s the British had destroyed the extended leadership of the army of Anupgiri by adroitly managing its family politics, and by dangling before its increasingly strapped representatives the prospect of an elusive "respectability." Significantly, just below the surface, and occasionally rising up to potentially bedevil any claims to a veneer of legitimacy, was the troubling memory of sexuality, the troublesome power of women, and the troubled memory of enslavement.

Importantly and in some ways paradoxically, the reduction of the *gosain* army was a process which a critical mass of Anupgiri's *gosain* "officer corps" embraced. Perhaps the lure of an officially sanctioned family legitimacy was too attractive a prospect for *gosain*s to let slip by, given the social death that underpinned the slaving world from which they had emerged. But it should be recognized that many *gosain*s, whether *sardar*s or *naga* rank-and-file, recoiled at the prospect of a settled retirement and, presumably, the false family aesthetic that went with it. No image captures this better than that of Kamptagiri (see figure 11), eyes downcast as he departs Daulat Rao Shinde's camp in 1809 in search of continued employment in the shrinking military labor market of the nineteenth century.

Kamptagiri would eventually give up his quest for continued military entrepreneurship along the dwindling frontier and would retire to a British pension. Others would seek to retain a shred of their predatory, entrepreneurial lifestyles. These men were dealt with in a different but not totally dissimilar way, via the police and courts: The Company-State quickly criminalized armed ascetics and, moreover, viewed with deep distrust any breed of ascetic itinerancy. Indeed, some of this discursive legal shift had begun even before the Company-State had allied itself with Anupgiri, during the insurgency in Bengal. But it achieved monumental force during the career of William Sleeman, who understood Hindu mendicancy as just another peculiarly Indian brand of criminality, not too dissimilar to the Kali-oriented "thuggee" that raged throughout the newly conquered tracts of the Gangetic north – and in the minds of imperial Victorians. Where Sleeman was right, perhaps, was in thinking armed, nomadic asceticism to be antithetical, in the long run, to British Indian imperial interests. He was joined in this in the late nineteenth and early twentieth centuries by a new breed of imperial ideologues, namely, Indian nationalists. For these men (and women), armed ascetics were icons of authentic, anti-foreign Indian patriotism, so much so that they modeled their nationalist organizations and symbols on an imagined past of *sanyasi* freedom-fighters in Bengal. One could even argue that Mohandas Gandhi, in gravitating toward an ascetic persona, was taking part in this religio-political discourse, especially if we accept the Mahatma's own admonition that non-violence was the most powerful weapon of all in the battle for *swaraj*, or self-rule. In this sense, Gandhi was a new and more potent breed of warrior ascetic, a fact that may explain his reception as a second Siva, multi-armed and dangerous. The ongoing martial culture that descended from eighteenth-century warrior asceticism, meanwhile, had evolved into a sideshow spectacle at the periodically occurring *kumbha mela* every three years – a kind of dangerous theatre of memory that occasionally exploded into sectarian violence, and also a stage

Figure 11. Kamptagiri and his men departing the camp of Daulat Rao Shinde, May 1809. From Thomas D. Broughton, *Letters Written in a Mahratta Camp during the Year 1809, Descriptive of the Character, Manners, Domestic Habits, and Religious Ceremonies of the Mahrattas* (London 1813).[2]

---

[2] Beneath the image an inscription reads as follows: "A Muhunt and Gosaeens. Etched by J. A. Atkinson from the original drawing by Deen Alee. Published April 5th, 1813, by J. Murray, Albemarle Street."

(or, rather, screen) upon which all manner of nationalist desires could be projected.

To sum up, the predatory, entrepreneurial warrior asceticism that was a long-standing feature of the Indian military and political landscape was domesticated and defanged by imperialism, an imperialism that was not simply military (no imperialism is), but religious as well – and therefore not simply British, but British-Indian. The most powerful weapon in the British arsenal did not involve gunpowder and was not measured in terms of caliber or troop strength. The most powerful weapon in the British arsenal was a way of thinking about religion, as private, devotional, and depoliticized – it was a conception of religion that Britons had inherited from the transformation of Christianity during the European Enlightenment. It was powerful and persuasive not because imperial military power stood behind it, ready to enforce it, but because it had a receptive, ready audience in India – an India that had long since embarked on its own journey of religious devotionalism and all that that entailed epistemologically. In this it was not unlike Gandhi's most powerful weapon, non-violence, which was effective not because an Indian nation stood behind it, ready to enforce it, but because it found a ready, receptive audience in a Christian Britain unsure of the moral implications of Empire.

Bibliography

PRIMARY SOURCES

GOVERNMENT RECORDS

India Office Records, Oriental and India Office Collection (OIOC), British Library, London
    Bengal Judicial Department, Criminal Proceedings (BJDCP)
    Bengal Political Consultations (BPC)
    Bengal Secret and Military Consultations (BSMC)
    Bengal Secret and Political Consultations (BSPC)
    Bengal Separate and Secret Consultations
    Board's Collection
    Fort William Legislative Department Proceedings
    Fort William Political Consultations (FWPC)
    India Political Consultations
    Indian States Residency Records (ISRR)
National Archives of India (NAI), New Delhi
    Foreign Department, Political Proceedings (FDPP)
    Foreign Department, Secret Proceedings (FDSP)
    Foreign Department, Select Committee Proceedings
    Home Department, Public Proceedings
Bihar State Archives, Patna
    Political Department, Special Section (PDSS)

UNPUBLISHED MANUSCRIPTS

Bhatt, Lala Bahadur, "Anupa Prakasa," 1894 translation into Hindi prose of Man Kavi, "Anupa Prakasa," MSS Hin. D.9(b), OIOC, British Library, London
Browne, James (Major), "Memorandum for Mr. Hastings, Respecting the State of Affairs in Hindostan, January 1, 1785," Add. MS 29,209, Manuscripts Reading Room, British Library, London
Buchanan, Francis, "An Account of the Northern Part of the District of Gorakhpur, 1812," MSS Eur. D.91–92, OIOC, British Library, London
"Correspondence of Thomas Brooke at Benares with Major M. Shawe, Secretary to Lord Wellesley, 1803–1805," Add. MS 37,281, Manuscripts Reading Room, British Library, London
Della Tomba, Marco, "Viaggio," Borg. Lat. 524, Vatican Library, Rome

Kavi, Man, "Anupa Prakasa," MSS Hin. D.9(a), OIOC, British Library, London

Marshall, John, "Marshall MSS," Harl. MS 4254, Manuscripts Reading Room, British Library, London

"Narrative of Events at Cawnpore by Nanukchund," trans. Doulut Pershad, no. 727, Home Miscellaneous Proceedings, OIOC, British Library, London

"Papers Relative to Bundelkhand," Add. MS 13,591, Manuscripts Reading Room, British Library, London

Rennell, James, "Typescript Copies of Personal Letters from Maj James Rennell (1742–1830), to his Guardian, Reverend Gilbert Burrington," MSS Eur. D.1073, OIOC, British Library, London

Skinner, James, "Skinner Papers," Photo. Eur. 173, OIOC, British Library, London (original held in the National Army Museum, London)

Skinner, James, "Tasrih-al-Akvam," Add. MS 27,255, Manuscripts Reading Room, British Library, London

"Tarikh-i-Khandan-i-Timuriya," Khuda Baksh Oriental Public Library, Patna

PUBLISHED PRIMARY SOURCES

Abu'l Fazl, *A'in-i-Akbari*, 3 volumes, translated by H. Blochmann and H. S. Jarrett, with corrections by Jadunath Sarkar, Calcutta 1927–1949, reprint Delhi 1989

—*Akbar Nama* 3 vols., trans. H. Beveridge, Calcutta 1902–1939

Adhyatmaramayana, with the commentaries of Narottama, Ramavarman and Gopala Chakravarti, ed. Nagendranath Siddhantaratna, Calcutta 1935

Baburnama: Memoirs of Babur, Prince and Emperor, trans., ed., and annot. by Wheeler M. Thackston, New York and Washington, DC, 1996

Badauni, *Muntakhabu't Tawarikh*, 3 vols. vol. I trans. George S. A. Ranking, vol. II trans. W. H. Lowe, vol. III trans. Sir Wolseley Haig (Thomas Wolseley) Calcutta 1884–1925, reprint New Delhi 1990

Banabhatta, *Harsa-carita*, trans. E. B. Cowell and F. W. Thomas, London 1897

Banda: A Gazetteer, vol. XXI of the District Gazetteers of Agra and Oudh, comp. and ed. D. L. Drake-Brockman, Allahabad 1909

Barbosa, Duarte, *A Description of the Coasts of East Africa and Malabar in the Beginning of the Sixteenth Century*, notes and preface by Henry E. J. Stanley, London 1866

Bernier, Francois, *Travels in the Mogul Empire, AD 1656–1668*, trans. I. Brock and A. Constable, 2nd edn, rev. and ed. V. A. Smith, London 1934, reprint Delhi 1994

Bhagvan Prasad, Sitaramsharan, *Goswami SriNabhaji krita SriBhaktamala Sri Priyadasji pranit Tika-Kavitta*, 7th edn Lucknow 1993

Bhaktamāla, by Nabhadas, *Bhaktisudhāsvād Vārtik Tilak* ed. with comm. and trans., Sitaramsharan Bhagvan Prasad, reprint, Lucknow 1993

Blacker, Valentine, *Memoir of the Operations of the British Army in India, During the Mahratta War of 1817, 1818, & 1819*, London 1821

Broughton, Thomas D., *Letters Written in a Mahratta Camp During the Year 1809, Descriptive of the Character, Manners, Domestic Habits, and Religious Ceremonies of the Mahrattas*, London 1813

Buchanan, Francis, *An Account of the Districts of Bihar and Patna in 1811–1812*, 2 vols., Patna 1934, reprint New Delhi 1986

—*An Account of the District of Bhagalpur in 1810–1811*, Patna 1939

—*An Account of the District of Purnea in 1809–1810*, Patna 1928, reprint New Delhi 1986

—*An Account of the District of Shahabad, 1812–1813*, Patna 1934, reprint New Delhi 1986

Carré, Barthélemy, *The Travels of the Abbé Carré in India and the Near East, 1672–1674*, London 1947–1948

Catalogue of Manuscripts in European Languages Belonging to the Library of the India Office, vol. II, part 2: Orme Collection, by S. C. Hill, London 1916

Cawnpore: A Gazetteer, volume XIX of the District Gazetteers of Agra and Oudh, comp. and ed. H. R. Nevill, Allahabad 1909

Chatterjee, Bankim Chandra, *Anandamath*, trans. Sree Aurobindo and Sree Barindra Kumar Ghosh, Calcutta n.d.

—*The Abbey of Bliss*, 5th edn, trans. of *Anandamatha* by Nares Chandra Sen Gupta, Calcutta 1906

Chatterji, Bankim Chandra, *Anandamath*, trans. and ad. B. K. Roy, New Delhi, 1992

The Collected Works of Mahatma Gandhi, 100 vols., Delhi 1958–1994

The Complete Kama Sutra, by Vatsyayana, trans. Alain Daniélou, Rochester, 1994

Dabistan-i-Mazahib, 3 vols. trans. David Shea and Anthony Troyer, Paris and London 1843

Delhi Gazette, 1850

Della Valle, Pietro, *The Pilgrim: The Travels of Pietro Della Valle*, abridged edn, trans. G. Bull, London 1989

du Jarric, Pierre, *Akbar and the Jesuits: An Account of the Jesuit Missions to the Court of Akbar*, trans. C. H. Payne, New York 1926

Elliot, H. M., *Memoirs on the History, Folk-lore, and Distribution of the Races of the North Western Provinces of India*, ed. John Beames, London 1869

Elliot, H. M., and J. Dowson, *The History of India as Told by its Own Historians*, 8 vols., London 1867–1877, reprint Delhi 1990

From Sepoy to Subadar: Being the Life and Adventures of a Native Officer of the Bengal Army Written and Related by Himself, 3rd edn, trans. J. T. Norgate, ed. D. C. Phillot, Calcutta 1911

"Godse's Statement," in *Gandhi Murder Trial: Official Account of the Trial of Godse, Apte, and Others for Murder and Conspiracy, with Verbatim Reports of Speeches by Godse and Savarkar*, special double issue of *The Word Quarterly* 1, 1 (Special Double Number, Spring 1950): 39–66

Growse, F. S., *Mathura: A District Memoir*, Allahabad 1882, reprint New Delhi 1993

Hamirpur: A Gazetteer, volume XXII of the District Gazetteers of the United Provinces of Agra and Oudh, comp. and ed. D. L. Drake-Brockman, Allahabad 1909

Hill, W. Douglas P., *The Holy Lake of the Acts of Rama: An English Translation of Tulsi Das's Ramcaritamanasa*, Oxford 1952

Hussain, Saiyyid Muhammad Tassaduq, *Kitab-i Sadhu*, Sadhaura, Umballa District, 1913

The Indian Travels of Thevenot and Careri, ed. Surendranath Sen, New Delhi 1949

Jahangirnama: Memoirs of Jahangir, Emperor of India, trans., ed., and annot. Wheeler M. Thackston, Washington, DC and New York 1999

John Marshall in India: Notes and Observations in Bengal 1668–1672, ed. Shafaat Ahmad Khan, London 1927

Kabir-bijak, ed. Shukdev Singh, Allahabad 1972

Kamasutra, by Vatsyayana Mallanaga, trans. Wendy Doniger and Sudhir Kakar, New York 2002

Kautilya, *Arthasastra*, Mysore 1929

Khan, Gholam Hossein, *Seir Mutaqherin, or a Review of Modern Times*, trans. Nota Manus (nom de plume for M. Raymond, also known as Hajee Mustapha) 4 vols. vol. III, Calcutta 1789, reprint Delhi 1990

Khosla, G. D., *The Murder of the Mahatma, and Other Cases from a Judge's Notebook*, London 1963, reprint Bombay 1965

Kularnava Tantra, ed. Taranatha Vidyaratna, with an introduction by Arthur Avalon (Sir John Woodroffe), Madras 1965, reprint Delhi 1975

Long, James, *Selections from Unpublished Records of Government for the Years 1748 to 1767 Inclusive*, Calcutta 1869

Madhava-Vidyaranya, *Sankara-dig-vijaya, The Traditional Life of Sri Sankaracharya*, trans. Swami Tapasyananda, Madras 1978

Manucci, Niccolao, *Storia do Mogor, or Mogul India, 1653–1708*, trans. W. Irvine, London 1907–1908, reprint Delhi 1990

Martin, R. Montgomery, *The History, Antiquities, Topography, and Statistics of Eastern India*, 5 vols. vol. II, London 1838

Memoirs of the Life of the Right Hon. Warren Hastings, First Governor-General of Bengal, 3 vols. vol. I, London 1841

Naqawi, Ghulam Ali Khan, *'Imad us-Sa'adat*, Lucknow 1864

Padmakar, *Himmatbahadur Virdavali*, ed. Bhagvandin, 2nd edn, Banaras n.d.

Ramayana of Valmiki, vol. I, Balakanda, trans. Robert P. Goldman, Princeton 1984

Report of the Committee Appointed by the Uttar Pradesh Government to Enquire into the Mishap which Occurred in the Kumbha Mela at Prayaga on the 3rd February 1954, Allahabad 1955

Saraswati, Swami Sahajanand, *Mera Jivan Sangharsh*, Bihta, Patna District, 1952

Shah, Hasan, *The Nautch Girl*, trans. Qurratulain Hyder, New Delhi 1993

Sharif, Ja'far, *Islam in India, or, the Qanun-i-Islam*, trans. G. A. Herklots, originally published as *Qanoon e Islam*, London 1832; rev. edn, London and New York 1921; reprint Delhi 1997

Shinde, Tarabai, *A Comparison between Women and Men*, ed. Rosalind O'Hanlon, Delhi 1994

Sitaram, *Ayodhya ka Itihas*, Prayag 1932

Skinner, James, *Military Memoir of Lieut.-Col. James Skinner*, ed. J. B. Fraser, 2 vols., London 1851, reprint Mussoorie 1955

Sleeman, William, *A Report on the System of Megpunnaism or, The Murder of Indigent Parents for their Young Children (Who are Sold as Slaves) as it Prevails in the*

Delhi Territories, and the Native States of Rajpootana, Ulwar, and Bhurtpore, Calcutta 1839

Steele, Arthur, *Summary of the Law and Custom of Hindoo Castes within the Dekhun Provinces Subject to the Presidency of Bombay, Chiefly Affecting Civil Suits*, Bombay? 1827, new edn London 1868, reprint Delhi 1986 as *The Hindu Castes, their Law, Religion and Customs*

Svatmarama, *The Hathayogapradipika of Svatmarama*, with the commentary *Jyotsnā* of Brahmananda and English translation, Madras 1972

Tantraloka of Abhinavagupta with Commentary by Rajanaka Jayaratha, ed. Mukund Ram Shastri, 12 vols. Allahabad 1918–1938, reprint with introduction and notes by R. C. Dwivedi and Navjivan Rastogi, 8 vols., Delhi 1987

Tavernier, Jean Baptiste, *Travels in India*, trans. V. Ball, London 1889

Terry, Edward, *Voyage to East India*, London, 1655, reprint London 1777

Textual Sources for the Study of Sikhism, ed. W. H. McLeod, Manchester 1984

Travels of Ludovico di Varthema (1503–1508), trans. and ed. John Winter Jones, notes and introduction by George Perry Badger, London 1863

Travels of Peter Mundy, in Europe and Asia, 1608–1667, vol. II, *Travels in Asia, 1628–1634*, ed. R. C. Temple, London 1914

Tulsidas, *Sri Ramacharitamanasa*, Gorakhpur 1968

Uttar Pradesh District Gazetteers: Hamirpur, comp. and ed. Balwant Singh, Lucknow and Allahabad 1988

Uttar Pradesh District Gazetteers: Mathura, comp. and ed. Esha Basanti Joshi, Lucknow 1968

Wilson, Horace Hayman, *Glossary of Judicial and Revenue Terms and of Useful Words Occurring in Official Documents Relating to the Administration of British India*, London 1855, reprint Delhi 1968

SECONDARY SOURCES

1857 in India: Mutiny or War of Independence?, ed. Ainslee T. Embree, Boston 1963

Alavi, Seema, "The Company Army and Rural Society: The Invalid Thana, 1780–1830," *Modern Asian Studies* 27,1 (1993): 147–178

— *The Sepoys and the Company: Tradition and Transition in Northern India, 1770–1830*, Delhi 1995

Alter, Joseph, *Gandhi's Body: Sex, Diet, and the Politics of Nationalism*, Philadelphia 2000

—*The Wrestler's Body: Identity and Ideology in North India*, Berkeley 1992

Amin, Shahid, *Event, Metaphor, Memory: Chauri Chaura, 1922–1992*, Delhi and Berkeley, 1995

—"Gandhi as Mahatma," in Ranajit Guha (ed.), *Subaltern Studies III: Writings on Indian History and Society*, Delhi 1984, pp. 1–61

Asad, Talal, "Anthropological Conceptions of Religion: Reflections on Geertz," *Man* n.s. 18, 2 (June 1983): 237–259

—"The Construction of Religion as an Anthropological Category," in Talal Asad, *Genealogies of Religion: Discipline and Reasons of Power in Christianity and Islam*, Baltimore 1993, pp. 27–54

Askari, S. H., "Dabistan-i-Mazahib and Diwan-i-Mubad," in Fathullah Mujtabai (ed.) *Indo-Iranian Studies Presented for the Golden Jubilee of the Pahlavi Dynasty of Iran*, New Delhi 1977

Athar Ali, M., "Suhl-i Kul and the Religious Ideas of Akbar," *Studies in History* 4, 1 (1982): 27–39

Bahura, Gopal Narayan and Chandramani Singh, *Catalogue of Historical Documents in the Kapad Dwara, Jaipur*, Amber–Jaipur 1988

Barnett, Richard, *North India Between Empires: Awadh, The Mughals, and the British, 1720–1801*, Berkeley 1987

Bayly, C. A., *Empire and Information: Intelligence Gathering and Social Communication in India, 1780–1870*, Cambridge 1996

— *Imperial Meridian: The British Empire and the World, 1780–1830*, London 1989

— *Origins of Nationality in South Asia: Patriotism and Ethical Government in the Making of Modern India*, Delhi 1998

— *Rulers, Townsmen and Bazaars: North Indian Society in the Age of British Expansion, 1770–1870*, Cambridge 1983

—(ed.) *An Illustrated History of Modern India, 1600–1947*, Delhi 1990

Bedi, Ramesh, and Rajesh Bedi, *Sadhus: The Holy Men of India*, New Delhi 1991

Behl, Aditya, "An Ethnographer in Disguise: Comparing Self and Other in Mughal India," in Laurie Patton and David Haberman (eds.), *Notes from a Mandala: Essays in Honor of Wendy Doniger*, New York 2003

Betz, Hans Dieter, "Christianity as Religion: Paul's Attempt at Definition in Romans," *The Journal of Religion* 71, 3 (July 1991): 315–344

Bhalla, P. N., "The Gosain Brothers," *Journal of Indian History* 23, 2 (August 1944): 128–136

Bizzocchi, Roberto, "Church, Religion, and State in the Early Modern Period," trans. Barbara Dooley, *Journal of Modern History*, 67, Supplement: "The Origins of the State in Italy, 1300–1600" (December 1995): 152–165

Bossy, John, *Christianity in the West, 1400–1700*, Oxford 1985

Briggs, G. W., *Gorakhnath and the Kanphata Yogis*, Calcutta 1938, reprint Delhi 1989

Brown, Peter, *The Cult of the Saints: its Rise and Function in Latin Christianity*, Chicago 1981

Burghart, Richard, "The Founding of the Ramanandi Sect," *Ethnohistory* 25, 2 (Spring 1978): 121–139

Bynum, Caroline Walker, *Holy Feast and Holy Fast: The Religious Significance of Food to Medieval Women*, Berkeley 1987

Chandra, A. N., *The Sannyasi Rebellion*, Calcutta 1977

Chandra, K. R., *A Critical Study of Paumacariyam*, Vaishali 1970

Chandra, Moti, *The World of Courtesans*, Delhi 1973

Chandra, Pramod, "Hindu Ascetics in Mughal Painting," in Michael Meister (ed.), *Discourses on Siva: Proceedings of a Symposium on the Nature of Religious Imagery*, Philadelphia 1984, 312–316

Chatterjee, Indrani, *Gender, Slavery and Law in Colonial India*, Delhi 1999

—"A Slave's Quest for Selfhood in Eighteenth-Century Hindustan," *Indian Economic and Social History Review* 37, 1 (2000): 53–86

—and Sumit Guha, "Slave-Queen, Waif-Prince: Slavery and Social Capital in Eighteenth-Century India," *Indian Economic and Social History Review* 36, 2 (1999): 165–186

Chatterjee, R., *Prayag or Allahabad, A Handbook*, Calcutta 1910

Chatterjee, Suranjan, "New Reflections on the Sannyasi, Fakir and Peasants War," *Economic and Political Weekly* 19 (28 January 1984): PE2–PE13

Chaudhuri, K. N., *Trade and Civilisation in the Indian Ocean: An Economic History from the Rise of Islam to 1750*, Cambridge 1985

Clémentin-Ojha, Catherine, *Le Trident au Palais: Une Cabale Anti-Vishnuite dans un Royaume Hindou à l'Époque Coloniale*, Paris 1999

Cohn, Bernard S., "The Role of the Gosains in the Economy of Eighteenth and Nineteenth Century Upper India," *Indian Economic and Social History Review* 1, 4 (1964): 175–183

Das Gupta, Atis K., *The Fakir and Sannyasi Uprisings*, Calcutta 1992

Dimmit, C., and J. A. B. Buitenen (eds.), *Classical Hindu Mythology: A Reader in the Sanskrit Puranas*, ed. Philadelphia 1978

Dirks, Nicholas, *Castes of Mind: Colonialism and the Making of Modern India*, Princeton 2001

—*The Hollow Crown: Ethnohistory of an Indian Kingdom*, Cambridge 1987

Dumont, Louis, *Homo Hierarchicus: The Caste System and its Implications*, trans. Mark Sainsbury, rev. edn, Chicago 1980

—"World Renunciation in Indian Religions," *Contributions to Indian Sociology* 4 (1960): 33–62

Duncan, Jonathan, "An Account of Two Fakeers, with their Portraits," *Asiatic Researches* 5 (1808): 45–46

Eaton, Richard, "(Re)imag(in)ing Otherness: A Postmortem for the Postmodern in India," *Journal of World History* 11, 1 (2000): 57–78

—*The Rise of Islam and the Bengal Frontier, 1204–1760*, Berkeley 1993

—"Temple Desecration in Pre-Modern India," *Frontline* (22 December 2000): 62–70, part 1, and "Temple Desecration and Indo-Muslim States," *Frontline* (5 January 2001): 70–77, part 2

Eliade, Mircea, *Yoga: Immortality and Freedom*, trans. W. Trask, 2nd edn, Princeton 1969

Farquhar, J. N., "The Fighting Ascetics of India," *Bulletin of the John Rylands Library* 9 (1925): 431–452

—"The Historical Position of Ramananda," *Journal of the Royal Asiatic Society* (April 1920): 185–192

—*Modern Religious Movements in India*, reprint New Delhi 1977

—"The Organization of the Sannyasis of the Vedanta," *Journal of the Royal Asiatic Society* (July 1925): 479–486

Fox, Richard, *Lions of the Punjab: Culture in the Making*, Berkeley 1985

Freitag, Sandria, "Contesting in Public: Colonial Legacies and Contemporary Communalism," in David Ludden (ed.), *Contesting the Nation: Religion, Community, and the Politics of Democracy in India*, Philadelphia 1996, pp. 211–234

Friedmann, Y., "Medieval Muslim Views of Indian Religions," *Journal of the American Oriental Society* 95, 2 (1975): 214–221

Ghosh, Jamini Mohan, *Sannyasi and Fakir Raiders in Bengal*, Calcutta 1930

Ghurye, G. S., *Indian Sadhus*, 2nd edn, Bombay 1964

Giri, Sadananda, *Society and Sannyasin (A History of the Dasnami Sannyasins)*, Rishikesh 1976

Gole, Susan, *Indian Maps and Plans, From the Earliest Times to the Advent of European Surveys*, New Delhi 1989

Gommans, Jos, "Indian Warfare and Afghan Innovation During the Eighteenth Century," *Studies in History* 11, 2, n.s. (1995): 261–281

—*The Rise of the Indo-Afghan Empire, c.1710–1780*, Leiden 1995

Gordon, Stewart, *The Marathas, 1600–1818*, Cambridge 1994

—"Scarf and Sword: Thugs, Marauders, and State-Formation in Eighteenth-Century Malwa," *Indian Economic and Social History Review* 6, 4 (1969): 403–429

Goswamy, B. N. and J. S. Grewal, *The Mughals and the Jogis of Jakhbar: Some Madad-i-Ma'ash and Other Documents*, Simla 1967

Gottschalk, Peter, *Beyond Hindu and Muslim: Multiple Identity in Narratives from Rural India*, New York 2000

Greenblatt, Stephen Jay, *Marvelous Possessions: The Wonder of the New World*, Chicago 1991

—(ed.), *New World Encounters*, Berkeley 1993

Gregory, Brad, *Salvation at Stake: Christian Martyrdom in Early Modern Europe*, Cambridge, MA 1999

Grierson, George, "Rukhada," in James Hastings (ed.), *Encyclopædia of Religion and Ethics*, New York and Edinburgh 1908–1926, vol. x, pp. 866–867

Guha, Ranajit, "The Prose of Counter-Insurgency," in Ranajit Guha (ed.), *Subaltern Studies: Writings on South Asian History and Society*, vol. ii (Delhi 1983), pp. 1–42

Hadi, Nabi, *Dictionary of Indo-Persian Literature*, New Delhi 1995

Hauser, Walter, "Swami Sahajanand and the Politics of Social Reform, 1907–1950," *Indian Historical Review* 18, 1–2 (July 1991 and January 1992): 59–75

Hawley, J. S., and Mark Juergensmeyer, *Songs of the Saints of India*, New York 1988

Hobson-Jobson: A Glossary of Colloquial Anglo-Indian Words and Phrases, and of Kindred Terms, Etymological, Historical, Geographical and Discursive, comp. Col. Henry Yule and A. C. Burnell, London 1903

Hodgson, Marshall G. S., *Venture of Islam: Conscience and History in a World Civilization*, 3 vols. vol. i, Chicago 1974

Horstmann, Monika, "The Ramanandis of Galta (Jaipur, Rajasthan)," in Lawrence Babb, Varsha Joshi and Michael Meister (eds.), *Multiple Histories: Culture and Society in the Study of Rajasthan*, Jaipur and New Delhi 2002, pp. 141–197

Irvine, W., *A History of the Bangash Nawabs of Farrukhabad, from 1713 to 1771 A.D.*, Calcutta 1879

Jones, Kenneth, *Socio-Religious Reform Movements in British India*, Cambridge 1989

Kane, P. V., *History of Dharmasastra: Ancient and Mediaeval Religious and Civil Law*, 5 vols., Poona 1974

Kaye, J. W., *A History of the Sepoy War in India, 1857–1858*, 2nd edn, London 1865

Keegan, John, *The Face of Battle*, New York 1976

—*A History of Warfare*, New York 1993

Keiser, R. Lincoln, *The Vice Lords: Warriors of the Streets*, New York 1969

Khan, Mohammad Ishaaq, *Kashmir's Transition to Islam: the Role of the Muslim Rishis*, New Delhi 1994

Khandalvala, Karl, Moti Chandra, and Pramod Chandra, *Miniature Painting: A Catalogue of the Exhibition of the Sri Motichand Khajanchi Collection*, New Delhi 1960

King, Richard, *Orientalism and Religion: Postcolonial Theory, India and 'the Mystic East,'* London 1999

Kolff, D. H. A., *Naukar, Rajput, and Sepoy: The Ethnohistory of the Military Labour Market in Hindustan, 1450–1850*, Cambridge 1990

—"Sanyasi Trader-Soldiers," *Indian Economic and Social History Review* 8, 2 (1971): 213–220

—"The End of an Ancien Régime: Colonial War in India, 1798–1818," in J. A. de Moor and H. L. Wesseling (eds.), *Imperialism and War: Essays on Colonial Wars in Asia and Africa*, Leiden 1989, pp. 22–49

S. Kossak, *Indian Court Painting: 16th-19th Century*, New York 1997

Kulke, Hermann, "Maharajas, Mahants and Historians: Reflections on the Early Historiography of Early Vijayanagara and Sringeri," in Hermann Kulke, *Kings and Cults: State Formation and Legitimation in India and Southeast Asia*, New Delhi 1993, pp. 208–239

Kumar, Radha, *The History of Doing: An Illustrated Account of Movements for Women's Rights and Feminism in India, 1800–1990*, New Delhi 1993

Lochtefeld, James, "The Vishva Hindu Parishad and the Roots of Hindu Militancy," *Journal of the American Academy of Religion* 42, 2 (Summer 1994): 587–602

Lorenzen, David, "Europeans in Late Mughal South Asia: The Perceptions of Italian Missionaries," *Indian Economic and Social History Review* 40, 1 (2003): 1–31

— "Warrior Ascetics in Indian History," *Journal of the American Oriental Society* 98 (1978): 61–75

—"Who Invented Hinduism?" *Comparative Studies in Society and History* 41, 4 (October 1999): 630–659

Lutgendorf, Philip, *The Life of a Text: Performing the Ramcaritmanas of Tulsidas*, Berkeley 1991

—"Monkey in the Middle: The Status of Hanuman in Popular Hinduism," *Religion* 27 (Oct 1997): 311–332

—"The Quest for the Legendary Tulsidas" in W. M. Callewaert and R. Snell (eds.) *According to Tradition: Hagiographical Writing in India*, Wiesbaden 1994, pp. 65–85

MacLean, Kama, "Making the Colonial State Work for You: The Modern Beginnings of the Ancient Kumbh Mela in Allahabad," *Journal of Asian Studies* 62, 3 (2003): 873–905

McLeod, W. H., *The Evolution of the Sikh Community*, Delhi 1975

McNeill, William, *The Pursuit of Power: Technology, Armed Forces, and Society since A.D. 1000*, Chicago 1982

Muztar, Bal Krishna, *History of Kurukshetra*, Kurukshetra, Haryana, n.d.

—*Kurukshetra: Political and Cultural History*, Delhi 1978

Nandy, Ashis, "Final Encounter: The Politics of the Assassination of Gandhi," in Ashis Nandy, *At the Edge of Psychology: Essays in Politics and Culture* (Delhi 1980), pp. 70–98

— *The Intimate Enemy: Loss and the Recovery of Self Under Colonialism*, Delhi 1983

Okada, Amina, *Indian Miniatures of the Mughal Court*, trans. Deke Dusinberre, New York 1992

Oldenburg, Veena Talwar, "Lifestyle as Resistance: The Case of the Courtesans of Lucknow," in V. Graff (ed.), *Lucknow: Memories of a City*, Delhi 1997, pp. 136–154

Oman, J. Campbell, *The Mystics, Ascetics, and Saints of India*, London 1903

Orr, W. G., "Armed Religious Ascetics in Northern India," *The Bulletin of the John Rylands Library* 25 (1940): 81–100

Pal, Pratapaditya and Vidya Dehejia, *From Merchants to Emperors: British Artists and India, 1757–1930*, Ithaca, NY 1986

Palsokar, R. D., *Bajirao I: An Outstanding Cavalry General*, New Delhi 1995

Pandey, Gyanendra, *The Construction of Communalism in Colonial North India*, Delhi 1990

Parker, Geoffrey, *The Military Revolution: Military Innovation and the Rise of the West*, Cambridge 1996

Patterson, Orlando, *Slavery and Social Death*, Cambridge, MA, 1982

Pinch, Vijay, "*Bhakti* and the British Empire," *Past & Present*, 179 (May 2003): 159–196

Pinch, William R. *Peasants and Monks in British India*, Berkeley 1996

—"Same Difference in India and Europe," *History and Theory* 38, 3 (October 1999): 389–407

—"History, Devotion, and The Search for Nabhadas of Galta," in Daud Ali (ed.), *Invoking the Past: The Uses of History in South Asia*, Delhi 1999, pp. 367–399

—"Soldier Monks and Militant Sadhus," in David Ludden (ed.), *Contesting the Nation: Religion, Community, and the Politics of Democracy in India*, Philadelphia 1996, pp. 140–162

Pingree, David, *Census of the Exact Sciences in Sanskrit*, vol. v, Philadelphia 1970

Pogson, W. R., *History of the Boondelas*, Calcutta 1828, reprint New Delhi 1974

Pollet, G., "Early Evidence on Tulsidas and his Epic," *Orientalia Lovaniensia Periodica* 5 (1974): 157–162

Potter, Karl, *Encyclopedia of Indian Philosophies*, vol. i, bibliography, 2nd rev. edn, Delhi 1983

Qaisar, A. J., *The Indian Response to European Technology and Culture: (A.D. 1498–1707)*, Delhi 1998

Ralston, David B., *Importing the European Army: The Introduction of European Military Techniques and Institutions into the Extra-European World, 1600–1914*, Chicago 1990

Ramanujan, A. K., "Three Hundred Ramayanas: Five Examples and Three Thoughts on Translation," in Paula Richman (ed.), *Many Ramayanas: The Diversity of a Narrative Tradition in South Asia*, Berkeley 1991

Raychaudhuri, Tapan, *Europe Reconsidered: Perceptions of the West in Nineteenth-Century Bengal*, Delhi 1988

Richards, John, *The Mughal Empire*, Cambridge 1993

Richman, Paula, *Many Ramayanas: The Diversity of a Narrative Tradition in South Asia*, Berkeley 1991

Rizvi, S. A. A., *The Religious and Intellectual History of Muslims in Akbar's Reign*, New Delhi 1975

Roy, A. K., *History of Jaipur City*, New Delhi 1978

Roy, Tapti, *The Politics of a Popular Uprising: Bundelkhand in 1857*, Delhi 1994

Rudolph, Lloyd and Susanne H., *The Modernity of Tradition: Political Development in India*, Chicago 1967

Saler, Benson, "*Religio* and the Definition of Religion," *Cultural Anthropology* 2, 3 (August 1987): 395–399

Saraswati, Baidyanath and Surajit Sinha, *Ascetics of Kashi: An Anthropological Exploration*, Varanasi 1978

Sarkar, Jadunath, *Fall of the Mughal Empire*, 4 vols., 4th edn, New Delhi 1991

—and Nirod Bhusan Roy, *History of the Dasnami Naga Sanyasis*, Allahabad, n.d.

Sarkar, Sumit, "The Decline of the Subaltern in Subaltern Studies," in Sumit Sarkar, *Writing Social History*, Delhi 1997

Sarkar, Sushobhan C., "A Note on Puran Giri Gosain," *Bengal Past & Present* 43 (April–June 1932): 83–87

Sarkar, Tanika, "Imagining Hindurashtra: The Hindu and the Muslim in Bankim Chandra's Writings," in David Ludden (ed.), *Contesting the Nation: Religion, Community, and the Politics of Democracy in India*, Philadelphia 1996, pp. 162–184

Schomer, Karine and W. H. McLeod (eds.), *Sants: Studies in a Devotional Tradition of India*, Delhi 1987

Seyller, John, *The Adventures of Hamza: Painting and Storytelling in India*, London and Washington, DC, 2002

Sharma, Sri Ram, *The Religious Policy of the Mughal Emperors*, 1st edn, London 1940; 3rd edn, New York 1972

Sinha, Bhagwati Prasad, *Ram Bhakti men Rasika Sampraday*, Balrampur 1957

Smith, Jonathan Z., "Religion, Religions, Religious," in Mark Taylor (ed.), *Critical Terms for Religious Studies*, Chicago 1998, pp. 269–284

Smith, Vincent, *Akbar the Great Mogul*, 2nd edn, Oxford 1919

Smith, Walter, "Hindu Ascetics in Mughal Painting under Akbar," *Oriental Art* n.s. 27, 1 (1981): 67–75

Srivastava, A. L, *The First Two Nawabs of Oudh*, Lucknow 1933

Streusand, Douglas, *The Formation of the Mughal Empire*, Delhi 1989

Subramanian, Anna N., *The Concept of Tapas in Valmiki Ramayana*, Madras 1977

Talbot, Cynthia, "Inscribing the Other, Inscribing the Self: Hindu-Muslim Identities in Pre-Colonial India," *Comparative Studies in Society and History* 37, 4 (October 1995): 692–722

Tharu, Susie and K. Lalita (eds.), *Women Writing in India*, vol. i, New York 1991

Thomas, Keith, *Religion and the Decline of Magic: Studies in Popular Beliefs in Sixteenth and Seventeenth Century England*, New York 1971

van der Veer, Peter, *Gods on Earth: The Management of Religious Experience and Identity in a North Indian Pilgrimage Center*, London 1988

—*Religious Nationalism: Hindus and Muslims in India*, Berkeley 1994

Vansina, Jan, "Once upon a Time: Oral Traditions as History in Africa," *Daedalus* 1971 100 (2): 442–468

—"Recording the Oral History of the Bakuba," *Journal of African History* 1, 1 (1960): 43–51, and 1, 2: 257–270

von Stietencron, H., "Hinduism: On the Proper Use of a Deceptive Term," in G. D. Sontheimer and H. Kulke (eds.), *Hinduism Reconsidered*, New Delhi 1989, pp. 11–27

Welch, S. C., *Imperial Mughal Painting*, New York 1978

Whaling, Frank, *The Rise of the Religious Significance of Rama*, Delhi 1980

White, David G., *Alchemical Body: Siddha Traditions in Medieval India*, Chicago 1996

—*Kiss of the Yogini: 'Tantric Sex' in its South Asian Contexts*, Chicago 2003

Index

Cambridge Studies in Indian History and Society

Other titles in the series